Student Study Guide
John Harris

Cost Accounting
Fourteenth Edition

Charles T. Horngren
Srikant Datar
Madhav Rajan

Prentice Hall

Boston   Columbus   Indianapolis   New York   San Francisco   Upper Saddle River

Amsterdam   Cape Town   Dubai   London   Madrid   Milan   Munich   Paris   Montreal   Toronto

Delhi   Mexico City   Sao Paulo   Sydney   Hong Kong   Seoul   Singapore   Taipei   Tokyo

Editor-in-Chief: Donna Battista
Executive Editor: Stephanie Wall
Editorial Project Manager: Christina Rumbaugh
Production Project Manager: Lynne Breitfeller
Senior Operations Specialist: Diane Peirano
Printer/Binder: OPM Digital Print Services
Cover Printer: OPM Digital Print Services

Prentice Hall
is an imprint of

www.pearsonhighered.com

10 9 8 7 6 5 4 3 2 1

ISBN-13: 978-0-13-210920-8
ISBN-10: 0-13-210920-4

Contents

Introduction

This *Student Guide* is a self-study aid to accompany the 13th edition of *Cost Accounting: A Managerial Emphasis*, by Horngren, Datar, and Rajan. The *Student Guide* has three purposes: (1) to reinforce and clarify your understanding of the textbook material, (2) to develop your analytical thinking skills, and (3) to help you review for exams effectively and efficiently. I designed the *Student Guide* to provide maximum benefit from your study time.

Each *Student Guide* chapter has the following sections:

- **Overview** is a one-paragraph description of the textbook chapter.
- **Highlights** is a comprehensive summary of the chapter presented in an easy-to-read paragraph style, with the textbook "Terms to Learn" in bold type.
- **Featured Exercise** covers key points in the textbook assignment material.
- **Review Questions and Exercises** consist of completion statements, true-false and multiple choice questions, short exercises, and an occasional crossword puzzle. They help you master the terms and concepts in the chapter. Most chapters include at least five questions/exercises from the Certified Public Accountant (CPA) and Certified Management Accountant (CMA) exams.
- **Answers and Solutions to Review Questions and Exercises**—located at the end of the chapter—allow you to check your work. This section provides complete explanations for each false statement and all multiple-choice answers, and easy-to-follow solutions to the exercises.
- **Check Figures for the Review Exercises** are at the end of the *Student Guide*.

How to Use the *Student Guide*

I recommend a six-step approach for using the *Student Guide* with the textbook:

1. Study the chapter in the textbook and solve the Problem for Self-Study included there.
2. Read the Overview and Highlights sections in the *Student Guide*. The Highlights refer only to *the most essential textbook exhibits and examples* (an average of three per chapter), so the *Student Guide* can almost be used in a stand-alone way at this stage of your study.
3. Prepare your solution to the Featured Exercise in the *Student Guide* and compare it to the solution provided there.
4. Answer the Review Questions and Exercises in the *Student Guide* and compare your answers with those provided at the end of the chapter.
   - Resist the temptation to look at the answers before preparing your own! This approach keeps you from developing a false sense of confidence about your knowledge of the material.
   - When your answers to an exercise do not agree with the Check Figures, first try reworking the exercise before you look at the complete solution.
5. Solve the homework problems assigned by your professor.
6. Use the *Student Guide* to review for exams. Concentrate on the Featured Exercises as well as the Review Questions and Exercises that you found to be most difficult.

As you study cost accounting, keep in mind that there is no substitute for hard work and a desire to learn. These qualities are key to your success.

Acknowledgments

For ideas and assistance, I am indebted to the textbook authors, Jim Payne of The University of Tulsa, and numerous students. I thank the American Institute of Certified Public Accountants and the Institute of Certified Management Accountants for permission to use their professional examination questions.

John K. Harris

CHAPTER 1

The Manager and Management Accounting

If you have not already read the Introduction (p. vii), do so now. It describes the purposes and contents of the *Student Guide* and recommends a six-step approach for using the *Student Guide* with the textbook.

Overview

Welcome to the study of cost accounting. This introductory chapter explains the intertwining roles of managers and management accountants in choosing an organization's strategy, and in planning and controlling its operations. Unlike the remainder of the textbook, this chapter has no "number crunching." Its main purpose is to emphasize the management accountant's role in providing information for managers.

Highlights

1. It is important to distinguish management accounting from financial accounting.

- **Management accounting** measures, analyzes, and reports financial and nonfinancial information that helps managers make decisions to fulfill the goals of an organization. Management accounting (a) emphasizes the future, (b) is designed to influence the behavior of managers and other employees in achieving the goals of an organization, and (c) does not have to follow generally accepted accounting principles (GAAP) but instead is based on cost-benefit analysis.
- **Financial accounting** focuses on reporting to external parties such as investors, government agencies, banks and suppliers. It measures and records business transactions and provides financial statements—the balance sheet, income statement, statement of cash flows, and statement of retained earnings—that are based on GAAP.

2. **Cost accounting** measures, analyzes, and reports financial and nonfinancial information relating to the costs of acquiring or using resources in an organization. Cost accounting provides information for both management accounting and financial accounting.

3. **Cost management** encompasses the approaches and activities of managers that use resources to increase value to customers and to achieve organizational goals. For example, rearranging the production-floor layout might reduce manufacturing costs, or additional product design costs might be incurred in an effort to increase revenues and profits.

4. **Strategy** specifies how an organization matches its own capabilities with the opportunities in the marketplace to accomplish its objectives. In other words, strategy describes how an organization will compete and the opportunities its employees should seek and pursue. Companies follow one of two broad strategies:

- *Cost leadership strategy*: Sell quality products or services at low prices. An example is Southwest Airlines.
- *Product differentiation strategy*: Sell differentiated or unique products or services at higher prices than charged by competitors. An example is Apple.

Deciding between these strategies is a critical part of what managers do. The term **strategic cost management** describes cost management that specifically focuses on strategic issues.

5. The **value chain** is the sequence of business functions in which customer usefulness is added to products. These business functions are **research and development (R&D); design of products and processes; production; marketing** including sales); **distribution;** and **customer service**. Managers in each of these six business functions of the value chain are customers of

management accounting information. Rather than proceeding sequentially through the value chain, companies gain if two or more business functions work concurrently as a team. For example, additional spending on R&D and product design might be more than offset by lower costs of production and customer service.

6. The term **supply chain** describes the flow of goods, services, and information from the initial sources of materials and services to the delivery of products to customers, regardless of whether those activities occur in the same organization or in other organizations. Cost management emphasizes integrating and coordinating activities across all companies in the supply chain, as well as across each business function in an individual company's value chain, to improve performance and reduce costs.

7. Customers want companies to use the value chain and supply chain to deliver ever improving levels of performance regarding four key success factors:

a. *Cost and efficiency*—Companies face continuous pressure to reduce the cost of the products they sell. An example is outsourcing one or more business functions to foreign countries.

b. *Quality*—Customers expect high levels of quality. The philosophy of total quality management (TQM) is to improve operations throughout the value chain to deliver products and services that exceed customer expectations.

c. *Time*—Time has many components. Examples include the time to develop and bring new products to market and the speed at which an organization responds to customer requests.

d. *Innovation*—A constant flow of innovative products or *services* is the basis for ongoing company success. A main source of innovations is R&D.

Management accountants help managers track performance of competitors on these key success factors. Tracking what is happening in other companies serves as a *benchmark* and alerts managers to market changes. Companies seek to *continuously improve* their critical operations.

8. Decision making is a five-step process: (i) identify the problem and uncertainties, (ii) obtain information, (iii) make predictions about the future, (iv) make decisions by choosing among alternatives, and (v) implement the decision, evaluate performance and learn. Collectively, the first four steps are *planning* and the last step is *control*.

9. **Planning** comprises (a) selecting organization goals, (b) predicting results under various alternative ways of achieving those goals, (c) deciding how to attain the desired goals, and (d) communicating the goals and how to attain them to the entire organization. **Control** comprises (a) taking actions that implement the planning decisions, (b) deciding how to evaluate performance, and (c) providing feedback and learning to help future decision making.

10. Budgeting is essential for planning and control. A **budget** is the quantitative expression of a proposed plan of action by management and is an aid to coordinating what needs to be done to execute that plan. Because the process of preparing a budget crosses business functions, it forces coordination and communication throughout the company, as well as with the company's suppliers and customers.

11. A performance report (see EXHIBIT 1-4, text p.10) spurs investigation and learning. **Learning** is examining past performance (the control function) and systematically exploring alternative ways to make better-informed decisions and plans in the future. Learning can lead to changes in goals, changes in strategies, changes in the range of information collected when making predictions, and sometimes changes in managers.

12. Three guidelines help management accountants provide the most value to their companies in strategic and operational decision making:

a. *Employ a* **cost-benefit approach**. This approach guides decision making: resources should be spent if the expected benefits to the company exceed the expected costs. For example, consider a budgeting system. The *expected costs* of a proposed budgeting system (such as personnel, software, and training) should be compared with its *expected benefits*, which are the collective decisions of managers that will better attain the company's goals. In particular, measurement of the expected benefits is not easy.

b. *Give full recognition to behavioral and technical considerations.* A management accounting system should have two simultaneous missions for *providing* information: (i) to help managers make wise economic decisions by providing them with desired information (the technical mission) and (ii) to help encourage managers and other employees to strive for achieving goals of the organization (the behavioral mission). Management is primarily a human activity that should focus on how to help individuals do their jobs better.

c. *Use different costs for different purposes.* To illustrate this guideline, consider how to account for advertising. For the purpose of preparing financial statements under GAAP, advertising is an expense in the accounting period when it is incurred. For the purpose of determining a product's selling price, its advertising costs, along with its other costs from all business functions of the value chain, should be taken into account as part of the total cost of the product.

13. Organizations distinguish **line management** from **staff management**. Line management (for example, production) is directly responsible for attaining the goals of the organization. Staff management (for example, accounting) provides advice and assistance to line management. Increasingly, organizations are using teams incorporating both line and staff management to achieve their objectives.

14. The **chief financial officer (CFO)** is the executive responsible for overseeing the financial operations of an organization, which usually include controllership, treasury, risk management, taxation, investor relations, and internal audit. The **controller** is the financial executive primarily responsible for management accounting and financial accounting. The controller "controls" the behavior of employees by exerting a force that impels managers toward making better-informed decisions as they implement their strategies.

15. Accountants have special obligations regarding ethics, given that they are responsible for the integrity of the financial information provided to internal and external parties. In the United States, the **Institute of Management Accountants (IMA)** has issued ethical guidelines on issues relating to *competence, confidentiality, integrity, and credibility.* EXHIBIT 1-7, text p.16, provides the IMA's guidance on issues relating to those four standards. EXHIBIT 1-8, text p.17, presents the IMA's guidance on how to resolve ethical conflict.

Featured Exercise

Exon Tackle Company manufactures a wide range of fishing equipment and supplies for the retail market. In the current fiscal year, Exon incurred the costs described below. For each of these costs, indicate the applicable business function of the value chain by putting the identifying number in the space provided.

Business Function of the Value Chain

1. Research and development
2. Design of products and processes
3. Production
4. Marketing
5. Distribution
6. Customer service

____ a. Cost of repairing reels that malfunctioned during the warranty period.
____ b. Cost of hooks used in making fishing lures.
____ c. Salary of a mechanical engineer working on the basic concept for the next generation of ultra-light fishing rods.
____ d. Cost of overnight delivery of rods and reels to winter boat shows.
____ e. Cost of running advertisements in fishing magazines.
____ f. Cost of printing operating instructions to be packaged with a new model of trolling motor.

Review Questions and Exercises

This section is designed to help determine how well you have mastered the textbook material. Try to answer all of these questions and exercises without using your textbook or the Highlights in the *Student Guide*. *In answering the Review Questions and Exercises, be sure to follow Step 4 of the study approach recommended in the Introduction, p.vii.* All answers are at the end of the chapter.

Completion Statements

Fill in the blank(s) to complete each statement.

1. _____ (a) emphasizes the future, (b) is designed to influence the behavior of managers and other employees in achieving the goals of an organization, and (c) does not have to follow generally accepted accounting principles (GAAP).

2. _____ is the approaches and activities of managers to use resources to increase value to customers and to achieve organizational goals.

3. Selecting organization goals, predicting results under various alternative ways of achieving these goals, and deciding how to attain the desired goals are aspects of _____.

4. A _____ is a quantitative expression of a proposed plan of action by management and is an aid to coordinating what needs to be done to execute that plan.

5. Name the six business functions in the value chain in their sequential order: _____
_____
_____
_____

6. The _____ approach helps guide managers' decision making.

7. The Institute of Management Accountants' four standards of ethical conduct for management accountants are _____
_____
_____.

True-False

Indicate whether each statement is true (T) or false (F).

____ 1. Management accounting does not have to follow generally accepted accounting principles.

____ 2. Cost accounting provides information for management accounting but not for financial accounting.

____ 3. Control is defined as the process of setting maximum limits on expenditures.

____ 4. Managers should proceed sequentially through the value chain of business functions.

____ 5. The term supply chain describes the flow of goods, services, and information from the initial sources of materials and services to the delivery of products to customers, regardless of whether those activities occur in the same organization or in other organizations.

____ 6. Learning is examining past performance (the control function) and systematically exploring alternative ways to make better informed decisions and plans in the future.

____ 7. The CFO, a line management function, is the executive responsible for overseeing the financial operations of an organization.

Multiple Choice

Select the best answer to each question.

____ 1. Control includes:
  a. selecting organization goals.
  b. implementing the planning decisions.
  c. deciding how to attain the desired results.
  d. preparing budgets.

____ 2. The primary responsibility of the controller is:
  a. risk management.
  b. overseeing the financial operations of an organization.
  c. management accounting and financial accounting.
  d. obtaining short-term and long-term financing.

____ 3. Maintaining records on traffic tickets issued by the city of Atlanta is performing what management accounting role?
  a. Scorekeeping
  b. Attention directing
  c. Problem solving
  d. Internal auditing

____ 4. The Institute of Management Accountants' *Standards of Ethical Conduct for Management Accountants* includes standards on:
  a. competence and responsibility.
  b. integrity and professionalism.
  c. objectivity and responsibility.
  d. competence and confidentiality.

Review Exercises

1. Define strategy. Then specify the two broad strategies that companies choose between.

_____

_____

_____

_____

_____

_____

_____

_____

_____

_____

_____

2. For each of the following actions by companies, identify the applicable key success factor.

____ a. Company X uses TQM to improve operations throughout the value chain to deliver products and services that exceed customer expectations.

____ b. Company Y keeps records on how long it takes a new product to be introduced to the market after the initial concept for the product is approved by management.

____ c. Company Z outsources its production to Mexico.

Answers to Chapter 1 Review Questions and Exercises

Completion Statements

1. Management accounting
2. Cost management
3. planning
4. budget
5. research and development (R&D); design of products and processes; production; marketing; distribution; customer service
6. cost-benefit
7. competence, confidentiality, integrity, credibility

True-False

1. T
2. F Cost accounting provides information for *both* management accounting and financial accounting. Cost accounting measures, analyzes, and reports financial and nonfinancial information relating to the cost of acquiring and using resources in an organization.
3. F Control comprises (a) taking actions that implement the planning decisions, (b) deciding how to evaluate performance, and (c) providing feedback and learning to help future decision making.
4. F Rather than proceeding sequentially through the value chain, companies gain if two or more business functions work concurrently as a team. For example, additional spending on R&D and product design might be more than offset by lower costs of production and customer service.
5. T
6. T
7. F The CFO, a *staff management* function (not a *line management* function), is the executive responsible for overseeing the financial operations of an organization, which usually include controllership, treasury, risk management, taxation, investor relations, and internal audit. Staff management provides advice and assistance to line management. Line management is directly responsible for attaining the goals of the organization.

Multiple Choice

1. b Control comprises (i) taking actions that implement the planning decisions, (ii) deciding how to evaluate performance, and (iii) providing feedback that will help future decision making. Answers (a), (c) and (d) are aspects of planning.
2. c The controller is the financial executive primarily responsible for management accounting and financial accounting.
3. d The IMA's *Standards* of *Ethical Conduct for Management Accountants* has four standards: competence, confidentiality, integrity, and credibility.

Review Exercise 1

Strategy specifies how an organization matches its own capabilities with the opportunities in the marketplace to accomplish its objectives. In other words, strategy describes how an organization will compete and the opportunities its employees should seek and pursue. Companies follow one of two broad strategies:

- Cost leadership strategy: Sell quality products or services at low prices. Examples are Wal-Mart and Southwest Airlines.
- Product differentiation strategy: Sell differentiated or unique products or services at higher prices than charged by competitors. Examples are Apple and Johnson & Johnson.

Deciding between these strategies is a critical part of what managers do. Management accountants work closely with managers in formulating strategy.

Review Exercise 2

a. quality   b. time   c. cost and efficiency

CHAPTER 2

An Introduction to Cost Terms and Purposes

Overview

This chapter introduces the basic terminology of cost accounting. Communication among managers and management accountants is greatly facilitated by having a common understanding of the meaning of cost terms and concepts. The chapter illustrates a major theme of the textbook: using different costs for different purposes. The chapter also provides a framework to help you understand cost accounting and cost management.

Highlights

1. Accountants define **cost** as a resource sacrificed (used) or forgone to achieve a specific objective. For example, it might *cost* $5,000 per month to rent retail space in a shopping center. To guide their decisions, managers often want to know how much a particular thing costs. This "thing" is called a **cost object**, anything for which a measurement of costs is desired. In the following questions, the cost object is in italics: How much does it cost to manufacture a *12-pack of Diet Pepsi*? Which *delivery truck* at the local Pepsi bottling company is the least expensive to operate?

2. Costing systems account for costs in two basic stages. The first stage is **cost accumulation**, the collection of cost data in some organized way by means of an accounting system. The second stage is **cost assignment**, a general term that encompasses both (a) tracing direct costs to a cost object and (b) allocating indirect costs to a cost object. Paragraph 3 defines *cost tracing* and *cost allocation*.

3. The key question in cost assignment is whether costs have a direct or an indirect relationship to the particular cost object.

- The **direct costs of a cost object** are related to the particular cost object and can be *traced* to it in an economically feasible (cost-effective) way. The term **cost tracing** describes the as-signment of *direct costs* to the particular cost object.

- The **indirect costs of a cost object** are related to the particular cost object but cannot be traced to it in an economically feasible way. The term **cost allocation** describes the assignment of *indirect costs* to the particular cost object.

Several factors affect the classification of a cost as direct or indirect: the materiality (relative importance) of the cost in question, available information-gathering technology, and design of operations.

4. Consider this question: Is the production department manager's salary a direct cost or an indirect cost? The answer: *It depends on the choice of the cost object*. For example, if the cost object is the production department, the salary is a direct cost because it can be *traced* to the cost object. But if the cost object is one of the many products manufactured in the production department, the salary is an indirect cost because it can be *allocated* (but cannot be traced) to the cost object.

5. Two basic types of cost-behavior patterns are found in accounting systems.

- A **variable cost** changes *in total* in proportion to changes in the related level of total volume. A variable cost does not change *on a per unit basis* when the related level of total volume changes.
- A **fixed cost** does not change *in total* over a normal range of volume for a given time span. A fixed cost increases (decreases) *on a per unit basis* when the related level of total volume decreases (increases).

Relevant range is the band of the normal level of volume in which there is a specific relationship between the level of volume and the total variable costs or total fixed costs in question. Exhibit 2-4, text p. 34, illustrates the relevant range for a fixed cost.

6. A **cost driver** is a variable, such as the level of volume, that causally affects costs over a given time span. In other words, a cause-and-effect relationship exists between a change in the level of volume and a change in the level of total costs.

- The cost driver of a variable cost is the level of volume whose change causes proportionate changes in that cost. For example, the number of trucks assembled is a cost driver of the cost of steering wheels for the trucks; that's because the more trucks produced, the more steering wheels needed.
- Costs that are fixed in the short run have no cost driver in the short run but may have a cost driver in the long run. For example, the equipment and staff costs of product testing typically are fixed in the short run with respect to changes in the volume of production. In the long run, however, the company increases or decreases these costs to the levels needed to support future production levels.

7. Accounting systems typically report both *total costs* and **unit costs** (also called **average costs**). A unit cost is computed by dividing some amount of total costs by the related number of units. Unit costs are regularly used in financial reports. Generally, however, *managers should think in terms of total costs rather than unit costs*. That's because fixed cost per unit changes when the related level of volume changes. Unit costs, therefore, should be interpreted with caution if they include a fixed-cost component. The Tennessee Products example, text p.35-36, illustrates this important point.

8. Companies in the manufacturing, merchandising, and service sectors of the economy are frequently referred to in the study of cost accounting.

- **Manufacturing-sector companies** purchase materials and components and convert them into various finished goods. These companies typically have one or more of three types of inventory: **direct materials inventory**, **work-in-process inventory**, and **finished goods inventory**.
- **Merchandise-sector companies** purchase and then sell tangible products without changing their basic form. These companies have one type of inventory: *merchandise inventory*.
- **Service-sector companies** provide services (intangible products)—for example, legal advice or audits—to their customers. These companies do not have an inventory of items for sale.

9. Three terms are widely used in describing manufacturing costs. In the following definitions, "the cost object" refers to "work in process inventory" and then "finished goods inventory."

- **Direct material costs** are the acquisition costs of all materials that eventually become part of the cost object and that can be traced to the cost object in an economically feasible way.
- **Direct manufacturing labor costs** include the compensation of all manufacturing labor that can be traced to the cost object in an economically feasible way. Direct manufacturing labor is typically hands-on assembly line labor.
- **Indirect manufacturing costs** (also called **manufacturing overhead costs** or **factory overhead costs**) are all manufacturing costs that are related to the cost object but that cannot be traced to it in an economically feasible way. Examples include power, indirect materials, indirect manufacturing labor, plant insurance, plant depreciation, and compensation of plant managers.

10. For companies with inventories, generally accepted accounting principles distinguish **inventoriable costs** from **period costs**.

- Inventoriable costs, according to GAAP and the IRS, are all costs of a product that are considered as assets in the balance sheet when they are incurred and that become cost of goods sold only when the product is sold. *For manufacturing companies, all manufacturing costs are inventoriable costs.* For merchandising companies, inventoriable costs are the costs of purchasing the merchandise. Because service companies have no inventories, they have no inventoriable costs.

- Period costs are all costs in the income statement other than cost of goods sold. Period costs are treated as expenses of the accounting period in which they are incurred.

11. In the income statement of a manufacturing company, cost of goods sold is computed as follows (figures assumed):

Beginning finished goods	$ 50,000
Add **cost of goods manufactured**	800,000
Cost of goods available for sale	850,000
Deduct ending finished goods	60,000
Cost of goods sold	$790,000

The line item, *cost of goods manufactured*, refers to the cost of goods brought to completion during the current accounting period, whether the the goods were started before or during the current accounting period. Cost of goods manufactured is often computed in a supporting schedule to the income statement as follows (figures assumed):

Beginning direct materials	$ 60,000
Add purchases of direct materials	510,000
Direct materials available for use	570,000
Deduct ending direct materials	50,000
Direct materials used	520,000
Add direct manufacturing labor	100,000
Add overhead manufacturing costs	230,000
Manufacturing costs incurred during the period	850,000
Add beginning work-in-process	120,000
Total manufacturing cost to account for	970,000
Deduct ending work-in- process	170,000
Cost of goods manufactured	$800,000

EXHIBIT 2-9, text p.42, shows the *flow of manufacturing costs*, from Work-in-Process Inventory to Finished Goods Inventory to Cost of Goods Sold.

12. Manufacturing costing systems use the terms **prime** costs and **conversion costs**.

- Prime costs are all direct manufacturing costs. Under the three-part classification of manufacturing costs in paragraph 9, prime costs are equal to direct material costs plus direct manufacturing labor costs. In cases where other direct manufacturing cost categories are used, they too are prime costs. For example, power costs could be classified as a direct cost if the power is metered to specific areas of a plant that are dedicated to manufacturing separate products.

- Conversion costs are all manufacturing costs other than direct material costs; they are incurred *to convert direct materials into finished goods*. Under the three-part classification of manufacturing costs, conversion costs are equal to direct manufacturing labor costs plus indirect manufacturing costs.

13. Indirect labor, a major component of manufacturing overhead, includes all manufacturing labor compensation other than direct labor. Examples include managers' salaries, department heads' salaries, and supervisors' salaries. Two main categories of indirect labor in manufacturing and service companies are **overtime premium** and **idle time**. Overtime premium is the wage rate paid to workers (for both direct labor and indirect labor) in *excess* of their straight-time wage rates. Overtime premium is classified as overhead when the overtime is attributable to the heavy overall volume of work. When a particular job, such as a rush order, is the sole reason for the overtime, the overtime premium is classified as a direct cost of that job. Idle time is wages paid for unproductive time caused by lack of orders, machine breakdowns, material shortages, poor scheduling, and the like.

14. Some manufacturing companies classify payroll fringe benefit costs of direct labor as overhead cost, whereas others classify them as direct labor cost. The latter approach is preferable because these payroll fringe benefit costs are a fundamental part of acquiring direct manufacturing labor services. To prevent disputes about cost items such as payroll fringe benefits, training time, overtime premium, idle time, vacations, and sick leave, contracts and laws should be as specific as feasible regarding definitions and measurements.

15. An important theme of the textbook is *using different costs for different purposes*. For ex-

ample, managers can assign different costs to a product depending on their purpose. A **product cost** is the sum of costs assigned to a product for a specific purpose. The product cost will be different if the purpose is (a) preparing financial statements for external reporting under generally accepted accounting principles (GAAP), (b) contracting with government agencies, or (c) pricing and product-mix decisions. For financial statements based on GAAP, a product cost includes only inventoriable costs. A product cost includes a broader set of costs for reimbursement under government contracts, or a still broader set of costs for pricing and product-mix decisions.

16. The three wide-ranging applications of cost accounting and cost management focus on:
a. Calculating the cost of products, services, and other cost objects
b. Obtaining information for planning and control and performance evaluation
c. Analyzing the relevant information for making
   decisions.

Chapters 3 through 12 explain these ideas, which also form the foundation for the study of various topics later in the textbook.

Featured Exercises

1. Whitaker Company's relevant range is between 8,000 units and 16,000 units. If 10,000 units are produced, variable costs are $200,000 and fixed costs are $450,000. Assuming production increases to 15,000 units, compute (a) total variable costs, (b) variable cost per unit, and (c) fixed cost per unit.

Solution

a. Variable cost per unit = $200,000 ÷ 10,000 = $20
   Total variable costs = $20 × 15,000 = $300,000
b. Variable cost per unit = $300,000 ÷ 15,000 = $20
c. Fixed cost per unit = $450,000 ÷ 15,000 = $30

2. The following information pertains to Thorpe Company's operations for January of the current year:

Inventories	Beginning	Ending
Direct materials	$18,000	$15,000
Work in proc-ess	9,000	6,000
Finished goods	27,000	36,000

Additional cost information for January: direct materials purchased $42,000, direct manufacturing labor $30,000, manufacturing overhead $40,000.

Compute cost of goods manufactured for January.

Solution

Direct materials used, $18,000 + $42,000 − $15,000	$ 45,000
Direct manufacturing labor	30,000
Manufacturing overhead	40,000
Manufacturing costs incurred during the period	115,000
Add beginning work-in-process inventory	9,000
Total manufacturing costs to account for	124,000
Deduct ending work-in-process inventory	6,000
Cost of goods manufactured	$118,000

Review Questions and Exercises

(All answers are at the end of the chapter.)

Completion Statements

Fill in the blank(s) to complete each statement.

1. For a given cost object, _____ costs are traced to it and _____ costs are allocated to it.
2. _____ is the band of the normal level of volume in which there is a specific relationship between the level of volume and the total variable costs or total fixed costs in question.
3. A _____ is a variable, such as the level of or volume, that causally affects costs over a given time span.
4. All costs of a product that are considered as assets when they are incurred and that become cost of goods sold only when the product is sold are called _____ costs.
5. _____ costs are all costs in the income statement other than cost of goods sold.
6. Indirect manufacturing costs are also known as _____ costs.
7. _____ costs are incurred to convert direct materials into finished goods.
8. Different costs are assigned to products for different purposes. Three of these purposes are:

   _____
   _____
   _____

True-False

Indicate whether each statement is true (T) or false (F).

____ 1. A cost object is a target level of costs to be achieved.
____ 2. Cost accumulation is a general term that encompasses both tracing costs to a cost object and allocating costs to that cost object.
____ 3. A given cost item can be a direct cost of one cost object and an indirect cost of another cost object.

____ 4. When graphed on a per unit basis, both variable costs and fixed costs are linear within the relevant range.
____ 5. When a manufacturer of soft drinks initially incurs television advertising and depreciation on bottle-capping machines, they are period costs.
____ 6. In the income statement of a manufacturing company, cost of goods manufactured refers to the cost of goods brought to completion during the current period, whether the goods were started before or during the current accounting period.
____ 7. The concept of inventoriable costs is applicable to manufacturing companies and merchandising companies, but not to service companies.
____ 8. Manufacturing costs incurred during the accounting period minus the decrease in work-in-process inventory during the period is equal to cost of goods manufactured.
____ 9. When a manufacturing plant becomes highly automated, the traditional three-part classification of manufacturing costs is not necessarily used.
____ 10. It is preferable to classify payroll fringe benefit costs of direct manufacturing labor as a manufacturing overhead cost.

Multiple Choice

Select the best answer to each question. Space is provided for computations after the quantitative questions.

____ 1. (CMA adapted) A fixed cost that would be considered a direct cost is:
   a. a controller's salary if the cost object is a unit of product.
   b. the cost of renting a warehouse to store inventory if the cost object is the Purchasing Department.
   c. an order clerk's salary if the cost object is the Purchasing Department.
   d. the cost of electricity if the cost object is the Internal Audit Department.

2. Booth Company has total fixed costs of $64,000 if 8,000 units are produced. The relevant range is 8,000 units to 16,000 units. If 10,000 units are produced, fixed costs are:
   a. $80,000 in total.
   b. $8 per unit.
   c. $48,000 in total.
   d. $6.40 per unit.

3. In general, costs that can be most reliably predicted are:
   a. fixed cost per unit.
   b. total cost per unit.
   c. total variable costs.
   d. variable cost per unit.

4. Oxley Company has total variable costs of $120,000 if 15,000 units are produced. The relevant range is 10,000 units to 20,000 units. If 12,000 units are produced, variable costs are:
   a. $10 per unit.
   b. $120,000 in total.
   c. $8 per unit.
   d. $90,000 in total.

5. (CPA adapted) The monthly cost of renting a manufacturing plant is:
   a. a prime cost and an inventoriable cost.
   b. a prime cost and a period cost.
   c. a conversion cost and an inventoriable cost.
   d. a conversion cost and a period cost.

6. (CPA adapted) Anthony Company has budgeted its cost of goods sold at $4,000,000, including fixed costs of $800,000. The variable cost of goods sold is expected to be 75% of revenues. Budgeted revenues are:
   a. $4,266,667.
   b. $4,800,000.
   c. $5,333,333.
   d. $6,400,000.

7. (CPA) For 2008, the gross margin of Dumas Company is $96,000; the cost of goods manufactured is $340,000; the beginning inventories of work in process and finished goods are $28,000 and $45,000, respectively; and the ending inventories of work in process and finished goods are $38,000 and $52,000, respectively. The revenues of Dumas Company for 2008 are:
   a. $419,000.
   b. $429,000.
   c. $434,000.
   d. $436,000.

8. Using the traditional three-part classification of manufacturing costs, prime costs and conversion costs have the common component of:
   a. direct material costs.
   b. direct manufacturing labor costs.
   c. variable manufacturing overhead costs.
   d. fixed manufacturing overhead costs.

9. An assembly worker at a manufacturing company earns $12 per hour for straight time and $18 per hour for time over 40 hours per week. In a given week, the assembler worked 47 hours. The overtime premium for the week is:
   a. $6.
   b. $42.
   c. $84.
   d. $126.

Review Exercises

Check Figures for these Review Exercises are at the end of the *Student Guide*. Solutions are at the end of the chapter.

1. (CMA adapted) Backus Company estimated its unit cost of producing and selling 12,000 units per month as follows:

Direct materials used	$32
Direct manufacturing labor	20
Variable manufacturing overhead	15
Fixed manufacturing overhead	6
Variable nonmanufacturing costs	3
Fixed nonmanufacturing costs	4
Total costs	$80

The cost driver for manufacturing costs is units produced. The cost driver for nonmanufacturing costs is units sold. The relevant range is 7,000 units to 14,000 units.

a. Compute fixed manufacturing overhead per unit for monthly production of 10,000 units.
b. Compute total costs (manufacturing and nonmanufacturing) for a month when 9,000 units are produced and 8,000 units are sold.

2. Yardley Corp. incurred the following manufacturing costs in 2010:

Variable manufacturing costs:	
Direct materials	$ 600,000
Direct manufacturing labor	560,000
Manufacturing overhead	40,000
Fixed manufacturing overhead	540,000
Total manufacturing costs	$1,740,000

In 2010, the total unit cost at production levels of 40,000 units and 60,000 units is $37.50 and $33.00, respectively. The relevant range is 35,000 units to 70,000 units.

Compute the number of units produced in 2010.

3. (CPA) The following information is from the records of Wiggins & Sons for 2010:

	Inventories	
	Ending	Beginning
Finished goods	$95,000	$110,000
Work in process	80,000	70,000
Direct materials	95,000	90,000

Costs Incurred During the Period	
Total manufacturing costs	$580,000
Manufacturing overhead	160,000
Direct materials used	190,000

a. Compute direct materials purchased.
b. Compute direct manufacturing labor costs.
c. Compute cost of goods sold.

Crossword Puzzle for Chapters 1 and 2

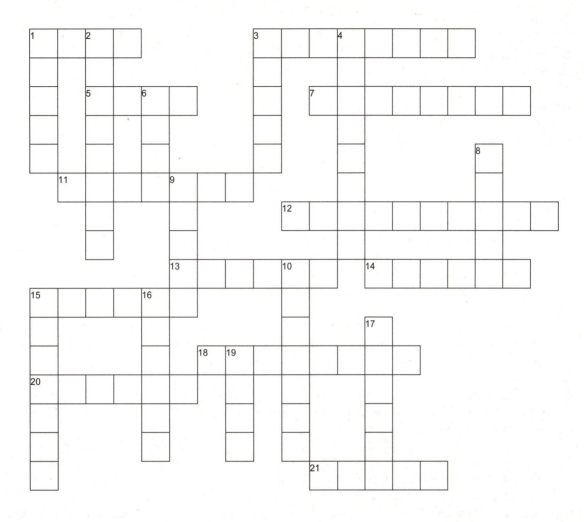

ACROSS

1. A resource sacrificed or forgone
3. Different costs for different _____
5. Management accounting's problem-solving _____
7. A _____ cost increases in total as more units are produced.
11. Cost-_____ approach
12. Chief accounting officer
13. Code of professional _____
14. A planning tool
15. All costs in the income statement except cost of goods sold
18. _____ focus
20. A cost _____ is a variable that causes costs to increase or decrease over a given time period.
21. Relevant _____

DOWN

1. Supply _____
2. Matches organization's capabilities to opportunities in marketplace
3. All direct manufacturing costs are _____ costs.
4. Includes selecting organization goals
6. _____ management versus staff management
8. _____ chain of business functions
9. A _____ cost decreases per unit as more units are produced.
10. Planning and _____ functions
15. _____ cost has three different meanings
16. Direct costs of a cost _____
17. Part of the value chain: _____ of products and processes
19. $100,000 ÷ 20,000 units = $5; $5 is the _____ cost

Answers and Solutions to Chapter 2 Review Questions and Exercises

Completion Statements

1. direct, indirect
2. Relevant range
3. cost driver
4. inventoriable
5. Period
6. manufacturing overhead (factory overhead)
7. Conversion
8. preparing financial statements, contracting with government agencies, pricing and product-mix decisions

True-False

1. F A cost object is anything for which a measurement of costs is desired. Examples of cost objects include products, customers, projects, and departments.
2. F The statement defines *cost assignment*, not *cost accumulation*. Cost accumulation is the collection of cost data in some organized way by means of an accounting system.
3. T
4. F Variable cost per unit does not change within the relevant range. Fixed cost per unit increases (decreases)—though not in a straight line—if the related level of volume decreases (increases). When graphed on a *total basis*, both variable costs and fixed costs are straight lines (linear) within the relevant range.
5. F When they are initially incurred, nonmanufacturing costs are period costs and manufacturing costs are inventoriable costs. Television advertising is a period cost, and depreciation on the bottle-capping machines is an inventoriable cost.
6. T
7. T
8. F When work-in-process inventory decreases during the accounting period (that is, the ending work-in-process inventory is less than the beginning work-in-process inventory), cost of goods manufactured exceeds total manufacturing costs incurred for the period. Cost of goods manufactured, therefore, is equal to manufacturing costs incurred during the period *plus* the decrease in work-in-process inventory. EXHIBIT 2-8, text p.40, shows the opposite case in which work-in-process inventory increased during the period.
9. T
10. F It is preferable to classify payroll fringe benefit costs of direct manufacturing labor as a direct manufacturing labor cost. That's because payroll fringe benefit costs are a fundamental aspect of acquiring the direct manufacturing labor services.

Multiple Choice

1. c Answers (a), (b), and (d) refer to indirect costs of their respective cost objects.
2. d $64,000 ÷ 10,000 = $6.40 per unit
3. d In general, variable cost *per unit* and fixed costs *in total* can be most reliably predicted because a forecast of the level of activity or volume is not required.
4. c $120,000 ÷ 15,000 = $8 per unit, which is also the variable cost per unit when 12,000 units are produced.
5. c Plant rent is part of manufacturing overhead costs. As a result, it is a conversion cost and an inventoriable cost.
6. a The variable portion of budgeted cost of goods sold is $4,000,000 − $800,000 = $3,200,000. Because this amount is 75% of revenues, budgeted revenues are $3,200,000 ÷ 0.75 = $4,266,667.

7. b

Beginning finished goods	$ 45,000
Cost of goods manufactured	340,000
Cost of goods available for sale	385,000
Ending finished goods	52,000
Cost of goods sold	$333,000

Revenues	$ R
Cost of goods sold	333,000
Gross margin	$ 96,000

$$R − \$333,000 = \$96,000$$
$$R = \$96,000 + \$333,000 = \$429,000$$

Note, the beginning and ending work-in-process inventories are not explicitly included in these computations. That's because the cost of goods manufactured, $340,000, includes the change in work-in-process inventory.

8. b Under the traditional three-part classification of manufacturing costs:
Prime costs = Direct material costs + Direct manufacturing labor costs
Conversion costs = Direct manufacturing labor costs + Manufacturing overhead costs
9. b Overtime premium = (47 − 40) × ($18 − $12) = 7 × $6 = $42

Review Exercise 1

   a. Fixed manufacturing overhead = 12,000 × \$6 = \$72,000

       Fixed manufacturing overhead per unit = \$72,000 ÷ 10,000 = \$7.20

   b. Variable manufacturing costs

9,000 × (\$32 + \$20 + \$15)	\$603,000
Fixed manufacturing costs, 12,000 × \$6	72,000
Variable nonmanufacturing costs, 8,000 × \$3	24,000
Fixed nonmanufacturing costs, 12,000 × \$4	48,000
Total costs	\$747,000

Review Exercise 2

Variable cost per unit:

  \$37.50 − (\$540,000 ÷ 40,000) = \$37.50 − \$13.50 = \$24.00

or

  \$33.00 − (\$540,000 ÷ 60,000) = \$33.00 − \$9.00 = \$24.00

Units produced = (\$600,000 + \$560,000 +\$40,000) ÷ \$24.00

                = \$1,200,000 ÷ \$24.00 = 50,000 units

Review Exercise 3

a. Direct materials costs:

Beginning inventory	$ 90,000
Add purchases	P
Available for use	?
Deduct ending inventory	95,000
Direct materials used	$190,000

$90,000 + P - \$95,000 = \$190,000$

$P = \$190,000 - \$90,000 + \$95,000 = \$195,000$

b.

Direct materials used	$190,000
Direct manufacturing labor costs	L
Manufacturing overhead costs	160,000
Manufacturing costs incurred during the period	$580,000

$\$190,000 + L + \$160,000 = \$580,000$

$L = \$580,000 - \$190,000 - \$160,000 = \$230,000$

c. Two steps are used to obtain the answer. First, compute cost of goods manufactured:

Manufacturing costs incurred during the period	$580,000
Add beginning work in process	70,000
Manufacturing costs to account for	650,000
Deduct ending work in process	80,000
Cost of goods manufactured	$570,000

Second, compute cost of goods sold:

Beginning finished goods	$110,000
Add cost of goods manufactured	570,000
Cost of goods available for sale	680,000
Deduct ending finished goods	95,000
Cost of goods sold	$585,000

C	O	S	T			P	U	R	P	O	S	E	S
H		T				R		L					
A		R	O	L	E	I		V	A	R	I	A	B	L	E
I		A		I		M		N					V
N		T		N		E		N				A
	B	E	N	E	F	I	T		I			V
	G		I		C	O	N	T	R	O	L	L	E	R
	Y		X			G			U
		E	T	H	I	C	S	B	U	D	G	E	T
P	E	R	I	O	D	O
R		B		N	D
O		J	C	U	S	T	O	M	E	R
D	R	I	V	E	R	N	R	S
U		C	I	O	I
C		T	T	L	G
T		R	A	N	G	E

Cost-Volume-Profit Analysis

Overview

This chapter explains a planning tool called **cost-volume-profit (CVP) analysis**. CVP analysis studies the behavior of total revenues, total costs, and operating income (profit) as changes occur in the units sold, the selling price, the variable cost per unit, or the fixed costs of a product. The reliability of the results from CVP analysis depends on the reasonableness of the underlying assumptions. The Appendix to the chapter gives additional insights about CVP analysis; it explains decision models and uncertainty.

Highlights

1.   Because managers want to avoid operating losses, they are interested in the **breakeven point** calculated using CVP analysis. The breakeven point is the quantity of output sold at which total revenues equal total costs. There is neither a profit nor a loss at the breakeven point. To illustrate, assume a company sells 2,000 units of its only product for $50 per unit, variable cost is $20 per unit, and fixed costs are $60,000 per month. Under these conditions, the company is operating at the breakeven point:

Revenues, 2,000 × $50	$100,000
Deduct:	
Variable costs, 2,000 × $20	40,000
Fixed costs	60,000
Operating income	$ -0-

This breakeven point can be expressed two ways: *2,000 units* and *$100,000 of revenues.*

2.   Under CVP analysis, the income statement above is reformatted to show a key line item, **contribution margin**:

Revenues, 2,000 × $50	$100,000
Variable costs, 2,000 × $20	40,000
Contribution margin	60,000
Fixed costs	60,000
Operating income	$ -0-

This format is called the **contribution income statement** because it groups costs into the variable and fixed categories to highlight contribution margin. *The contribution income statement is used extensively in this chapter and throughout the textbook.*

3.   Contribution margin can be expressed three ways: *in total, on a per unit basis,* and *as a percentage of revenues.* In our example, total contribution margin is $60,000. **Contribution margin per unit** is the difference between selling price and variable cost per unit: $50 − $20 = $30. Contribution margin per unit is also equal to contribution margin divided by the number of units sold: $60,000 ÷ 2,000 = $30. **Contribution margin percentage** (also called **contribution margin ratio**) is contribution margin per unit divided by selling price: $30 ÷ $50 = 60%; it is also equal to contribution margin divided by revenues: $60,000 ÷ $100,000 = 60%. This contribution margin percentage means that 60 cents in contribution margin is gained for each $1 of revenues.

4.   In our example, compute the breakeven point (BEP) *in units* and *in revenues* as follows:

$$\text{BEP units} = \frac{\text{Total fixed costs}}{\text{Contribution margin per unit}}$$

$$\text{BEP units} = \frac{\$60,000}{\$30} = 2,000 \text{ units}$$

$$\text{BEP revenues} = \frac{\text{Total fixed costs}}{\text{Contribution margin percentage}}$$

$$\text{BEP revenues} = \frac{\$60,000}{0.60} = \$100,000$$

5. The CVP analysis above is based on the following assumptions:

a. Changes in the levels of revenues and costs arise only because of changes in the number of product (or service) units sold (that is, the number of output units is the only driver of revenues and costs).
b. Total costs can be separated into a fixed component that does not vary with units sold and a component that is variable with respect to units sold.
c. When represented graphically, the behaviors of total revenues and total costs are linear (straight lines) in relation to the units sold within a relevant range (and time period).
d. Selling price, variable cost per unit, and total fixed costs (within a relevant range and time period) are known and constant.

6. While the breakeven point is often of interest to managers, CVP analysis considers a broader question: What amount of sales in units or in revenues is needed to achieve a specified *target operating income*? The answer is easily obtained by adding target operating income to total fixed costs in the numerator of the formulas above. Assuming target operating income (TOI) is $15,000:

$$\text{Unit sales to achieve TOI} = \frac{\$60,000 + \$15,000}{\$30} = 2,500 \text{ units}$$

$$\text{Revenues to achieve TOI} = \frac{\$60,000 + \$15,000}{0.60} = \$125,000$$

7. Because for-profit organizations are subject to income taxes, their CVP analyses must include this factor. For example, if a company earns $50,000 before income taxes and the tax rate is 40%, then:

Operating income	$50,000
Deduct incomes taxes (40%)	20,000
Net income	$30,000

To state a target *net income* figure in terms of *operating income*, divide target net income by $1 -$ tax rate: $\$30,000 \div (1 - .40) = \$50,000$. Note, the income-tax factor does not change the breakeven point because no income taxes arise if operating income is $0.

8. Managers use CVP analysis to guide their decisions, many of which are strategic decisions. For example, CVP analysis helps managers decide how much to spend on advertising, whether or not to reduce selling price, whether or not to expand into new markets, and which features to add to existing products. Of course, different choices can affect fixed costs, variable cost per unit, selling prices, units sold, and operating income.

9. Single-number "best estimates" of input data for CVP analysis are subject to varying degrees of **uncertainty**, the possibility that an actual amount will deviate from an expected amount. One approach to deal with uncertainty is to use *sensitivity analysis* (discussed in paragraphs 10 through 12). Another approach is to compute *expected values* using probability distributions (discussed in paragraph 18).

10. **Sensitivity analysis** is a "what if" technique that managers use to calculate how an outcome will change if the original predicted data are not achieved or if an underlying assumption changes. In the context of CVP analysis, sensitivity analysis calculates how operating income (or the breakeven point) changes if the predicted data for selling price, variable cost per unit, fixed costs, or units sold are not achieved. The sensitivity to various possible outcomes broadens managers' perspectives as to what might actually occur *before* they make cost commitments. Electronic spreadsheets, such as Excel, enable managers to conduct CVP-based sensitivity analyses in a systematic and efficient way.

11. An aspect of sensitivity analysis is **margin of safety**, the amount by which budgeted (or actual) revenues exceed breakeven revenues. The margin of safety answers the "what-if" question: If budgeted (or actual) revenues are above breakeven revenues and drop, how far can they fall below budgeted (or actual) revenues before breakeven revenues are reached?

12. CVP-based sensitivity analysis highlights the risks and returns that an existing cost structure holds for a company. This insight may lead managers to consider alternative cost structures. For example, compensating a salesperson on the basis

of a sales commission (a variable cost) rather than a salary (a fixed cost) decreases the company's downside risk if demand is low but decreases its return if demand is high. The risk-return tradeoff across alternative cost structures can be measured as **operating leverage**. Operating leverage describes the effects that fixed costs have on changes in operating income as changes occur in units sold and contribution margin. Companies with a high proportion of fixed costs in their cost structures have high operating leverage; consequently, small changes in units sold cause large changes in operating income. *At any given level of sales*:

$$\text{Degree of operating leverage} = \frac{\text{Contribution margin}}{\text{Operating income}}$$

Knowing the degree of operating leverage at a given level of sales helps managers calculate the effect of changes in sales on operating income.

13. The time horizon being considered for a decision affects the classification of costs as variable or fixed. The shorter the time horizon, the greater the proportion of total costs that are fixed. For example, virtually all the costs of an airline flight are fixed one hour before takeoff. When the time horizon is lengthened to one year and then five years, more and more costs become variable. This example underscores the point that which costs are fixed in a specific decision situation depends on the length of the time horizon and the relevant range.

14. **Sales mix** is the quantities (or proportions) of various products (or services) that constitute total unit sales of a company. If the sales mix changes and the overall unit sales target is still achieved, however, the effect on the breakeven point and operating income depends on how the original proportions of lower or higher contribution margin products have shifted. Other things being equal, for any given total quantity of units sold, the breakeven point decreases and operating income increases if the sales mix shifts toward products with higher contribution margins.

15. In multiple product situations, CVP analysis assumes a given sales mix of products remains constant as the level of total units sold changes.

The breakeven point is some number of units of each product, depending on the sales mix. To illustrate, assume a company sells two products, A and B. The sales mix is 4 units of A and 3 units of B. The contribution margins per unit are $80 for A and $40 for B. Fixed costs are $308,000 per month. To compute the breakeven point:

$$\text{Let } 4X = \text{No. of units of A to break even}$$
$$\text{Then } 3X = \text{No. of units of B to break even}$$

$$\text{BEP in X units} = \frac{\$308,000}{4(\$80)+3(\$40)}$$

$$\text{BEP in X units} = \frac{\$308,000}{\$440} = 700 \text{ bundles}$$

A units to break even $= 4 \times 700 = 2,800$ units

B units to break even $= 3 \times 700 = 2,100$ units

Proof of breakeven point:

A: 2,800 × $80	$224,000
B: 2,100 × $40	84,000
Total contribution margin	308,000
Fixed costs	308,000
Operating income	$ -0-

16. CVP analysis can be applied to service organizations and nonprofit organizations. The key is measuring their output. Unlike manufacturing and merchandising companies that measure their output in units of product, the measure of output differs from one service industry (or nonprofit organization) to another. For example, airlines measure output in passenger miles and hotels/motels use room-nights occupied. Government welfare agencies measure output in number of clients served and universities use student credit-hours.

17. *Contribution margin*, a key concept in this chapter, contrasts with *gross margin* discussed in Chapter 2. Gross margin is an important line item in the GAAP income statements of merchandising and manufacturing companies. *Gross margin* is total revenues minus cost of goods sold, whereas *contribution margin* is total revenues minus total variable costs (from the entire value chain). Gross margin and contribution margin will be different amounts (except in the highly unlikely case that cost of goods sold and total variable costs are equal). For example, a manufacturing company

deducts fixed manufacturing costs that have become a period cost from revenues in calculating gross margin (but not in calculating contribution margin); it deducts sales commissions from revenues in calculating contribution margin (but not in calculating gross margin because sales commissions are a period cost).

18. (Appendix) A *probability distribution* incorporates uncertainty into a *decision model*. This approach provides additional insights about CVP analysis. A decision model, a formal method for making a choice, usually includes five steps: (a) identify a *choice criterion* such as maximize income, (b) identify the set of alternative actions (choices) that can be taken, (c) identify the set of *events* (possible occurrences) that can occur, (d) assign a *probability* to each event that can occur, and (e) identify the set of possible *outcomes* (the predicted economic result of each action-event combination). Uncertainty is present in a decision model because for each alternative action there are two or more possible events, each with a probability of occurrence. The correct decision is to choose the action with the best **expected value**. Expected value is the weighted average of the outcomes, with the probability of each outcome serving as the weight. Although the expected value criterion helps managers make *good decisions*, it does not prevent *bad outcomes* from occurring.

Featured Exercise

In its budget for next month, Karney Company has revenues of $500,000, variable costs of $350,000, and fixed costs of $135,000.

a. Compute contribution margin percentage.
b. Compute total revenues needed to break even.
c. Compute total revenues needed to achieve a target operating income of $45,000.
d. Compute total revenues needed to achieve a target net income of $48,000, assuming the income tax rate is 40%.

Solution

a. Contribution margin percentage = ($500,000 − $350,000) ÷ $500,000

$$= \$150{,}000 \div \$500{,}000 = 30\%$$

Note, variable costs as a percentage of revenues = $\$350{,}000 \div \$500{,}000 = 70\%$

b. Breakeven point = $\$135{,}000 \div 0.30 = \$450{,}000$

Proof of breakeven point:

Revenues	$450,000
Variable costs, $450,000 × 0.70	315,000
Contribution margin	135,000
Fixed costs	135,000
Operating income	$ -0-

c. Let X = Total revenues needed to achieve target operating income of $45,000

$$X = \frac{\$135{,}000 + \$45{,}000}{0.30} = \frac{\$180{,}000}{0.30} = \$600{,}000$$

d. Two steps are used to obtain the answer. First, compute operating income when net income is $48,000:

$$\frac{\$48{,}000}{1 - 0.40} = \frac{\$48{,}000}{0.60} = \$80{,}000$$

Second, compute total revenues needed to achieve a target operating income of $80,000 (that is, a target net income of $48,000), which is denoted by Y:

$$Y = \frac{\$135{,}000 + \$80{,}000}{0.30} = \frac{\$215{,}000}{0.30} = \$716{,}667$$

Review Questions and Exercises

(All answers are at the end of the chapter.)

Completion Statements

Fill in the blank(s) to complete each statement.

1. _____ is equal to selling price minus variable cost per unit.
2. The financial report that highlights the contribution margin as a line item is called the _____.
3. The possibility that an actual amount will deviate from an expected amount is called _____.
4. _____ is a "what if" technique that, when used in the context of CVP analysis, calculates how an outcome such as operating income will change if the original predicted data are not achieved or if an underlying assumption changes.
5. The quantities (or proportions) of various products (or services) that constitute total unit sales of a company is called the _____.
6. _____ describes the effects that fixed costs have on changes in operating income as changes occur in units sold and, hence, in contribution margin.
7. (Appendix) In a decision model, the correct decision is to choose the action with the best _____, which is the weighted average of the outcomes with the probability of each outcome serving as the weight.

True-False

Indicate whether each statement is true (T) or false (F).

_____ 1. Generally, the breakeven point in revenues can be easily determined by simply summing all costs in the company's contribution income statement.

_____ 2. At the breakeven point, total fixed costs always equals contribution margin.

_____ 3. The amount by which budgeted (or actual) revenues exceed breakeven revenues is called the margin of forecasting error.

_____ 4. An increase in the income tax rate increases the breakeven point.

_____ 5. Trading off fixed costs in a company's cost structure for higher variable cost per unit decreases downside risk if demand is low and decreases return if demand is high.

_____ 6. At any given level of sales, the degree of operating leverage is equal to contribution margin divided by operating income.

_____ 7. If the budget appropriation for a government social welfare agency is reduced by 15% and its cost-volume relationships remain the same, the client service level would decrease by 15%.

_____ 8. The longer the time horizon in a decision situation, the lower the percentage of total costs that are variable.

_____ 9. Cost of goods sold in manufacturing companies is a variable cost.

_____ 10. (Appendix) The probability distribution for the mutually exclusive and collectively exhaustive set of events in a decision model sums to 1.00.

_____ 11. (Appendix) Even if a manager makes a good decision, a bad outcome may still occur.

Multiple Choice

Select the best answer to each question. Space is provided for computations after the quantitative questions.

_____ 1. (CPA) CVP analysis _does not_ assume that:
a. selling prices remain constant.
b. there is a single driver of both revenue and cost.
c. total fixed costs vary inversely with the output level.
d. total costs are linear within the relevant range.

_____ 2. Given for Winn Company in 2010: revenues $530,000, manufacturing costs $220,000 (one-half fixed), and marketing and administrative costs $270,000 (two-thirds variable). The contribution margin is:
a. $40,000.
b. $240,000.
c. $310,000.
d. $330,000.

_____ 3. Using the information in question 2 and ignoring inventories, the gross margin for Winn Company is:
a. $40,000.
b. $240,000.
c. $310,000.
d. $330,000.

_____ 4. (CPA) Koby Company has revenues of $200,000, variable costs of $150,000, fixed costs of $60,000, and an operating loss of $10,000. By how much would Koby need to increase its revenues in order to achieve a target operating income of 10% of revenues?
a. $200,000
b. $231,000
c. $251,000
d. $400,000

5. (CPA) The following information pertains to Nova Co.'s CVP relationships:

Breakeven point in units	1,000
Variable cost per unit	$500
Total fixed costs	$150,000

How much will be contributed to operating income by the 1,001st unit sold?
a. $650
b. $500
c. $150
d. $0

6. (CPA) During 2010, Thor Lab supplied hospitals with a comprehensive diagnostic kit for $120. At a volume of 80,000 kits, Thor had fixed costs of $1,000,000 and an operating income of $200,000. Due to an adverse legal decision, Thor's liability insurance in 2011 will increase by $1,200,000. Assuming the volume and other costs are unchanged, what should the selling price be in 2011 if Thor is to earn the same operating income of $200,000?
a. $120
b. $135
c. $150
d. $240

7. In the fiscal year just completed, Varsity Shop reported net income of $24,000 on revenues of $300,000. The variable costs as a percentage of revenues are 70%. The income tax rate is 40%. What is the amount of fixed costs?
a. $30,000
b. $50,000
c. $66,000
d. $170,000

8. The amount of total costs probably will not vary significantly in decision situations in which:
a. the time span is quite short and the change in units of output is quite large.
b. the time span is quite long and the change in units of output is quite large.
c. the time span is quite long and the change in units of output is quite small.
d. the time span is quite short and the change in units of output is quite small.

9. (CPA) Product Cott has revenues of $200,000, a contribution margin of 20%, and a margin of safety of $80,000. What are Cott's fixed costs?
a. $16,000
b. $24,000
c. $80,000
d. $96,000

10. For a multiple-product company, a shift in sales mix from products with high contribution margin percentages toward products with low contribution margin percentages causes the breakeven point to be:
a. lower.
b. higher.
c. unchanged.
d. different but undeterminable.

11. (Appendix, CMA) The College Honor Society sells large pretzels at the home football games. The following information is available:

Unit Sales	Probability
2,000 pretzels	.10
3,000 pretzels	.15
4,000 pretzels	.20
5,000 pretzels	.35
6,000 pretzels	.20

The pretzels are sold for $2.00 each, and the cost per pretzel is $0.60. Any unsold pretzels are discarded because they will be stale before the next home game. Considering the probability information and other factors, the decision is made to stock 4,000 pretzels for this week's game. If only 3,000 of those pretzels are sold, the operating income would be:

a. $5,600.
b. $4,200.
c. $3,600.
d. $900.
e. none of the above.

Review Exercises

> Check Figures for these Review Exercises are at the end of the *Student Guide*. Solutions are at the end of the chapter.

1. (CMA) The income statement for Davann Co. presented below shows the operating results for the fiscal year just ended. Davann had sales of 1,800 tons of product during that year. The manufacturing capacity of Davann's facilities is 3,000 tons of product.

Revenues		$900,000
Variable costs:		
Manufacturing	$315,000	
Nonmanufacturing	180,000	495,000
Contribution margin		405,000
Fixed costs:		
Manufacturing	90,000	
Nonmanufacturing	157,500	247,500
Operating income		157,500
Income taxes (40%)		63,000
Net income		$ 94,500

a. If the sales volume is estimated to be 2,100 tons for next year, and if the selling price and cost-behavior patterns remain the same next year, how much net income does Davann expect to earn next year?

b. Assume Davann estimates the selling price per ton will decline 10% next year, variable cost will increase by $40 per ton, and total fixed costs will not change. Compute how many tons must be sold next year to earn net income of $94,500.

2. Valdosta Manufacturing Co. produces and sells two products:

	T	U
Selling price	$25	$16
Variable cost per unit	20	13

Total fixed costs are $40,500.

Compute the breakeven point in units for products T and U, assuming the sales mix is five units of U for each unit of T.

3. (CPA) Dallas Corporation wishes to market a new product at a selling price of $1.50 per unit. Fixed costs for this product are $100,000 for less than 500,000 units of output and $150,000 for 500,000 or more units of output. The contribution margin percentage is 20%.

Compute how many units of this product must be sold to earn a target operating income of $100,000.

4. (Appendix, CMA) The ARC Radio Company is trying to decide whether to introduce a new product, a wrist "radiowatch" designed for shortwave reception of the exact time as broadcast by the National Bureau of Standards. The radiowatch would be priced at $60, which is exactly twice the variable cost per unit to manufacture and sell it. The fixed costs to introduce the radiowatch are $240,000 per year. The following probability distribution estimates the demand for the product:

Annual Demand	Probability
6,000 units	.20
8,000 units	.20
10,000 units	.20
12,000 units	.20
14,000 units	.10
16,000 units	.10

a. Compute the expected value of demand for the radiowatch.
b. Compute the probability that the introduction of the radiowatch will not increase the company's operating income.

Answers and Solutions to Chapter 3 Review Questions and Exercises

Completion Statements

1. Contribution margin per unit
2. contribution income statement
3. uncertainty
4. Sensitivity analysis
5. sales mix
6. Operating leverage
7. expected value

True-False

1. F The breakeven point in revenues is computed by dividing total fixed costs by contribution-margin percentage. The computation described in the statement gives breakeven revenues *only if* the company happened to be operating at the breakeven point.
2. T
3. F The amount by which budgeted revenues exceed the breakeven quantity is called the *margin of safety*.
4. F The breakeven point is unaffected by income taxes because operating income at the breakeven point is $0 and, hence, no income taxes arise.
5. T
6. T
7. F If the budget appropriation for a government social welfare agency is reduced by 15% and the cost-volume relationships remain the same, the client service level would decrease by more than 15% because of the existence of fixed costs. For example, the illustration, text pp.80-81, has a 21.4% decrease in the service level when the budget appropriation is reduced by 15%.
8. F The longer the time horizon in a decision situation, the lower the percentage of total costs that are fixed and the higher the percentage of total costs that are variable.
9. F Cost of goods sold in manufacturing companies includes both variable and fixed manufacturing costs.
10. T
11. T

Multiple Choice

1. c One of the assumptions in CVP analysis is that total fixed costs remain the same within the relevant range. In other words, fixed cost per unit varies inversely with the output level within the relevant range.
2. b Contribution margin = $530,000 − $220,000(1/2 variable) − $270,000(2/3 variable)
$$= \$530,000 - \$110,000 - \$180,000 = \$240,000$$
3. c Gross margin = $530,000 − $220,000 = $310,000
4. a Let R = Revenues needed to earn a target operating income of 10% of revenues
$$R - (\$150,000 \div \$200,000)R - \$60,000 = 0.10R$$
$$R - 0.75R - 0.10R = \$60,000$$
$$0.15R = \$60,000$$
$$R = \$60,000 \div 0.15 = \$400,000$$

Because current revenues are $200,000, an *increase in revenues* of $200,000 is needed to earn a target operating income of 10% of revenues.

5. c Total costs at breakeven $= (1,000 \times \$500) + \$150,000 = \$650,000$

Selling price $= \$650,000 \div 1,000$ units $= \$650$

Contribution margin per unit $= \$650 - \$500 = \$150$

6. b The selling price in 2011 to earn the same operating income of \$200,000 is the selling price in 2010, \$120, increased by the amount of the higher liability insurance in 2009, \$1,200,000, spread over the 80,000-unit sales volume:

Selling price in 2011 $= \$120 + (\$1,200,000 \div 80,000) = \$120 + \$15 = \$135$

7. b Three steps are used to obtain the answer. First, compute contribution margin.

Contribution margin percentage $= 100\% -$ Variable costs percentage of $70\% = 30\%$.

Contribution margin $= \$300,000 \times 0.30 = \$90,000$. Second, compute operating income:

$$\frac{\$24,000}{1-0.40} = \frac{\$24,000}{0.60} = \$40,000$$

Third, the difference between contribution margin and operating income is fixed costs:

$\$90,000 - \$40,000 = \$50,000$

8. d An example of this decision situation is deciding whether to add a passenger to an airline flight that has empty seats and will depart in one hour. Variable cost for the passenger is negligible. Virtually all the costs in this decision situation are fixed.

9. b Margin of safety answers the what-if question: If budgeted revenues exceed the breakeven point and drop, how far can they fall below the budget before the breakeven point is reached?

$$\begin{aligned} \text{Breakeven point} &= \$200,000 - \$80,000 = \$120,000 \\ \text{Variable costs} &= \$120,000 \times (1-0.20) \\ &= \$120,000 \times 0.80 = \$96,000 \\ \text{Fixed costs} &= \$120,000 - \$96,000 = \$24,000 \end{aligned}$$

Proof of breakeven point: $\$24,000 \div 0.20 = \$120,000$

10. b A shift in the sales mix from high contribution margin percentage products toward low ones decreases the overall contribution margin percentage of the sales mix. That change increases the breakeven point.

11. c Operating income $= 3,000(\$2.00) - 4,000(\$0.60) = \$6,000 - \$2,400 = \$3,600$

Review Exercise 1

a. Three steps are used to obtain the answer. First, compute selling price: $\$900,000 \div 1,800 = \$500$. Second, compute variable cost per ton: $\$495,000 \div 1,800 = \$275$. Third, prepare a contribution income statement at the 2,100-ton level of output:

Revenues, $2,100 \times \$500$	\$1,050,000
Variable costs, $2,100 \times \$275$	577,500
Contribution margin	472,500
Fixed costs	247,500
Operating income	225,000
Income taxes (40%)	90,000
Net income	$\underline{\$\ \ 135,000}$

b. Let Q = Number of tons to break even next year

$$\$500Q(1-0.10) - (\$275Q + \$40Q) - \$247,500 = \frac{\$94,500}{1-0.40}$$

$$\$450Q - \$315Q = \$247,500 + \$157,500$$
$$\$135Q = \$405,000$$
$$Q = 3,000 \text{ tons}$$

Review Exercise 2

Let T = Number of units of T to be sold to break even
Then 5T = Number of units of U to be sold to break even
$$\$25T + \$16(5T) - \$20T - \$13(5T) - \$40,500 = \$0$$
$$\$25T + \$80T - \$20T - \$65T = \$40,500$$
$$\$20T = \$40,500; \ T = 2,025 \text{ units}; \ 5T = 2,025 \times 5 = 10,125 \text{ units}$$
Proof: $\$25(2,025) + \$16(10,125) - \$20(2,025) - \$13(10,125) - \$40,500 = \$0$
$$\$50,625 + \$162,000 - \$40,500 - \$131,625 - \$40,500 = \$0$$
$$\$0 = \$0$$

Review Exercise 3

Two steps are used to obtain the answer. First, determine if fixed costs will be $100,000 or $150,000. If fixed costs are $100,000, the *maximum* operating income is attained at 499,999 units:

Revenues, 499,999 × $1.50	$749,998.50
Variable costs, 80% of revenues	599,998.80
Contribution margin, 20% of revenues	149,999.70
Fixed costs	100,000.00
Operating income	$ 49,999.70

Because this operating income is below the target of $100,000, the output level needs to be greater than 499,999 units and, hence, fixed costs will be $150,000. Second, compute the required output level:

Let Q = Number of units to be sold to earn a target operating income of $100,000
$$\$1.50Q - (1 - 0.20)(\$1.50)Q - \$150,000 = \$100,000$$
$$\$1.50Q - \$1.20Q = \$100,000 + \$150,000$$
$$\$0.30Q = \$250,000$$
$$Q = 833,333.33, \text{ rounded to } 833,334 \text{ units}$$

Review Exercise 4

a.

6,000 × .20 =	1,200
8,000 × .20 =	1,600
10,000 × .20 =	2,000
12,000 × .20 =	2,400
14,000 × .10 =	1,400
16,000 × .10 =	1,600
Expected value of demand in units	10,200

b. If the number of units sold each year is *equal to or less than* the breakeven point, the radiowatch will not increase the company's operating income. At the breakeven point,

Revenues – Variable costs – Fixed costs = $0
Let Q = Number of units to be sold to break even
$$\$60Q - (\$60 \div 2)Q - \$240,000 = \$0$$
$$\$60Q - \$30Q = \$240,000$$
$$\$30Q = \$240,000$$
$$Q = \$240,000 \div \$30 = 8,000 \text{ units}$$

Because the company's operating income will not increase if 8,000 units or 6,000 units are sold, the probability of *either* of these events occurring is equal to the sum of their individual probabilities: 0.20 + 0.20 = 0.40.

CHAPTER	Job Costing
4	

Overview

This chapter explains how job-costing systems determine the cost of products or services. Managers use job-costing information for pricing, product-mix, and cost management decisions and (in the case of manufacturing companies) inventory valuation. The major illustration in the chapter demonstrates, on a transaction-by-transaction basis, the flow of manufacturing costs through the accounts in the general and subsidiary ledgers.

Highlights

1. The building block concepts of costing systems are *cost object*, *direct costs of a cost object*, *indirect costs of a cost object* (terms introduced in Chapter 2), **cost pool**, and **cost-allocation base** (terms introduced in this chapter). Products, services, and customers are often used as cost objects in costing systems. For example, if product X is the chosen cost object, the direct costs will be *traced* to X and the indirect costs will be *allocated* to X. In order to allocate indirect costs to product X, (i) individual indirect cost items are grouped into one or more *cost pools* and (ii) a *cost-allocation base* is chosen for each cost pool.

2. There are two basic types of costing systems used to assign costs to products or services: a **job-costing system** and a **process-costing system**.

- In a job-costing system, the cost object is a unit or multiple units of a *distinct* product or service called a **job**. The product or service is often custom-made, such as a construction job or an advertising campaign, and direct and indirect costs are assigned to each job.
- In a process-costing system, the cost object is masses of *identical or similar* units of a product or service. Examples are barrels of oil refined or bank deposits processed. Each period the total costs of producing this type of product or service are divided by the total number

of units produced to obtain the average cost per unit.

3. Job-costing systems use a seven-step procedure to assign costs to individual jobs:

Step 1: Identify the job that is the chosen cost object.

Step 2: Identify the direct costs of the job.

Step 3: Select the cost-allocation bases to use for allocating indirect costs to the job.

Step 4: Identify the indirect costs associated with each cost-allocation base.

Step 5: Compute the rate per unit of each cost-allocation base used to allocate indirect costs to the job.

Step 6: Compute the indirect costs allocated to the job.

Step 7: Compute the total cost of the job by adding all direct and indirect costs assigned to the job.

To illustrate this procedure, assume a custom-made piece of equipment (the job) is the chosen cost object. After performing Steps 2 through 6 (explained below), the result for Step 7 is as follows:

Direct material costs	$ 7,000
Direct manufacturing labor costs	2,500
Indirect manufacturing costs	8,800
Total manufacturing costs of equipment	$18,300

Details about performing Steps 2 through 6:

- For each direct cost traced to the job, the actual quantity used is multiplied by the actual cost rate. Assume that several types of direct materials were used in various quantities. The total cost of all the direct materials is $7,000.
- Machine-hours was selected as the only cost-allocation base for allocating indirect manufacturing costs (manufacturing overhead) to the job.

- All $220,000 of the company's indirect manufacturing costs were grouped into a single cost pool and allocated based on a total of 2,000 machine-hours. The **indirect-cost rate** = $220,000 ÷ 2,000 = $110 per machine-hour.
- Eighty machine-hours were used to produce the custom-made equipment, so indirect manufacturing costs of $8,800 (80 × $110) were allocated to the job.

4. In our example, the indirect-cost rate is computed as follows:

$$\frac{\$220,000}{2,000 \text{ machine-hours}} = \$110 \text{ per machine-hour}$$

In developing such rates, most companies use a period of *one year*. There are two important reasons for this practice. First, *the numerator reason*: the period for the $220,000 must be long enough to lessen or eliminate the effect of the four seasons as well as erratic items such as repairs. Second, *the denominator reason*: the period for the 2,000 machine-hours must be long enough to spread the monthly fixed costs over fluctuating levels of monthly output.

5. Managers and accountants gather information that goes into their costing systems via **source documents**, which are the original records that support journal entries in an accounting system. The main source document in a job-costing system is a **job-cost record** (also called a **job-cost sheet**). This document records and accumulates all the costs assigned to a specific job, starting when work begins. Source documents also exist for individual items in a job-cost record. A **materials-requisition record** is a source document that contains information about the cost of direct materials used for a specific job and in a specific department. A **labor-time record** is a source document that contains information about the amount of labor time used for a specific job and in a specific department. In many costing systems, the source documents exist only in the form of computer records. Bar coding and other forms of online information recording reduce human intervention and improve the accuracy of the records of materials and labor time for individual jobs.

6. **Actual costing** and **normal costing** are two systems for determining the cost of a job.
- Actual costing is a system that (i) traces direct costs to the cost object by using the actual direct-cost rates times actual quantities of the direct-cost inputs and (ii) allocates indirect costs based on actual indirect-cost rates times actual quantities of the cost-allocation bases. Actual costing is not commonly found in practice, however, because it requires waiting until all the indirect costs are known at year-end before allocating them to jobs.
- Normal costing is a system that approximates actual costing but provides information on a timely basis. *Normal costing differs from actual costing in only one respect*: a **budgeted indirect-cost rate** is computed at the *beginning* of the fiscal year and used to allocate indirect costs to jobs as work on them progresses *during* the year.

Our example above is actual costing if the $110 indirect-cost rate is an *actual rate*; it is normal costing if the $110 is a *budgeted rate*.

7. For manufacturing companies using job costing, seven summary transactions explain the *flow of manufacturing costs* through the accounts in the general and subsidiary ledgers. These transactions arise from purchasing materials and converting them into finished goods. Each general-ledger account with the word "Control" in its title is supported by a subsidiary ledger. For example, the subsidiary ledger for Materials Control contains details on the quantity and cost per unit of each type of material in inventory. The job-cost record for each unfinished job is the subsidiary ledger for Work-in-Process Control. The following transactions and related journal entries are in the normal costing example, beginning text p.113.

(1) Purchases of direct and indirect materials on credit in February was $89,000.

Materials Control	89,000	
Accounts Payable Control		89,000

(2) Materials-requisition records for February showed $81,000 of direct materials and $4,000 of indirect materials. (Indirect materi-

als are part of manufacturing overhead, hereafter abbreviated MOH).

Work-in-Process Control	81,000	
MOH Control	4,000	
Materials Control		85,000

(3) Total manufacturing payroll incurred in February was $39,000 for direct labor and $15,000 for indirect labor.

Work-in-Process Control	39,000	
MOH Control	15,000	
Cash Control		54,000

(4) Additional MOH incurred in February was $44,000 for engineering and supervisory salaries; $13,000 for utilities, repairs, and insurance; and $18,000 for depreciation.

MOH Control	75,000	
Cash Control		57,000
Accumulated Dep. Control		18,000

(5) MOH allocated to all jobs worked on during February was $80,000 (2,000 actual direct manufacturing labor-hours × $40 budgeted rate).

Work-in-Process Control	80,000	
MOH Allocated		80,000

(6) Transfer to finished goods the individual jobs that were completed during February at a total cost of $188,800.

Finished Goods Control	188,800	
Work-in-Process Control		188,800

(7) Cost of goods sold in February was $180,000.

Cost of Goods Sold	180,000	
Finished Goods Control		180,000

In addition to these seven transactions for manufacturing costs, journal entries also are made to record nonmanufacturing costs and revenues.

8. In the journal entries above, the actual MOH incurred during February is $94,000

($4,000 in entry 2 + $15,000 in entry 3 + $75,000 in entry 4). Entry 5 shows $80,000 of MOH allocated to jobs during February. The difference of $14,000 ($94,000 − $80,000) is **underallocated** (also called **underapplied** or **underabsorbed**) MOH. That is, in this example the amount of MOH allocated is *less than* the amount of MOH incurred. Had the allocated amount been *greater than* the amount incurred, MOH would be **overallocated** (**overapplied** or **overabsorbed**).

9. The balances of MOH Control and MOH Allocated are carried forward each month. *At the end of the fiscal year*, underallocated or overallocated MOH must be disposed of using one of the three approaches described below. To illustrate, assume the *year-end* balances are MOH Control $1,215,000 and MOH Allocated $1,080,000, which means MOH is underallocated by $135,000. Each of the three approaches results in a journal entry to close MOH Control and MOH Allocated.

a. Write-off to Cost of Goods Sold:

Cost of Goods Sold	135,000	
MOH Allocated	1,080,000	
MOH Control		1,215,000

This is the simplest approach and is widely used. Because inventory balances of job-costing companies are usually relatively small, this approach is unlikely to cause significant distortions in the financial statements.

b. **Proration** spreads underallocated or overallocated MOH among Work-in-Process Control, Finished Goods Control, and Cost of Goods Sold:

Work-in-Process Control	X	
Finished Goods Control	Y	
Cost of Goods Sold	Z	
MOH Allocated	1,080,000	
MOH Control		1,215,000

The amounts X, Y, and Z above, which will total $135,000, depend on whether proration is based on (i) the total amount of manufacturing overhead allocated (before proration) in the ending balances of these three accounts or (ii) the total ending balances (before proration) of these accounts. Method (i) is more accurate but (ii) is simpler to use. The example, text pp.119-121, shows computations for these two methods.

c. **Adjusted allocation rate** uses actual cost rates to restate all allocated MOH entries in the general-ledger (Work-in-Process Control, Finished Goods Control, and Cost of Goods Sold), and in the subsidiary ledgers of all jobs worked on during the year.

Same journal entry as in proration method (i).

Procedurally, these restatements are based on the difference between the actual overhead rate determined at the end of the fiscal year and the budgeted overhead rate used for normal costing during the year. The widespread adoption of computerized accounting systems has greatly reduced the cost of using the adjusted allocation-rate approach.

10. Under generally accepted accounting principles, only manufacturing costs are inventoriable costs; nonmanufacturing costs are period costs. Despite this difference, companies often assign nonmanufacturing costs to individual jobs (just as they do manufacturing costs) for pricing, product-mix, and cost management decisions.

11. Although this chapter focuses on manufacturing, job costing is also useful in the service sector: accounting firms, law firms, advertising agencies, auto repair shops, and the like. For example, in an accounting firm, each audit is a job. The costs of an audit are accumulated in a job-cost record using the seven-step procedure described in paragraph 3. Some service and **manufacturing** companies use a variation of normal costing in which *both* direct costs and indirect costs are charged to jobs by means of budgeted rates.

Featured Exercise

Madison Company has overallocated manufacturing overhead (MOH) of $45,000 for the year ended December 31, 2010. Before disposing of the overallocated MOH, selected year-end balances from Madison's general ledger are as follows:

MOH Control	$435,000
MOH Allocated	480,000
Work-in-Process Control	24,000
Finished Goods Control	56,000
Cost of Goods Sold	720,000

At year-end, the company prorates underallocated or overallocated MOH to the last three accounts listed above based on their ending balances (before proration).

a. Compute the amount of overallocated MOH to be prorated to each of the three accounts and compute their balances after proration.
b. Prepare a journal entry to record the proration.

Solution (on next page)

Solution

a.

	Account Balance (Before Proration) (1)		Proration of $45,000 Overallocated MOH (2)	Account Balance (After Proration) (3) = (1) − (2)
Work in process	$ 24,000	3%	0.03 × $45,000 = $ 1,350	$ 22,650
Finished goods	56,000	7%	0.07 × $45,000 = 3,150	52,850
Cost of goods sold	720,000	90%	0.90 × $45,000 = 40,500	679,500
	$800,000	100%	$45,000	$755,000

The prorated amounts of overallocated MOH are *deducted from* the account balances before proration because too much MOH was allocated to the accounts during the year.

b. The journal entry to record this proration is:

MOH Allocated	480,000	
Work-in-Process Control		1,350
Finished Goods		3,150
Cost of Goods Sold		40,500
MOH Control		435,000

Review Questions and Exercises

(All answers are at the end of the chapter.)

Completion Statements

Fill in the blank(s) to complete each statement.

1. A _____ is a factor that is the common denominator for systematically linking an indirect cost or group of indirect costs to a cost object.
2. In a _____ system, the cost object is a unit or multiple units of a distinct product or service, whereas the cost object is masses of identical or similar units of a product or service in a _____ _____ system.
3. Under _____ costing, a manufacturing company debits Work-in-Process Control for the amount of the budgeted overhead rates multiplied by the actual quantity used of the cost-allocation bases.
4. In a job-costing system, the source document used to record all costs assigned to a specific job is called a _____.

5. The supporting detail for a general-ledger control account is called a _____ _____.

True-False

Indicate whether each statement is true (T) or false (F).

_____ 1. A canning company would use a job-costing system.
_____ 2. One reason that budgeted overhead rates are developed annually rather than monthly is to overcome the volatility in unit costs caused by seasonal fluctuations in the level of the cost-allocation base.
_____ 3. Overallocated overhead arises when the balance of Manufacturing Overhead Control is less than the balance of Manufacturing Overhead Allocated.
_____ 4. In general, the amount of underallocated or overallocated overhead is greater at year-end than at any month-end during the year.

5. If a company uses normal costing and the actual level of production is substantially less than the budgeted level, overhead will most likely be overallocated.

6. In using the proration approach to dispose of underallocated or overallocated overhead, it is conceptually superior to prorate based on the amount of allocated overhead (before proration) in the ending balances of Work-in-Process Control, Finished Goods Control, and Cost of Goods Sold rather than to prorate based on the ending balances (before proration) of these accounts.

7. Assume a manufacturing company has underallocated overhead at the end of its fiscal year. The year's operating income will be lower if the underallocated overhead is prorated to the appropriate accounts rather than written off to Cost of Goods Sold.

Multiple Choice

Select the best answer to each question. Space is provided for computations after the quantitative questions.

1. A budgeted rate for allocating manufacturing overhead costs to products is preferred to an actual rate if the objective is:
   a. timeliness but not accuracy.
   b. accuracy but not timeliness.
   c. both accuracy and timeliness.
   d. neither timeliness nor accuracy.

2. (CPA adapted) Avery Co. uses a budgeted manufacturing overhead rate based on machine-hours. For the month of October, Avery's budgeted overhead was $300,000 based on a budgeted allocation base of 10,000 machine-hours. Actual overhead incurred amounted to $325,000 and 11,000 actual machine-hours were used. How much was the underallocated or overallocated overhead?
   a. $30,000 overallocated
   b. $30,000 underallocated
   c. $5,000 overallocated

d. $5,000 underallocated

3. Shadwick Company used a budgeted manufacturing overhead rate of $0.175 per machine-hour during 2010. Two machine-hours were budgeted per unit produced. For 2010, actual manufacturing overhead incurred was $350,000 and overhead was overallocated by $10,500. How many units were produced in 2010?
   a. 970,000
   b. 1,030,000
   c. 1,940,000
   d. 2,060,000

4. (CPA) In a job-costing system, issuing indirect materials to production increases which account?
   a. Materials Control
   b. Work-in-Process Control
   c. Manufacturing Overhead Control
   d. Manufacturing Overhead Allocated

5. (CPA) In a job-costing system, the dollar amount of the journal entry transferring inventory from Work-in-Process Control to Finished Goods Control is the sum of the costs debited to all jobs:
   a. started in production during the period.
   b. in production during the period.
   c. completed and sold during the period.
   d. completed during the period.

6. Under generally accepted accounting principles, the appropriate approach for disposing of underallocated or overallocated manufacturing overhead at the end of the fiscal year:
   a. is to write it off to Cost of Goods Sold.
   b. is to prorate it to Work-in-Process Control, Finished Goods Control, and Cost of Goods Sold.

c. is to restate the overhead rate and use this rate to restate the balances of Work-in-Process Control, Finished Goods Control, and Cost of Goods Sold as well as the job cost record of every job worked on during the year.

d. depends on the significance of the amount.

___ 7. (CPA) Worley Company has overallocated overhead of $45,000 for the year ended December 31, 2010. Before disposing of the overallocated overhead, selected December 31, 2010, balances from Worley's accounting records are as follows:

Cost of Goods Sold	720,000
Inventories:	
Materials Control	36,000
Work-in-Process Control	54,000
Finished Goods Control	90,000

Under Worley's accounting system, underallocated or overallocated overhead is prorated to applicable inventories and Cost of Goods Sold based on their year-end balances (before proration). In its 2010 income statement, Worley should report Cost of Goods Sold of:

a. $682,500.
b. $684,000.
c. $756,000.
d. $757,500.

Revenues	$1,200,000

Review Exercises

Check Figures for these Review Exercises are at the end of the *Student Guide*. Solutions are at the end of the chapter.

1. (CMA adapted) Sanger Company provides the following information:

Department 203 Costs Incurred for 2010

Identified With Specific Jobs	Materials	Labor	Other	Total
Job 1376	$ 1,000	$ 7,000		$ 8,000
Job 1377	26,000	53,000		79,000
Job 1378	12,000	9,000		21,000
Job 1379	4,000	1,000		5,000
Not Identified With Specific Jobs				
Indirect materials and supplies	15,000			15,000
Indirect manufacturing labor		53,000		53,000
Employee fringe benefits			$23,000	23,000
Depreciation			12,000	12,000
Supervision		20,000		20,000
Total	$58,000	$143,000	$35,000	$236,000

Department 203 Budgeted Overhead Rate for 2010

Budgeted overhead:
Variable	
Indirect materials and supplies	$ 16,000
Indirect manufacturing labor	56,000
Employee fringe benefits	24,000
Fixed	
Depreciation	12,000
Supervision	20,000
Total	$128,000

Budgeted direct manufacturing labor costs	$80,000
Budgeted manufacturing overhead rate	
$128,000 ÷ $80,000	160%

Department 203 Work in Process at Beginning of 2010

Job No.	Direct Materials	Direct Labor	Overhead	Total
1376	$17,500	$22,000	$33,000	$72,500

Assume Job 1376 was the only job completed during 2010. It was sold upon completion.

a. Compute underallocated or overallocated overhead for Department 203 for 2010.
b. Compute cost of goods sold for 2010.
c. Compute the cost of work-in-process inventory at the end of 2010.
d. Ignoring your answer in part (a), assume overhead is underallocated by $14,000 in Department 203. If underallocated overhead is prorated to Cost of Goods Sold and applicable inventories based on 2010's amount of allocated overhead (before proration) in the ending balances of these accounts, compute the amount of underallocated overhead that should be debited to Work-in-Process Control at year-end.

2. Rigdon Company uses a job-costing system. The following accounts are from Rigdon's general ledger:

AP:	Accounts Payable Control
AD:	Accumulated Depreciation Control
C:	Cash Control
COGS:	Costs of Goods Sold
FG:	Finished Goods Control
MOHA:	Manufacturing Overhead Allocated
MOHC:	Manufacturing Overhead Control
M:	Materials Control
WP:	Wages Payable Control
WIP:	Work-in-Process Control

Enter the identifying letters in the debit and credit columns to record each transaction.

	Debits(s)	Credit(s)
a. Indirect materials requisitioned	_____	_____
b. Depreciation on manufacturing equipment	_____	_____
c. Manufacturing overhead allocated to jobs	_____	_____
d. Direct manufacturing labor costs	_____	_____
e. Completion of jobs	_____	_____
f. Dispose of an immaterial amount of underallocated overhead	_____	_____

3. (CPA) Worrell Corporation uses a job-costing system. The following debits (credits) appeared in the general-ledger account Work-in-Process Control for March 2010:

March 1, balance	$ 12,000
March 31, direct materials	40,000
March 31, direct manufacturing labor	30,000
March 31, manufacturing overhead allocated	27,000
March 31, transferred to finished goods	(100,000)

Worrell allocates overhead to jobs at a budgeted rate of 90% of direct manufacturing labor costs. Job 232, the only job still in process at the end of March 2010, has $2,250 of manufacturing overhead allocated to it.

Compute the amount of direct materials debited to Job 232.

Crossword Puzzle for Chapters 3 and 4

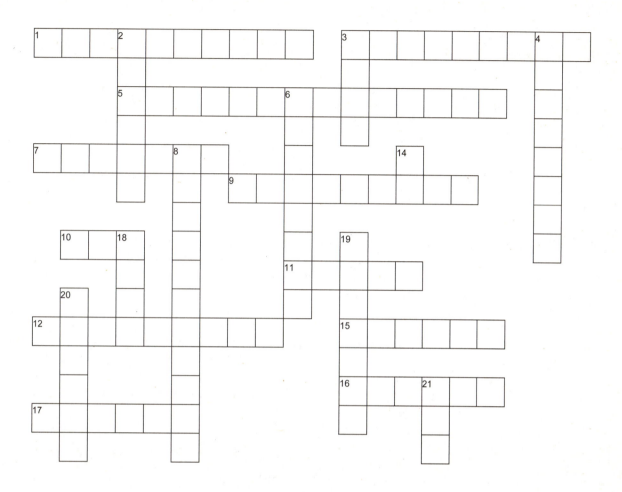

1. General ledger and _____ ledgers

3. A method that can be used to dispose of overallocated manufacturing overhead.

5. When actual manufacturing overhead (MOH) exceeds MOH allocated, MOH is _____.

7. In this costing system the cost object is masses of identical or similar units of a product or service.

9. Margin of safety is the amount of budgeted revenues over and above _____ revenues.

10. In this costing system the cost object is an individual unit, batch, or lot of a distinct product or service.

11. Contribution margin versus _____ margin

12. _____ requisition record

15. _____ operating income

16. _____ costing uses budgeted indirect-cost rates.

17. The type of manufacturing labor costs debited to Work-in-Process Control.

DOWN

2. _____ documents are the original records that support journal entries in an accounting system.

3. A cost _____ is a grouping of individual cost items.

4. Debit Work-in-Process Control and credit Manufacturing _____ Allocated.

6. Operating _____ measures the risk-return trade-off across alternative cost structures.

8. _____ analysis that is a "what if" technique.

14. A graph showing the impact on operating income of changes in the output level

18. Allocate indirect costs to jobs based on the rate per unit of each cost-allocation _____.

19. _____ systems should be tailored to the underlying operations, and not vice versa.

20. Contribution _____ per unit

21. Sales _____ is the relative combination of products that constitutes total unit sales.

Answers and Solutions to Chapter 4 Review Questions and Exercises

Completion Statements

1. cost-allocation base
2. job-costing, process-costing
3. normal
4. job-cost record
5. subsidiary ledger

True-False

1. F   A canning company, being a producer of masses of similar units of products, would use a process-costing system.
2. T
3. T
4. F   In general, the amount of underallocated or overallocated overhead is *less* at year-end than at any month-end during the year because the effect of all four seasons has been recorded by year-end.
5. F   If the actual level of production is substantially less than the budgeted level, overhead will most likely be underallocated. That's because the fixed portion of overhead allocated would be substantially less than the fixed portion of actual overhead incurred.
6. T
7. F   When a manufacturing company disposes of *underallocated* overhead at the end of its fiscal year, the Cost of Goods Sold account *increases*, regardless of the approach used. Cost of Goods Sold, however, *increases less* under proration than under write-off. Therefore, operating income is *higher* if underallocated overhead is prorated to Work-in-Process Control, Finished Goods Control, and Cost of Goods Sold rather than written off to Cost of Goods Sold.

Multiple Choice

1. a   A budgeted overhead rate is more timely but an actual overhead rate is more accurate.
2. c   Budgeted overhead rate = $300,000 ÷ 10,000 hours = $30 per machine-hour

Actual overhead incurred	$325,000
Overhead allocated, 11,000 × $30	330,000
Overallocated overhead	$ 5,000

3. b   Three steps are used to obtain the answer. First, compute overhead allocated: $350,000 + $10,500 = $360,500. Second, compute the budgeted overhead rate *per unit of output*: $0.175 per machine-hour × 2 machine-hours per unit = $0.35 per unit. Third, compute the production in units: $360,500 ÷ $0.35 = 1,030,000 units.
4. c   The cost of indirect materials used increases (is a debit to) Manufacturing Overhead Control and decreases (is a credit to) Materials Control.
5. d   The journal entry described is triggered by the completion of jobs.
6. d   Under GAAP, write off underallocated or overallocated manufacturing overhead to Cost of Goods Sold if the amount is insignificant (immaterial). If the amount is material, use the approach described in either answer (b) or (c).
7. a   Two steps are used to obtain the answer. First, compute the share of the overallocated overhead to be allocated to Cost of Goods Sold: $720,000 ÷ ($54,000 + $90,000 + $720,000) = $720,000 ÷ $864,000 = 5/6. Second, *decrease* Cost of Goods Sold by its share of the overallocated overhead: $720,000 − 5/6($45,000) = $682,500.

Review Exercise 1

a. Actual overhead for 2010:

Indirect materials and supplies	$ 15,000
Indirect manufacturing labor	53,000
Employee fringe benefits	23,000
Depreciation	12,000
Supervision	20,000
Total	$123,000

Actual direct manufacturing labor costs for 2010:

Job 1376	$ 7,000
Job 1377	53,000
Job 1378	9,000
Job 1379	1,000
Total	$70,000

Actual overhead incurred	$123,000
Overhead allocated, $70,000 × 160%	112,000
Underallocated overhead	$ 11,000

b. In this case, cost of goods sold is equal to the cost of Job 1376.
Cost of goods sold = $72,500 + $1,000 + $7,000 + ($7,000 × 160%) = $91,700
Note that, for use in answer (d) below, overhead allocated to cost of goods sold during 2008 = $7,000 × 160% = $11,200.

c.

	Job 1377	Job 1378	Job 1379	Total
Direct materials	$ 26,000	$12,000	$4,000	$ 42,000
Direct manufacturing labor	53,000	9,000	1,000	63,000
Overhead allocated				
(Direct manuf. labor costs × 160%)	84,800	14,400	1,600	100,800
Work in process at year-end	$163,800	$35,400	$6,600	$205,800

d. Overhead allocated during 2010:

Portion to cost of goods sold (from answer b)	$ 11,200
Portion to work in process (from answer c)	100,800
Total overhead allocated	$112,000

Let X = Underallocated overhead debited to ending Work-in-Process Control
$$X = (\$100,800 \div \$112,000) \times \$14,000$$
$$X = 0.90 \times \$14,000 = \$12,600$$

Review Exercise 2

	Debit(s)	Credit(s)
a.	MOHC	M
b.	MOHC	AD
c.	WIP	MOHA
d.	WIP	WP
e.	FG	WIP
f.	MOHA, COGS	MOHC

Three steps are used to obtain the answer. First, compute the March 31 balance of Work-in-Process Control: $12,000 + $40,000 + $30,000 + $27,000 − $100,000 = $9,000. This balance is also the balance of Job 232 because it is the only unfinished job. Second, compute the direct manufacturing labor (DML) debited to Job 232:

$$0.90DML = \$2,250$$
$$DML = \$2,250 \div 0.90 = \$2,500$$

Third, compute the amount of direct materials debited to Job 232:

$$\$9,000 − \$2,250 − \$2,500 = \$4,250$$

Solution to Crossword Puzzle
for Chapters 3 and 4

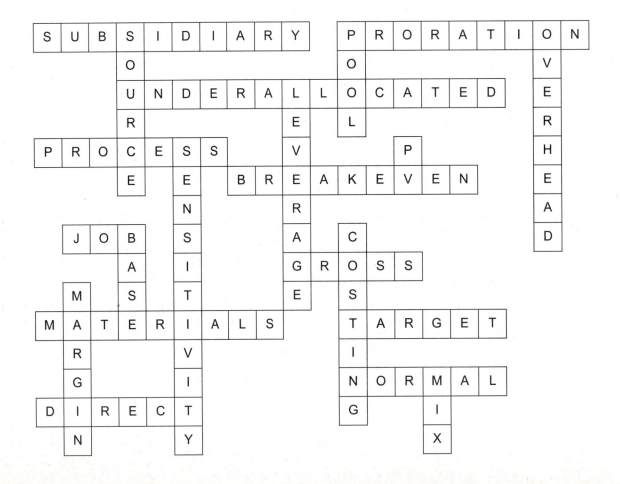

CHAPTER 5 | Activity-Based Costing and Activity-Based Management

Overview

This chapter explains why and how companies refine the basic job-costing system introduced in Chapter 4. To refine their costing systems, many companies around the world have implemented activity-based costing (ABC). ABC helps managers make better informed pricing and product-mix decisions, and also assists them in cost management.

Highlights

1. The colorful term *peanut-butter costing* describes a particular costing approach that uses broad averages for assigning (or spreading, as in spreading peanut butter) the cost of resources uniformly to cost objects (such as products or services) when the individual products or services may, in fact, use those resources in nonuniform ways. Peanut-butter costing leads to undercosting or overcosting of products (or services). **Product undercosting** occurs when a product consumes a high level of resources but is reported to have a low cost per unit. **Product overcosting** occurs when a product consumes a low level of resources but is reported to have a high cost per unit. **Product-cost cross-subsidization** means that if a company undercosts one of its products, then it will overcost at least one of its other products.

2. In the example, beginning text p.141, Plastim Corporation's existing costing system traces direct costs to products S3 (a simple lens) and CL5 (a complex lens) and allocates indirect costs to them by using a single indirect-cost rate, similar to the system described in Chapter 4. Under this system, S3 costs $58.75 per unit and CL5 costs $97.00 per unit. These costs, however, are counter-intuitive because they indicate Plastim is not competitive on S3 where it believes it has strong capabilities, and is very profitable on the newer, less-established CL5 product. In this situation, the key question is: How might Plastim's costing system be refined?

3. A **refined costing system** reduces the use of broad averages for assigning the cost of resources to cost objects (such as jobs, products, and services) and provides better measurement of the costs of indirect resources used by different cost objects—no matter how differently various cost objects use indirect resources. Increasing product diversity, increasing indirect costs, and competition in the product market have accelerated these refinements. Three guidelines for refining a costing system are:

a. *Direct-cost tracing.* Identify as many of the total costs as direct costs of the cost object as is economically feasible. This guideline aims to reduce the amount of costs classified as indirect, and thereby to minimize the extent to which costs have to be allocated, rather than traced.

b. *Indirect-cost pools.* Expand the number of indirect-cost pools until each of these pools is more homogeneous. *In a homogeneous cost pool*, all of the costs have the same or a similar cause-and-effect (or benefits-received) relationship with a single cost-allocation base.

c. *Cost-allocation bases.* Use the cause-and-effect criterion, when possible, to identify the cost-allocation base (the cause) for each homogenous indirect-cost pool (the effect).

4. One of the best tools for refining a costing system is **activity-based costing (ABC)**. ABC refines a costing system by identifying individual activities as the fundamental cost objects. An **activity** is an event, task, or unit of work with a specified purpose—for example, designing products, setting up machines, operating machines, and distributing products. ABC calculates the costs of individual activities and assigns costs to cost objects such as products and services on the basis of the activities needed to produce each product or service.

5. A key step in implementing ABC is to identify activities that help explain why an organi-

zation incurs the costs that it currently classifies as indirect. In the Plastim example in the textbook, a cross-functional team identifies seven major activities needed to design, manufacture, and distribute lenses—(i) design products and processes, (ii) set up molding machines, (iii) operate molding machines, (iv) clean and maintain molds, (v) prepare batches of finished lenses for shipment, (vi) distribute lenses to customers, and (vii) administer and manage all processes. The costs of the cleaning and maintenance activity cost pool can be traced directly to S3 and CL5, whereas the costs of the other six activities are indirect costs of the products. Because ABC provides a greater level of detail in understanding how Plastim uses its resources, the costs of products S3 and CL5 will be more accurate.

6.　An important feature of ABC is how it highlights the different levels of activities in a **cost hierarchy**. A cost hierarchy categorizes various activity cost pools on the basis of different types of cost drivers or cost-allocation bases, or different degrees of difficulty in determining cause-and-effect (or benefits-received) relationships. ABC commonly uses a cost hierarchy having four levels:

a.　**Output unit-level costs** are the costs of activities performed on each individual unit of a product or service. In the Plastim example, machine operations costs related to the activity of running the automated molding machines (such as energy, machine depreciation, and repair) are output unit-level costs. That is, over time the costs of this activity increase with additional units of output produced (or machine-hours used).
b.　**Batch-level costs** are the costs of activities related to a group of units of products or services rather than to each individual unit of product or service. In the Plastim example, setup costs for a production run are batch-level costs.
c.　**Product-sustaining costs** (or **service-sustaining costs**) are the costs of activities undertaken to support individual products (or services) regardless of the number of units or batches in which the units are produced. In the Plastim example, design costs for a specific

product are product-sustaining costs.
d.　**Facility-sustaining costs** are the costs of activities that cannot be traced to individual products or services but that support the organization as a whole. In the Plastim example, general administration costs (such as top management compensation, rent, and building security) are facility-sustaining costs.

EXHIBIT 5-4, text p.151, summarizes the calculation of Plastim's activity-cost rates for the six indirect-cost pools in its ABC system; column 2 of the exhibit shows the product cost hierarchy category for each activity.

7.　Compare Plastim's cost per unit for products S3 and CL5:

	S3	CL5
Single indirect-cost rate system	$58.75	$ 97.00
ABC system	49.98	132.07
Difference	$ 8.77	$(35.07)

Because the ABC system provides more accurate costs, this comparison shows the single indirect-cost rate system *overcosts* S3 by $8.77 and *undercosts* CL5 by $35.07. The ABC information makes it clear that selling S3 at a price of, say, $53 will be only marginally profitable.

8.　These are telltale signs of when ABC systems are likely to provide the most benefits: (a) significant amounts of indirect costs are allocated using only one or two cost pools, (b) all or most indirect costs are identified as output unit-level costs (that is, few indirect costs are described as batch-level, product-sustaining, or facility-sustaining costs), (c) products make diverse demands on resources because of differences in volume, process steps, batch size, or complexity, (d) products that a company is well suited to make and sell show small profits, whereas products that a company is less suited to make and sell show large profits, and (e) the operations staff has substantial disagreements with the reported costs of manufacturing and marketing products and services.

9. Managers choose the level of detail in their costing systems by comparing the expected costs of the system with the expected benefits of using the information to make better informed decisions. The main costs and limitations of ABC are the measurements necessary to implement the system and to keep activity-cost rates updated regularly. Improvements in information technology and related declines in measurement costs have enabled ABC to be practical in many organizations. As these trends continue, ABC should be better able to pass the cost-benefit test.

10. **Activity-based management (ABM)** is a method of management decision-making that uses ABC information to improve customer satisfaction and profitability. ABM includes decisions about pricing and product mix, how to reduce costs, how to improve processes, and decisions relating to product design. For example, the table, text p.157, shows how Plastim used process and efficiency improvements to reduce the distribution cost of S3 by $0.75 per unit and CL5 by $1.50 per unit.

11. In many companies, costing systems have evolved from using a single indirect-cost rate to using separate indirect-cost rates for each department. Department costing approximates ABC in a department if the department has a single activity or a single cause-and-effect cost-allocation base for different activities, or if individual products use the activities of the department in the same proportions. In companies where none of these conditions are met, department costing can be refined using ABC.

12. Although ABC originated in manufacturing companies, it has many applications in service and merchandising companies. In fact, the Plastim example illustrates the application of ABC to a service activity—design—and a merchandising activity—distribution. Companies in the banking, telecommunications, railroad, and as well as retail and wholesale industries have implemented some form of ABC to identify profitable product mixes, improve efficiency, and satisfy customers.

Featured Exercise

A. H. Church, Inc. manufactures a variety of wooden toys for young children. The company uses ABC. The manufacturing activities and related data are as follows:

Activity Area	Cost-Allocation Base	Indirect Cost per Unit of Cost-Allocation Base
Materials handling	Board feet of lumber	$ 0.10
Forming and sanding	Direct manuf. labor-hours	10.00
Painting	Number of painted sets	0.30
Inspection	Number of finished sets	0.04
Packaging	Number of finished sets	0.20

Two types of wooden blocks were manufactured in September, alphabet cubes and numeric shapes. Quantities and per-set data are as follows:

	Alphabet Cubes	Numeric Shapes
Number of sets produced	12,000	2,000
Direct material costs per set	$1.20	$2.00
Board feet of lumber per set	1.50	2.00
Direct manufacturing labor-hours per set	0.05	0.10
Number of sets painted	12,000	none

Compute the manufacturing cost per set for each product.

Solution

	Alphabet Cubes	Numeric Shapes
Direct material costs,		
12,000 × $1.20; 2,000 × $2.00	$14,400	$4,000
Indirect costs:		
Materials handling,		
12,000 × 1.5 × $0.10; 2,000 × 2.0 × $0.10	1,800	400
Forming and sanding,		
12,000 × 0.05 × $10; 2,000 × 0.10 × $10	6,000	2,000
Painting, 12,000 × $0.30	3,600	
Inspection, 12,000 × $0.04; 2,000 × $0.04	480	80
Packaging, 12,000 × $0.20; 2,000 × $0.20	2,400	400
Total manufacturing costs	$28,680	$6,880
Divide by number of sets produced	÷12,000	÷2,000
Manufacturing cost per set	$ 2.39	$ 3.44

Review Questions and Exercises

(All answers are at the end of the chapter.)

Completion Statements

Fill in the blank(s) to complete each statement.

1. _____ occurs when a product consumes a high level of resources but is reported to have a low total cost.

2. A _____ reduces the use of broad averages for assigning the cost of resources to cost objects (such as jobs, products, and services), and provides better measurement of the costs of indirect resources used by different cost objects—no matter how differently the different cost object use indirect resources.

3. Three guidelines for refining a costing system are: (a) identify as many of the total costs as _____ costs of the cost object as is economically feasible, (b) expand the number of indirect-cost pools until each of these pools is more _____, and (c) use the cause-and-effect criterion, when possible, to identify the _____ (the cause) for each homogenous indirect-cost pool (the effect).

4. A _____ categorizes various activity cost pools on the basis of different types of cost drivers or cost-allocation bases, or different degrees of difficulty in determining cause-and-effect (or benefits-received) relationships.

True-False

Indicate whether each statement is true (T) or false (F).

____ 1. A main factor driving refinement of costing systems is increasing competition in the marketplace.

____ 2. ABC identifies activities as the fundamental cost object and assigns the costs of products or services to those activities.

____ 3. In ABC, the costs of activities are always indirect costs of products.

____ 4. ABC seeks to identify all costs used by products regardless of whether the costs are variable or fixed in the short run.

____ 5. Output unit-level costs are the costs of activities undertaken to support individual products or services regardless of the number of units or batches in which the units are produced.

____ 6. ABC systems can be particularly beneficial if a simple system shows that complex products are very profitable and simple products are unprofitable.

7. A major reason why low-volume products are often overcosted is the batch-level costs and product-sustaining costs of those products are allocated as if they were output unit-level costs of all products.

Multiple Choice

Select the best answer to each question. Space is provided for computations after the quantitative questions.

1. If a costing system uses a single cost-allocation base:
   a. products that use more of this base in comparison with the resources they actually consume tend to be undercosted.
   b. products that use less of this base in comparison with the resources they actually consume tend to be overcosted.
   c. products that use more of this base in comparison with the resources they actually consume tend to be overcosted.
   d. products that use none of this base tend to be overcosted.

2. (CPA) What is the usual effect on the number of cost pools and cost-allocation bases when activity-based costing replaces a simple costing system?

	Cost Pools	Cost-Allocation Bases
a.	No effect	No effect
b.	Increase	No effect
c.	No effect	Increase
d.	Increase	Increase

3. Which of the following *is not* a characteristic of ABC?
   a. Operating personnel play a key role in identifying the individual activities.
   b. It is usually difficult to find a good cause-and-effect relationship between a cost-allocation base and facility-sustaining costs.
   c. There are many homogenous indirect-cost pools.

d. Cost-allocation bases of indirect-cost pools are usually financial in nature.

4. Procurement costs, which include the costs of placing orders for materials and paying suppliers, are classified as:
   a. an output unit-level cost.
   b. a batch-level cost.
   c. a product-sustaining cost.
   d. a facility-sustaining cost.

5. (CMA) Zeta Company is preparing its annual profit plan. As part of its analysis of the profitability of individual products, the controller estimates the amount of manufacturing overhead that should be allocated to the individual product lines from the information given below.

	Wall Mirrors	Specialty Windows
Units produced	25	25
Material moves per product line	5	15
Direct manufacturing labor-hours per unit	200	200

Budgeted material-handling costs are $50,000.

Under a costing system that allocates manufacturing overhead on the basis of direct manufacturing labor-hours, the material-handling costs allocated to one wall mirror are:
   a. $1,000.
   b. $500.
   c. $2,000.
   d. $5,000.
   e. $0.

6. Using the information in question 5, the material-handling costs allocated to one wall mirror under ABC are:
   a. $1,000.
   b. $500.
   c. $1,500.
   d. $2,500.
   e. $0.

7. ABC tends to pass the cost-benefit test for companies with:

a. operations that are relatively simple.
b. many products that use different amounts of resources.
c. many products that use about the
same amount of resources.
d. few products that use about the same amount of resources.

Review Exercises

Check figures for these Review Exercises are at the end of the *Student Guide*. Solutions are at the end of the chapter.

1. (CMA adapted) New-Rage Cosmetics uses ABC. The following data describe New-Rage's indirect costs of producing 200 cases of Satin Sheen makeup:

Activity	Activity-Cost Rate	Quantity of Activity Used
Incoming material inspection	$11.50 per type of material	12 types of material
Production setup	$30 per setup-hour	16 setup-hours
In-process inspection	$3 per case	200 cases
Product certification	$24 per order	4 orders
Distribution	$1 per pound	2,000 pounds
General administration	$8 per direct manufacturing labor-hour	50 direct manufacturing labor-hours

The direct costs of the 200 cases of Satin Sheen makeup total $8,200.

Compute the cost per case of Satin Sheen makeup.

2. Four managers of Torchlight Company had dinner together. Details of their restaurant bill are as follows:

Diner	Entrée	Dessert	Drinks	Total
Jason	$17	$8	$19	$ 44
Kent	24	3	10	37
Lynne	15	4	6	25
Marci	31	6	5	42
				$148

Jason put the entire bill on his credit card. A few days later, he billed each of the other diners for the average cost per diner.

   a. Compute the amount by which Jason's billing approach undercosts or overcosts each of the diners. Assume the four diners shared the gratuity at the restaurant by paying cash.
   b. What is the fundamental difference between costing the diners in this exercise and costing products in a manufacturing company?

3. Jay & Associates, a CPA firm, has many audit clients. The following information is available for two of Jay's recent audits:

	Fuentes Footwear	Detrick Properties
Direct professional labor-hours		
Partner time used	30 hours	75 hours
Staff time used	150 hours	105 hours
Travel time	0.5 hours	3.0 hours
Phone calls and faxes (estimated hours, detailed records are not kept)	Under 20	Over 100

The existing costing system uses (i) a single direct cost category, direct professional labor-hours (DPLH), costed at $120 per DPLH and (ii) a single indirect-cost rate of $80 per DPLH.

   a. Without making computations, which audit do you think actually costs Jay more? Explain.
   b. Compute the costs assigned to each audit under the existing costing system.
   c. Explain what is wrong with the existing costing system.
   d. What is a likely outcome of using the existing costing system?
   e. In general, how could the existing costing system be improved?

4. Wescott Foods manufactures many different types of breakfast cereal at its St. Louis plant. The following costs are incurred to produce 28,000,000 boxes of cereal in 2010:

- New-product developments costs—costs of adding new cereals to those already being produced. In 2010, "Wheat Flakes" was added at a cost of $5,684,000.
- Material-handling costs—costs of handling grain, sugar, packaging materials, and the like ($6,628,000). The cost-allocation base is hours of material-handling time, which is highly correlated with hours of production time.
- Material-purchase costs—costs of materials acquired from suppliers ($8,852,000). These are direct costs traced to individual products and are variable with respect to the number of boxes produced.
- Manufacturing labor costs—direct costs traced to (i) individual products on a per-box basis ($7,263,000), or (ii) setups for products when the production line switches from one type of cereal to another ($2,385,000).
- Energy costs—costs of heat, light, and power ($1,029,000). The cost-allocation base is hours of production time.
- Plant administration costs—costs such as salaries, depreciation, insurance, and building security ($6,295,000).

The number of boxes of cereal produced is highly correlated with hours of production time.

a. Classify each of Wescott's manufacturing costs as output unit-level, batch-level, product-sustaining, or facility-sustaining.
b. Compute the manufacturing output unit-level cost per box.
c. Compute the total manufacturing cost per box.
d. For what purpose might Wescott use the information in part (b)? In part (c)?

Answers and Solutions to Chapter 5 Review Questions and Exercises

Completion Statements

1. Product undercosting
2. refined costing system
3. direct, homogeneous, cost-allocation base
4. cost hierarchy

True-False

1. T
2. F The last part of the statement is reversed. ABC assigns the costs of activities to products or services.
3. F In ABC, the costs of activities are often indirect costs of products but can be direct costs of products. For example, EXHIBIT 5-3, text p.150, shows that the mold cleaning and maintenance activity is a direct cost of products S3 and CL5, whereas the other six activities are indirect costs of these products.
4. T
5. F The statement describes *product-sustaining costs* rather than *output unit-level costs*. Output unit-level costs are the costs of activities performed on each individual unit of product or service (for example, energy cost to run a molding machine).
6. T
7. F The statement describes a major reason why low-volume products are often *undercosted*.

Multiple Choice

1. c If a costing system uses a single cost-allocation base, products that use more (less) of that base in comparison to the resources they actually consume will be overcosted (undercosted). The reason: all indirect costs are allocated via the base. The costing system described in the question results in peanut-butter costing.
2. d ABC uses more cost pools, each with its own cost-allocation base. For example, compare the simple costing system in EXHIBIT 5-1, text p.142, with the ABC system in EXHIBIT 5-3, text p.150.
3. d In ABC, the cost-allocation bases of indirect-cost pools are usually nonfinancial variables. Some examples are setup-hours, number of shipments, and cubic feet of packages shipped.
4. b Procurement costs are a batch-level cost because they are related to the number of orders placed rather than the quantity or value of materials purchased.
5. a Two steps are used to obtain the answer. First, compute the budgeted materials-handling cost rate per direct manufacturing labor-hour (DMLH):

$$\frac{\$50,000}{(25 \times 200) + (25 \times 200)} = \frac{\$50,000}{5,000 + 5,000} = \frac{\$50,000}{10,000} = \$5 \text{ per DMLH}$$

Second, compute the material-handling costs allocated to one wall mirror:
200 DMLH × \$5 = \$1,000

6. b Two steps are used to obtain the answer. First, compute the budgeted material-handling cost rate per material move: \$50,000 ÷ (5 + 15) = \$50,000 ÷ 20 = \$2,500 per move. Second, compute the material-handling costs allocated to one wall mirror:
(\$2,500 × 5 moves) ÷ 25 units = \$12,500 ÷ 25 = \$500

7. b ABC tends to pass the costs-benefit test for companies meeting one or more of the conditions listed in paragraph 8 of the Highlights.

Review Exercise 1

Direct costs	$ 8,200
Indirect costs:	
Incoming material inspection, 12 × $11.50	138
Production setup, 16 × $30	480
In-process inspection, 200 × $3	600
Product certification, 4 × $24	96
Distribution, 2,000 × $1	2,000
General administration, 50 × $8	400
Total costs	$11,914

Cost per case = $11,914 ÷ 200 = $59.57

Review Exercise 2

a. Average cost per diner = $148 ÷ 4 = $37
    Jason: $44 − $37 = $7 undercosted
    Kent: $37 − $37 = $0 (that is, accurately costed, but only by coincidence)
    Lynne: $25 − $37 = $12 overcosted
    Marci: $42 − $37 = $5 undercosted
b. The fundamental difference in this example is that each cost in the restaurant bill is a *direct cost* that can be traced to one of the diners, whereas many manufacturing costs are *indirect costs* that must be allocated to products. An indirect cost would arise in the example if two or more of the diners shared an item such as an appetizer or bottle of wine.

Review Exercise 3

a. The audit of Detrick Properties actually costs Jay more because, although both audits use 180 DPLH, a much higher proportion of *partner hours* is used for Detrick: 75/180 versus 30/180. Also, Detrick uses much more of the travel and communication resources.
b. Fuentes audit = (180 × $120) + (180 × $80) = $21,600 + $14,400 = $36,000
    Detrick audit = (180 × $120) + (180 × $80) = $21,600 + $14,400 = $36,000
c. With only one direct-cost category and only one indirect-cost pool, the existing costing system does not accurately measure the cost of resources used by each audit. The Fuentes audit is overcosted because it used a lower proportion of the more expensive partner hours as well as relatively less travel and communication. For the opposite reasons, the Detrick audit is undercosted.
d. By misstating the cost of the audits, Jay could easily lose Fuentes as a client. A competing CPA firm with a better costing system might make a lower bid for the Fuentes audit.
e. The costing system could be refined by following three guidelines: (1) classify as many of the total costs as direct costs of audits as is economically feasible, (2) expand the number of indirect-cost pools until each of these pools is more homogeneous, and (3) use the cause-and-effect criterion, when possible, to identify the cost-allocation base (the cause) for each indirect-cost pool (the effect).

a.   New-product development costs are product-sustaining costs.
     Material-handling costs are output unit-level costs.
     Material-purchase costs are output unit-level costs.
     Manufacturing labor costs directly traced to individual products are output unit-level costs.
     Manufacturing labor costs traced directly to production setups are batch-level costs.
     Energy costs are output unit-level costs.
     Plant administration costs are facility-sustaining costs.

b. | | |
     |---|---:|
     | Material-handling costs | $ 6,628,000 |
     | Material-purchase costs | 8,852,000 |
     | Direct manufacturing labor costs | 7,263,000 |
     | Energy costs | 1,029,000 |
     | Total output unit-level costs | $23,772,000 |

$$\text{Output unit-level cost per box} = \frac{\$23,772,000}{28,000,000} = \$0.849 \text{ per box}$$

c. | | |
     |---|---:|
     | Output unit-level costs (from part b) | $23,772,000 |
     | Batch-level costs | |
     | Production setup costs | 2,385,000 |
     | Product-sustaining costs | |
     | New-product development costs | 5,684,000 |
     | Facility-sustaining costs | |
     | Plant administration costs | 6,295,000 |
     | Total manufacturing costs | $38,136,000 |

$$\text{Total manufacturing cost per box} = \frac{\$38,136,000}{28,000,000} = \$1.362 \text{ per box}$$

d.   Wescott could use the manufacturing output unit-level cost per box for developing budgets at different levels of output and for evaluating performance of managers. Total manufacturing cost per box is the inventoriable cost for reporting under generally accepted accounting principles. (Note that some value-chain costs not included in this exercise—such as marketing, distribution, and customer service—are not inventoriable costs, but they would be classified in the cost hierarchy in part a.)

CHAPTER 6

Master Budget and Responsibility Accounting

Overview

This chapter explains the key role budgets play in the planning and control of operations. The chapter has a dual focus: (1) how to prepare the operating budget, a key component of the master budget, and (2) how managers use responsibility accounting to facilitate planning and control. The Appendix to the chapter illustrates how to prepare the cash budget.

Highlights

1. A *budget* is a quantitative expression of a proposed plan of action by management for a specified period and is an aid to coordinating what needs to be done to implement that plan. A budget generally includes both financial and nonfinancial aspects of the plan and it serves as a blueprint for the company to follow in the upcoming period. When administered wisely, budgets compel strategic planning, promote coordination and communication among subunits within the company, provide a framework for judging performance, and motivate managers and other employees.

2. Budgeting is most useful when it is integrated with the company's strategy. *Strategy* specifies how an organization matches its own capabilities with the opportunities in the marketplace to accomplish its objectives. An organization's strategic plans lead to the formulation of budgets.

3. Well-managed companies usually cycle through the following budgeting steps during the course of the fiscal year:

a. Managers and management accountants plan the performance of the company as a whole and the performance of its subunits.
b. Senior managers give subordinate managers a frame of reference, a set of specific financial or nonfinancial expectations against which actual results will be compared.
c. Management accounts help managers investi-

gate variations from plans and, if necessary, take corrective action.
d. Managers and management accountants plan for the next period, taking into account market feedback and changed conditions.

4. The most frequently used budget period is one year. The annual budget is often subdivided into months and quarters. Companies are increasingly using **rolling budgets** (also called **continuous budgets**). A rolling budget is a budget that is always available for a specified future period by continually adding a month, quarter, or year to the period that just ended.

5. The **master budget** expresses management's operating and financial plans for a specified period (usually a fiscal year), and it includes a set of budgeted financial statements. The two main components of the master budget are the **operating budget** and the **financial budget**. The operating budget is the budgeted income statement and its supporting budget schedules. The financial budget consists of the capital expenditures budget, the cash budget (discussed in paragraph 18 below), the budgeted balance sheet, and the budgeted statement of cash flows. EXHIBIT 6-2, text p.190, provides an overview of the master budget.

6. Manufacturing companies commonly use nine basic steps for developing the operating budget:

Step 1: Prepare the revenues budget.
Step 2: Prepare the production budget (in units).
Step 3: Prepare the direct materials usage budget and direct materials purchases budget.
Step 4: Prepare the direct manufacturing labor costs budget.
Step 5: Prepare the manufacturing overhead costs budget.
Step 6: Prepare the ending inventories budget.
Step 7: Prepare the cost of goods sold budget.
Step 8: Prepare the nonmanufacturing costs budget.

Step 9: Prepare the budgeted income statement.

In performing Step 1, the usual starting point is to base revenues on expected demand. Occasionally, however, factors other than demand limit budgeted revenues. For example, when demand exceeds available production capacity, the revenues budget would be based on the maximum units that could be produced. Steps 2 and 3 are illustrated below using assumed amounts. Step 2 uses the following schedule:

	Product Units
Budgeted sales	104,000
Add target ending inventory	6,000
Total requirements	110,000
Deduct beginning inventory	10,000
Budgeted production	100,000

Step 3 uses the following schedule *for each type of direct material*:

	Material A (in gallons)
Budgeted production usage (100,000 units above × 2.5 gallons per unit)	250,000
Add target ending inventory	11,000
Total requirements	261,000
Deduct beginning inventory	12,500
Budgeted purchases	248,500

Steps 4-9 are all straightforward.

7. Historically, budgets have used a small number of cost drivers that are predominantly output-based (units produced, units sold, or revenues). Due to the use of activity-based costing, companies incorporate activity-based cost drivers into their budgets. **Activity-based budgeting (ABB)** focuses on the budgeted cost of activities necessary to produce and sell products and services. ABB formulates budgets for each activity area. An activity-based budget is prepared by multiplying budgeted usage of the cost driver for each activity times the respective budgeted cost rate, and then summing the budgeted costs of the activities. The more detailed information available from ABB gives managers additional insight into ways they can better manage future costs.

8. **Financial planning models** are mathematical representations of the relationships among operating activities, financing activities, and other factors that affect the master budget. These computer-based models enable managers to prepare the first draft of the master budget, and conduct "what if" (sensitivity) analysis of the effects on this budget of changes in the original predicted data or in the underlying assumptions. Sensitivity analysis is especially valuable for examining the effects of multiple changes to parameters in the master budget; EXHIBIT 6-4, text p.197, illustrates sensitivity analysis.

9. Budgeting is much more than the mechanical tool implied in paragraphs 6 through 8. Human factors play a crucial part in budgeting. Each manager, regardless of his or her level in the company, is in charge of a **responsibility center**. A responsibility center is a part, segment, or subunit of an organization whose manager is accountable for a specified set of activities. The higher the manager's level, the broader the responsibility center and, generally, the larger the number of his or her subordinates. Four types of responsibility centers are:

Type	Manager Is Accountable For
Cost center	Costs only
Revenue center	Revenues only
Profit center	Revenues and costs
Investment center	Investments, revenues & costs

10. **Responsibility accounting** is a system that measures the plans, budgets, actions, and actual results of each responsibility center. The *performance report* for each responsibility center shows by line item the actual result, the budgeted amount, and the *variance* (the difference between the actual result and the budgeted amount). Performance reports for higher levels of management combine lower-level reports but limit the amount of detail; as a result, performance reports for higher-level managers include more total dollars but less detail than lower-level reports.

11. Managers and accountants tend to "play the blame game"—using variances in performance reports for responsibility centers to pinpoint fault for operating problems. When variances occur, the initial focus should be on which manager to *ask*,

not which manager to *blame*. Variances should be used to raise questions and direct attention to the managers who are expected to have essential information and knowledge. Fixing the blame for a variance occurs only when the manager's performance is judged to be unsatisfactory.

12. **Controllability** is the degree of influence that a specific manager has over costs, revenues, or related items for which he or she is responsible. A **controllable cost** is any cost that is primarily subject to the influence of a given responsibility center manager for a given period. A responsibility accounting system could either exclude all uncontrollable costs from a manager's performance report or segregate such costs from the controllable costs.

13. Managers should avoid overemphasizing controllability. Responsibility accounting is more far-reaching. It focuses on information and knowledge, not only on control. The key question is: Which person knows the most about the specific item in question, regardless of his or her ability to exert personal control over that item? For example, a purchasing manager may be held accountable for total purchase costs, not because she can affect market prices, but because of her ability to predict uncontrollable prices and explain uncontrollable price changes.

14. Pressures often exist within companies for budgeted revenues to be overestimates and/or budgeted costs to be underestimates of the expected amounts. For example, some companies set high budgets for revenues and/or low budgets for costs in an attempt to motivate managers and other employees to put forth extra effort and achieve better performance. In other cases, budgets may require below-average effort to be attained. **Budgetary slack** describes the practice of underestimating budgeted revenues, or overestimating budgeted costs, to make budgeted targets more easily achievable. Budgetary slack provides managers with a hedge against unexpected adverse circumstances. A major challenge in budgeting is providing managers with incentives to make honest budget forecasts.

15. Research shows that achievable budgets serve as goals and improve performance. That's because people view an inability to meet budgeted numbers as a failure. Individuals are motivated to work hard to avoid failure more so than they are motivated to achieve success. As individuals get closer to a goal, they work harder to achieve it. For these reasons, many executives like to set challenging but achievable goals for their subordinates. Creating a little discomfort among managers and other employees improves performance, whereas unachievable budgets increase discomfort without motivation because individuals cannot avoid failure.

16. A key issue facing companies today is continuous improvement or *kaizen* in Japanese. **Kaizen budgeting** explicitly incorporates continuous improvement anticipated *during the budget period* into the budget numbers. Unless a company using kaizen budgeting meets its continuous improvement targets, actual costs will exceed budgeted costs.

17. Multinational companies need to budget for foreign exchange rates (for example, converting the euro to U.S. dollars) and the effect of each country's tax laws. When multinational companies operate in very uncertain environments, it is often necessary for them to make budget revisions. As a result, senior managers evaluate performance more subjectively, based on how well subordinate managers have managed under these conditions.

18. (Appendix) The **cash budget** is a key component of the financial budget. The cash budget is a schedule of expected cash receipts and disbursements. (Note, depreciation is excluded from this budget because it does not require a current period cash disbursement.) The cash budget helps prevent unexpected cash deficiencies or idle cash, thereby keeping the cash balance in line with needs. Like other budgets, the quality of the cash budget is enhanced by conducting sensitivity analysis of the effects on this budget of changes in the original predicted data or in the underlying assumptions. EXHIBIT 6-6, text p.208, shows a cash budget by quarters; it includes the cash flows associated with obtaining and repaying a bank loan.

Featured Exercises

1. Cobb Company budgets sales of Product A at 200,000 units for October 2011. Production of one unit of this product requires three pounds of Material Y and two gallons of Material Z. Actual beginning inventories and budgeted ending inventories for the month are as follows:

	October 1	October 31
Product A	25,000 units	8,000 units
Material Y	23,000 pounds	19,000 pounds
Material Z	16,000 gallons	21,000 gallons

Compute the number of gallons of Material Z the company needs to purchase during October 2011.

Solution

Two steps are used to obtain the answer. First, compute the budgeted production of Product A in units:

Budgeted sales	200,000
Add target ending inventory	8,000
Total requirements	208,000
Deduct beginning inventory	25,000
Budgeted production in units	183,000

Second, compute budgeted purchases of Material Z in gallons:

Budgeted production usage, 183,000 × 2	366,000
Add target ending inventory	21,000
Total requirements	387,000
Deduct beginning inventory	16,000
Budgeted purchases in gallons	371,000

2. (Relates to the Chapter Appendix) Information pertaining to Noskey Corporation's sales revenues is as follows:

	November 2010 (Actual)	December 2010 (Budget)	January 2011 (Budget)
Cash sales	$ 80,000	$100,000	$ 60,000
Credit sales	240,000	360,000	180,000
Total sales	$320,000	$460,000	$240,000

Management estimates that 5% of credit sales are uncollectible. Of the credit sales that are collectible, 60% are collected in the month of sale and the remainder in the month following sale. Purchases of inventory are equal to next month's sales, and gross margin is 30%. All purchases of inventory are on credit; 25% are paid in the month of purchase, and the remainder are paid in the month following purchase.

a. Compute budgeted cash receipts for January 2011.
b. Compute budgeted cash disbursements for purchases for December 2010.

Solution

a. Budgeted cash receipts for January 2011:
   From credit sales in December
   $360,000 (1 − 0.05)(1 − 0.60) $136,800
   From credit sales in January
   $180,000 (1 − 0.05)(0.60)   102,600
   From cash sales in January   60,000
   Total $299,400

b. Budgeted cash disbursements for purchases for December 2010:
   From purchases in November
   $460,000 (1 − 0.30)(1 − 0.25) $241,500
   From purchases in December
   $240,000 (1 − 0.30)(0.25)   42,000
   Total $283,500

Review Questions and Exercises

Completion Statements

Fill in the blank(s) to complete each statement.

1. A _____ budget is a budget that is always available for a specified future period by continually adding a month, quarter, or year to the period that just ended.
2. The practice of underestimating budgeted revenues, or overestimating budgeted costs, to make budgeted targets more easily achievable creates what is called _____ _____.
3. The master budget consists of two main components: _____ and _____.
4. _____ are computer-based mathematical representations of the relationships among operating activities, financing activities, and other factors that affect the master budget.
5. _____ budgeting explicitly incorporates continuous improvement anticipated during the budget period into the budgeted numbers.
6. A subunit (segment) of an organization whose manager is accountable for a specified set of activities is called a _____ _____.
7. Any cost that is primarily subject to the influence of a given responsibility center manager for a given period is called a _____ cost.
8. _____ is a system that measures the plans, budgets, actions, and actual results of each responsibility center.

True-False

Indicate whether each statement is true (T) or false (F).

_____ 1. The preferable basis for evaluating the actual results of a cost center for the current month is the center's actual results for the same month in the preceding year.

_____ 2. The financial budget component of the master budget consists of the capital expenditures budget, cash budget, operating budget, and budgeted balance sheet.

_____ 3. The usual constraint on the budgeted level of operations is the company's ability to produce products and services.

_____ 4. From the sales staff's standpoint, budgetary slack is a hedge against unexpected adverse circumstances.

_____ 5. The more detailed information used in activity-based budgeting gives managers additional insight into ways to better manage future costs.

_____ 6. The organization structure that results if operations are divided into increasingly smaller areas of responsibility at increasingly lower levels is shaped like a pyramid with top management at the peak.

_____ 7. Variances, the differences between actual results and budgeted amounts, should initially be used to fix the blame on the managers who are responsible for the variances.

_____ 8. (Appendix) Depreciation is excluded from the cash budget.

Multiple Choice

Select the best answer to each question. Space is provided for computations after the quantitative questions.

_a_ 1. In formulating the operating budget, the last step is usually the preparation of the:
   a. budgeted income statement.
   b. budgeted balance sheet.
   c. budgeted statement of cash flows.
   d. cash budget.

_c_ 2. (CPA) Mien Co. is budgeting sales of 53,000 units of product Nous for October 2010. The manufacture of one unit of Nous requires four kilos of chemical Loire. During October 2010, Mien plans to reduce the inventory of Loire by 50,000 kilos and increase the finished goods inventory of Nous by 6,000 units. There is no work-in-process inventory of Nous. How many kilos of Loire is Mien budgeting to purchase in October 2010?
   a. 138,000
   b. 162,000
   c. 186,000
   d. 238,000

_c_ 3. (CPA adapted) The Zel Company, a wholesaler, budgets $150,000 of credit sales and $20,000 of cash sales for next month. All merchandise is marked up to sell at 125% of its invoice cost. The budgeted cost of goods sold for next month is:
   a. $127,500.
   b. $132,500.
   c. $136,000.
   d. $140,000.

_b_ 4. (CMA adapted) Rokat Corporation manufactures tables that are sold to schools, hotels, and other institutions. Rokat plans to produce 1,800 tables next month. It takes 20 minutes of labor time to assemble a table. How many employees will be required next month for this assembly work? (Fractional employees are acceptable because employees can be hired on a part-time basis. Assume a 40-hour week and a 4-week month.)
   a. 1.5 employees
   b. 3.75 employees
   c. 15 employees
   d. 60 employees
   e. 600 employees

_b_ 5. (CPA) When used for evaluating the performance of a production department manager, performance reports in a responsibility accounting system *should not*:
   a. be related to the company structure.
   b. include allocated fixed manufacturing overhead costs.
   c. include variances between actual results and budgeted amounts of controllable costs.
   d. distinguish controllable costs from uncontrollable costs.

_c_ 6. Performance reports prepared for successively higher management levels in a company should include:
   a. less total dollars and more detail.
   b. less total dollars and less detail.
   c. more total dollars and less detail.
   d. more total dollars and more detail.

7. (Appendix) During the budget period, Bama Manufacturing Company expects to make $219,000 of sales on credit and collect $143,500 in cash from customers. Assume no other cash inflows are expected, total cash payments during the budget period are expected to be $179,000, and an increase of $10,000 is desired in the cash balance. How much cash needs to be borrowed during the budget period?
- a. $45,500
- b. $44,500
- c. $24,500
- d. $23,500

 8. (Appendix, CPA) Steven Corporation began operations in 2010. Steven provides the following information:

Total merchandise purchases for the year	$350,000
Merchandise inventory at December 31, 2010	70,000
Collections from customers	200,000

All merchandise is marked up to sell at 40% above cost. Assuming all sales are on credit and all receivables are collectible, the balance in accounts receivable on December 31, 2010 is:
- a. $50,000.
- b. $192,000.
- c. $250,000.
- d. $290,000.

Review Exercises

1. (CMA) Berol Company plans to sell 200,000 units of Product X in July 2011 and anticipates a growth rate in unit sales of 5% per month. The target monthly ending inventory in units of Product X is 80% of the next month's budgeted sales. There are 150,000 units of Product X in inventory on June 30, 2011. Each unit of Product X requires four pounds of direct materials at a cost of $1.20 per pound. There are 800,000 pounds of direct materials in inventory on June 30, 2011.

   a. Compute the budgeted production of Product X in units for the quarter ending September 30, 2011.
   b. Compute the budgeted cost of direct material purchases for the quarter ending September 30, 2011, assuming direct materials inventory at the end of the quarter is to equal 25% of the usage during that quarter.

2. Kern Company had the following actual results for 2010.

Revenues (1,000,000 units)	$20,000,000
Cost of goods sold	14,000,000
Gross margin	6,000,000
Operating costs (includes straight-line depreciation of $900,000)	4,200,000
Operating income	$ 1,800,000

The selling price for 2011 is expected to increase by 3%, and sales volume in units is expected to increase by 5%. Kern uses kaizen budgeting. Under the kaizen approach in 2011, cost of goods sold per unit is expected to decrease by 4%, and total operating costs (excluding depreciation) are expected to decline by 6%.

Prepare the budgeted income statement for 2011.

3. (Appendix, CMA adapted) Super Connect manufactures products for computer networks. Information regarding Super Connect's operations includes the following:
   - Revenues are budgeted at $520,000 for December 2010 and $500,000 for January 2011.
   - Purchased components comprise 40% of cost of goods sold. Eighty percent of the network components are purchased in the month prior to the month of sale, and 20% are purchased in the month of sale.
   - Payment for the components is made in the month following purchase.
   - Cost of goods sold is 80% of revenues.

Compute the budgeted balance of accounts payable on December 31, 2010.

Answers and Solutions to Chapter 6 Review Questions and Exercises

Completion Statements

1. rolling (continuous)
2. budgetary slack
3. operating budget, financial budget
4. Financial planning models
5. Kaizen
6. responsibility center
7. controllable
8. Responsibility accounting

True-False

1. F   The preferable basis for evaluating the actual results of a cost center for the current month is the center's budget for the current month. Past performance is generally not a good basis for evaluating current performance because (i) past performance may have been at a low level and/or (ii) current operating conditions may differ significantly from those in the past.
2. F   The financial budget component of the master budget consists of the capital expenditures budget, cash budget, budgeted balance sheet, and budgeted statement of cash flows. The operating budget is the other component of the master budget.
3. F   The usual constraint on the budgeted level of operations is the company's ability to *sell* products and services (that is, sales are limited by demand). Occasionally, however, factors other than demand limit sales. For example, if demand exceeds available production capacity, the revenues budget is based on the maximum number of units that can be produced.
4. T
5. T
6. T
7. F   When a variance occurs, the initial focus should be on which manager to *ask*, not which manager to *blame*. A variance should be used to raise questions and to direct attention to the manager who is expected to have the essential information and knowledge. Fixing the blame for a variance occurs only if the manager's performance is judged to be unsatisfactory.
8. T

Multiple Choice

1. a   As shown in EXHIBIT 6-2, p.190, preparing the budgeted income statement is the last step in developing the operating budget. The cash budget, budgeted balance sheet, and budgeted statement of cash flows are components of the financial budget.
2. c   Two steps are used to obtain the answer. First, compute the budgeted production in units:

	Units
Budgeted sales	53,000
Add budgeted increase in finished goods inventory	6,000
Budgeted production	59,000

Second, compute budgeted purchases in kilos:

	Kilos
Budgeted production requirement, 59,000 × 4	236,000
Deduct budgeted decrease in chemicals inventory	50,000
Budgeted purchases	186,000

Note in the example, text pp.191-195, both beginning and ending inventories are given for finished goods and direct materials. In this multiple-choice question, however, only the *changes* in inventories are given.

3. c Let X = Budgeted cost of goods sold for next month

$$\frac{1.25}{X} = \frac{\$170,000}{X}$$

X = $170,000 ÷ 1.25 = $136,000

4. b It takes 20 minutes or 1/3 labor-hour to assemble a table.

Assembly-hours for next month = 1,800 tables × 1/3 = 600 hours

Hours worked by a full-time employee per month = 40 hours × 4 weeks = 160 hours

Employees required for next month = 600 ÷ 160 = 3.75 employees

5. b Allocated fixed manufacturing overhead costs are generally not controllable by a production department manager. A responsibility accounting system could either exclude all noncontrollable costs from the production department manager's performance report or segregate those costs from the controllable costs. The latter approach could change the manager's behavior in a direction that top management desires. For example, if fixed manufacturing overhead costs are allocated on the basis of direct manufacturing labor-hours, the manager will be motivated to use less labor-hours.

6. c Performance reports prepared for successively higher management levels in a company combine lower-level reports but limit the amount of detail. As a result, performance reports for higher-level managers include more total dollars but less detail than lower-level reports.

7. a
Cash receipts from customers		$143,500
Deduct:		
Cash payments	$179,000	
Desired increase in cash balance	10,000	189,000
Cash deficiency (the borrowing required)		$ 45,500

8. b Cost of goods sold = $350,000 − $70,000 = $280,000

Revenues = $280,000 × 1.40 = $392,000

Accounts receivable balance on December 31, 2010 = $392,000 − $200,000 = $192,000

Review Exercise 1

a. $$\text{Production requirement in units of finished goods} = \text{Budgeted sales} + \text{Target ending finished goods inventory} - \text{Beginning finished goods inventory}$$

Budgeted sales: July = 200,000; August = 200,000(1.05) = 210,000; September = 210,000(1.05) = 220,500; October = 220,500(1.05) = 231,525

Budgeted production of finished units
for the quarter ending September 30, 2011:

July	200,000 + 210,000(0.80) − 150,000	218,000
August	210,000 + 220,500(0.80) − 210,000(0.80)	218,400
September	220,500 + 231,525(0.80) − 220,500(0.80)	229,320
Total		665,720

b. $\quad$ $\begin{array}{c}\text{Purchases} \\ \text{in} \\ \text{pounds}\end{array}$ $=$ $\begin{array}{c}\text{Production} \\ \text{requirement} \\ \text{in pounds}\end{array}$ $+$ $\begin{array}{c}\text{Target ending} \\ \text{materials inventory}\end{array}$ $-$ $\begin{array}{c}\text{Beginning materials} \\ \text{inventory}\end{array}$

Budgeted purchases in pounds = 665,720(4) + 665,720(4)(0.25) − 800,000
Budgeted purchases in pounds = 2,662,880 + 665,720 − 800,000 = 2,528,600
Budgeted cost of direct material purchases = 2,528,600 × $1.20 = $3,034,320

Review Exercise 2

Selling price in 2010 = $20,000,000 ÷ 1,000,000 = $20 per unit
Cost of goods sold in 2010 = $14,000,000 ÷ 1,000,000 = $14 per unit

Budgeted income statement for 2011:

Revenues, 1,000,000(1.05) × $20(1.03)	$21,630,000
Cost of goods sold, 1,000,000(1.05) × $14(1 − 0.04)	14,112,000
Gross margin	7,518,000
Operating costs	
($4,200,000 − $900,000)(1 − 0.06) + $900,000	4,002,000
Operating income	$ 3,516,000

Review Exercise 3

Budgeted balance of accounts payable on December 31, 2010:

From December purchases related to December sales	
$520,000 × 0.80 × 0.40 × 0.20	$ 33,280
From December purchases related to January sales	
$500,000 × 0.80 × 0.40 × 0.80	128,000
Total	$161,280

Flexible Budgets, Direct-Cost Variances, and Management Control

Overview

This chapter and the next explain the key role of flexible budgets and variances in the planning and control of operations. The chapter focuses on: (1) how to prepare flexible budgets and compute direct cost variances and (2) the insight managers gain regarding why actual results differ from budgeted amounts. The chapter features a *columnar format*, which is a helpful and intuitive approach to compute variances. The Appendix to the chapter explains the market-share and market-size variances.

Highlights

1. A **variance** is the difference between an actual result and the expected performance, which is also called **budgeted performance**. Variances assist managers in implementing their strategies by enabling **management by exception**, which is the practice of focusing management attention on areas that are not operating as expected (such as a large shortfall in sales of a product) and devoting less time to areas operating as expected. In other words, by highlighting the areas that have deviated most from expectations, variances enable managers to focus their efforts on the most critical areas.

2. Variances can be computed using amounts from a **static budget** or a **flexible budget**.

- The static budget is based on the level of output *planned (or units sold) at the start of the budget period*. (The master budget described in Chapter 6 is a static budget.) When variances are computed from a static budget at the end of the budget period, no adjustment is made to the budgeted revenue or budgeted cost amounts, regardless of the actual level of output achieved in the budget period.
- The flexible budget calculates budgeted revenues and budgeted costs based on the *actual output in the budget period*. The flexible budget enables managers to compute a more informative set of variances than does a static budget.

3. Assuming output units is the only revenue and cost driver, four data items are needed to prepare the static budget of operating income: (a) budgeted selling price, (b) budgeted variable cost per output unit, (c) budgeted quantity of output units, and (d) budgeted fixed costs. The same data items are used to prepare the flexible budget of operating income, except the *actual* quantity of output units is used instead of the *budgeted* quantity of output units.

4. Variances are labeled as favorable or unfavorable. A **favorable variance** (denoted F in the textbook and *Student Guide*) has the effect, when considered in isolation, of *increasing* operating income relative to the budgeted amount. An **unfavorable variance** (denoted U) has the effect, when considered in isolation, of *decreasing* operating income relative to the budgeted amount.

5. Both static budgets and flexible budgets can differ in the level of detail they report. Companies present budgets with broad summary figures that can be broken down into increasingly more detailed figures. The increasing level of detail pertains to both the number of line items included in the income statement and the number of variances computed. The term "level" followed by a number denotes the amount of detail shown by a variance analysis. Level 0 reports the least detail, level 1 provides more detail, and so on. Level 0 and level 1 analyses use static budgets only. Level 2 and higher analyses use flexible budgets.

6. The **static-budget variance** is the difference between the actual result and the corresponding budgeted amount in the static budget. Under level 0 analysis, the static-budget variance for operating income is computed by subtracting the static-budget amount of operating income from actual operating income. With the additional detail of level 1 analysis, static-budget variances are

computed for revenues, variable costs, contribution margin, fixed costs, and operating income. EXHIBIT 7-1, text p.229, computes the level 1 variances.

7. Level 2 analysis provides more insight into the causes of variances by using a flexible budget in the computation of variances. Level 2 analysis subdivides the static-budget variance into the **flexible-budget variance** and the **sales-volume variance**. The flexible-budget variance is the difference between an actual result and the corresponding flexible-budget amount based on the actual output level in the budget period. The sales-volume variance is the difference between a flexible-budget amount and the corresponding static-budget amount. As a result, sales-volume variances arise solely because the actual quantity of output differs from the budgeted quantity of output.

8. Flexible-budget variances and sales-volume variances are computed for revenues, variable costs, contribution margin, fixed costs, and operating income. The flexible-budget variance for revenues, called the **selling-price variance**, arises solely because actual selling price differs from budgeted selling price. It is favorable (unfavorable) if the actual selling price of a product or service is greater (less) than the budgeted selling price. EXHIBIT 7-2, text p.231, presents the computation of these level 2 variances in a columnar format.

9. Level 3 analysis subdivides the flexible-budget variance for direct material costs or direct manufacturing labor costs into the **price variance** and the **efficiency variance**. Price variances are sometimes called **rate variances**, especially when they are for direct labor. Efficiency variances are

sometimes called **usage variances**. The formulas for computing the price and efficiency variances are in the box below. The price variance is favorable (unfavorable) if the actual price of the input is less (greater) than its budgeted price. The efficiency variance is favorable (unfavorable) if the actual quantity of input used is less (greater) than the budgeted quantity of input that should have been used based on the actual output level in the budget period. EXHIBIT 7-3, text p.238, presents the computation of these level 3 variances in a columnar format.

10. In computing price and efficiency variances, budgeted input prices and budgeted input quantities are often based on standards. The term **standard** refers to a carefully determined price, cost, or quantity that is used as a benchmark for judging performance. Standards are usually expressed on a per-unit basis. For example, engineering studies can determine standard quantities of direct materials and direct manufacturing labor-hours per unit of output. To illustrate, assume an engineering study determines 0.80 direct manufacturing labor-hours (DMLH) is the standard time allowed to produce a unit of output. Assume the standard wage rate is $20 per DMLH. The **standard cost** per unit of output is $16 (0.80 × $20). Assuming 10,000 units of output are produced in April, the flexible budget for direct manufacturing labor costs for April is $160,000 (10,000 × $16). In this example, the 0.80 DMLH per unit of output is a **standard input**. Generally, a standard input amount is most useful when it (a) excludes past inefficiencies and (b) takes into account the changes expected to occur in the budget period.

11. Managers consider many possible causes for price variances and efficiency variances. Here are some examples.

$$\begin{array}{l} \text{Price} \\ \text{variance} \end{array} = \left(\begin{array}{l} \text{Actual price} \\ \text{of input} \end{array} - \begin{array}{l} \text{Budgeted price} \\ \text{of input} \end{array} \right) \times \begin{array}{l} \text{Actual quantity} \\ \text{of input} \end{array}$$

$$\begin{array}{l} \text{Efficiency} \\ \text{variance} \end{array} = \left(\begin{array}{l} \text{Actual} \\ \text{quantity of} \\ \text{input used} \end{array} - \begin{array}{l} \text{Budgeted quantity} \\ \text{of input allowed} \\ \text{for actual output} \end{array} \right) \times \begin{array}{l} \text{Budgeted price} \\ \text{of input} \end{array}$$

- A favorable materials-price variance occurs if the purchasing manager bought in larger order sizes than budgeted, thereby obtaining quantity discounts.
- An unfavorable labor-price variance occurs because wage rates for highly skilled workers unexpectedly increase.
- An unfavorable materials-efficiency variance results from inadequate training of the labor force.
- A favorable labor-efficiency variance occurs because budgeted time standards for highly skilled workers are not set tight enough.

12. The most important task in variance analysis is to identify the causes of variances and use this knowledge to improve future performance. Often the causes of variances are interrelated. For example, an unfavorable materials efficiency variance is likely to be related to a favorable materials price variance when the purchasing manager buys lower-priced, lower-quality materials. It is always best to consider possible interdependencies among variances rather than to interpret them in isolation of each other. In some cases, the causes of variances are in different parts of the company's value chain or in other companies in the supply chain. For example, an unfavorable labor-efficiency variance could be caused by the marketing manager obtaining a large number of rush orders that disrupts the normal flow of production. If rush orders caused the variance, top management could establish a policy limiting the number of rush orders or could increase the selling price for those orders.

13. Standard costs can be recorded in the journal entries made for direct materials (DM) and direct manufacturing labor (DML). In these entries, *unfavorable variances are recorded as debits* because they decrease operating income relative to the budgeted amount; *favorable variances are recorded as credits* for the opposite reason. The journal entries in the example, text p.240, are:

DM Control	666,000	
DM Price Variance		44,400
Accounts Payable Control		621,600
Work-in-Process Control	600,000	
DM Efficiency Variance	66,000	
DM Control		666,000
Work-in-Process Control	160,000	
DML Price Variance	18,000	
DML Efficiency Variance	20,000	
Wages Payable Control		198,000

- Materials Control is debited (actual quantity *purchased* × standard price) and then credited (actual quantity *used* × standard price). Accounts Payable Control is credited for actual quantity purchased × actual price.
- Work-in-Process Control is debited for standard input (DM and DML, respectively) allowed for actual output produced × standard price. Wages Payable Control is credited for actual hours worked × actual wage rate.

14. Managers often use variance analysis when evaluating the performance of their subordinates. **Effectiveness** and **efficiency** are two attributes of performance. Effectiveness is the degree to which a predetermined objective or target is met. Efficiency is the relative amount of inputs used to achieve a given output level. *Performance can be both effective and efficient, but either condition can exist without the other.* For example, assume a company's static budget calls for production and sales of 12,000 units. If the company produces and sells 15,000 units, performance is effective. Given the 25% increase in output, performance would be inefficient, however, if the usage of direct materials and direct manufacturing labor inputs exceeds the static-budget amounts by more than 25%.

15. Managers must decide when to investigate variances. They often use rules of thumb such as "investigate all variances exceeding $5,000 or 5% of budgeted cost, whichever is lower." This approach recognizes that the budget represents a *range of possible acceptable outcomes* rather than a single acceptable outcome. Variances within this range are considered to be "in-control occurrences" and call for no investigation or action by managers.

16. Companies use both financial and nonfinancial performance measures. Managers exercise control on the production floor by observing workers and by focusing on nonfinancial measures, such as the percentage of jackets started and completed without requiring rework. Financial measures summarize the economic impact of diverse physical activities in a way managers readily understand. Moreover, managers are often evaluated based on actual results compared to budgets expressed in financial terms.

17. **Benchmarking** is the continuous process of comparing the levels of performance in producing products and services and executing activities against the best levels of performance in competing companies or in companies having similar processes. For example, an airline could use benchmarking to compare itself to the best performance in the industry across various operating measures. Obtaining comparable numbers is a challenging aspect of any benchmarking effort. Moreover, understanding why cost or revenue differences exist across companies can be a difficult task.

18. (Appendix) Managers gain more insight into the sales-quantity variance by subdividing it into the **market-share variance** and **market-size variance**.

- The market-share variance is the difference in budgeted contribution margin for actual market size in units caused solely by *actual* market share being different from *budgeted* market share.
- The market-size variance is the difference in budgeted contribution margin at budgeted market size caused solely by *actual* market size in units being different from *budgeted* market size in units.

EXHIBIT 7-7, text p. 248, presents the computation of these level 3 variances in a columnar format. Be aware that reliable information on market size and market share is available in some industries (for example, automobiles and computers) but not others (for example, management consulting and personal financial planning).

Featured Exercises

1. Vermillion Company's actual results and static budget for last month are as follows:

	Actual Results	Static Budget
Units sold	12,000	10,000
Revenues	$119,200	$100,000
Variable costs	68,800	60,000
Contribution margin	50,400	40,000
Fixed costs	34,000	30,000
Operating income	$ 16,400	$ 10,000

a. Compute the flexible-budget operating income.
b. Compute the static-budget variance for operating income and indicate whether it is favorable or unfavorable.
c. Compute the flexible-budget variance for operating income and indicate whether it is favorable or unfavorable.
d. Compute the sales-volume variance for operating income and indicate whether it is favorable or unfavorable.
e. Compute the selling-price variance and indicate whether it is favorable or unfavorable.
f. Without using any of the variances computed in (b) through (e), present computations to explain why actual operating income exceeds static-budget operating income by $6,400.

Solution (on next page)

Solution

(F denotes a favorable variance and U denotes an unfavorable variance.)

a. Budgeted selling price = $100,000 ÷ 10,000 units = $10
    Budgeted variable cost per unit = $60,000 ÷ 10,000 units = $6

	Flexible Budget
Units sold	12,000
Revenues, 12,000 × $10	$120,000
Variable costs, 12,000 × $6	72,000
Contribution margin	48,000
Fixed costs	30,000
Operating income (OI)	$ 18,000

b. Static-budget variance for OI = $16,400 − $10,000 = $6,400, or $6,400 F
c. Flexible-budget variance for OI = $16,400 − $18,000 (from answer a) = −$1,600, or $1,600 U
d. Sales-volume variance for OI = $18,000 − $10,000 = $8,000, or $8,000 F
e. Selling-price variance = $119,200 − $120,000 (from answer a) = −$800, or $800 U
f. Actual contribution margin per unit = $50,400 ÷ 12,000 units = $4.20
    Static-budget contribution margin per unit = $40,000 ÷ 10,000 units = $4.00

Higher-than-expected contribution margin from actually selling 12,000 units rather than 10,000 units in the static budget, 2000 × $4.00	$8,000
Higher-than-expected contribution margin for the actual level of units sold, 12,000 × ($4.20 − $4.00)	2,400
Higher-than-expected fixed costs, $34,000 − $30,000	(4,000)
Actual operating income exceeds static-budget operating income	$6,400

---

2. Randall Company's data for direct manufacturing labor for last month are as follows:

Actual hours worked	20,000
Standard hours allowed for actual output	21,000
Price variance − unfavorable	$3,000
Payroll liability	$126,000

Compute the efficiency variance for direct manufacturing labor.

Solution

Three steps are used to obtain the answer. First, compute the cost of actual hours worked times the standard wage rate (denoted by X):

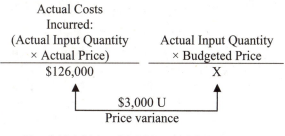

Actual Costs
Incurred:
(Actual Input Quantity   Actual Input Quantity
× Actual Price)   × Budgeted Price
$126,000   X

$3,000 U
Price variance

$$X = \$126,000 - \$3,000 = \$123,000$$

Because the price variance is *unfavorable*, it is *subtracted* in the equation from the actual payroll of $126,000 to equal actual input times budgeted price.

Second, compute the standard wage rate: $123,000 ÷ 20,000 = $6.15 per hour

Third, compute the efficiency variance:

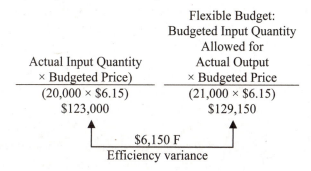

                              Flexible Budget:
                              Budgeted Input Quantity
                              Allowed for
Actual Input Quantity   Actual Output
× Budgeted Price)   × Budgeted Price
(20,000 × $6.15)   (21,000 × $6.15)
$123,000 $129,150

$6,150 F
Efficiency variance

Review Questions and Exercises

Completion Statements

Fill in the blank(s) to complete each statement.

1. A variance is the difference between an _____ and the _____.

2. _____ is the practice of focusing management attention on areas that are not operating as expected and devoting less time to areas operating as expected.

3. The _____ is developed using budgeted revenue or budgeted cost amounts based on the actual output level in the budget period.

4. The term _____ refers to a carefully determined price, cost, or quantity that is usually expressed on a per-unit basis.

5. The relative amount of inputs used to achieve a given output level is the measure of _____.

6. The continuous process of comparing the levels of performance in producing products and services and executing activities against the best levels of performance in competing companies or in companies having similar processes is called _____.

7. (Appendix) The sales-quantity variance subdivides into which two variances? _____ and _____.

True-False

Indicate whether each statement is true (T) or false (F).

____ 1. Favorable variances for revenue items and cost items mean that "good" performance has been achieved.

____ 2. When computing the flexible-budget variance for operating income, fixed costs can be ignored.

____ 3. To facilitate control, direct materials price variances are usually based on actual quantities of inputs used.

____ 4. Generally, the same manager has primary responsibility for the direct materials price variance and the direct materials efficiency variance.

____ 5. Managers usually have more control over efficiency variances than price variances.

____ 6. As performance measures, price and efficiency variances should be interpreted independently.

____ 7. When standard costs are used in journal entries, direct manufacturing labor costs are credited to Wages Payable Control at standard costs.

____ 8. Performance can be both effective and efficient, but either condition can exist without the other.

____ 9. When variances are considered to be "in-control occurrences," managers are not called to investigate them.

____ 10. In a standard-costing system, unfavorable variances should be recorded as debits in journal entries.

____ 11. The best levels of performance used in benchmarking are often found within the company that is using benchmarking.

____ 12. (Appendix) Marketing managers generally find the market-size variance is more controllable than the market-share variance.

____ 13. (Appendix) Reliable industry statistics needed to compute market-share and market-size variances are available in almost all industries.

Multiple Choice

Select the best answer to each question. Space is provided for computations after the quantitative questions.

____ 1. (CPA adapted) The static budget for a given cost during a given accounting period was $80,000. The actual cost for the period was $72,000. Assuming this cost is controllable by the production manager, it can be concluded that the manager did a better-than-expected job in controlling the cost if the cost is:
   a. variable, and actual production was 90% of budgeted production.
   b. variable, and actual production was 80% of budgeted production.
   c. variable, and actual production equaled budgeted production.
   d. fixed, and actual production equaled budgeted production.

____ 2. (CPA) The standard direct-material cost to produce a unit of Lem is 4 meters of material at $2.50 per meter. During the current month, 4,200 meters of material costing $10,080 were purchased and used to produce 1,000 units of Lem. The material price variance for the current month is:
   a. $400 favorable.
   b. $420 favorable.
   c. $80 unfavorable.
   d. $480 unfavorable.

3. (CPA) Information on Rex Co.'s direct materials for the current month is as follows:

Actual quantity of direct materials purchased and used	30,000 lbs.
Actual cost of direct materials	$84,000
Unfavorable direct materials efficiency variance	$3,000
Standard quantity of direct materials allowed for July production	29,000 lbs.

For July, Rex's direct materials price variance is:
a. $2,800 favorable.
b. $2,800 unfavorable.
c. $6,000 unfavorable.
d. $6,000 favorable.

4. (CMA) ChemKing uses a standard-costing system in the manufacturing of its only product. The 35,000 units of direct materials in inventory were purchased for $105,000, and two units of direct materials are required to produce one unit of finished product. In May, the company produced 12,000 finished units. The standard cost allowed for direct materials is $60,000, and there is an unfavorable efficiency variance of $2,500. ChemKing's standard price for one unit of direct materials is:
a. $2.00.
b. $2.50.
c. $3.00.
d. $5.00.
e. $6.00.

5. Using the information in question 4, the units of direct materials used to produce May's output total:
a. 12,000 units.
b. 12,500 units.
c. 23,000 units.
d. 24,000 units.
e. 25,000 units.

6. (CMA adapted) In evaluating the performance within a company, a materials efficiency variance can be caused by all of the following *except* the:
a. quantity of actual output produced.
b. performance of the workers using the materials.
c. quality of the materials.
d. skill level of the workers using the materials.

7. (CPA) Lab Corp. uses a standard costs. Direct manufacturing labor information for Product CER for the month of October is as follows:

Standard price	$6.00 per hour
Actual price	$6.10 per hour
Standard hours allowed for actual output produced	1,500 hours
Direct manufacturing labor efficiency variance—unfavorable	$600

How many actual hours were worked?
a. 1,400
b. 1,402
c. 1,598
d. 1,600

8. If direct material price variances are recorded in the general-ledger accounts at the time materials are purchased, the inventory of direct materials is carried on the books at:
a. actual quantities at actual prices.
b. standard quantities at standard prices.
c. actual quantities at standard prices.
d. standard quantities at actual prices.

Review Exercises

1. Cyrus Medical Products, Inc. uses standard costs and provides the following data concerning one of its products for the month just completed:

Units of output produced	300 units
Standard pounds of direct materials (DM) allowed per unit of output	10 pounds
Standard DM price per pound	$2.00
Actual DM purchase price per pound	$1.80
Actual quantity of DM purchased	4,000 pounds
Actual quantity of DM used in production	3,500 pounds
Direct manufacturing labor (DML) payroll	$6,050
DML price variance	$550 favorable
DML efficiency variance	$600 unfavorable

a. Compute the DM variances in the columnar format below, assuming the price variance is isolated when DM are purchased. Use F for favorable variances and U for unfavorable variances.

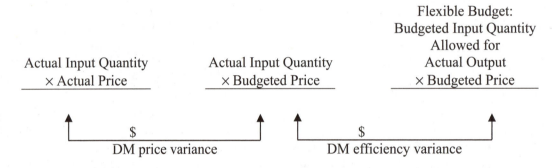

b. Prepare journal entries to record the DM variances and DML variances.

General Journal	Debit	Credit

2. (CMA adapted) Dash Company uses standard costs. The standard costs for the direct costs of manufacturing its only product are as follows:

Direct materials (DM)
    8 kilograms @ $5.00 per kilogram $40.00
Direct manufacturing labor (DML)
    3 hours @ $16.40 per hour   49.20

The following operating data are for the month just completed:

Actual output	6,300 units
Budgeted output	6,000 units
Purchases of DM	50,000 kilograms
Actual DML costs	$300,760
Actual hours of DML	18,250 hours
DM efficiency variance	$1,500 unfavorable
DM price variance	$750 favorable

Compute the following:
a. DML price variance
b. DML efficiency variance
c. Actual kilograms of DM used in the production process
d. Actual price per kilogram of DM, assuming the DM price variance is isolated at the time of purchase
e. Total amount of DM cost transferred to finished goods
f. Total amount of DML cost transferred to finished goods

3. (Appendix) Stover Company manufactures fine chocolate candies. The following sales information is for its industry and its operations for 2009:

	Number of Cases
Budgeted industry volume	550,000
Actual industry volume	560,000
Stover's budgeted volume	88,000
Stover's actual volume	84,000

For 2009, budgeted contribution margin per composite unit for the budgeted mix is $300 per case.

a. Compute the market-share variance and market-size variance.
b. Compute the sales-volume variance, assuming the sales-mix variance is $40,000 favorable.

Answers and Solutions to Chapter 7 Review Questions and Exercises

Completion Statements

1. actual result, expected performance (also called budgeted performance)
2. Management by exception
3. flexible budget
4. standard
5. efficiency
6. benchmarking
7. market-share variance, market-size variance

True-False

1. F   Favorable variances for revenue items and cost items have the effect of increasing operating income relative to the budgeted amount. Favorable variances, however, *do not necessarily* mean "good" performance has been achieved. For example, a favorable materials price variance is not good performance if the materials are of such poor quality that they increase scrap, rework, and customer-service costs by more than the amount of the price variance.
2. T
3. F   To facilitate control, direct materials price variances are usually based on actual quantities of inputs *purchased*, not *used*. This approach isolates the price variance at the earlier time.
4. F   The purchasing manager is responsible for acquisition of direct materials while the production manager is responsible for usage of direct materials.
5. T
6. F   As performance measures, price and efficiency variances should not be interpreted independently because their causes can be interrelated. For example, an unfavorable direct materials efficiency variance can be related to a favorable direct materials price variance when the purchasing manager buys lower-priced, lower-quality materials. It is always best to consider possible interdependencies among variances rather than interpreting them in isolation from each other.
7. F   When standard costs are used in journal entries, direct manufacturing labor costs are debited to Work-in-Process Control at standard costs and are credited to Wages Payable Control at *actual costs*. Any difference between the actual costs and standard costs is recorded as a price variance and/or an efficiency variance.
8. T
9. T
10. T
11. F   The best levels of performance used in benchmarking are often found in competing companies or in companies having similar processes.
12. F   Marketing managers generally find the market-share variance is more controllable than the market-size variance. Pricing and sales promotion decisions are more likely to affect market share than industry market size. When market size and demand for an industry's products are largely influenced by economic conditions, the market-size variance is less controllable by marketing managers.
13. F   Reliable industry statistics needed to compute market-share and market-size variances are not available in many industries.

Multiple Choice

1. c   The production manager's performance is properly evaluated by means of the flexible-budget variance. A performance report for each of the four answers is as follows:

	Actual Cost Incurred	Flexible Budget Based on Actual Output Produced	Flexible-Budget Variance
a.	$72,000	$72,000 (90% of $80,000)	$ -0-
b.	$72,000	$64,000 (80% of $80,000)	$8,000 U
c.	$72,000	$80,000 (100% of $80,000)	$8,000 F
d.	$72,000	$80,000 (100% of $80,000)	$8,000 F

While answers (c) and (d) give the same favorable variance of $8,000, the latter is misleading. Incurring less than the amount budgeted for a fixed cost (such as an employee training program) could result from failing to carry out the plan as budgeted or a poor estimate of the amount of the cost to be incurred. Answer (a) refers to a situation where the manager did exactly *as well as* expected in controlling cost.

2. b

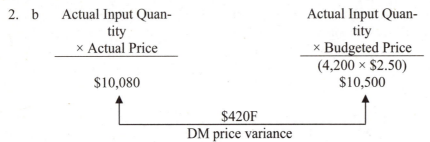

3. d   Standard cost per lb. = $3,000 ÷ (30,000 − 29,000) = $3,000 ÷ 1,000 = $3
DM price variance   = $84,000 − (30,000 × $3)
                            = $84,000 − $90,000 = −$6,000, or $6,000 F

4. b   Standard price of DM per finished unit = $60,000 ÷ 12,000 = $5
Each finished unit requires two units of DM. As a result, the standard price per unit of DM = $5 ÷ 2 = $2.50. Note, the actual purchase price of DM is $3.00 per unit ($105,000 ÷ 35,000).

5. e
Standard cost of DM allowed for actual output produced	$60,000
Add unfavorable DM efficiency variance	2,500
Actual quantity used × standard price	$62,500

Units of DM used = $62,500 ÷ $2.50 = 25,000 units

6. a   The quantity of actual output produced is used in computing the DM efficiency variance, but it is not a *cause* of this variance.

7. d   Let X = Actual hours worked

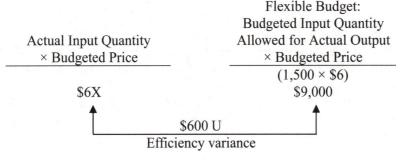

$6X − $600 = $9,000
$6X = $9,600
X = $9,600 ÷ $6 = 1,600

Because the efficiency variance is *unfavorable*, in the equation it is *subtracted* from $6X to equal the flexible-budget amount of $9,000.

8. c   When direct materials are purchased, DM Control is debited for the actual quantities purchased at standard prices. When direct materials are issued to production, DM Control is credited for the actual quantities used at standard prices. The balance of DM Control, therefore, is carried on the books at actual quantities at standard prices.

Review Exercise 1

a.

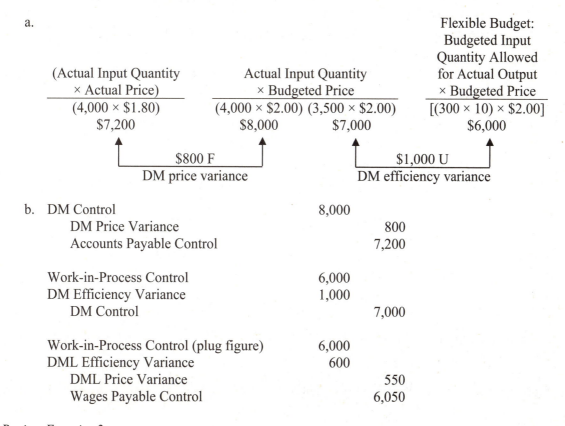

(Actual Input Quantity × Actual Price)	Actual Input Quantity × Budgeted Price		Flexible Budget: Budgeted Input Quantity Allowed for Actual Output × Budgeted Price
(4,000 × $1.80)	(4,000 × $2.00)	(3,500 × $2.00)	[(300 × 10) × $2.00]
$7,200	$8,000	$7,000	$6,000

$800 F
DM price variance

$1,000 U
DM efficiency variance

b.

DM Control	8,000	
DM Price Variance		800
Accounts Payable Control		7,200

Work-in-Process Control	6,000	
DM Efficiency Variance	1,000	
DM Control		7,000

Work-in-Process Control (plug figure)	6,000	
DML Efficiency Variance	600	
DML Price Variance		550
Wages Payable Control		6,050

Review Exercise 2

a.   Actual DML wage rate   = $300,760 ÷ 18,250 = $16.48 per hour
     DML price variance   = 18,250 × ($16.48 − $16.40)
                          = 18,250 × ($0.08) = $1,460, or $1,460 U

b.   Standard DML allowed   = 6,300 × 3 = 18,900 hours
     DML efficiency variance   = (18,250 − 18,900) × $16.40
                               = −650 × $16.40 = −$10,660, or $10,660 F

c.   Standard DM allowed   = 6,300 × 8 = 50,400 kilograms
     Actual DM used   = 50,400 + ($1,500 unfavorable efficiency variance ÷ $5)
                      = 50,400 + 300 = 50,700 kilograms

d.   Actual purchase price of DM = [(50,000 × $5) − $750 favorable variance] ÷ 50,000
                                 = ($250,000 − $750) ÷ 50,000
                                 = $249,250 ÷ 50,000 = $4.985 per kilogram

e.   Total DM cost transferred to finished goods   = 6,300 × 8 × $5 = $252,000

f.   Total DML cost transferred to finished goods = 6,300 × 3 × $16.40 = $309,960

Review Exercise 3

a.

$$\underset{\text{variance}}{\text{Market-share}} = \underset{\substack{\text{Actual} \\ \text{market size} \\ \text{in units}}}{} \times \left(\underset{\substack{\text{Actual} \\ \text{market} \\ \text{share}}}{} - \underset{\substack{\text{Budgeted} \\ \text{market} \\ \text{share}}}{} \right) \times \underset{\substack{\text{Budgeted} \\ \text{contribution margin} \\ \text{per composite unit} \\ \text{for budgeted mix}}}{}$$

$$= 560{,}000(0.15 - 0.16) \times \$300$$
$$= 560{,}000(-0.01) \times \$300 = -\$1{,}680{,}000, \text{ or } \$1{,}680{,}000 \text{ U}$$

The market-share variance is unfavorable because actual market share is less than budgeted market share.

$$\underset{\text{variance}}{\text{Market-size}} = \left(\underset{\substack{\text{Actual} \\ \text{market size} \\ \text{in units}}}{} - \underset{\substack{\text{Budgeted} \\ \text{market size} \\ \text{in units}}}{} \right) \times \underset{\substack{\text{Budgeted} \\ \text{market} \\ \text{share}}}{} \times \underset{\substack{\text{Budgeted} \\ \text{contribution margin} \\ \text{per composite unit} \\ \text{for budgeted mix}}}{}$$

$$= (560{,}000 - 550{,}000) \times 0.16 \times \$300$$
$$= 10{,}000 \times 0.16 \times \$300 = \$480{,}000, \text{ or } \$480{,}000 \text{ F}$$

The market-size variance is favorable because actual market size is greater than budgeted market size.

b. Two steps are used to obtain the answer. First, compute the sales-quantity variance, which is the algebraic sum of the two variances computed above:

Sales-quantity variance = $1,680,000 U + $480,000 F = $1,200,000 U

Second, compute the sales-volume variance, which is the algebraic sum of the sales-mix variance and sales-quantity variance:

Sales-volume variance = $40,000 F + $1,200,000 U = $1,160,000 U

Flexible Budgets, Overhead Cost Variances, and Management Control

Overview

This chapter uses concepts introduced in Chapter 7 to explain the key role flexible budgets and variances play in planning and control of overhead costs. The chapter focuses on (1) how to compute variances for variable and fixed manufacturing overhead costs and (2) how to interpret these variances. The chapter features a *columnar format*, which is a helpful and intuitive approach to compute variances.

Highlights

1. Effective planning of variable overhead costs involves two challenges: (a) undertake only those activities that add value for customers and (b) perform the value-adding activities efficiently. For example, because a clothing manufacturer's customers know sewing is a value-adding activity, maintenance activities for the sewing machines (included in variable overhead costs) are also value-adding activities. Such maintenance should be done in a cost-effective way.

2. Effective planning of fixed overhead costs involves three challenges: (a) undertake only value-adding activities, (b) perform the value-adding activities efficiently, and (c) choose the appropriate level of capacity that will benefit the company in the long run. Consider a clothing manufacturer that leases sewing machines, each of which has a fixed cost per year. Failure to lease sufficient machine capacity will result in an inability to meet demand (and hence in lost sales). On the other hand, if the company overestimates demand, it will incur additional fixed leasing costs on machines not fully utilized during the year.

3. In the example, beginning text p.263, Webb Company uses **standard costing**. Standard costing is a system that (a) traces direct costs to output produced by multiplying standard prices or rates times the standard quantities of inputs allowed for actual outputs produced and (b) allocates overhead costs on the basis of standard overhead-cost rates times the standard quantities of allocation bases allowed for the actual outputs produced. Chapter 7 described (a) and this chapter describes (b). Once standards have been set, the costs of using standard costing can be low relative to actual costing or normal costing.

4. The *budgeted variable overhead cost rate* plays a key role in variable overhead (VOH) variance analysis. To compute this rate, divide budgeted VOH costs by the budgeted quantity of the cost-allocation base. It is preferable to use the cause-and-effect criterion for selecting the cost-allocation base. A manufacturing company can express the VOH cost rate on an *input basis* or *output basis*. In the Webb Company example, the budgeted VOH cost rate on an input basis is $30 per machine-hour. Because 0.40 machine-hours are budgeted per jacket, the budgeted VOH cost rate on an output basis is $12 per jacket ($30 × 0.40).

5. There are three VOH cost variances. The **VOH flexible-budget variance**, a level 2 variance, subdivides into two level 3 variances: the **VOH spending variance** and the **VOH efficiency variance**.

*   The VOH flexible-budget variance is the difference between actual VOH costs incurred and VOH costs in the flexible budget. This variance is favorable (unfavorable) if the actual VOH costs incurred are less (greater) than the flexible-budget VOH costs. The amount of the VOH flexible-budget variance is the same as the amount of underallocated or overallocated VOH. If the VOH flexible-budget variance is

favorable (unfavorable), VOH is overallocated (underallocated).

- The formula for the VOH spending variance is in Panel A of the box on the next page. The variance is favorable (unfavorable) if the actual VOH cost rate is less (greater) than the budgeted VOH cost rate.
- The formula for the VOH efficiency variance is also in Panel A of the box. This variance is favorable (unfavorable) if the actual quantity of the VOH cost-allocation base used for actual output produced is less (greater) than the budgeted quantity of this base allowed for actual output produced.
- The VOH flexible-budget variance is equal to the amount of underallocated or overallocated VOH. When this variance is favorable (unfavorable), VOH is overallocated (underallocated).

Panel B of the box shows the computation of the three VOH variances presented in a columnar format.

6. Interpreting the VOH efficiency is straightforward, but the VOH spending variance is difficult to interpret.

- First consider the computation of the VOH efficiency variance in Panel B of the box. This variance is unfavorable simply because *more* machine-hours were used (4,500) than were allowed in the flexible budget to produce the actual output of 10,000 jackets: $0.40 \times 10,000 = 4,000$. Possible causes for using the additional 500 machine-hours include: (a) workers were underskilled in the use of machines than expected and (b) the machines were not maintained in good working condition. Cause (a) has implications for the employee-hiring practices and training procedures. Cause (b) has implications for scheduling and/or performing plant maintenance.
- Now consider the computation of the VOH spending variance in Panel B of the box. This variance is favorable because actual VOH cost per machine-hour ($29) is *less than* budgeted VOH cost per ma-

chine-hour ($30). To understand this variance, consider the question: Why is the actual cost rate less than the budgeted cost rate? Answer: relative to the flexible budget, the percentage increase in the actual quantity of machine-hours used versus the budgeted amount $[(4,500 - 4,000) \div 4,000 = 12.5\%]$ is *more than* the percentage increase in the actual VOH costs incurred versus the budgeted amount $[(\$130,500 - \$120,000) \div \$120,000 = 8.75\%]$. Because actual VOH costs incurred increased relatively *less than* machine-hours, the actual VOH cost rate per machine-hour is *less than* the budgeted cost rate. Two main reasons could explain why actual VOH costs incurred increased less than machine-hours in the example: (a) the actual prices of individual items included in VOH, such as the purchase prices of energy, indirect materials, and/or indirect manufacturing labor, are *less than* the budgeted prices and (b) relative to the flexible budget, the percentage increase in the actual quantity of individual VOH items used (such as kilowatt-hours of energy used) is *less than* the percentage increase in machine-hours used.

7. Consider another example on interpreting the VOH efficiency and spending variances. Suppose energy is the only item of VOH and machine-hours is the cost-allocation base. Assume actual machine-hours used to produce actual output equals budgeted machine-hours and the actual price of energy equals the budgeted price. *In this case there is no VOH efficiency variance but there might be a VOH spending variance.* The company has been efficient with respect to the number of machine-hours used to produce actual output. However, the company could have used too much energy—for example, if energy was wasted. The cost of this higher energy usage is measured by the spending variance.

The amounts in this box are from the Webb Company example, text p.267.

Panel A: Formulas for VOH Variances

$$\begin{matrix} \text{VOH} \\ \text{spending} \\ \text{variance} \end{matrix} = \left(\begin{matrix} \text{Actual VOH} \\ \text{cost per unit of} \\ \text{cost-allocation base} \end{matrix} - \begin{matrix} \text{Budgeted VOH} \\ \text{cost per unit of} \\ \text{cost-allocation base} \end{matrix} \right) \times \begin{matrix} \text{Actual quantity of} \\ \text{VOH cost-allocation base} \\ \text{used for actual output} \end{matrix}$$

$$= (\$29 - \$30) \times 4,500$$
$$= -\$1 \times 4,500 = -\$4,500, \text{ or } \$4,500 \text{ F}$$

$$\begin{matrix} \text{VOH} \\ \text{efficiency} \\ \text{variance} \end{matrix} = \left(\begin{matrix} \text{Actual quantity} \\ \text{of VOH cost-} \\ \text{allocation based used} \\ \text{for actual output} \end{matrix} - \begin{matrix} \text{Budgeted quantity of} \\ \text{VOH cost-allocation} \\ \text{base allowed} \\ \text{for actual output} \end{matrix} \right) \times \begin{matrix} \text{Budgeted VOH} \\ \text{cost per unit} \\ \text{of cost-} \\ \text{allocation base} \end{matrix}$$

$$= [4,500 - (0.40 \times 10,000)] \times \$30$$
$$= (4,500 - 4,000) \times \$30$$
$$= 500 \times \$30 = \$15,0000, \text{ or } \$15,000 \text{ U}$$

Panel B: VOH Variance Analysis in Columnar Format

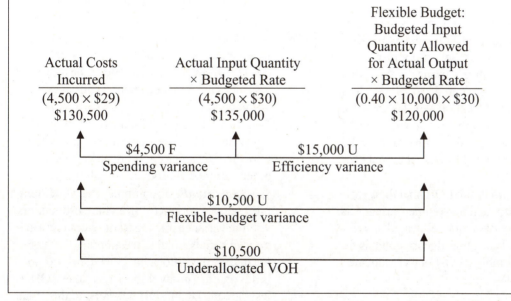

Actual Costs Incurred	Actual Input Quantity × Budgeted Rate	Flexible Budget: Budgeted Input Quantity Allowed for Actual Output × Budgeted Rate
(4,500 × $29)	(4,500 × $30)	(0.40 × 10,000 × $30)
$130,500	$135,000	$120,000

$4,500 F $15,000 U
Spending variance   Efficiency variance

$10,500 U
Flexible-budget variance

$10,500
Underallocated VOH

8. Fixed overhead (FOH) costs are, by definition, a lump-sum amount that remains unchanged in total for a given period over a wide range in output. To compute the *budgeted FOH cost rate*, divide budgeted FOH costs by the **denominator level** of the cost-allocation base. Manufacturing companies commonly call the denominator level the **production-denominator level**. Using amounts in the Webb Company example, text p.266, budgeted FOH costs are $3,312,000 per year and the production-denominator level is 57,600 machine-hours. The budgeted FOH cost rate = $3,312,000 ÷ 57,600 = $57.50 *per machine-hour*. Because 0.40 machine-hours are budgeted per jacket, the budgeted fixed overhead *on an output basis* is $23 per jacket ($57.50 × 0.40).

9. There are two FOH costs variances: the **FOH spending variance** (also called **FOH flexible-budget variance**) and the **production-volume variance**. Another term for the latter variance is **denominator-level variance**.

- The FOH spending variance is the difference between actual FOH costs and the FOH costs in the flexible budget. Within the relevant range, this flexible-budget amount is the same as the amount of FOH costs in the static budget (that is, no adjustment is required for any difference between actual output and budgeted output). The FOH spending variance is favorable (unfavorable) if actual FOH costs incurred are less (greater) than the flexible-budget amount. In the Webb Company example, investigation revealed that the unfavorable FOH spending variance of $9,000 is attributable to an unexpected increase in equipment leasing costs. Management concluded, however, that the higher lease rates are competitive with those available elsewhere.
- The production-volume variance is the difference between budgeted FOH and FOH allocated on the basis of actual output produced. The production-volume variance is favorable (unfavorable) if budgeted FOH is less (greater) than the FOH allocated. To calculate FOH allocated, multiply the budgeted FOH cost rate by the budgeted quantity of the FOH allocation base allowed for actual output produced.
- The algebraic sum of the FOH spending variance and the production-volume variance is equal to the amount of underallocated or overallocated FOH. When this algebraic sum is favorable (unfavorable), FOH is overallocated (underallocated).

EXHIBIT 8-2, text p.272, shows the computation of the FOH variances presented in a columnar format.

10. Assume a manager in the Webb Company example is interpreting the unfavorable production-volume variance of $46,000. Although this variance tells us budgeted FOH is $46,000 greater than FOH allocated, the cause of the variance is not apparent. Additional insight is provided by knowing the underlying relationship: an unfavorable (favorable) production-volume variance arises whenever actual production is less (greater) than the production-denominator level used to compute the budgeted FOH cost rate. (Computing this cost rate is explained in paragraph 8.) Management should not attribute much economic significance to this variance for two reasons. First, the plant capacity may exceed the production-denominator level (as explained in Chapter 9). Second, the production-volume variance focuses only on costs; it does not take into account any reduction in the selling price necessary to spur customer demand that would, in turn, make use of idle capacity.

11. There are four ways to analyze overhead variances, depending on the amount of detail desired:

- *4-variance analysis* consists of these variances: VOH spending, FOH spending, VOH efficiency, and production volume. EXHIBIT 8-4, text p.277, shows 4-variance analysis.
- *3-variance analysis* combines the VOH and FOH spending variances into the total overhead (TOH) spending variance. The other two variances are VOH efficiency and production volume.
- *2-variance analysis* combines the TOH spending variance and the VOH efficiency variance into the TOH flexible-budget variance. The other variance is production volume.
- *1-variance analysis* combines the TOH flexible-budget variance and the production-volume variance into the **total-overhead variance**, which is equal to the amount of underallocated or overallocated TOH. This variance is favorable (unfavorable) if actual TOH is less (greater) than TOH allocated to the actual output produced.

12. Variable and fixed manufacturing overhead (MOH) costs are used for two main purposes of cost accounting: (a) planning and control and (b) inventory costing under generally accepted accounting principles (GAAP).
- For variable MOH, the budgeted cost rate serves both purposes. At a given level of pro-

duction, therefore, the flexible-budget amount of variable MOH is the same as the amount of variable MOH allocated as an inventoriable cost under GAAP.

- For fixed MOH, the budgeted cost for planning and control is the same lump-sum amount within the relevant range. The amount of fixed MOH allocated as an inventoriable cost under GAAP, however, behaves *as if* it were a variable cost; this amount is equal to the fixed overhead cost rate per unit of output multiplied by the quantity of actual output produced.

13. The separate analysis of variable and fixed MOH costs requires the use of separate MOH Control accounts and separate MOH Allocated accounts in the general ledger. *Variable and fixed MOH costs are each recorded by means of the same set of three summary journal entries.* Entry 1 records the actual variable (fixed) MOH incurred.

(1) Variable (Fixed) MOH Control   X
    Accounts Payable and
    various other accounts   X

Entry 2 records the variable (fixed) MOH allocated as an inventoriable cost under GAAP.

(2) Work-in-Process Control   Y
    Variable (Fixed) MOH
    Allocated   Y

Entry 3 closes the variable (fixed) MOH accounts from the preceding entries and records the variable (fixed) overhead variances.

(3) Variable (Fixed) MOH
    Allocated   Y
    Variable (Fixed) MOH
    Unfavorable Variances   U
       Variable (Fixed) MOH Control   X
       Variable (Fixed) MOH
       Favorable Variances   F

14. Variance analysis can be applied to activity-based costing (ABC) systems. Interpreting a cost variance for an activity area requires an understanding of the cost hierarchy introduced in Chapter 5. The Lyco Brass works example, beginning text p. 281, explains how to compute and interpret variances for materials-handing labor costs (a variable batch-level direct cost) and setup costs (a fixed batch-level overhead cost). EXHIBIT 8-5, text p. 283, and EXHIBIT 8-6, text p. 284, present the computation of these level 3 variances in a columnar format.

15. The overhead variances described in this chapter are examples of financial performance measures. Managers also find nonfinancial measures provide useful information. In fact, many overhead variances initially appear as nonfinancial measures. For example, the difference between actual and budgeted energy usage per machine-hour probably would be reported on the production floor daily or even hourly. Expressing nonfinancial variances in financial terms informs managers of their relative importance.

16. In some cases, managers find it useful to use the variance analysis framework described in this chapter for overhead costs in *nonmanufacturing* areas. For example, in industries where distribution costs are high, using standard costs to compute variable distribution overhead spending and efficiency variances may be cost effective. Moreover, variance analysis of fixed distribution overhead costs or other nonmanufacturing costs can be useful in capacity planning and utilization decisions.

Featured Exercise

Franklin Company provides the following information about its manufacturing operations for the month just ended:

Actual machine-hours used	22,000
Budgeted total overhead	$900,000
Actual variable overhead incurred	$352,000
Actual fixed overhead incurred	$575,000

Budgeted production is 200,000 units of output and actual production is 198,000 units of output. One-tenth of a machine-hour is budgeted per unit of output. The budgeted fixed overhead cost rate is $30 per machine-hour. The company uses 4-variance analysis for overhead.

a. Using the columnar format below, compute the variable overhead spending and efficiency variances. Indicate whether each variance is favorable or unfavorable. Use F for favorable variances and U for unfavorable variances.

b. Using the columnar format below, compute the fixed overhead spending and production-volume variances. Indicate whether each variance is favorable or unfavorable. Use F for favorable variances and U for unfavorable variances.

c. Is total overhead underallocated or overallocated? By what amount?

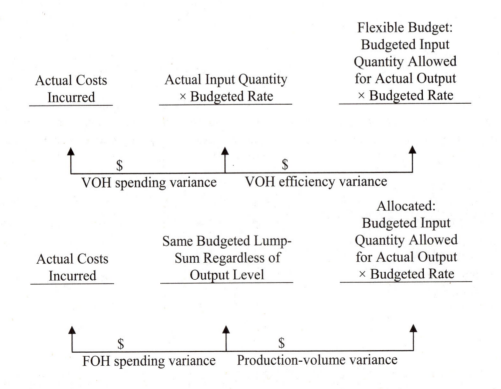

Solution

a. Three steps are used to compute the variable overhead variances. First, compute budgeted variable overhead.

Budgeted total overhead	$900,000
Deduct budgeted fixed overhead, 200,000 × (0.10 × $30)	600,000
Budgeted variable overhead	$300,000

Second, compute the budgeted variable overhead cost rate per machine-hour.

$$\text{Budgeted variable overhead cost rate} = \frac{\$300,000}{200,000 \times 0.10} = \$15 \text{ per machine-hour}$$

Third, compute the variances and indicate whether each is favorable or unfavorable.

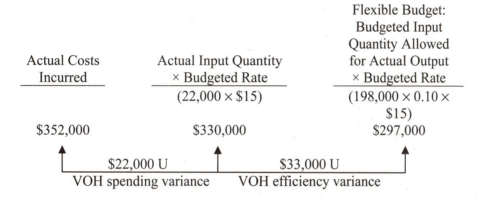

Actual Costs Incurred	Actual Input Quantity × Budgeted Rate (22,000 × $15)	Flexible Budget: Budgeted Input Quantity Allowed for Actual Output × Budgeted Rate (198,000 × 0.10 × $15)
$352,000	$330,000	$297,000

↑————— $22,000 U —————↑————— $33,000 U —————↑
VOH spending variance   VOH efficiency variance

b. The budgeted fixed overhead, $600,000, is computed in part (a).

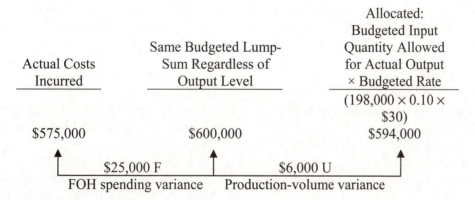

Actual Costs Incurred	Same Budgeted Lump-Sum Regardless of Output Level	Allocated: Budgeted Input Quantity Allowed for Actual Output × Budgeted Rate (198,000 × 0.10 × $30)
$575,000	$600,000	$594,000

↑————— $25,000 F —————↑————— $6,000 U —————↑
FOH spending variance   Production-volume variance

c. Variable overhead allocated is $297,000, the flexible-budget amount from column 3 in part (a). Fixed overhead allocated is $594,000 from column 3 in part (b).

	Variable	Fixed	Total
Actual overhead incurred	$352,000	$575,000	$927,000
Allocated overhead	297,000	594,000	891,000
Underallocated (overallocated)	$ 55,000	$(19,000)	$ 36,000

Note that, because total overhead is underallocated by $36,000, the total overhead variance is $36,000 U.

Review Questions and Exercises

Completion Statements

Fill in the blank(s) to complete each statement.

1. The variable overhead flexible-budget variance subdivides into which two variances?

   _____ and

   _____

2. To compute the budgeted variable overhead cost rate for a manufacturing company, divide budgeted variable overhead costs by the budgeted quantity of the _____

   _____.

3. To compute the budgeted fixed overhead cost rate for a manufacturing company, divide budgeted fixed overhead costs by the _____ of the cost-allocation base.

4. The _____ variance is the difference between budgeted FOH and the FOH allocated on the basis of actual output produced.

5. Manufacturing companies treat fixed manufacturing overhead *as if* it were a variable cost for which purpose of cost accounting?

   _____

6. Fixed overhead is underallocated if the general-ledger balance of the Fixed Manufacturing Overhead Control account is _____ than the balance of the Fixed Manufacturing Overhead Allocated account.

7. The amount of underallocated or overallocated total overhead is the same as the amount of the _____ variance.

8. Interpreting a cost variance for an activity area requires an understanding of the _____ used in ABC systems.

True-False

____ 1. Budgeted overhead cost rates can be expressed as an amount per unit of output or per unit of input.

____ 2. There is no fundamental difference between the budgeted variable-overhead cost rate per unit of input and the budgeted price of individual direct materials.

____ 3. The variable-overhead spending variance is unfavorable if the actual variable overhead cost rate per unit of input (the cost-allocation base) is greater than the budgeted variable overhead cost rate per unit of input.

____ 4. The variable overhead efficiency variance is computed similarly to the direct-labor efficiency variance, and the meaning and interpretation of these variances are basically the same.

____ 5. If variable overhead is underallocated, this means the flexible-budget variance for variable overhead is unfavorable.

____ 6. The total amount of budgeted fixed manufacturing overhead is affected by the production-denominator level chosen.

____ 7. The fixed manufacturing overhead cost per unit is inversely related to the production-denominator level.

____ 8. The production-volume variance is zero if actual output produced is equal to the production-denominator level.

____ 9. The production-volume variance is generally a good measure of the operating income forgone by having unused capacity.

____ 10. In 2-variance analysis of overhead costs, there is only one spending variance.

____ 11. Computing variances for fixed setup costs under an ABC system parallels the computation of variances for fixed overhead costs under a non-ABC system.

Multiple Choice

Select the best answer to each question. Space is provided for computations after the quantitative questions.

____ 1. (CPA) Information on Fire Company's overhead costs is as follows:

Actual variable overhead	$73,000
Actual fixed overhead	$17,000
Budgeted hours allowed for actual output produced	32,000
Budgeted variable overhead cost rate per machine-hour	$2.50
Budgeted fixed overhead cost rate per machine-hour	$0.50

The total overhead variance is:
a. $1,000 unfavorable.
b. $6,000 favorable.
c. $6,000 unfavorable.
d. $7,000 favorable.

____ 2. (CPA adapted) Geyer Company uses standard costing. For the month of April 2009, total overhead is budgeted at $80,000 based on using 20,000 machine-hours. At standard, each finished unit of output requires 2 machine-hours. The following data are available for April 2011:

Actual units of output produced	9,500
Machine-hours used	19,500
Total overhead incurred	$79,500

What total amount of variable and fixed overhead should Geyer credit to the Manufacturing Overhead Allocated account for April 2011?
a. $76,000
b. $78,000
c. $79,500
d. $80,000

____ 3. The following information is for Pappillon Corporation's variable manufacturing overhead costs last month: favorable flexible-budget variance of $3,000, unfavorable efficiency variance of $2,500. The spending variance is:
a. $500 favorable.
b. $5,500 unfavorable.
c. $5,500 favorable.
d. none of the above.

____ 4. (CPA) Fawcett Company prepared the following information on its manufacturing operations for 2010:

	Static Budget	Maximum Capacity
Percent of capacity	80%	100%
Machine-hours	3,200	4,000
Variable overhead	$64,000	$80,000
Fixed overhead	$160,000	$160,000

Fawcett operated at 90% of maximum capacity during 2010. Actual manufacturing overhead for 2010 is $252,000. Fawcett uses the 2-variance analysis of manufacturing overhead. The total overhead flexible-budget variance for the year is:
a. $36,000 unfavorable.
b. $0.
c. $18,000 unfavorable.
d. $20,000 unfavorable.

5. (CMA adapted) Edney Company uses standard costing. The standard cost of its product is as follows:

Direct materials	$14.50
Direct manufacturing labor	16.00
Manufacturing overhead	
2 machine-hours @ $11	22.00
Total standard cost	$52.50

The manufacturing overhead cost rate is based on a denominator level of 600,000 machine-hours. Edney planned to produce 25,000 units each month during 2010. The budgeted manufacturing overhead for 2010 is as follows:

Variable	$3,600,000
Fixed	3,000,000
Total	$6,600,000

During November 2010, Edney Company produced 26,000 units. Edney used 53,500 machine-hours in November. Actual manufacturing overhead for the month is $315,000 variable and $260,000 fixed. The total manufacturing overhead allocated during November is $572,000. The variable overhead spending variance for November is:
a. $9,000 unfavorable.
b. $4,000 unfavorable.
c. $11,350 unfavorable.
d. $9,000 favorable.
e. $6,000 favorable.

6. Using the information in question 5, the variable overhead efficiency variance for November is:
a. $3,000 unfavorable.
b. $9,000 unfavorable.
c. $1,000 favorable.
d. $12,000 unfavorable.
e. $0.

7. Using the information in question 5, the fixed overhead flexible-budget (spending) variance for November is:
a. $10,000 favorable.
b. $10,000 unfavorable.
c. $6,000 favorable.
d. $4,000 unfavorable.
e. $0.

8. Using the information in question 5, the production-volume variance for November is:
a. $10,000 favorable.
b. $10,000 unfavorable.
c. $3,000 unfavorable.
d. $22,000 favorable.
e. $0.

9. Considering questions 5 through 8, Edney Company is using which type of overhead variance analysis?
a. 1-variance analysis
b. 2-variance analysis
c. 3-variance analysis
d. 4-variance analysis

Review Exercises

1. Regal Company provides the following information on its manufacturing operations for April:

Production in output units	400
Budgeted variable overhead cost rate per output unit	$3
Actual machine-hours used	700
Actual variable overhead costs	$1,350
Budgeted machine-hours allowed per output unit	1.50

   a. Compute the budgeted variable overhead cost rate per machine-hour.

   b. Compute the budgeted machine-hours allowed for actual output produced.

   c. Using the columnar format below, compute the variable overhead spending and efficiency variances. Use F for favorable variances and U for unfavorable variances.

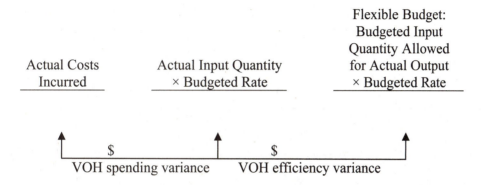

Actual Costs Incurred	Actual Input Quantity × Budgeted Rate	Flexible Budget: Budgeted Input Quantity Allowed for Actual Output × Budgeted Rate

$\qquad$ $ $\qquad$ $ $\qquad$

VOH spending variance   VOH efficiency variance

   d. Prepare the journal entries to record variable overhead incurred, variable overhead allocated, and the variable overhead spending and efficiency variances.

General Journal	Debit	Credit

2. The following information pertains to the manufacturing operations of Payton Corporation:

Budgeted fixed overhead	$1,800
Actual fixed overhead costs	$1,750
Denominator level in machine-hours	300
Budgeted machine-hours allowed for actual output produced	280

a. Compute the budgeted fixed overhead cost rate per machine-hour.
b. Using the columnar format below, compute the fixed overhead spending and production-volume variances. Use F for favorable variances and U for unfavorable variances.

Actual Costs Incurred	Same Budgeted Lump-Sum Regardless of Output Level	Allocated: Budgeted Input Quantity Allowed for Actual Output × Budgeted Rate

```
      ↑             ↑                 ↑
     |___$_____|___$_____|
    Spending variance   Production-volume variance
```

3. (CPA) The following information relates to the manufacturing operations of Herman Company for March:

Actual total overhead costs	$178,500
Flexible-budget formula based on machine-hours (MH)	$110,000 + $0.50 per MH
Budgeted total overhead cost rate per MH	$1.50 per MH
Total overhead spending variance	$8,000 unfavorable
Production-volume variance	$5,000 favorable

Herman uses the 3-variance analysis of overhead costs.

a. Compute the actual machine-hours used.
b. Compute the budgeted machine-hours allowed for actual output produced.

Crossword Puzzle for Chapters 7 and 8

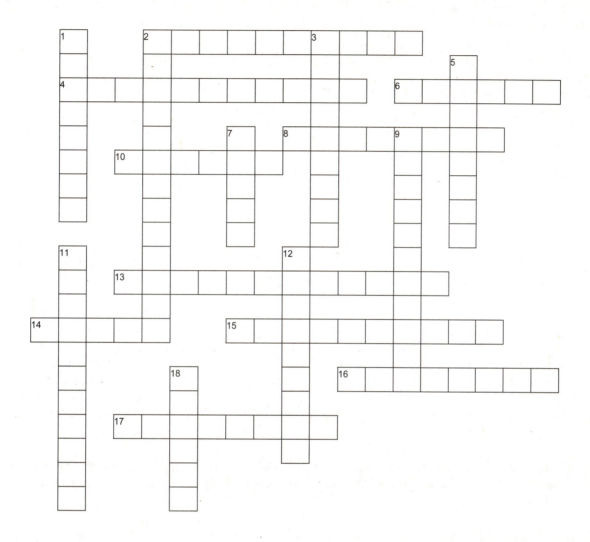

ACROSS

2. For direct manufacturing labor: Price variance + _____ variance = Flexible-budget variance

4. Finance and nonfinancial _____ measures

6. Budgeted quantity of input allowed for actual _____

8. Variable overhead flexible-budget variance = Variable overhead _____ variance + Variable overhead efficiency variance

10. A type of budget based on the output level planned at the start of the budget period

13. The continuous process of measuring products, services, and activities against the best levels of performance

14. Flexible-budget variance + _____-volume variance = Static-budget variance

15. Budgeted fixed overhead − Fixed overhead allocated using budgeted input allowed for actual output units produced = _____-volume variance

16. The difference between an actual result and a budgeted amount

17. A type of budget based on the actual output level for the budget period

DOWN

1. Companies plan their plant _____ strategically on the basis of expected usage over some future time horizon.

2. The degree to which a predetermined objective or target is met

3. Management by _____ is the practice of concentrating on areas not operating as anticipated and giving less attention to areas operating as anticipated.

5. A carefully predetermined price, cost, or quantity amount

7. _____ overhead never has an efficiency variance.

9. The _____ level of the allocation base is used in computing the budgeted fixed overhead cost rate.

11. These variances decrease operating income relative to the budgeted amount.

12. Do not automatically interpret a _____ variance as "good news."

18. A favorable variance is a _____ in a journal entry.

Answers and Solutions to Chapter 8 Review Questions and Exercises

Completion Statements

1. variable overhead spending variance, variable overhead efficiency variance
2. cost-allocation base
3. production-denominator level (denominator level)
4. production-volume
5. Inventory costing purpose
6. greater
7. total overhead
8. cost hierarchy

True-False

1. T
2. F The budgeted VOH cost rate includes the cost of *many diverse* overhead items, whereas each type of direct material has its own individual budgeted price.
3. T
4. F The variable overhead efficiency variance and the direct-labor efficiency variance are computed in a similar manner (for example, compare EXHIBIT 8-1, text p.268, and EXHIBIT 7-3, text p.238). The meaning and interpretation of these variances, however, is fundamentally different. Consider the case when both of the variances are unfavorable. An unfavorable direct-labor efficiency variance arises from inefficient use of direct labor-hours. In contrast, an unfavorable variable overhead efficiency variance means that the cost-allocation base was used inefficiently. The example, text p.268, lists five possible causes of the unfavorable variable overhead efficiency variance; this unfavorable variance is due to the fact that actual machine-hours exceeded budgeted machine-hours.
5. T
6. F Budgeted fixed overhead is a lump-sum amount that does not change within the relevant range. The choice of the production-denominator level has no effect on the total amount of budgeted fixed manufacturing overhead.
7. T
8. T
9. F Two reasons explain why the production-volume variance *is not* a good measure of the operating income forgone by having unused capacity. First, the plant capacity may exceed the production-denominator level. Second, a reduction in the selling price may be necessary to spur customer demand that would, in turn, make use of idle capacity.
10. F In 2-variance analysis of overhead costs, there is no spending variance. The two variances are total overhead flexible-budget variance and production-volume variance.
11. T

Multiple Choice

1. b Total overhead variance = Total overhead incurred − Total overhead allocated
   Total overhead variance = ($73,000 + $17,000) − 32,000($2.50 + $0.50)
   Total overhead variance = $90,000 − $96,000 = − $6,000, or $6,000 F
2. a Budgeted total overhead cost rate = $80,000 ÷ 20,000 = $4 per machine-hour
   Budgeted hours allowed for actual output produced = 9,500 × 2 = 19,000 machine-hours
   Manufacturing overhead allocated = 19,000 × $4 = $76,000

3. c $\quad$ VOH flexible-budget vari-ance $=$ VOH spending variance $+$ VOH efficiency variance

$$\$3,000 \text{ F} = \text{VOH spending variance} + \$2,500 \text{ U}$$
$$\text{VOH spending variance} = \$3,000 \text{ F} - (\$2,500 \text{ U})$$
$$= \$3,000 \text{ F} + \$2,500 \text{ F} = \$5,500 \text{ F}$$

Proof: VOH spending variance $\quad\quad$ \$5,500 $\quad$ F
$\quad\quad\quad$ VOH efficiency variance $\quad\quad\quad$ 2,500 $\quad$ U
$\quad\quad\quad$ VOH flexible-budget variance $\quad$ \$3,000 $\quad$ F

4. d $\quad$ Budgeted VOH cost rate $= \$64,000 \div 3,200 = \$20$ per machine-hour
$\quad\quad\quad\quad$ (or $\$80,000 \div 4,000 = \$20$ per machine-hour)
$\quad$ TOH flexible-budget variance $= \$252,000 - [\$160,000 + (4,000 \times 0.90)(\$20)]$
$\quad\quad\quad\quad\quad\quad\quad = \$252,000 - (\$160,000 + \$72,000)$
$\quad\quad\quad\quad\quad\quad\quad = \$252,000 - \$232,000 = \$20,000, \text{ or } \$20,000 \text{ U}$

5. e $\quad$ Budgeted VOH cost rate $= \$3,600,000 \div (25,000 \times 2 \text{ machine-hours} \times 12 \text{ months})$
$\quad\quad\quad\quad\quad\quad = \$3,600,000 \div 600,000 = \$6$ per machine-hour

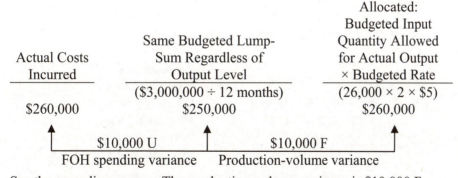

Actual Costs Incurred	Actual Input Quantity × Budgeted Rate (53,500 × \$6)	Flexible Budget: Budgeted Input Quantity Allowed for Actual Output × Budgeted Rate (26,000 × 2 × \$6)
\$315,000	\$321,000	\$312,000

$\quad\quad\quad\quad$ \$6,000 F $\quad\quad\quad\quad\quad\quad$ \$9,000 U
$\quad\quad$ VOH spending variance $\quad\quad$ VOH efficiency variance

6. b $\quad$ See the preceding answer. The VOH efficiency variance is \$9,000 U.
7. b $\quad$ Budgeted FOH cost rate $= \$3,000,000 \div 600,000 = \$5$ per machine-hour

Actual Costs Incurred	Same Budgeted Lump-Sum Regardless of Output Level (\$3,000,000 ÷ 12 months)	Allocated: Budgeted Input Quantity Allowed for Actual Output × Budgeted Rate (26,000 × 2 × \$5)
\$260,000	\$250,000	\$260,000

$\quad\quad\quad\quad$ \$10,000 U $\quad\quad\quad\quad\quad\quad$ \$10,000 F
$\quad\quad$ FOH spending variance $\quad\quad$ Production-volume variance

8. a $\quad$ See the preceding answer. The production-volume variance is \$10,000 F.
9. d $\quad$ Edney Company uses 4-variance analysis because four overhead variances are isolated:

VOH spending variance	\$ 6,000	F
VOH efficiency variance	9,000	U
FOH spending variance	10,000	U
Production-volume variance	10,000	F
TOH variance	\$ 3,000	U

$\quad$ Since the TOH variance is \$3,000 U, this means TOH is underallocated by \$3,000.

Review Exercise 1

a. Budgeted VOH cost rate = $3 ÷ 1.50 = $2 per machine-hour
b. Budgeted machine-hours allowed for actual output produced = 400 × 1.50 = 600 hours
c.

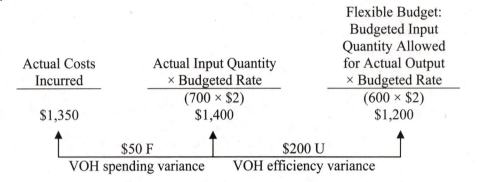

d. In the following journal entries, MOH denotes manufacturing overhead:

Variable MOH Control	1,350	
Accounts Payable Control and other accounts		1,350
Work-in-Process Control	1,200	
Variable MOH Allocated		1,200
Variable MOH Allocated	1,200	
Variable MOH Efficiency Variance	200	
Variable MOH Control		1,350
Variable MOH Spending Variance		50

Review Exercise 2

a. Budgeted FOH cost rate = $1,800 ÷ 300 = $6 per machine-hour
b.

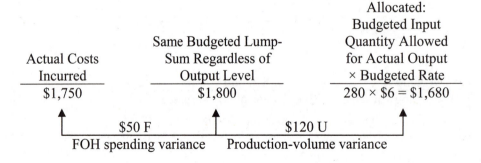

Review Exercise 3

a. Let X = Actual machine-hours used:

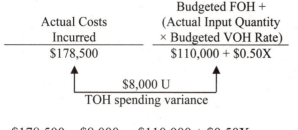

Actual Costs Incurred	Budgeted FOH + (Actual Input Quantity × Budgeted VOH Rate)
$178,500	$110,000 + $0.50X

$8,000 U
TOH spending variance

$$\$178,500 - \$8,000 = \$110,000 + \$0.50X$$
$$\$0.50X = \$178,500 - \$8,000 - \$110,000$$
$$\$0.50X = \$60,500$$
$$X = 121,000 \text{ machine-hours}$$

Because the TOH spending variance is *unfavorable*, in the equation it is *subtracted* from the actual costs incurred to equal the flexible-budget amount of $110,000 + $0.50X.

b. Let Y = Budgeted machine-hours allowed for actual output produced:

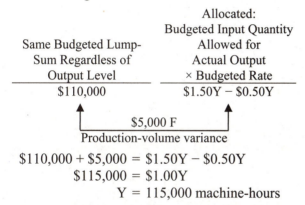

Same Budgeted Lump-Sum Regardless of Output Level	Allocated: Budgeted Input Quantity Allowed for Actual Output × Budgeted Rate
$110,000	$1.50Y − $0.50Y

$5,000 F
Production-volume variance

$$\$110,000 + \$5,000 = \$1.50Y - \$0.50Y$$
$$\$115,000 = \$1.00Y$$
$$Y = 115,000 \text{ machine-hours}$$

Because the production-volume variance is *favorable*, in the equation it is *added* to the flexible-budget amount of $110,000 to equal the FOH allocated amount of $1.50Y − $0.50Y.

The solution to the crossword puzzle is on the next page.

Solution to Crossword Puzzle
Chapters 7 and 8

```
C       E  F  F  I  C  I  E  N  C  Y
A       F                 X              S
P  E  R  F  O  R  M  A  N  C  E     O  U  T  P  U  T
A       E                 E              A
C       C        F     S  P  E  N  D  I  N  G
I       S  T  A  T  I  C     T     E     D
Y       I        X        I     N     A
        V        E        O     O     R
        E        D        N     M     D
U       N              F        I
N       B  E  N  C  H  M  A  R  K  I  N  G
F       S              V        A
S  A  L  E  S        P  R  O  D  U  C  T  I  O  N
V                       R        O
O             C         A        V  A  R  I  A  N  C  E
R             R         B
A       F  L  E  X  I  B  L  E
B             D         E
L             I
E             T
```

Inventory Costing and Capacity Analysis

Overview

This chapter examines how the operating income of manufacturing companies is affected by cost accounting choices related to inventories. The focus is on two basic choices: inventory costing for manufacturing companies and denominator-level capacity concepts. The Appendix to the chapter extends Chapter 3's calculation of the breakeven point.

Highlights

1. *Inventoriable costs* for manufacturing companies are all the manufacturing costs of a product that are considered as assets in the balance sheet when they are incurred. Inventoriable costs become cost of goods sold when the product is sold.

2. **Variable costing** and **absorption costing** are the two common methods of costing inventories in manufacturing companies.

- Variable costing includes *all variable manufacturing costs* as inventoriable costs; all fixed manufacturing costs are excluded from inventoriable costs and are treated as costs of the period in which they are incurred.
- Absorption costing includes *all variable manufacturing costs* and *all fixed manufacturing costs* as inventoriable costs.

Under both methods, the respective amount of inventoriable costs becomes cost of goods sold when the products are sold.

3. *Variable costing and absorption costing differ in how they account for fixed manufacturing costs*. To illustrate, assume a company beginning its operations in May 2011, budgets and incurs $120,000 of fixed manufacturing costs for the month in producing 8,000 units. Assume also the denominator level (used in calculating the budgeted fixed manufacturing overhead cost rate) is 8,000 units per month, and sales in May are 6,000 units. Under variable costing, the fixed cost of $120,000 is deducted as an expense in May's income statement; as a result, *variable costing never has a production-volume variance*. Under absorption costing, the $120,000 is an inventoriable cost—initially recorded as work in process and then transferred to finished goods—at the cost of $15 ($120,000 ÷ 8,000) per output unit produced. Because 6,000 units are sold in May, $90,000 (6,000 × $15) is transferred from finished goods to cost of goods sold; the fixed manufacturing cost component of the ending balance of finished goods is $30,000 ($120,000 − $90,000, or 2,000 units unsold × $15). When these 2,000 units are sold, the $30,000 will be transferred to cost of goods sold. In other words, the $120,000 gets written off in the income statement under either variable costing or absorption costing, but *the timing differs if there is any inventory at the end of the period*.

4. Absorption costing (but not variable costing) is a generally accepted accounting principle for external reporting purposes. Absorption costing recognizes that both variable and fixed manufacturing costs are necessary to produce finished goods. The role of variable costing is to help companies avoid undesirable buildups of inventory (explained in paragraphs 8 and 9).

5. Variable costing uses the contribution income statement, which separates variable costs from fixed costs. Absorption costing uses the conventional income statement, which separates manufacturing costs from nonmanufacturing costs. EXHIBIT 9-1, text p.304, presents income statements for variable costing and absorption costing.

6. Although variable costing is sometimes called **direct costing**, this term is inappropriate for two reasons. First, all variable manufacturing costs—both direct and indirect—are inventoriable under variable costing. Second, not all direct costs are inventoriable under variable costing. Only di-

rect variable manufacturing costs are inventoriable. Direct fixed manufacturing costs and direct nonmanufacturing costs are not inventoriable under variable costing.

7. In general, choosing between variable costing and absorption costing affects period-to-period operating income *whenever the unit level of inventory changes*. The reason: absorption costing transfers fixed manufacturing costs into inventory when the unit level of inventory increases or out of inventory when it decreases. Assuming budgeted fixed manufacturing cost per unit is constant from period to period and the production-volume variance is written off as a period cost,

ACOI > VCOI when the unit level of inventory
                increases
ACOI = VCOI when the unit level of inventory
                remains the same
ACOI < VCOI when the unit level of inventory
                decreases

where:

ACOI = Absorption-costing operating income
VCOI = Variable-costing operating income

For many accounting periods combined, total ACOI tends to equal total VCOI because total units produced will be approximately the same as total units sold (that is, the unit level of inventory will be virtually unchanged over a period of several years).

8. VCOI is *driven by the unit level of sales*, assuming a constant contribution margin per unit and constant fixed costs. As a result, managers cannot increase VCOI by producing more units. The clear-cut relationship between units sold and VCOI helps managers gear the production schedule to the expected level of customer demand. On the other hand, ACOI is *driven by three factors: unit level of sales, unit level of production, and denominator level*, assuming a constant contribution margin and constant fixed costs. Consequently, managers can increase ACOI in the short-run simply by increasing production. Such decisions are manipulative when the expected level of customer demand does not justify increased production and are called "producing for inventory".

9. Criticism of absorption costing increasingly emphasizes its potentially undesirable incentive for managers to produce for inventory in the short run. One way of avoiding those excessive inventories is to evaluate managers' performance based on VCOI in-stead of ACOI, because the unit level of production does not affect VCOI. An alternative is to base the evaluation on ACOI along with nonfinancial performance measures, such as period-to-period tracking of the unit level of inventory in relation to the unit level of sales.

10. Another inventory costing method, **throughput costing** (also called **super-variable costing**), includes *only direct material costs* as inventoriable costs; all other costs are treated as costs of the period in which they are incurred. Because a smaller amount of cost is inventoried under throughput costing than under absorption costing or variable costing, throughput costing operating income is less (greater) than ACOI or VCOI when units produced are greater (less) than units sold. An important subtotal in the throughput-costing income statement is throughput contribution: revenues minus direct materials cost of the goods sold. EXHIBIT 9-5, text p.312, presents the income statement for throughput costing.

11. (Appendix) There is a *single* breakeven point under variable costing and *multiple* breakeven points under absorption costing. Variable costing dovetails precisely with cost-volume-profit (CVP) analysis introduced in Chapter 3. Target VCOI ($0 or some other specified amount) is a function of the unit level of sales; *the unit level of production does not affect target VCOI*. In contrast, target ACOI depends on the combination of three factors: unit level of sales, unit level of production, and denominator level. Many combinations of these three factors cause target ACOI to be $0 or some other specified amount. The illustration, text p.327, provides the formulas for these computations under variable costing and absorption costing.

12. The denominator level chosen for allocating fixed manufacturing costs under absorption costing can greatly impact the amount of inventoriable costs, the magnitude of the favorable or

unfavorable production-volume variance, and the amount of ACOI. A manufacturing company can use any one of four denominator-levels capacity concepts: **theoretical capacity**, **practical capacity**, **normal capacity utilization**, and **master-budget capacity utilization**. Both theoretical capacity and practical capacity measure the denominator level in terms of how much output a manufacturing plant can *supply*, whereas normal capacity utilization and master-budget capacity utilization measure the denominator level in terms of *demand* for the plant's output. In many cases, demand is considerably less than potential supply.

13. Theoretical capacity is the level of capacity based on producing at full efficiency *all the time*. This capacity is theoretical in the sense it does not allow for such things as plant maintenance and machine breakdowns. Practical capacity is the level of capacity that reduces theoretical capacity by considering unavoidable operating interruptions, such as scheduled maintenance time, shutdowns for holidays, and so on.

14. Normal capacity utilization is the level of capacity utilization that satisfies average customer demand over a period (say, two or three years) that includes seasonal, cyclical, and trend factors. Master-budget capacity utilization is the level of capacity utilization that managers expect for the current budget period, which is typically one year. A key reason for choosing master-budget capacity utilization instead of normal capacity utilization is the difficulty of forecasting normal capacity utilization in industries with long-run cyclical patterns.

15. The higher (lower) the denominator level chosen, the lower (higher) the fixed manufacturing costs allocated per unit of output as an inventoriable cost, and the lower (higher) ACOI will be. For example, using the highest denominator level (theoretical capacity) results in the lowest inventoriable costs and the lowest ACOI. That is, the smallest amount of fixed manufacturing costs is allocated to inventory when theoretical capacity is the denominator level. EXHIBIT 9-7, text p.322, compares the income statement effects of using the four alternative denominator levels.

16. Managers face uncertainty about customer demand for their products and need to consider this factor in their capacity planning decisions. For example, practical capacity is often larger than demand in the current period, in part to provide the capacity to meet possible surges in demand. Even if demand surges do not occur in a given period, it is erroneous to conclude that all unused capacity in a given period is wasted resources. The gain from meeting sudden demand surges in some periods may well require having unused capacity in other periods.

17. When large differences exist between practical capacity and master-budget capacity utilization, some companies classify the difference as *planned unused capacity*. There are two main reasons for this approach. One reason relates to using responsibility accounting for performance evaluation. Top management decides on the amount of practical capacity by focusing on demand over, say, the next five years. In contrast, marketing managers—middle management—make pricing decisions by focusing on the potential customer base in the current year. If the accounting system tracks separately the costs of planned unused capacity, marketing managers can focus on the controllable costs they are responsible for in the current period. That is, their controllable costs will not be commingled with the costs of planned unused capacity. The second reason for tracking separately the costs of planned unused capacity relates to the connection between cost-based pricing and avoiding the **downward demand spiral**. The downward demand spiral for a company is the continuing reduction in demand for its products that occurs when competitor prices are not met; as demand declines further, higher and higher unit costs result in greater reluctance to meet competitors' prices. If the costs of planned unused capacity are excluded from the unit costs a manager considers to set selling prices, a downward demand spiral is less likely to develop.

18. For tax reporting purposes in the U.S., the Internal Revenue Service permits companies to use practical capacity to calculate budgeted fixed manufacturing cost per unit. At year-end, any variances must be prorated between inventories and cost of goods sold, unless the variances are immaterial in amount.

Featured Exercise

The following information is for Carthage Manufacturing Company's first year of operations:

Revenues	$1,400,000
Manufacturing costs	
Variable	$272,000
Fixed	$630,000
Operating costs	
Variable	$140,000
Fixed	$198,000
Units manufactured	68,000
Units sold	60,000
Work in process, ending inventory	None

To better focus on concepts, this exercise assumes actual costs are equal to budgeted costs.

Assume the company uses variable costing:
a. Compute the cost of ending finished goods inventory
b. Compute operating income.

Assume the company uses absorption costing and the denominator level is 70,000 units per year:
c. Compute the cost of ending finished goods inventory.
d. Compute the production-volume variance.
e. Compute operating income.

Solution (on next page)

Solution

a. Variable manufacturing cost per unit = $272,000 ÷ 68,000 = $4
    Finished goods, ending inventory = (68,000 − 60,000) × $4 = $32,000
b. Variable-costing income statement:

Revenues		$1,400,000
Variable costs		
Variable cost of goods sold:		
60,000 × $4	$240,000	
Variable operating costs	140,000	
To al variable costs		380,000
Contribution margin		1,020,000
Fixed costs		
Fixed manufacturing costs	630,000	
Fixed operating costs	198,000	
Total fixed costs		828,000
Operating Income		$ 192,000

c. Variable manufacturing cost per unit,

from part (a)	$ 4
Fixed manufacturing cost per unit	
for the denominator level:	
$630,000 ÷ 70,000	9
Total manufacturing cost per unit	$13

Finished goods, ending inventory = (68,000 − 60,000) × $13 = $104,000

d. Production-volume variance = (68,000 − 70,000) × $9 = $18,000, or $18,000 U

This variance is unfavorable because the actual production is *less than* the denominator level. Note, the production-volume variance exists only under absorption costing; all fixed manufacturing costs are written off as an expense of the period under variable costing.

e. Absorption-costing income statement:

Revenues		$1,400,000
Cost of goods sold		
Before considering variances:		
60,000 × $13	$780,000	
Add unfavorable production-		
volume variance	18,000	
After adjusting for variances		798,000
Gross margin		602,000
Operating costs		
Variable costs	140,000	
Fixed costs	198,000	
Total operating costs		338,000
Operating Income		$ 264,000

Note: absorption-costing operating income is greater than variable-costing operating income by $72,000 ($264,000 − $192,000). That's because production exceeds sales by 68,000 − 60,000 = 8,000 units, and each unit of the inventory increase is allocated $9 of fixed manufacturing cost under absorption costing: 8,000 × $9 = $72,000.

Review Questions and Exercises

Completion Statements

Fill in the blank(s) to complete each statement.

1. Variable-costing operating income is greater than absorption-costing operating income for an accounting period when the inventory level _____ during the period.
2. Absorption-costing operating income decreases for a given period when either units sold or _____ decrease (with the other one held constant, or when both of these quantities decrease).
3. Only direct material costs are inventoriable costs under _____ costing.
4. _____ is the level of capacity utilization that satisfies average customer demand over a period (say, two or three years) that includes seasonal, cyclical, and trend factors.
5. The continuing reduction in demand for a company's products that occurs when competitor prices are not met; as demand declines further, higher and higher unit costs result in greater reluctance to meet competitors' prices, is a phenomenon called the _____.

True-False

Indicate whether each statement is true (T) or false (F).

____ 1. The fundamental difference between absorption costing and variable costing is that absorption costing treats fixed manufacturing costs as inventoriable costs, whereas variable costing treats fixed manufacturing costs as an expense of the period they are incurred.
____ 2. A company's gross margin is the same under absorption costing, variable costing, and throughput costing.
____ 3. There is no production-volume variance under variable costing.
____ 4. Assume a single-product company holds its selling price constant and its fixed and variable costs follow their cost-behavior patterns. If the company uses absorption costing and the denominator level remains the same from period to period, its operating income could not decrease if more units are sold in the current period compared to last period.
____ 5. Variable costing motivates managers to produce more units than needed to meet customer demand.
____ 6. (Appendix) There are many combinations of the unit level of sales, the unit level of production, and the denominator level that are breakeven points under absorption costing, but there is a single breakeven point under variable costing.
____ 7. Choosing a denominator-level capacity concept is only applicable to absorption costing.
____ 8. The use of practical capacity rather than master-budget capacity utilization generally results in higher operating income, assuming all variances are written off to cost of goods sold at the end of the fiscal year.
____ 9. If normal capacity utilization is used to compute the budgeted fixed manufacturing overhead cost rate, inventoriable cost per unit tends to fluctuate because of year-to-year differences in the utilization of capacity.
____ 10. If a manager excludes the costs of planned unused capacity from unit costs in setting selling prices, a downward demand spiral is less likely to develop.

Multiple Choice

Select the best answer to each question. Space is provided for computations after the quantitative questions.

____ 1. During its first year of operations, Vintage Co. made 4,000 units of a product and sold 3,000 units for $600,000. There was no ending work in process. Total costs were $600,000: $250,000 of direct materials and direct manufacturing labor, $200,000 of manufacturing overhead costs (50% fixed), and $150,000 of nonmanufacturing costs (100% variable). The cost of the 1,000 units of ending finished goods inventory under variable costing is:
   a. $112,500.
   b. $125,000.
   c. $87,500.
   d. none of the above.

____ 2. Using the information in question 1, the cost of ending finished goods inventory under absorption costing is:
   a. $112,500.
   b. $150,000.
   c. $25,000.
   d. none of the above.

____ 3. Using the information in question 1, the contribution margin is:
   a. $337,500.
   b. $187,500.
   c. $100,000.
   d. none of the above.

____ 4. Using the information in question 1, the gross margin is:
   a. $100,000.
   b. $150,000.
   c. $262,500.
   d. none of the above.

____ 5. (CPA adapted) Indiana Corporation began its operations on January 1, 2010, and produces a single product that sells for $9.00 per unit. Production is 100,000 units and 90,000 units are sold in 2010. There is no work-in-process inventory at December 31, 2010. Manufacturing, marketing, and administrative costs for 2010 are as follows:

	Total Fixed Costs	Variable Cost Per Unit
Direct materials		$1.75
Direct manufacturing labor		1.25
Indirect manufacturing costs	$100,000	.50
Nonmanufacturing costs	70,000	.60

The cost driver for manufacturing costs is units produced, and the cost driver for nonmanufacturing costs is units sold. Indiana's operating income for 2010 using variable costing is:
   a. $181,000.
   b. $271,000.
   c. $281,000.
   d. $371,000.

6. (CPA adapted) Variable-costing operating income is higher than absorption-costing operating income:
   a. when the amount of fixed manufacturing costs in beginning inventory is greater than the corresponding amount in ending inventory.
   b. when the amount of fixed manufacturing costs in beginning inventory equals the corresponding amount in ending inventory.
   c. when the amount of fixed manufacturing costs in beginning inventory is less than the corresponding amount in ending inventory.
   d. under no circumstances.

7. (CPA adapted) Edmond Company has operating income of $50,000 for 2010 under variable costing. Beginning and ending inventories of finished goods for 2010 are 13,000 units and 18,000 units, respectively. There is no work-in-process inventory at the beginning or end of 2010. If the fixed manufacturing cost is $2.00 per unit of output in 2009 and 2010, operating income for 2010 under absorption costing is:
   a. $40,000.
   b. $50,000.
   c. $60,000.
   d. $70,000.

8. (CPA) The budgeted variable manufacturing overhead cost rate under the denominator-level concepts of normal capacity utilization, practical capacity, and master-budget capacity utilization is:
   a. the same except for normal capacity utilization.
   b. the same except for practical capacity.
   c. the same except for master-budget capacity utilization.
   d. the same for all three denominator levels.

9. (CPA adapted) Dean Company is preparing a flexible budget for the coming year and the following practical capacity estimates for Department M are available:

	At practical capacity
Direct manufacturing labor-hours (DMLH)	60,000
Variable manufacturing overhead	$150,000
Fixed manufacturing overhead	$240,000

Assume Department M's normal capacity utilization, which is 80% of practical capacity, is used as the denominator level. Using normal capacity utilization based on DMLH, the total overhead cost rate in the flexible budget is:
   a. $6.00.
   b. $6.50.
   c. $7.50.
   d. $8.13.

Review Exercises

1. (CMA adapted) Denham Company began operations in January 2010. Standard costs were established at that time. The budgeted fixed manufacturing overhead cost rate is based on a denominator level of 160,000 units. During 2010, Denham produced only 140,000 units of output and sold 100,000 units at a selling price of $180 per unit. Variable costs total $7,000,000, of which 60% are manufacturing. Fixed costs total $11,200,000, of which 50% are manufacturing. Denham has no materials or work-in-process inventories at December 31, 2010. Actual input prices per unit of output and actual input quantities per unit of output are equal to the standard amounts.

    a. Compute the cost of finished goods inventory at December 31, 2010, under variable costing.
    b. Compute the cost of finished goods inventory at December 31, 2010, under absorption costing.
    c. Compute operating income for 2010 under variable costing.
    d. Compute the production-volume variance for 2010 under absorption costing.
    e. Compute operating income for 2010 under absorption costing.
    f. Reconcile by formula the difference between operating income for 2010 under variable costing and absorption costing (that is, the difference between the answers for parts (c) and (e) above).
    g. Assume in the coming year (2011) that sales increase by 1,000 units and production increases by 1,000 units (over 2010). Assume selling price, variable manufacturing cost per unit, total fixed manufacturing costs, and denominator level remain the same. Without preparing an income statement, compute the increase or decrease in operating income in 2011 under variable costing.
    h. Using the data in part (g) and assuming the denominator level remains the same as in 2010, compute the increase or decrease in operating income in 2011 under absorption costing.
    i. (Appendix) Under variable costing, how many units must be sold in 2010 to break even? Show a proof of your answer.
    j. (Appendix) Under absorption costing, how many units must be sold in 2010 to break even? Show a proof of your answer.

2. Bouchard Company provides the following data for 2010:

Fixed manufacturing costs:	
Budgeted	$720,000
Actual	$740,000
Practical capacity in machine-hours	20,000 hours
Normal capacity utilization in machine-hours	16,000 hours
Master-budget capacity utilization in machine-hours	12,000 hours
Budgeted input allowed for actual output produced	13,000 hours

    a. Using master-budget capacity utilization:

       (1) Compute the budgeted fixed-manufacturing cost rate.

       (2) Compute the fixed manufacturing costs allocated.

       (3) Are fixed manufacturing costs underallocated or overallocated? By what amount?

       (4) Compute the production-volume variance.

    b. Compute the production-volume variance using normal capacity utilization.

    c. Compute the production-volume variance using practical capacity.

Answers and Solutions to Chapter 9 Review Questions and Exercises

Completion Statements

1. decreases
2. units produced
3. throughput (super-variable)
4. Normal capacity utilization
5. downward demand spiral

True-False

1. T
2. F   Gross margin is a key line item in the income statement only under absorption costing. Contribution margin is a key line item in the variable-costing income statement, and throughput contribution is a key line item in the throughput-costing income statement.
3. T
4. F   Under absorption costing with an unchanging denominator level from period to period, operating income is driven by *both units sold and units produced*. If the increase in operating income from selling more units in the current period is more than offset by the decrease in operating income from producing fewer units, the net effect is a decrease in operating income for the current period.
5. F   Because variable-costing operating income is not affected by the quantity of units produced, managers are not motivated to produce more units than needed to meet demand. Under absorption costing, however, managers can increase operating income in the short run by producing more units (called "producing for inventory").
6. T
7. T
8. F   Practical capacity is generally larger than master-budget capacity utilization. Accordingly, practical capacity results in a lower fixed overhead cost rate and lower operating income because a smaller portion of fixed overhead costs is allocated to units in inventory.
9. F   The budgeted fixed manufacturing overhead cost rate is equal to budgeted fixed manufacturing overhead divided by the denominator level of capacity. Normal capacity utilization is the level of capacity utilization that satisfies average customer demand over a period (say, two or three years) that includes seasonal, cyclical, and trend factors. Year-to-year differences in utilization of capacity, therefore, do not affect the budgeted manufacturing overhead cost rate and do not affect inventoriable cost per unit.
10. T

Multiple Choice

1. c   Total variable manufacturing costs =$250,000 + $200,000(0.50) = $350,000, which is
              $87.50 ($350,000 ÷ 4,000) per unit
       Cost of ending finished goods inventory = (4,000 − 3,000) × $87.50 = $87,500
2. a   Total manufacturing cost per unit = ($250,000 + $200,000) ÷ 4,000 = $112.50
       Cost of ending finished goods inventory = (4,000 − 3,000) × $112.50 = $112,500
3. b   Using amounts from answer 1 above:
       Variable cost of goods sold = $350,000 − $87,500 = $262,500
       Contribution margin = Revenues − (Variable COGS + Variable nonmanufacturing costs)
       Contribution margin = $600,000 − ($262,500 + $150,000) = $187,500
       Note, ending finished goods inventory of $87,500 is deducted in these computations because it is an asset carried forward to the next accounting period.

4. c   Cost of goods sold = 3,000 × \$112.50 (from answer 2 above) = \$337,500
       Gross margin = \$600,000 − \$337,500 = \$262,500

5. b   \$9.00 − (\$1.75 + \$1.25 + \$0.50 + \$0.60) = \$9.00 − \$4.10 = \$4.90;
    (90,000 × \$4.90) − (\$100,000 + \$70,000) = \$441,000 − \$170,000 = \$271,000

6. a

$$\text{ACOI} - \text{VCOI} = \left(\begin{array}{c}\text{Fixed manufacturing costs}\\\text{in ending inventory}\\\text{under absorption costing}\end{array}\right) - \left(\begin{array}{c}\text{Fixed manufacturing costs}\\\text{in beginning inventory}\\\text{under absorption costing}\end{array}\right)$$

    If the amount of fixed manufacturing costs in beginning inventory is greater than the corresponding amount in ending inventory, the right-hand side of the equation is negative. This result means that VCOI is greater than ACOI.

7. c   Substituting amounts from this question into the equation in the preceding answer:
    ACOI − \$50,000 = (18,000 × \$2) − (13,000 × \$2)
         ACOI = \$36,000 − \$26,000 + \$50,000 = \$60,000

8. d   The budgeted *variable* manufacturing overhead cost rate is not affected by the denominator level chosen. Of course, the budgeted *fixed* manufacturing overhead cost rate is affected by the choice.

9. c   The budgeted variable overhead cost rate remains the same within the relevant range.

$$\frac{\text{Budgeted variable}}{\text{overhead cost rate}} = \frac{\$150,000}{60,000\ \text{DMLH}} = \$2.50 \text{ per DMLH}$$

$$\frac{\text{Budgeted variable}}{\text{overhead cost rate}} = \frac{(0.80)\$150,000}{(0.80)60,000\ \text{DMLH}} = \frac{\$120,000}{48,000\ \text{DMLH}} = \$2.50 \text{ per DMLH}$$

    The budgeted fixed overhead cost rate is computed by dividing budgeted fixed manufacturing overhead by the denominator level of capacity:

$$\frac{\text{Budgeted fixed}}{\text{overhead cost rate}} = \frac{\$240,000}{(0.80)60,000\ \text{DMLH}} = \frac{\$240,000}{48,000\ \text{DMLH}} = \$5.00 \text{ per DMLH}$$

    The budgeted total overhead cost rate = \$2.50 + \$5.00 = \$7.50 per DMLH

Review Exercise 1

a.   \$7,000,000 × 0.60 = \$4,200,000; \$4,200,000 ÷ 140,000 = \$30;
    (140,000 − 100,000) × \$30 = \$1,200,000

b.   \$11,200,000 × 0.50 = \$5,600,000; \$5,600,000 ÷ 160,000 = \$35;
    (140,000 − 100,000) × (\$30 + \$35) = 40,000 × \$65 = \$2,600,000

c.   \$7,000,000 × 0.40 = \$2,800,000; \$2,800,000 ÷ 100,000 = \$28;

Revenues, 100,000 × \$180	\$18,000,000
Variable costs, 100,000 × (\$30 + \$28)	5,800,000
Contribution margin	12,200,000
Fixed costs	11,200,000
Operating income	\$ 1,000,000

d.   Budgeted fixed manufacturing overhead = \$11,200,000 × 0.50 = \$5,600,000
    Budgeted fixed manufacturing overhead cost = \$5,600,000 ÷ 160,000 = \$35 per unit
    Production-volume variance = (160,000 − 140,000) × \$35 = \$700,000, or \$700,000 U

e.

Revenues, 100,000 × $180		$18,000,000
Cost of goods sold		
At standard, 100,000 × ($30 + $35)	$6,500,000	
Add unfavorable production-volume variance	700,000	7,200,000
Gross margin		10,800,000
Nonmanufacturing costs		
Variable, $7,000,000 × 0.40	2,800,000	
Fixed, $11,200,000 × 0.50	5,600,000	8,400,000
Operating income		$ 2,400,000

f.
$$\text{ACOI} - \text{VCOI} = \text{Change in unit level of inventory} \times \text{Fixed overhead cost rate}$$
$$\$2,400,000 - \$1,000,000 = (140,000 - 100,000) \times \$35$$
$$\$1,400,000 = 40,000 \times \$35$$
$$\$1,400,000 = \$1,400,000$$

g. Variable-costing operating income (VCOI) is driven by units sold (units produced have no effect):

$$\text{Effect on VCOI} = 1,000 \times [\$180 - (\$30 + \$28)]$$
$$= 1,000 \times \$122 = \$122,000 \text{ increase}$$

h. Absorption-costing operating income (ACOI) is driven by units sold, units produced, and the denominator level:

$$\text{Effect on ACOI} = 1,000 \times [\$180 - (\$30 + \$28)] + 1,000(\$35)$$
$$= (1,000 \times \$122) + \$35,000$$
$$= \$122,000 + \$35,000 = \$157,000 \text{ increase}$$

i. Variable manufacturing cost per unit = ($7,000,000 × 0.60) ÷ 140,000 = $30
Variable nonmanufacturing cost per unit = ($7,000,000 × 0.40) ÷ 100,000 = $28

Let X = Breakeven sales in units
X = $11,200,000 ÷ [$180 − ($30 + $28)]
X = $11,200,000 ÷ $122 = 91,804 units (rounded up)

Proof:

Revenues, 91,804 × $180	$16,524,720
Variable costs, 91,804 × ($30 + $28)	5,324,632
Contribution margin	11,200,088
Fixed costs	11,200,000
Operating income (not zero due to rounding)	$ 88

j. Budgeted fixed manufacturing overhead cost rate = ($11,200,000 × 0.50) ÷ 160,000
= $5,600,000 ÷ 160,000 = $35 per unit

Using the formula, text p.320, and letting X = Breakeven sales in units:

$$X = \frac{\$11,200,000 + \$35(X - 140,000)}{\$180 - (\$30 + \$28)}$$

$$X = \frac{\$11,200,000 + \$35X - \$4,900,000}{\$122}$$

$$\$122X = \$6,300,000 + \$35X$$
$$\$87X = \$6,300,000$$
$$X = 72,414 \text{ units (rounded up)}$$

Proof:

Revenues, 72,414 × $180		$13,034,520
Cost of goods sold		
At standard, 72,414 × ($30 + $35)	$4,706,910	
Add unfavorable production-volume variance		
(160,000 − 140,000) × $35	700,000	5,406,910
Gross margin		7,627,610
Marketing and administrative costs		
Variable, 72,414 × $28	2,027,592	
Fixed, $11,200,000 × 0.50	5,600,000	7,627,592
Operating income (not zero due to rounding)		$ 18

Review Exercise 2

a. (1) $720,000 ÷ 12,000 = $60 per machine-hour
   (2) 13,000 × $60 = $780,000
   (3) $740,000 − $780,000 = $40,000 overallocated
   (4) $720,000 − (13,000 × $60) = $720,000 − $780,000 = −$60,000, or $60,000 F

b. and c.

	Normal Capacity Utilization	Practical Capacity
Budgeted fixed manufacturing cost rate		
$720,000 ÷ 16,000; $720,000 ÷ 20,000	$45	$36
Fixed manufacturing costs allocated		
13,000 × $45; 13,000 × $36	$585,000	$468,000
Production-volume variance		
($720,000 − $585,000); ($720,000 − $468,000)	$135,000 U	$252,000 U

CHAPTER 10

Determining How Costs Behave

Overview

This chapter explains how regression analysis and other methods can be used to estimate cost functions. Cost functions help managers make better informed strategic and operating decisions. Although most cost functions are assumed to be linear, the learning curve and step costs are important nonlinear cost functions. The Appendix to the chapter provides details on choosing among cost functions developed by regression analysis.

Highlights

1. A **cost function** is a mathematical description of how a cost changes with changes in the level of an activity relating to that cost. Cost functions can be plotted on a graph by measuring the levels of an activity on the horizontal axis (x-axis) and the corresponding amounts of total cost on the vertical axis (y-axis).

2. Estimating cost functions often relies on two basic assumptions: (i) variations in the level of a *single* activity—the cost driver—explain the variations in the related total costs and (ii) cost behavior is approximated by a **linear cost function**. The graph of a linear cost function is a straight line within the relevant range. *These two assumptions apply to all of the paragraphs below except 15 through 18, and 24.*

3. The general form of a linear cost function is:

$$y = a + bX$$

where:

y = estimated total cost
a = **constant** (also called the **intercept**), the component of total cost that does not vary with changes in the level of an activity
b = **slope coefficient**, the amount by which total cost changes when a one-unit change occurs in the level of an activity
X = actual level of an activity within the relevant range

Three types of linear cost functions are *variable cost, y = bX; fixed cost, y = a;* and **mixed cost** (also called a **semivariable cost**), which has both fixed and variable elements, *y = a + bX.* In the equation for a mixed cost, the constant is an estimate of fixed cost *only if the zero level of an activity (shutdown) is within the relevant range.*

4. Measuring a relationship based on data from past costs and the related level of an activity is called **cost estimation**. Managers are interested in estimating past cost-behavior functions because these estimates can help them make more accurate **cost predictions** (forecasts) of future costs. Cost estimation and cost prediction underlie major cost accounting topics such as CVP analysis and flexible budgets.

5. The most important issue in estimating a cost function is to determine whether a *cause-and-effect relationship* exists between the level of an activity and the cost in question. For example, producing more units *causes* more direct materials and more direct manufacturing labor to be used. In contrast, the usage of direct materials and direct manufacturing labor move together (are highly correlated), *but neither causes the other.* Only a true cause-and-effect relationship—one that is logical to the operating manager and the management accountant—establishes *economic plausibility* between the level of an activity and a cost. *In such cases, the activity measure is called a cost driver.* Because economic plausibility is essential for cost estimation, the terms *level of an activity* and *cost driver* are used interchangeably when estimating cost functions.

6. *Four methods to cost estimation are the industrial engineering method, the conference method, the account analysis method, and the quantitative* analysis *method* (which takes different forms). Many organizations use a combination of these methods.

7. The **industrial engineering method** (also called the **work-measurement method**) estimates cost functions by analyzing the relationship between inputs and outputs in physical terms. To illustrate, assume a time-and-motion study *determines* 0.20 direct manufacturing labor-hours are required per unit of output. If labor is expected to cost $20 per hour, the estimated cost function is $4 ($20 × 0.20) per unit of output. The industrial engineering method is a very thorough way to estimate a cost function when there is a physical relationship between inputs and outputs, but it can be very time-consuming. Some government contracts mandate its use.

8. The **conference method** estimates cost functions on the basis of analysis and opinions about costs and their drivers gathered from various departments of a company. Because this method does not require detailed analysis of data, cost functions can be developed quickly. The emphasis on opinions rather than systematic estimation, however, means that the accuracy of the cost estimates depends largely on care and skill of the individuals providing the inputs.

9. The **account analysis method** estimates cost functions by classifying various cost accounts as variable, fixed, or mixed with respect to the identified level of an activity. Typically, managers use qualitative rather than quantitative analysis when making these cost classifications. The account analysis method is widely used because it is reasonably accurate, cost-effective, and easy to use.

10. *Quantitative analysis* uses a formal mathematical method to fit cost functions to past data observations. There are six steps in estimating a cost function using quantitative analysis of a past cost relationship:

Step 1: Choose the **dependent variable**, the particular cost to be predicted.
Step 2: Identify the **independent variable**, or cost driver.
Step 3: Collect data on the dependent variable and the cost driver.
Step 4: Plot the data.
Step 5: Estimate the cost function.

Step 6: Evaluate the cost driver of the estimated cost function.

In performing Step 2, the idea is to find an economically plausible relationship between the cost driver and the cost to be predicted. Collecting data is usually the most difficult step in the analysis. Common problems in data collection include missing data, recording errors, a changing relationship over time between the cost driver and the cost, and distortions caused by inflation. Plotting the data not only depicts the relationship between the cost driver and the cost, but also highlights observations outside the general pattern the analyst should check for errors or unusual events. The two most common forms of quantitative analysis for estimating a cost function are the *high-low method* and *regression analysis*. The four criteria for evaluating the cost driver of the estimated cost function are listed in paragraph 13.

11. The **high-low method** is the simplest method of quantitative analysis to estimate cost functions. This method computes the equation for a straight line by using only the highest and lowest observed values of the cost driver within the relevant range and their respective costs. This equation is the estimated cost function; however, if the two observations chosen are not a representative high and a representative low, there is an obvious danger of relying on the high-low method.

12. **Regression analysis** is a statistical method that measures the average amount of change in the dependent variable associated with a unit change in one or more independent variables. **Simple regression** analysis estimates the relationship between the dependent variable and *one* independent variable. **Multiple regression** analysis estimates the relationship between the dependent variable and *two or more* independent variables. Regression analysis uses all observations to estimate the cost function. This cost function is more accurate than the one obtained from only two observations under the high-low method.

13. Computer software such as Excel makes it quick and inexpensive to develop numerous simple and multiple regressions. As a result, the question is this: Which regression cost function should

be chosen? *Four criteria are used for choosing among cost functions: (i) economic plausibility, (ii) goodness of fit, (iii) significance of independent variable, and (iv) specification analysis.* Economic plausibility was discussed in paragraph 5. The other three criteria are discussed in paragraphs 19 through 24.

14. When using activity-based costing (ABC), operating managers and cost analysts identify key activities and their cost drivers. To estimate cost functions, ABC uses a variety of methods—industrial engineering, conference, and regression analysis. Generally, ABC emphasizes long-run relationships between the cost drivers and their corresponding costs. The long-run focus means more costs are variable, which strengthens cause-and-effect relationships.

15. In practice, cost functions are not always linear. The graph of a **nonlinear cost function** for a single cost driver is not a straight line within the relevant range. A **step cost function** is one type of nonlinear cost function: this cost remains the same over various ranges of the level of an activity, but the cost increases by discrete amounts—that is, increases in steps—as the level of an activity increases from one range to the next. If the steps are narrow, it is a *step variable-cost function*. If the steps are wide, it is a *step fixed-cost function*.

16. **Learning curves** are another type of nonlinear cost function. A learning curve measures how labor-hours per unit decline as units of production increase because workers are learning and becoming better at their jobs. Managers use learning curves to predict how labor-hours (or labor costs) will change as more units are produced. The **experience curve** extends the learning curve beyond manufacturing to other business functions in the value chain. The experience curve measures the decline in cost per unit in various business functions of the value chain—marketing, distribution, and so on—as the amount of those activities increases.

17. Two models of the learning curve are the **cumulative average-time learning model** and the **incremental unit-time learning model**. In the cumulative average-time learning model, cumula-

tive average time per unit declines by a constant percentage each time the cumulative quantity of units produced doubles. In the incremental unit-time learning model, incremental time needed to produce the last unit declines by a constant percentage each time the cumulative quantity of units produced doubles. Assuming the same learning rate in both models, the incremental unit-time model predicts that a higher cumulative total time is required to produce two or more units than does the cumulative average-time model. The preferable model to use is the one that more accurately approximates cost behavior; this choice can only be made on a case-by-case basis. EXHIBITS 10-10 and 10-11, text pp.359-360, present the detailed computations under the two models of the learning curve.

18. The lower costs brought about by the learning curve (and experience curve) can have a major influence on decisions. For example, a company might set a low selling price on its product in order to generate high demand. As the company's production increases to meet this growing demand, cost per unit declines. The company "rides the product down the learning curve" as it establishes a higher market share and earns more operating income per unit. Another example is a company incorporating learning-curve effects into budgets and standards to provide a better means of evaluating performance.

19. (Appendix, paragraphs 19-24) It is important to understand how to choose among cost functions developed by regression analysis. Specifically, the Appendix discusses three of the four criteria identified in paragraph 13—goodness of fit, significance of independent variables(s), and specification analysis.

20. *Goodness of fit* measures how well the predicted values of a cost match the actual cost observations. The closer the regression line estimates of cost are to actual cost amounts, the better the goodness of fit. A statistical measure of goodness of fit is the **coefficient of determination (r^2)**, which is the percentage of variation in the dependent variable (the cost) explained by the independent variable (the cost driver). If the estimated costs exactly equal the actual costs, $r^2 = 1$. Generally, an

r^2 of 0.30 or higher passes the goodness-of-fit test. This test is meaningful, however, only if economic plausibility has been established between the cost driver and the cost. *A high r^2 between two variables does not imply or prove that a cause-and-effect relationship exists; it merely indicates that these variables move together.*

21. *Significance of independent variable(s)* focuses on this question: Is the slope of the regression line, the estimated value *b*, statistically significant (that is, statistically different from zero)? The answer depends on the *t*-value of the slope coefficient, which is equal to *b* divided by the **standard error of the estimated coefficient**. This standard error indicates how much of the estimated value *b* is likely to be affected by random factors. If the *t*-value of this slope coefficient is greater than 2.00, a statistically significant relationship exists between the independent variable (the cost driver) and the dependent variable (the cost).

22. When simple regression is used, **specification analysis** tests four assumptions: (i) linearity within the relevant range, (ii) constant variance of residuals, (iii) independence of residuals, and (iv) normality of residuals. A **residual term** measures the vertical distance in a graph between actual cost and estimated cost for each observation of the cost driver.

a. The assumption of *linearity within the relevant range* can be tested by studying the data in a scatter diagram. This assumption holds in EXHIBIT 10-6, p.352. (A scatter diagram can be prepared in the case of simple regression but not for multiple regression.)

b. *Constant variance of residuals* can also be tested by studying the data in a scatter dia-gram. For this assumption to hold, there must be a uniform scatter (dispersion) of the data points around the regression line. This assumption holds in Panel A of EXHIBIT 10-15, p.370, but does not hold in Panel B.

c. *Independence of residuals* can be tested by studying a plot of the residuals. For this assumption to hold, the residual for an observation must not be related to the residual for any other observation. Residuals are not independent if, when considered sequentially, they have a systematic pattern. This condition is *serial correlation* (also called *autocorrelation*). Serial correlation does not exist in Panel A of EXHIBIT 10-16, p.370, but does exist in Panel B. Serial correlation can be measured by the *Durbin-Watson statistic*. For samples of 10 to 20 observations, this statistic falling in the 1.10 to 2.90 range indicates that the residuals are independent.

d. The assumption of *normality of residuals* means the residuals are normally distributed around the regression line.

23. EXHIBIT 10-14, p.369, presents a convenient format for summarizing the regression results. EXHIBIT 10-18, p.372, presents a comprehensive comparison of two cost functions using the four criteria.

24. In multiple regression, specification analysis must also test the assumption that there is no **multicollinearity**. Multicollinearity exists when two or more independent variables are highly correlated with each other. For the no-multicollinearity assumption to hold, the coefficient of correlation (*r*) between any pair of independent variables cannot exceed 0.70.

Featured Exercise

Kenton Corporation predicts its monthly energy cost by using simple regression analysis. The cost driver is degree-days, which is the absolute difference between 65 degrees and the average daily temperature. The regression results are as follows:

Constant	$2,000
Slope coefficient	$3
Standard error of the estimated coefficient	$1
Coefficient of determination	.73
Durbin-Watson statistic	1.82

a. Specify the regression equation.
b. Compute the predicted energy cost if there are 320 degree-days in a particular month.
c. How much does the predicted energy cost increase from one additional degree-day?
d. Is the constant in the regression equation an acceptable estimate of the fixed cost of energy? Explain.
e. (Appendix) Comment on the goodness of fit.
f. (Appendix) Compute the t-value of the slope coefficient.
g. (Appendix) Comment on the significance of the independent variable.
h. (Appendix) Comment on the independence of residuals, assuming 18 monthly observations were used in the regression analysis.

Solution (on the next page)

Solution

a. $y = \$2,000 + \$3X$

b. $y = \$2,000 + \$3(320) = \$2,000 + \$960 = \$2,960$

c. $\$3$, the slope coefficient

d. No, the constant is not an acceptable estimate of the fixed cost of energy, unless the zero level of the cost driver is within the relevant range (which is not logical in this case). Therefore, the constant here is a component of the regression equation that provides the best linear approximation of how energy cost behaves within the relevant range.

e. This regression meets the goodness-of-fit test because the r^2 of 0.73 satisfies the requirement of $r^2 \geq 0.30$.

f. $\$3 \div \$1 = 3.00$

g. The independent variable, degree-days, is statistically significant; that is, the slope coefficient is significantly different than zero because the t-value is greater than 2.00, as calculated in part (f). An alternative approach is to determine the confidence interval for b: $\$3 \pm (2.00 \times \$1)$, or a range of $\$1$ to $\$5$. That is, there is about a 5% chance that the true value of the degree-days coefficient of $\$3$ falls outside that range; therefore, the likelihood that $b = \$0$ is remote.

h. The residuals are independent (that is, serial correlation is not a problem) because the Durbin-Watson statistic lies in the acceptable range of 1.10 to 2.90 for sample sizes of 10 to 20 observations.

Review Questions and Exercises

Completion Statements

Fill in the blank(s) to complete each statement.

1. It is often assumed that a cost function is _____ within the relevant range of a single activity.

2. The _____ in an estimated cost function is the component of total cost that does not vary with changes in the level of an activity.

3. The _____ in an estimated cost function is the amount by which total cost changes when a one-unit change occurs in the level of an activity.

4. The most important issue in estimating a cost function is to determine whether or not a _____ relationship exists between an activity and the cost in question.

5. The _____ method estimates cost functions by analyzing the relationship between inputs and outputs in physical terms.

6. A statistical method that measures the average amount of change in the dependent variable associated with a unit change in one or more independent variables is _____ _____.

7. A _____ remains the same over various ranges of the level of an activity, but increases by discrete amounts as the level of an activity increases from one range to the next.

8. (Appendix) A statistical measure of goodness of fit is the _____, which is the percentage of variation in the dependent variable (the cost) explained by the independent variable (the cost driver).

9. (Appendix) The vertical distance in a graph between actual cost and estimated cost for each observation of the cost driver is called a _____.

Indicate whether each statement is true (T) or false (F).

___ 1. The main purpose for estimating cost functions is to improve the accuracy of cost predictions.

___ 2. In the regression equation $y = a + bX$, the constant a is an estimate of fixed costs.

___ 3. To obtain reliable estimated cost functions using the account analysis method, the cost-classification decisions should be made by individuals thoroughly knowledgeable about the operations.

___ 4. Usually, data collection is the most difficult step in estimating a cost function based on quantitative analysis.

___ 5. If the high-low method is used, the constant in the cost function equation is always computed after computing the slope coefficient.

___ 6. The closer the predicted amounts of y in a cost function are to the actual cost amounts, the better the economic plausibility.

___ 7. The main purpose of the learning curve is to assist managers in developing techniques for increasing the speed and efficiency of production.

___ 8. A higher learning-curve percentage indicates a faster pace of learning.

___ 9. (Appendix) If the t-value of the slope coefficient is less than 2.00, the independent variable is not a cost driver.

___ 10. (Appendix) When simple regression is used, specification analysis tests the assumption regarding the reliability of data collection procedures.

___ 11. (Appendix) In simple regression, a scatter diagram is useful to check for constant variance of residuals.

___ 12. (Appendix) Multicollinearity exists whenever residuals, considered sequentially, have a systematic pattern.

Multiple Choice

Select the best answer to each question. Space is provided for computations after the quantitative questions.

___ 1. (CPA) Jackson, Inc., is preparing a flexible budget for the coming year and requires the cost of steam used in its plant to be divided into its fixed and variable elements. The following data on the cost of steam used and direct manufacturing labor-hours (DMLH) used are available for the last six months:

Month	Cost of Steam	DMLH
July	$ 15,850	3,000
August	13,400	2,050
September	16,370	2,900
October	19,800	3,650
November	17,600	2,670
December	18,500	2,650
Total	$101,520	16,920

Assuming Jackson uses the high-low method, the estimated variable cost of steam per DMLH is:

a. $4.00.
b. $5.42.
c. $5.82.
d. $6.00.

___ 2. Using the information in question 1 and assuming Jackson uses the high-low method, the estimated amount of the constant is:

a. $6,400.
b. $0.
c. $5,200.
d. none of the above.

___ 3. In a step cost function where the steps are narrow, the cost behavior approaches the pattern of a:

a. fixed cost.
b. variable cost.
c. mixed cost.
d. semivariable cost.

4. (CPA) Adams Corporation developed the following flexible budget for annual indirect manufacturing labor cost:

$$\text{Total cost} = \$4{,}800 + \$0.50 \text{ (machine-hours)}$$

The operating budget for the current month is based on 20,000 machine-hours. Indirect manufacturing labor cost included in the monthly flexible budget is:
   a. $14,800.
   b. $10,000.
   c. $14,400.
   d. $10,400.

5. (CPA) Quo Co. rented a building to Hava Fast Food. Each month Quo receives a fixed rental amount plus a variable rental amount based on Hava's revenues for that month. As revenues increase so does the variable rental amount, but at a reduced rate. Which of the following curves reflects the monthly rentals under the agreement?

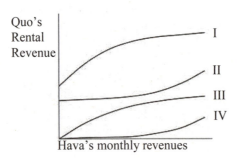

   Quo's Rental Revenue

   I
   II
   III
   IV

   Hava's monthly revenues

   a. I
   b. II
   c. III
   d. IV

6. (CMA) Ace Manufacturing Corporation found that the production of a certain product is subject to an 80% learning curve. The product is produced in lots of 100 units and 8 labor-hours are required for the first lot. Assuming Ace uses the cumulative average-time learning model, total time required to produce 400 units is:
   a. 32 hours.
   b. 20.48 hours.
   c. 25.6 hours.
   d. 19.52 hours.
   e. none of the above.

7. Using the information in question 6 and assuming Ace uses the cumulative average-time learning model, the incremental time required to produce the second lot of 100 units is:
   a. 0.0640 hours per unit.
   b. 12.80 hours.
   c. 0.0480 hours per unit.
   d. 0.1120 hours per unit.
   e. none of the above.

8. (Appendix) Serial correlation is measured by:
   a. the standard error of the slope coefficient.
   b. the coefficient of determination.
   c. the t-value of the slope coefficient.
   d. the Durbin-Watson statistic.

Review Exercises

1. Barnes Company estimated the cost function for its maintenance cost. The cost function has a variable element and a step fixed element that increases by $10,000 for each additional 20,000 units of output between 40,000 and 80,000 units of output. Total maintenance cost would be $130,000 at 40,000 units of output and $180,000 at 60,000 units of output.

   Compute the variable cost per unit of output in this cost function.

2. Addison Construction Company has begun paving roads for the Illinois highway system. Each paving project is similar. Recently, the company completed its first paving project in 20,000 hours. Direct labor is paid $20 per hour. The company needs to predict its direct labor cost for purposes of making a competitive bid on a contract for three additional paving projects. Addison's experience indicates that a 90% learning curve is appropriate for these projects.

   a. Using the cumulative average-time learning model, compute the predicted direct labor cost for the contract of three additional paving projects.
   b. Using the incremental unit-time learning model, compute the predicted direct labor cost for the contract of three additional paving projects, assuming a 90% learning curve.

3. (Appendix) Steve Kovzan was given the task of developing a cost function for predicting indirect manu-facturing costs (manufacturing overhead) for the Kansas City personal computer plant of Electronic Horizons. The plant is highly automated. The following information has been collected:

Month	Indirect Manufacturing Costs	Machine-Hours	Direct Manufacturing Labor-Hours (DMLH)
January	$2,530	2,730	324
February	1,900	1,810	210
March	4,710	3,403	347
April	1,270	2,200	331
May	4,380	3,411	272
June	4,020	2,586	202
July	3,730	3,364	342
August	3,070	2,411	247
September	4,980	3,964	347
October	3,310	2,897	328
November	1,270	2,207	293
December	3,510	2,864	307

Kovzan estimates two cost functions using regression analysis:

Regression Model A: Indirect manufacturing costs = f(Machine-hours)

Variable	Coefficient	Standard Error	t-Value
Constant	−1,707.70	912.94	−1.87
Independent variable:			
Machine-hours	1.75	0.32	5.47

$r^2 = .75$; Standard error of residuals = 657.44; Durbin-Watson statistic = 2.59

Regression Model B: Indirect manufacturing costs = f(Direct manufacturing labor-hours)

Variable	Coefficient	Standard Error	t-Value
Constant	1,914.10	2,264.60	0.85
Independent variable:			
DMLH	4.43	7.55	0.59

$r^2 = .03$; Standard error of residuals = 1,300.77; Durbin-Watson statistic = 2.45

Which cost function should Kovzan use for predicting indirect manufacturing costs? Present your answer in the following format, as used in EXHIBIT 10-18, text p.372. State your conclusion in the space below this table.

Criterion	Regression Model A (Machine-hours)	Regression Model B (Direct manufacturing labor-hours)
1.		
2.		
3.		
4. Specification analysis a.		
b.		
c.		
d.		

Conclusion:

Answers and Solutions to Chapter 10 Review Questions and Exercises

Completion Statements

1. linear
2. constant (intercept)
3. slope coefficient
4. cause-and-effect
5. industrial engineering (work measurement)
6. regression analysis
7. step cost function
8. coefficient of determination (r^2)
9. residual term

True-False

1. T
2. F   The constant *a* is an estimate of fixed cost *only if* the zero level of an activity (shutdown) is within the relevant range. Otherwise, the constant in the regression equation provides the best linear approximation of how total cost behaves within the relevant range.
3. T
4. T
5. T
6. F   The statement refers to *goodness of fit*, not *economic plausibility*. Only a true cause-and-effect relationship—one that is logical to the operating manager and the management accountant—establishes economic plausibility between the level of an activity and a cost. In such cases, the activity measure is called a cost driver.
7. F   Managers use learning curves to predict how labor-hours (or labor costs) change as more units are produced. Such predictions have a major influence on decisions about setting selling prices, budgets, and standards.
8. F   A higher learning-curve percentage indicates a *slower* pace of learning. To illustrate, assume a company uses the cumulative average-time learning model with an 80% learning curve. If the first unit requires 10 labor-hours, the second unit requires 8 (10×0.80) labor-hours. The total time for the first 2 units = $10 + 8 = 18$ labor-hours. Under a 90% learning curve, the total time for the first 2 units = $10 + 10(0.90) = 19$ labor-hours.
9. T
10. F   If simple regression is used, specification analysis tests four assumptions: linearity within the relevant range, constant variance of residuals, independence of residuals, and normality of residuals.
11. T
12. F   The statement describes *serial correlation* (also called *autocorrelation*), not *multicollinearity*. Multicollinearity exists in multiple regression when two or more independent variables are highly correlated with each other. Multicollinearity is not a problem if the coefficient of correlation (r) between any pair of independent variables does not exceed 0.70.

Multiple Choice

1. a   The highest and lowest observations of DMLH are 3,650 and 2,050, respectively:
    ($19,800 − $13,400) ÷ (3,650 − 2,050) = $6,400 ÷ 1,600 = $4 per hour
2. c   At the high point, $19,800 − 3,650($4) = $5,200
    At the low point, $13,400 − 2,050($4) = $5,200

3. b   Where the steps in a step cost function are narrow, the cost behavior approaches the pattern of a variable cost. In contrast, the steps are wide in a step fixed-cost function.

4. d   The key point is that the flexible-budget equation is for a *year*, whereas the flexible budget in the question is for a *month*. Therefore, $4,800 \div 12 = $400 per month; $400 + 20,000($0.50) = $10,400.

5. a   The monthly rentals are increasing at a decreasing rate as the cost driver increases.

6. b

Cumulative Number of Units	Cumulative Average Hours Per Unit		Cumulative Total Hours	
100	$8.0 \div 100$	$= 0.0800$	$100 \times 0.0800 =$	8.00
200	$0.0800 \times 80\%$	$= 0.0640$	$200 \times 0.0640 =$	12.80
400	$0.0640 \times 80\%$	$= 0.0512$	$400 \times 0.0512 =$	20.48

7. c   Using amounts from the computations in the preceding answer, $12.80 - 8.00 = 4.80$ hours; $4.80 \div$ the second lot of 100 units $= 0.0480$ hours per unit.

8. d   Serial correlation is measured by the Durbin-Watson statistic. This statistic falling in the 1.10 to 2.90 range for samples of 10 to 20 observations indicates that the residuals are independent.

Review Exercise 1

Increase in total cost = $180,000 - $130,000 = $50,000 (of which $10,000 is fixed cost)
Increase in variable cost = $50,000 - $10,000 = $40,000
Variable cost per unit = $40,000 \div (60,000 - 40,000) = $40,000 \div 20,000 = $2

Proof:

At 60,000 units, fixed cost = $180,000 - (60,000 \times $2)	= $60,000
At 40,000 units, fixed cost = $130,000 - (40,000 \times $2)	= 50,000
Increase (that is, the step) in fixed cost	$10,000

Review Exercise 2

a.

Cumulative Number of Projects	Cumulative Average Hours Per Project	Cumulative Total Hours
1	20,000	20,000
2	18,000 (20,000 × 0.9)	36,000
4	16,200 (18,000 × 0.9)	64,800

Predicted direct labor cost for the contract of 3 additional (4 − 1) projects:
    (64,800 − 20,000) × $20 = $896,000

b.

Cumulative Number of Projects	Individual Project Hours for Xth Project	Cumulative Total Hours
1	20,000	20,000
2	18,000 (20,000 × 0.9)	38,000
3	16,924*	54,924
4	16,200 (18,000 × 0.9)	71,124

*This amount is computed by using logarithms, as illustrated in the bottom section of EXHIBIT 10-11, text p.360.

Predicted direct labor cost for the contract of three additional projects:

$$(71,124 - 20,000) \times \$20 = \$1,022,480$$

Review Exercise 3

Plots of the scatter diagram for each regression model are as follows:

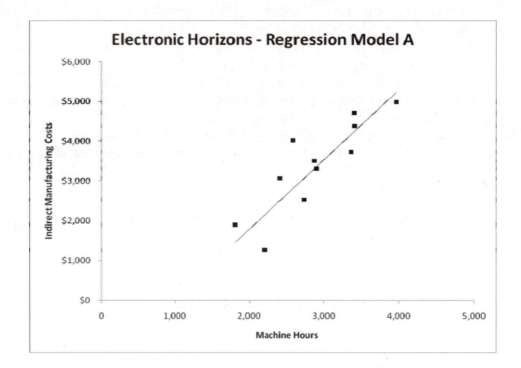

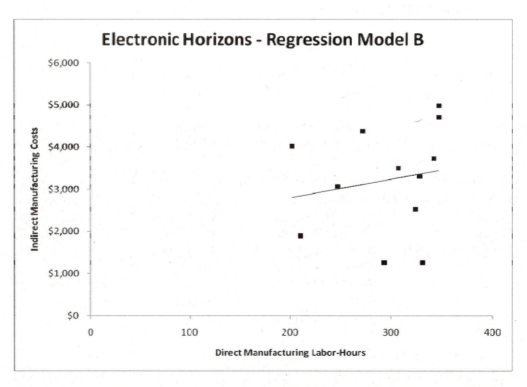

A comparison of the cost functions is on the next page.

Criterion	Regression Model A (Machine-hours)	Regression Model B (Direct manufacturing labor-hours)
1. Economic plausibility	Positive relationship between indirect manufacturing costs and machine-hours is economically plausible in a highly automated plant.	Positive relationship between indirect manufacturing costs and DMLH is economically plausible, but less so than machine-hours on a month-by-month basis.
2. Goodness of fit	$r^2 = 0.75$ Excellent goodness of fit.	$r^2 = 0.03$ Very poor goodness of fit.
3. Significance of independent variable	t-value for machine-hours of 5.47 is significant.	t-value for DMLH of 0.59 is not significant.
4. Specification analysis		
a. Linearity within the relevant range	Appears reasonable from a plot of the data, but inferences drawn from only 12 observations are not reliable.	Appears questionable from a plot of the data, but inferences drawn from only 12 observations are not reliable.
b. Constant variance of residuals	Appears reasonable from the plot of the data, but inferences drawn from only 12 observations are not reliable.	Appears questionable from the plot of the data, but inferences drawn from only 12 observations are not reliable.
c. Independence of residuals	Durbin-Watson statistic = 2.59, thus the assumption of independence is not rejected.	Durbin-Watson statistic = 2.45, thus the assumption of independence is not rejected.
d. Normality of residuals	Database is too small to make reliable inferences.	Database is too small to make reliable inferences.

Conclusion: The cost function using machine-hours as the cost-allocation base is clearly preferred. In this exercise, however, the cost function using machine-hours as the cost-allocation base is imperfect. That's because the database of 12 observations is too small to make reliable inferences about linearity within the relevant range, constant variance of residuals, and normality of residuals. It is important to realize that the cost analyst often must make a choice among "imperfect" cost functions. Generally, the data of any particular cost function will not perfectly meet all of the criteria for choosing among regressions.

CHAPTER 11

Decision Making and Relevant Information

Overview

This chapter focuses on several types of management decisions including: accepting or rejecting a one-time-only special order, insourcing or outsourcing (making or buying) a product or service, choosing a product mix, keeping or discontinuing a customer or business segment, and keeping or replacing equipment. Management accountants help managers make these decisions by clearly distinguishing relevant revenues and costs from irrelevant ones. The Appendix to the chapter explains linear programming, an optimization technique for making product-mix decisions where there are multiple constraints.

Highlights

1. Managers normally follow a **decision model** for choosing among alternative courses of action. A decision model is a formal method of making a choice that often involves both quantitative and qualitative analyses. Management accountants work with managers by analyzing and presenting relevant data to guide decisions.

2. In the decision process, managers proceed through a sequence of five steps: (a) identify the problem and uncertainties, (b) obtain information, (c) make predictions about the future, (d) make decisions by choosing among alternatives, and (e) implement the decision, evaluate performance and learn. The last step, in turn, can affect any of the first four steps in making future decisions.

3. The most important decision-making concepts in this chapter are **relevant costs** and **relevant revenues**. Relevant costs (revenues) must meet two criteria: *(a) they must occur in the future and (b) they must differ among the alternative courses of action being considered*. Only *future* costs (revenues) can be relevant to decisions because *nothing can be done to alter what happened in the past*. While past (historical) costs are always irrelevant to decisions, they can be a useful basis to predict future costs. *There are two common pitfalls in relevant-cost analysis:*

(a) assuming all variable costs are relevant and (b) assuming all fixed costs are irrelevant.

4. To determine the change in total operating income between two alternatives, compare all future revenues and costs or compute the difference in relevant future revenues and costs. While *both* approaches provide the same result, the latter one has the advantage of focusing the manager's attention only on relevant items. EXHIBIT 11-2, text p.393, illustrates the two approaches.

5. Due consideration must be given to both **quantitative factors** and **qualitative factors** in management decisions. Quantitative factors are outcomes that are measured in numerical (financial or nonfinancial) terms. Qualitative factors are outcomes that are difficult to measure accurately in numerical terms (for example, employee morale). Cost analysis generally emphasizes quantitative factors that can be expressed in financial terms. Just because qualitative factors and quantitative nonfinancial factors cannot be measured easily in financial terms, however, does not make them unimportant. Managers must at times give more weight to these factors.

6. If a company has idle production capacity, it may be advisable to accept a **one-time-only special order** at a price below the normal selling price. The phrase "one time only" highlights the point that a special order has no long-run implications. A one-time-only special order should be accepted if its additional revenues exceed its additional costs. EXHIBIT 11-5, text p.396, presents the analysis of a one-time-only special order: additional revenues are $55,000, additional costs are $37,500, so additional operating income is $17,500.

7. In a one-time-only special order decision (as in all decisions), *total costs should be used rather than unit costs*. Reliance on unit-cost numbers that include a fixed cost component can mislead managers about the effect that increasing output has on operating income. Unit costs also are misleading if any variable costs are irrelevant; for example, variable

marketing costs often remain the same whether a one-time-only special order is accepted or rejected.

8. Organizations must decide between **insourcing** and **outsourcing** various products or services. Insourcing is producing goods or providing services within the organization rather than outsourcing, which is purchasing the same goods or services from outside vendors. For example, a company might decide to insource a component part for one of its products and outsource payroll processing. Decisions on insourcing or outsourcing are also called **make-or-buy decisions**. The main quantitative factor in these decisions is cost. The most important qualitative factors are quality of the products or services and dependability of vendors. In some cases, despite the cost and other advantages of insourcing, companies outsource in order to focus on their own core competencies.

9. Two commonly used terms in decision making are **incremental cost** and **differential cost**. An incremental cost is the additional total cost incurred for an activity. A differential cost is the difference in total cost between two alternatives. To illustrate, consider the following make-or-buy decision:

	Make	Buy
Total relevant costs	$130,000	$119,000
Difference in favor of buying	$11,000	

The incremental cost of making is $130,000. The incremental cost of buying is $119,000. The differential cost (in favor of buying) is $11,000. Two parallel terms, **incremental revenue** and **differential revenue**, are defined in a corresponding manner. Incremental revenue is the additional total revenue from an activity. Differential revenue is the difference in total revenue between two alternatives.

10. Whenever a manufacturing company is deciding between making or buying a component part, technically the buy alternative should be stated as *how best to use the available production facilities*. The facilities that would have been used to manufacture the part in question could be idle, used for other production purposes, or rented out. Fixed costs are relevant in the analysis if they are avoidable when buying from an outside vendor. EXHIBIT 11-6, text p.399, presents the analysis of a make-or-buy decision.

11. Deciding to use a resource in a particular way causes the manager to give up the opportunity to use the resource in alternative ways. The lost opportunity is a cost that the manager must take into account in making a decision. **Opportunity cost** is the contribution to operating income that is forgone (given up) by not using a limited resource in its next-best alternative use. For example, suppose a company uses some of its production capacity to make a product that increases operating income by $20,000 rather than renting out the space for $16,000, the next-best alternative. The company's opportunity cost of making the product is $16,000. *Opportunity costs are not recorded in financial accounting systems because those systems are limited to transactions involving alternatives actually selected*; when alternatives are rejected, they do not qualify as transactions.

12. If a multiple-product plant is operating at capacity, managers must often make **product-mix decisions**—which products to sell and in what quantities. These decisions have a short-run focus because the level of capacity can be expanded in the long run. The criterion that maximizes operating income when operating at capacity is to choose the product with *the highest contribution margin per unit of the resource (factor)*—that's the resource that limits the production or sale of products. To illustrate, assume the demand for one of a company's products, product A, uses all the production capacity. A's contribution margin per unit is $100 and the limiting factor is machine-hours. Four machine-hours are required to make a unit of A, so its contribution margin per machine-hour is $25 ($100 ÷ 4). If the contribution margin per machine-hour for each of the company's other products is less than $25, short-run operating income is maximized by manufacturing only product A. If a company has a variety of products and faces more than one limiting factor, the most profitable product mix can be determined by using linear programming (discussed in paragraph 16).

13. In addition to making choices among individual products, managers must often make decisions about adding or discontinuing a product line, a cus-

tomer, or a business segment. The key question in each of these decisions is this: What are the relevant revenues and relevant costs? Relevant costs can be affected by one or more cost drivers. In making these decisions, managers should ignore allocated overhead costs and focus instead on how *total* overhead costs differ among the alternatives.

14. Another important type of decision is keeping or replacing equipment. These decisions focus on relevant costs over the useful life of the equipment; for simplicity in this chapter, time value of money and income taxes are ignored. **Book value** (original cost minus accumulated depreciation) of existing ("old") equipment is irrelevant to these decisions because it is a past cost (also called a **sunk cost**). A sunk cost is unavoidable and cannot be changed no matter what action is taken. The book value of the old equipment is written off in the income statement either at the time of replacement or as depreciation each year if the equipment is kept. The disposal value of old equipment and the acquisition cost of replacement ("new") equipment are relevant because they are future amounts that differ between the keep and replace alternatives.

15. On the surface, keeping or replacing equipment seems like a straightforward decision: the manager analyzes the relevant costs and chooses the lower-cost alternative. In reality, however, the manager tends to favor the alternative that makes his or her short-run performance look better. To illustrate, assume (a) relevant costs are lower for replacing an old machine, (b) a significant loss on disposal of the old machine would be reported in the income statement for the year of replacement, and (c) the manager's annual performance bonus is based on each year's operating income. (Of course, there is no loss on disposal if the old machine is kept for its entire useful life.) Under these conditions, the manager's temptation to *not replace* the old machine is overwhelming. Resolving this conflict between the *decision model* and the *performance evaluation model* is often a baffling problem in practice. The practical difficulty is that accounting systems rarely track each decision separately. Performance evaluation focuses on responsibility centers for a specific period, not on individual items of equipment over their entire useful lives.

16. (Appendix) **Linear programming (LP)** is an optimization technique used to maximize the objective function (for example, total contribution margin of a mix of products) when there are multiple constraints. In cases involving only two products and a small number of constraints, the trial-and-error or graphic approach can be used to formulate and solve LP problems. While these approaches provide insight about LP, computer software packages are used to solve most real-world LP problems.

Featured Exercises

1. Sedona Corporation has an annual plant capacity of 2,800,000 units of output. Its regular operations for the year are budgeted as follows:

Revenues, 2,000,000 units at $38 each	$76,000,000
Manufacturing costs	
Variable	$25 per unit
Fixed	$18,000,000
Marketing and administrative costs	
Variable (sales commissions)	$6 per unit
Fixed	$2,000,000

    Sedona has been contacted about supplying a one-time-only special order of 60,000 units at a selling price of $32, subject to half the usual sales commission per unit.

    Assuming this special order will have no effect on regular sales, should Sedona accept the order? Show your computations.

Solution

Yes, accept this special order because operating income would increase $240,000.

Incremental revenues, 60,000 × $32		$1,920,000
Incremental costs (all variable in this case):		
Manufacturing, 60,000 × $25	$1,500,000	
Sales commission, 60,000 × $3	180,000	1,680,000
Incremental operating income		$ 240,000

2. Cardinal Company needs 20,000 units of Part K28 to use in its production cycle. The following information is available:

Cost to Cardinal to make a unit of Part K28:
Direct materials	$ 4
Direct manufacturing labor	16
Variable overhead allocated	8
Fixed overhead allocated	10
Total cost	$38

Cost to buy the part from
Oriole Company $36

If Cardinal buys the part from Oriole instead of making it, the released facilities will be idle. Sixty percent of the fixed overhead allocated will continue if the part is bought from Oriole.

Should Cardinal make or buy Part K28? Show your computations.

Solution

Relevant Items	Make	Buy
Outside purchase of part, 20,000 × $36		$720,000
Direct materials, 20,000 × $4	$ 80,000	
Direct manufacturing labor, 20,000 × $16	320,000	
Variable overhead, 20,000 × $8	160,000	
Fixed overhead, 20,000 × $10(1 − 0.60)	80,000	
Total relevant costs	$640,000	$720,000

Difference in favor of making $80,000

Fixed overhead that cannot be avoided = 20,000 × ($10 × 0.60) = $120,000. This amount is irrelevant to the decision because it is the same under both alternatives.

Review Questions and Exercises

Completion Statements

Fill in the blank(s) to complete each statement.

1. A _____ is a formal method of making a choice, often involving both quantitative and qualitative analysis.
2. In a one-time-only special order decision, the relevant costs are the _____ costs that _____ between the "accept" and "reject" alternatives.
3. In management decisions, outcomes that are difficult to measure accurately in numerical terms are called _____ factors.
4. Producing goods or providing services within the organization rather than purchasing the same goods or services from outside vendors is called _____.
5. _____ is the contribution to operating income that is forgone (given up) by not using a limited resource in its next-best alternative use.
6. In equipment replacement decisions, an item that is always irrelevant is the _____ _____.
7. (Appendix) _____ is an optimization technique used to maximize the objective function when there are multiple constraints.

True-False

Indicate whether each statement is true (T) or false (F).

____ 1. In general, all variable costs are relevant to decisions, and all fixed costs are irrelevant to decisions.

____ 2. Past (historical) costs are always irrelevant to decisions but they can be helpful in predicting future costs.

____ 3. A car rental company is comparing two makes of cars to decide which one to purchase for its fleet. Miles per gallon of fuel consumption is a qualitative factor in this decision.

____ 4. Assuming sufficient idle production capacity is available, a one-time-only special order should not be accepted at a selling price below the total manufacturing cost per unit.

____ 5. Opportunity costs do not entail cash receipts or disbursements.

____ 6. Incremental cost and differential cost have the same meaning.

____ 7. In deciding among three alternatives for the sale of units held in finished goods inventory, the manager should regard past cost of the inventory as irrelevant, whether or not the inventory is obsolete.

____ 8. If there is an inconsistency between the decision model and the performance evaluation model in a decision to keep or replace some "old" equipment, the manager's choice tends to be influenced more by the decision model.

____ 9. (Appendix) The LP model is not applicable to situations where there are more than three constraints.

____ 10. (Appendix) The area of feasible solutions in an LP graphic solution shows the boundaries of those combinations of the two products that satisfy all constraints.

Multiple Choice

Select the best answer to each question. Space is provided for computations after the quantitative questions.

____ 1. (CPA) Light Company has 2,000 obsolete light fixtures that were manufactured at a cost of $30,000. If the fixtures are reworked for $10,000, they can be sold for $18,000. Alternatively, the fixtures can be sold for $3,000 to a jobber. Assuming the fixtures are reworked and sold, the opportunity cost is:
a. $3,000.
b. $5,000.
c. $10,000.
d. $30,000.

2. (CPA) The manufacturing capacity of Jordan Company's facilities is 30,000 units of a product per year. A summary of operating results for the year ended December 31, 2010, is as follows:

Revenues,	
18,000 units × $100	$1,800,000
Variable costs	990,000
Contribution margin	810,000
Fixed costs	495,000
Operating income	$ 315,000

A foreign distributor has offered to buy 15,000 units at $90 per unit during 2011. Assume all of Jordan's costs will have the same behavior patterns in 2011 as in 2010. If Jordan accepts this offer and rejects 3,000 units of business from regular customers so as not to exceed its capacity, total operating income for 2009 is:

a. $855,000.
b. $840,000.
c. $705,000.
d. $390,000.

4. Which one of the following items is relevant to an equipment replacement decision?
a. Original cost of the old equipment
b. Disposal value of the old equipment
c. Gain or loss on disposal of the old equipment
d. Book value of the old equipment

5. (CPA) Maxwell Company has an opportunity to acquire a new machine to replace one of its old machines. The new machine costs $90,000 and has an estimated useful life of five years, with a zero terminal disposal value. Variable operating costs are $100,000 per year. The old machine has a book value of $50,000 and a remaining life of five years. Its disposal value now is $5,000 but would be zero after five years. Variable operating costs are $125,000 per year. Considering the five years in total, but ignoring time value of money and income taxes, what is the difference in operating income by replacing the old machine?
a. $10,000 decrease
b. $15,000 decrease
c. $35,000 increase
d. $40,000 increase

3. (CPA) Gata Co. plans to discontinue a division with a $48,000 contribution margin, and allocated fixed costs of $96,000, of which $42,000 cannot be eliminated. What is the effect on Gata's operating income of discontinuing this division?
a. Increase of $48,000
b. Decrease of $48,000
c. Increase of $6,000
d. Decrease of $6,000

6. (Appendix, CMA adapted) Pleasant Valley Company makes two products, ceramic vases (V) and ceramic bowls (B). Each vase requires two pounds of direct materials and three hours of direct manufacturing labor. Each bowl requires two pounds of direct materials and one hour of direct manufacturing labor. During the next production week, 100 pounds of direct materials and 60 hours of direct manufacturing labor are available to make vases and bowls. Each pound of direct material costs $4 and each hour of direct manufacturing labor costs $10. All manufacturing overhead is fixed and is estimated to be $200 per week for this production process. Pleasant Valley sells vases for $50 each and bowls for $35 each. The objective function for total contribution margin is:

a. $50V + $35B.
b. $12V + $17B.
c. $38V + $18B.
d. $12V + $17B − $200.

7. Using the information in question 6, one of the constraints is:

a. 2V + 2B ≤ 60.
b. 2V + 2B ≤ $400.
c. 3V + B ≤ 60.
d. V + 3B ≤ 100.
e. $8V + $8B ≤ 600.

Review Exercises

1. Edgewood Corporation has 1,440 machine-hours of plant capacity available during a particular period for manufacturing two products with the following characteristics:

	T	L
Selling price	$42	$75
Variable cost per unit	$20	$25
Units that can be manufactured per machine-hour	8	3
Demand in units	13,500	6,000

Compute the number of available machine-hours that should be used to manufacture each product.

2. (CMA) Richardson Motors uses ten units of Part T305 each month in the production of large diesel engines. The cost to manufacture one unit of T305 is as follows:

Direct materials	$ 2,000
Materials handling	
(20% of direct material costs)	400
Direct manufacturing labor	16,000
Manufacturing overhead	
(150% of direct manufacturing labor cost)	24,000
Total manufacturing cost	$42,400

Materials handling, a separate cost category that is not included in manufacturing overhead, represents those direct variable costs of the Receiving Department that are allocated to direct materials and purchased components on the basis of their cost. Richardson's annual manufacturing overhead budget is one-third variable and two-thirds fixed. Simpson Castings, one of Richardson's reliable vendors, offers to supply T305 at a unit price of $30,000. Assume Richardson Motors could rent out all its idle production capacity for $50,000 per month.

Compute how much Richardson's monthly cost of T305 increases/decreases if the company purchases the ten units from Simpson Castings.

3. (CPA) Bradshaw Manufacturing Company is reviewing the profitability of the company's four products and the potential of several proposals for improving the profitability of the product mix. An income statement and other data follow:

	Total	Product W	Product X	Product Y	Product Z
Revenues	$62,600	$10,000	$18,000	$12,600	$22,000
Cost of goods sold	44,274	4,750	7,056	13,968	18,500
Gross margin	18,326	5,250	10,944	(1,368)	3,500
Operating costs	12,012	1,990	2,976	2,826	4,220
Operating income	$ 6,314	$ 3,260	$ 7,968	$ (4,194)	$ (720)
Units sold		1,000	1,200	1,800	2,000
Selling price		$ 10.00	$ 15.00	$ 7.00	$ 11.00
Variable cost of goods sold per unit		$ 2.50	$ 3.00	$ 6.50	$ 6.00
Variable operating cost per unit		$ 1.17	$ 1.25	$ 1.00	$ 1.20

Each of the following proposals is to be considered independently. Consider only the product changes stated in each proposal; the production and sales levels of the other products remain the same.

a. Compute the effect on operating income if Y is dropped.
b. Compute the total effect on operating income if Y is dropped and a resulting loss of customers causes a decrease of 200 units in the production and sales of X.
c. Assume the area of the plant in which W is manufactured can easily be adapted to the production of Z, but changes in quantities produced necessitate changes in selling prices. Compute the total effect on operating income if production of W is reduced to 500 units (to be sold at $12 each) and production of Z is increased to 2,500 units (to be sold at $10.50 each).

Answers and Solutions to Chapter 11 Review Questions and Exercises

Completion Statements

1. decision model
2. expected future, differ
3. qualitative
4. insourcing
5. Opportunity cost
6. book value of the existing ("old") equipment
7. Linear programming (LP)

True-False

1. F Only *expected future costs (whether variable or fixed)* that *differ* between the alternatives under consideration are relevant to a decision. In EXHIBIT 11-2, text p.393, direct material costs (a variable cost) are irrelevant to the decision, and reorganization costs (a fixed cost) are relevant to the decision.

2. T

3. F Miles per gallon of fuel consumption is a quantitative factor because it is an outcome that is measured in numerical terms. An example of a qualitative factor in the decision is the expected comfort of each make of car.

4. F In the example, text pp. 394-396 , total manufacturing cost is $12 per unit. At a selling price of $11 per unit, accepting the one-time-only special order *adds* $17,500 of operating income.

5. T

6. F In the solution to the Featured Exercise, p.141, the incremental cost of the make alternative is $640,000, and the incremental cost of the buy alternative is $720,000. The differential cost (in favor of making) is $80,000.

7. T

8. F Managers tend to favor the alternative that makes their performance look better. Therefore, they focus on the measure(s) used in the performance evaluation model.

9. F The LP model is applicable to situations where there are any number of constraints. If there are only two products and the number of constraints is small, the optimal solution can be found by trial and error or graphically. If the LP problem is more complex, computer software packages are used to compute the optimal solution.

10. T

Multiple Choice

1. a The following analysis shows there is a $5,000 advantage of reworking the fixtures:

	Rework and Sell	Sell As Is
Revenue	$18,000	$3,000
Deduct costs	10,000	-0-
Operating income	$ 8,000	$3,000

Difference in favor of reworking $5,000

The *difference* in operating income between the alternatives, however, *is not* the opportunity cost. Opportunity cost is the contribution to income that is forgone (given up) by not using a limited resource in its next-best alternative use. If the fixtures (a limited resource) are reworked and sold, the opportunity cost is the rejected alternative of selling them "as is" for $3,000.

2. c

Revenues, (15,000 × $100) + (15,000 × $90)	$2,850,000
Variable costs, ($990,000 ÷ 18,000) × 30,000	1,650,000
Contribution margin	1,200,000
Fixed costs	495,000
Operating income	$ 705,000

Note, although opportunity cost is *not explicitly shown* in this income statement, it is present in this situation because the short-run capacity of 30,000 units is insufficient to accommodate both the regular business of 18,000 units and the special order of 15,000 units (that is, 3,000 units of regular business must be forgone in order to accept the special order). Knowing that variable cost per unit is $55 ($990,000 ÷ 18,000), the opportunity cost can be *shown explicitly* in an incremental analysis as follows:

Increase in contribution margin from the special order itself, 15,000 × ($90 − $55)	$525,000
Deduct forgone contribution margin from the regular business, 3,000 × ($100 − $55)	135,000
Increase in operating income from accepting the special order	390,000
Add operating income before considering the special order	315,000
Operating income	$705,000

3. c

	Before Discontinuing	After Discontinuing
Contribution to fixed costs	$ 48,000	$ 0
Deduct allocated fixed costs	96,000	42,000
Operating income of division	$(48,000)	$(42,000)
Difference in favor of discontinuing the division		$6,000

4. b   Disposal value of the old equipment is relevant because it is an expected future cash flow that differs between the keep and replace alternatives. Gain or loss on disposal of the old equipment is the difference between the irrelevant book value of the old equipment and the relevant disposal value.

5. d

Relevant Items	Keep	Replace
Variable operating costs		
$125,000 × 5; $100,000 × 5	$625,000	$500,000
Cost of new machine		90,000
Disposal value of old machine		(5,000)
Total relevant costs	$625,000	$585,000
Difference in favor of replacing old machine		$40,000

	Vase	Bowl
Selling price	$50	$35
Variable cost per unit		
Direct materials		
2 lbs. × $4; 2 lbs. × $4	8	8
Direct manufacturing labor		
3 hrs. × $10; 1 hr. × $10	30	10
Total variable cost per unit	38	18
Contribution margin per unit	$12	$17

6. c $38V + $18B.

7. c   Constraint for direct materials: $2V + 2B \leq 100$
        Constraint for direct manufacturing labor: $3V + B \leq 60$

Review Exercise 1

	T	L
Selling price	$ 42	$ 75
Variable cost per unit	20	25
Contribution margin per unit	22	50
Multiply by number of units that		
can be manufactured per hour	× 8	× 3
Contribution margin per hour of		
plant capacity	$176	$150

All 1,440 machine-hours should be used to manufacture product T, because T has the higher contribution margin per unit of the limited resource (machine-hours) *and* producing 11,520 units of T (1.440 × 8) does not exceed the demand for T of 13,500 units.

Review Exercise 2

Relevant Costs	Make	Buy
Direct materials, $2,000 × 10	$ 20,000	
Materials handling, $20,000 × 20%	4,000	
Direct manufacturing labor, $16,000 × 10	160,000	
Variable manufacturing overhead		
($24,000 × 1/3) × 10	80,000	
Outside purchase of T305		
$30,000 × 10		$300,000
Rental income		(50,000)
Total relevant costs per month	$264,000	$250,000
Monthly decrease in cost		
from buying T305	$14,000	

Review Exercise 3

a. Effect on operating income of dropping Y:

Loss of revenues, 1,800 units × $7	$(12,600)
Savings of variable costs,	
1,800 units × ($6.50 + $1.00)	13,500
Increase in operating income	$ 900

This analysis includes *relevant items only*. The same answer can also be obtained by including *both* relevant and irrelevant items, albeit much more time consuming. Under that presentation (not shown), the company's income statement without Y would show operating income of $7,214, which is $900 more than the present level of $6,314. Note that when the product mix changes, total fixed costs (which are the same with or without Y) would merely be allocated (reallocated) to the new mix of products W, X and Z.

b. Effect on operating income of changes in Y and X:

Increase in operating income from	
dropping Y (from answer a)	$ 900
Loss of part of X's contribution margin	
200 units × ($15.00 − $3.00 − $1.25)	(2,150)
Increase (decrease) in operating income	$(1,250)

c. Effect on operating income of changes in W and Z:

Loss of present contribution margin	
W: 1,000 units × ($10.00 − $2.50 − $1.17)	$(6,330)
Z: 2,000 units × ($11.00 − $6.00 − $1.20)	(7,600)
Addition of proposed contribution margin	
W: 500 units × ($12.00 − $2.50 − $1.17)	4,165
Z: 2,500 units × ($10.50 − $6.00 − $1.20)	8,250
Increase (decrease) in operating income	$(1,515)

CHAPTER 12

Pricing Decisions and Cost Management

Overview

This chapter focuses on the important role that cost data play in pricing decisions. These strategic decisions challenge managers because there is no single way of computing a product cost that is suitable for both short-run and long-run time horizons. The relevant-revenue and relevant-cost analysis introduced in Chapter 11 helps managers make pricing decisions.

Highlights

1. The three major influences on pricing decisions are *customers*, *competitors*, and *costs* ("the three C's"). Customers influence price through their effect on demand. Competitors offer alternative or substitute products that may affect demand and price. Costs influence price through their effect on supply. Knowing how costs behave when the level of one or more cost drivers changes provides insight into the predicted operating income from various price-volume combinations for a product.

2. Surveys of how managers make pricing decisions reveal that companies consider customers, competitors, and costs differently. For companies selling similar commodity-type products in highly competitive markets, the market sets the price. In these cases, cost data help managers to decide on the output level that maximizes operating income. In less competitive markets, products are differentiated and managers have some discretion in setting prices. In these cases, the pricing decision depends on the value that customers place on the product, the prices competitors charge for their products, and the costs of producing and delivering the product.

3. In determining the costs that are relevant for a pricing decision, managers must consider costs in all six business functions of the value chain, from R&D to customer service, as well as whether the time horizon is short run (less than a year) or long run. A classic short run pricing decision is a one-time-only special order with no long run implications. There are two key differences in pricing for the long run compared to the short run: (a) costs that are irrelevant for short run pricing decisions, such as fixed costs that cannot be changed, are generally relevant in the long run and (b) prices are often set to earn an acceptable return on investment in the long run while short run pricing is more opportunistic—in the short run, prices are decreased if demand is weak and increased if demand is strong.

4. Long-run pricing decisions can be market-based or cost-based.

- The *market-based approach to long-run pricing* starts by asking this: Given what our customers want and how our competitors will react to what we do, what price should we charge? This approach first considers customers and competitors and then looks at costs.
- The *cost-based approach to long-run pricing* starts by asking this: Given what it costs us to make this product, what price should we charge that will recoup our costs and achieve a required return on investment? This approach first considers costs and then looks at customers and competitors.

Both approaches consider the three C's; only their *starting points* differ.

5. One form of the market-based approach is target pricing. A **target price** is the estimated price for a product or service that potential customers are willing to pay. This estimate is based on an understanding of customers' perceived value for a product or service and how competitors will price competing products or services. The target price forms the basis for calculating **target cost per unit**. Target cost per unit is the target price minus **target operating income per unit**. Target operating income per unit is the operating income that a company aims to earn per unit of a product

or service sold. Target cost per unit is the estimated long-run cost per unit of a product or service that enables the company to achieve its target operating income per unit when selling at the target price. All future costs, both variable and fixed, are relevant to target cost calculations because the time horizon is long run. Because target cost per unit is often lower than the existing full cost per unit of the product, target cost per unit really is a target the company must aim for.

6. Companies use five steps in developing target prices and target costs for a product:

Step 1: Develop a product that satisfies the needs of potential customers.
Step 2: Choose a target price.
Step 3: Derive a target cost per unit by subtracting target operating income per unit from the target price.
Step 4: Perform cost analysis.
Step 5: Perform **value engineering** to achieve target cost.

Value engineering is a systematic evaluation of all aspects of the value chain, whose key objective is to reduce costs and achieve a quality level that satisfies customers.

7. To implement value engineering, managers distinguish value-added activities and costs from nonvalue-added activities and costs in producing a product or service. A **value-added cost** is a cost that, if eliminated, would reduce the actual or perceived value or utility (usefulness) customers experience from using the product or service. Examples are costs of specific product features and attributes desired by customers, such as preloaded software on a personal computer, product reliability, and prompt customer service. A **nonvalue-added cost** is a cost that, if eliminated, would not reduce the actual or perceived value or utility (usefulness) customers gain from using the product or service. An example is the cost of reworking defective products. Value engineering seeks to reduce nonvalue-added costs by reducing the usage of cost drivers on nonvalue-added activities. Value engineering also aims to achieve greater efficiency in

value-added activities in order to reduce value-added costs.

8. To do value engineering, managers must distinguish **cost incurrence** from **locked-in costs** (also called **designed-in costs**). Cost incurrence describes when a resource is consumed (or benefit forgone) to meet a specific objective. The accrual basis of accounting records costs when they are incurred. Locked-in costs are costs that have not yet been incurred but, based on decisions that have already been made, will be incurred in the future. For example, a product's direct material costs are incurred when each unit is manufactured and sold, but these costs are locked-in much earlier—at the time the product is designed. It is important to distinguish when costs are locked-in from when they are incurred because locked-in costs are difficult to reduce. EXHIBIT 12-3, text p.443, shows a typical pattern for a product: wide divergence between the time when costs are locked-in and the time when those costs are incurred.

9. Costs are not always locked-in at the design stage. In some industries, such as legal and consulting, costs are locked-in and incurred as the services are performed. If costs are not locked-in early, cost reduction can be achieved up to the time when costs are incurred. In these industries, the key to lowering costs is improved operating efficiency and productivity rather than better design.

10. The cost-based approach to long-run pricing is often called *cost-plus pricing*. Under this approach, a company chooses a cost base it regards as reliable and a markup component to recover its costs and earn a target rate of return on investment. The basic formula is:

$$\frac{\text{Cost}}{\text{base}} + \frac{\text{Markup}}{\text{component}} = \frac{\text{Prospective}}{\text{selling price}}$$

Although several cost bases are usually available for pricing decisions, surveys indicate that most managers use *full cost of the product*—the sum of all the variable and fixed costs of all the business functions in the value chain. Managers cite three advantages for using this cost base: full recovery of all costs of the product, price stability, and simplicity. The markup component is often based on **target rate of return on investment**. To illustrate, assume this rate is 18%, invested capital (total assets) required for the product is $96,000,000, and sales are expected to be 200,000 units per year. The target annual operating income is $17,280,000 (18% × $96,000,000), and the markup component per unit is $86.40 ($17,280,000 ÷ 200,000). Assuming the cost base is $720 per unit, the prospective selling price is $806.40 ($720 + $86.40). In these computations it is important to distinguish the target rate of return on investment, 18%, from the markup component expressed as a percentage of the cost base, $86.40 ÷ $720 = 12%.

11. The selling prices computed under cost-plus pricing are *prospective* prices. Customer and competitor reactions to the original price may cause it to be reduced. Also, the product may be redesigned to cut costs. The eventual design and cost-plus price chosen must balance the conflicting tensions among costs, markup, and customer reactions.

12. The target pricing approach (discussed in paragraphs 5 and 6) reduces the need to go back and forth among prospective cost-plus prices, customer reactions, and design modifications. Instead, target pricing first determines product characteristics and target price on the basis of customer preferences and expected competitor responses. Market considerations and the target price then serve to focus and motivate managers to reduce costs and achieve target cost per unit and target operating income per unit.

13. Companies sometimes need to consider how to cost and price a product over its multiyear life cycle. The **product life cycle** spans the time from initial R&D on a product to when customer service and support is no longer offered for that product—typically a period of several years or more. Using **life-cycle budgeting**, managers estimate the revenues and business function costs across the entire value chain from a product's initial R&D to its final customer service and support. **Life-cycle costing** tracks and accumulates business function costs across the entire value chain from a product's initial R&D to its final customer service and support. A key benefit of life-cycle costing is that the full set of costs associated with each product becomes visible rather than being buried in the traditional income statement.

14. Life-cycle costs for individual products reinforce the importance of locked-in costs, target costing, and value engineering in pricing decisions and cost management. The earlier in a product's life-cycle that costs are locked-in (before there is much information on the likelihood of the product being successful in the marketplace), the riskier the product in terms of profitability.

15. A different notion of life-cycle costs is **customer life-cycle costs**. Here the focus is on the total costs incurred *by a customer* to acquire, use, maintain and dispose of a product or service. Customer life-cycle costs influence pricing decisions. For example, manufacturers of washing machines and air conditioners charge higher prices for models that save electricity and have low maintenance costs.

16. Many pricing decisions are driven by factors other than cost. Two examples are **price discrimination** and **peak-load pricing**.

- Price discrimination is the practice of charging different customers different prices for the same product or service. Airlines use price discrimination because, in contrast to pleasure travelers, business travelers are relatively insensitive to price.
- Peak-load pricing is the practice of charging a higher price for the same product or service when demand for it approaches the physical limit of the capacity to produce that product or service. A main user of peak-load pricing is the electric utility industry; higher rates are charged during the summer months when air conditioning creates peak-load demand for electricity.

17. Another factor affecting pricing decisions is the U.S. antitrust laws, including the Sherman Act, the Clayton Act, the Federal Trade Commission Act, and the Robinson-Patman Act. These laws prohibit **predatory pricing**. A company engages in predatory pricing when it deliberately

prices below its costs in an effort to drive competitors out of the market and restrict supply, and then raises prices rather than enlarge demand.

18. U.S. antitrust laws also prohibit **dumping** and **collusive pricing**. Dumping is closely related to predatory pricing. Dumping occurs when a non-U.S. company sells a product in the U.S. at a price below the market value in the country where it is produced, and this lower price materially injures or threatens to materially injure an industry in the U.S. Collusive pricing occurs when companies in an industry conspire in their pricing and production decisions to achieve a price above the competitive price and so restrain trade.

19. Companies that have concerns about their conformance to antitrust laws: (a) should collect data and keep detailed records of variable costs for all business functions in the value chain and (b) should review all proposed prices below variable costs in advance, with a presumption that claims of predatory intent will occur.

Featured Exercise

E. Berg & Sons build custom-made pleasure boats that range in price from $150,000 to $1,500,000. For the past 30 years, Ed Berg Sr. has determined the selling price of each boat by estimating the cost of direct materials, direct manufacturing labor, an allocated portion of total overhead (which includes nonmanufacturing cost), and adding a 20% markup to the total of this cost. For example, a recent price quotation was determined as follows:

Direct materials	$ 60,000
Direct manufacturing labor	96,000
Total overhead	24,000
Total estimated cost	180,000
Markup, 20% × $180,000	36,000
Selling price	$216,000

The total overhead figure is determined by budgeting total overhead costs for the year and allocating them at 25% of direct manufacturing labor costs.

If a customer rejects the price and business is slack, Ed Berg Sr. often reduces his markup to as little as 5% of total estimated cost. The average markup for the year is expected to be 15%.

Ed Berg Jr. just completed a course on pricing in which contribution margin was emphasized. He feels this approach will help in determining the selling prices of his company's boats.

Total overhead for the year has been budgeted at $3,600,000 of which $2,160,000 is fixed and the remainder varies in proportion to direct manufacturing labor costs.

a. Assume the customer in the example rejects the $216,000 quotation and also rejects a $189,000 quotation (5% markup) during a slack period. The customer counters with a $180,000 offer. Compute the minimum selling price Ed Berg Jr. could quote without decreasing or increasing operating income.
b. What is the main disadvantage of emphasizing contribution margin in pricing decisions?

Solution (on next page)

Solution

a. Two steps are used to obtain the selling price that would have no effect on operating income. First, compute the budgeted variable overhead rate (denoted by X):

$$X = \frac{\text{Budgeted variable overhead costs}}{\text{Budgeted direct manufacturing labor costs}}$$

$$X = \frac{\$3,600,000 - \$2,160,000}{\$3,600,000 \div 0.25} = \frac{\$1,440,000}{\$14,400,000} = 10\%$$

Second, compute the relevant cost of the boat. Only the variable cost is relevant in this case.

Direct materials	$ 60,000
Direct manufacturing labor	96,000
Variable overhead,	
$96,000 \times 10\%$	9,600
Total relevant cost	$165,600

Selling the boat for $165,600 would have no effect on operating income.

b. Focusing exclusively on contribution margin in pricing decisions ignores fixed costs. Although fixed costs are often irrelevant in the short-run, they must be recovered in the long-run, along with a target return on investment, for the company to stay in business.

Review Questions and Exercises

Completion Statements

Fill in the blank(s) to complete each statement.

1. The estimated long-run cost per unit of a product or service that enables the company to achieve the target operating income per unit when selling at the target price is called the _____.

2. _____ is a systematic evaluation of all aspects of the business functions in the value chain, whose key objective is to reduce costs and achieve a quality level that satisfies customers.

3. Costs that have not yet been incurred but, based on that decisions that have already been made, will be incurred in the future are called _____ costs.

4. _____ tracks and accumulates the business function costs across the entire value chain from a product's initial R&D to its final customer servicing and support.

5. The practice of charging different customers different prices for the same product or service is called _____.

6. The practice of charging a higher price for the same product or service when demand for it approaches the physical limit of the capacity to produce that product or service is called _____.

7. A company engages in _____ _____ when it deliberately prices below its costs in an effort to drive competitors out of the market and restrict supply, and then raises prices rather than enlarge demand.

True-False

Indicate whether each statement is true (T) or false (F).

____ 1. The three major influences on pricing decisions are customers, competitors, and costs.

____ 2. A company should accept a one-time-only special order when the order's total contribution margin is positive.

____ 3. Value engineering is usually constrained

by locked-in costs.

_____ 4. The target rate of return on investment for a product is the same as the product's markup as a percentage of its full unit cost.

_____ 5. The cost of preparing an owner's manual and including it in each product package is a value-added cost.

_____ 6. One reason managers use the full cost of products as the cost base in their pricing decisions is to promote price stability.

_____ 7. Life-cycle costing highlights manufacturing costs more than the costs of other business functions in the value chain.

_____ 8. When there is price discrimination, pricing is not linked closely to the cost of the product.

_____ 9. Under the U.S. Robinson-Patman Act, a manufacturing company cannot price discriminate between two customers if its intent is to lessen or prevent competition.

_____ 10. Setting prices above average variable costs is regarded as pricing that is non-predatory.

_____ 11. Collusive pricing occurs when a non-U.S. company sells a product in the U.S. at a price below the market value in the country where it is produced, and this lower price materially injures or threatens to materially injure an industry in the U.S.

Multiple Choice

Select the best answer to each question. Space is provided for computations after the quantitative questions.

_____ 1. In regard to supply and demand, demand is affected by:
a. customers, competitors, and costs.
b. customers and competitors.
c. customers and costs.
d. competitors and costs.

_____ 2. (CPA) Relay Corporation manufactures batons. Relay can manufacture 300,000 batons a year at variable costs of $750,000 and fixed costs of $450,000. Fixed costs will remain the same between 200,000 and 300,000 batons. Based on Relay's predictions, 240,000 batons will be sold at the regular price of $5.00 each. In addition, a one-time-only special order was received for 60,000 batons to be sold at a 40% discount off the regular price. By what amount does operating income increase or decrease as a result of accepting the special order?
a. $30,000 increase
b. $60,000 decrease
c. $36,000 increase
d. $180,000 increase

_____ 3. (CPA) Nile Co.'s cost allocation and product-costing procedures follow activity-based costing principles. Activities related to each product have been identified and classified as being either value-adding or nonvalue-adding. Which of the following activities, used in Nile's production process, is nonvalue-adding?
a. Design engineering activity
b. Heat treatment activity
c. Drill press activity
d. Materials storage activity

_____ 4. For a company manufacturing personal computers, a graph of locked-in costs and incurred costs shows:
a. locked-in costs rising much faster initially than incurred costs, but dropping to zero after the product is manufactured.
b. locked-in costs rising much faster initially than incurred costs, but joining the incurred cost line at the completion of the value-chain functions.
c. the two cost lines running parallel until the end of the production process, where they join.
d. no differences unless the product is

manufactured inefficiently.

____ 5. (CPA) Purvis Company manufactures a product that has a variable cost of $50 per unit. Fixed costs total $1,000,000 and are allocated on the basis of the number of units produced. Selling price is computed by adding a 10% markup to full cost of the product. How much should the selling price per unit be for 100,000 units?
   a. $55
   b. $60
   c. $61
   d. $66

____ 6. (CPA) Diva Co. wants to establish a selling price that will yield a gross margin of 40% on the revenues of a product whose cost is $12.00 per unit. The selling price should be:
   a. $16.80.
   b. $19.20.
   c. $20.00.
   d. $30.00.

____ 7. (CPA) Briar Co. signed a government construction contract providing for a formula price of actual cost plus 10% of cost. In addition, Briar was to receive one-half of any savings resulting from the formula price being less than the target price of $2,200,000. Briar's actual costs incurred were $1,920,000. How much should Briar receive from the contract?
   a. $2,060,000
   b. $2,112,000
   c. $2,156,000
   d. $2,200,000

____ 8. Peak-load pricing is:
   a. an illegal form of price discrimination.
   b. a legal form of price discrimination.
   c. illegal, but is not a form of price discrimination.
   d. legal, but is not a form of price discrimination.

Review Exercises

1. Silverthorne Inc. is deciding on the price for a new product. The company uses cost-plus pricing based on target return on investment. The following information is available for the product:

Invested capital	$25 million
Target rate of return on investment	20%
Full cost of the product (per unit) at the output level of 125,000 units	$200
Full cost of the product (per unit) at the output level of 80,000 units	$250

   a. Compute the prospective selling price, assuming the predicted output level is 125,000 units.
   b. Compute markup as a percentage of full cost of the product, assuming the predicted output level is 80,000 units.

2. Appletree Inc. is analyzing the profitability of two of its accounting software packages. Summary data on the packages over their two-year product life cycle are as follows:

Package	Selling Price	Sales in Units	
Quick Tax	$250	Year 1	4,000
		Year 2	16,000
Fast Audit	$200	Year 1	10,000
		Year 2	6,000

The life-cycle revenue and cost information is (in thousands):

	Quick Tax		Fast Audit	
	Year 1	Year 2	Year 1	Year 2
Revenues	$1,000	$4,000	$2,000	$1,200
Costs:				
R&D	1,400	0	480	0
Product design	370	30	160	32
Manufacturing	150	450	286	130
Marketing	280	720	480	416
Distribution	30	120	120	72
Customer service	100	650	440	776

Appletree is particularly concerned with increases in R&D and product design costs for many of its software packages in recent years. Consequently, major efforts have been made to reduce these costs on the Fast Audit package.

a. Prepare a product life-cycle income statement for each software package.
b. Compare the two packages in terms of their profitability and cost structure. State your conclusions.

Answers and Solutions to Chapter 12 Review Questions and Exercises

Completion Statements

1. target cost per unit
2. Value engineering
3. locked-in (designed-in)
4. Life-cycle costing
5. price discrimination
6. peak-load pricing
7. predatory pricing

True-False

1. T
2. F   A one-time-only special order should be accepted when it increases a company's operating income. A special order increases operating income when its total contribution margin is positive *and* exceeds the relevant fixed costs (if any) related to the order. Of course, when the positive total contribution margin is less than the relevant fixed costs, the special order decreases operating income and should be rejected.
3. F   Value engineering aims to control costs *before* they are locked-in (designed-in), with the objective of reducing costs and achieving a quality level that satisfies customers.
4. F   *Target rate of return on investment* and *markup* are not the same. In the example, text pp.445-446, target return on investment for the product is 18% while the product's markup is 12% of its full cost per unit.
5. T
6. T
7. F   Life-cycle costing tracks and accumulates business function costs across the entire value chain from a product's initial R&D to its final customer service and support. The costs of each business function in the value chain are highlighted.
8. T
9. T
10. T
11. F   The statement refers to *dumping*, not *collusive pricing*. Collusive pricing occurs when companies in an industry conspire in their pricing and production decisions to achieve a price above the competitive price and so restrain trade.

Multiple Choice

1. b   Customers, competitors, and costs are all important factors in setting prices. The value customers place on the product and the prices competitors charge for competing products affect demand, while the costs of producing and delivering the product influence supply.
2. a   For the special order:

Selling price, $5.00(1 − 0.40)	$3.00 per baton
Incremental cost, $750,000 ÷ 300,000	2.50 per baton
Increase in operating income	$0.50 per baton × 60,000 batons = $30,000

3. d   A nonvalue-added activity is an activity that, if eliminated, does not reduce the value customers gain from using a particular product or service. The materials storage activity fits this definition. The other answers are examples of value-added activities (that is, activities that, if eliminated, reduce the value customers gain from using particular products or services).

4. b   In this graph, locked-in costs rise much faster than incurred costs during R&D and product design, incurred costs accelerate during production while locked-in costs are nearly flat; both costs are equal at the completion of the value-chain functions. EXHIBIT 12-3, text p.438, presents this graph for a company manufacturing personal computers.

5. d   Full cost of the product = $50 + ($1,000,000 ÷ 100,000) = $50 + $10 = $60
Selling price = $60 + $60(0.10) = $60 + $6 = $66

6. c   Let X = Selling price
$$X - \$12.00 = 0.40X$$
$$0.60X = \$12.00$$
$$X = \$12.00 \div 0.60 = \$20.00$$
Proof: $20.00 − $12.00 = $8.00; $8.00 ÷ $20.00 = 40%

7. c   Two steps are used to obtain the answer. First, determine if the formula price is less than the target price, in which case savings result:

Target price	$2,200,000
Deduct formula price	
$1,920,000 + $1,920,000(0.10)	2,112,000
Savings	$ 88,000

Second, compute the amount to be received from the contract:

Formula price (from above)	$2,112,000
Add one-half of savings	
$88,000 × 50%	44,000
Amount to be received	$2,156,000

8. b   Peak-load pricing is the practice of charging a higher price for the same product or service when demand for it approaches the physical limit of the capacity to produce that product or service. Peak-load pricing is a legal form of price discrimination that occurs in the telephone, telecommunications, electric utility, hotel, and car rental industries.

Review Exercise 1

a.   Total target return on investment = $25,000,000 × 0.20 = $5,000,000
Target return on investment per unit = $5,000,000 ÷ 125,000 = $40
Prospective selling price = $200 + $40 = $240

b.   Total target return on investment = $25,000,000 × 0.20 = $5,000,000
Target return on investment per unit = $5,000,000 ÷ 80,000 = $62.50
Markup as a percentage of full cost of the product = $62.50 ÷ $250 = 25%

Review Exercise 2

a. and b. (dollars in thousands)	Quick Tax		Fast Audit	
Revenues (two-year totals)	$5,000		$3,200	
Costs (two-year totals):		%		%
R&D	1,400	32.5	480	14.1
Product design	400	9.3	192	5.7
Manufacturing	600	14.0	416	12.3
Marketing	1,000	23.3	896	26.4
Distribution	150	3.5	192	5.7
Customer service	750	17.4	1,216	35.8
Total costs	4,300	100.0	3,392	100.0
Operating income	$ 700		$ (192)	

Quick Tax is profitable, whereas Fast Audit is unprofitable. The product life-cycle report highlights possible causal relationships among costs classified by business function in the value chain. The relatively much lower R&D and product design costs of Fast Audit might be the reason for this outcome. Quick Tax has 41.8% of its costs in R&D and product design compared to 19.8% for Fast Audit. Also, customer service costs are relatively much higher for Fast Audit (35.8% versus 17.4%), which suggests the customer service problems most likely relate to the lower costs of Fast Audit's R&D and product design.

CHAPTER 13

Strategy, Balanced Scorecard, and Strategic Profitability Analysis

Overview

This chapter explores the use of management accounting information in implementing and evaluating an organization's strategy. The chapter describes the balanced scorecard approach to implementing strategy, presents an analysis of operating income for evaluating strategy, and explains the strategic initiatives of productivity improvement, reengineering and downsizing. The Appendix to the chapter explains how to measure productivity and interpret the results.

Highlights

1. *Strategy* specifies how an organization matches its own capabilities with the opportunities in the marketplace to accomplish its objectives. In formulating its strategy, an organization must first thoroughly understand its industry. Industry analysis focuses on five forces: (a) competitors, (b) potential entrants into the market, (c) equivalent products, (d) bargaining power of customers, and (e) bargaining power of input suppliers. The collective effect of these forces shapes an organization's profit potential.

2. Organizations use two basic strategies: **product differentiation** and **cost leadership**.

- Product differentiation is an organization's ability to offer products or services perceived by its customers to be superior and unique relative to the products or services of its competitors. Product differentiation increases brand loyalty and the willingness of customers to pay higher prices.
- Cost leadership is an organization's ability to achieve lower costs relative to competitors through productivity and efficiency improvements, elimination of waste, and tight cost control. For companies that are cost leaders, lower selling prices—rather than unique products or services—provide a competitive advantage.

Being successful at product differentiation or cost leadership generally increases market share and helps a company to grow.

3. The **balanced scorecard** translates an organization's mission and strategy into a set of performance measures that provides the framework for implementing its strategy. The balanced scorecard gets its name because it balances financial and nonfinancial performance measures to evaluate both short-run and long-run performance in a single report. The balanced scorecard reduces managers' emphasis on short-run financial performance, such as quarterly earnings, because nonfinancial and operational measures track longer-run changes that a company is making. The financial benefits of these changes may not be captured in short-run earnings, but strong improvements in nonfinancial and operational measures are an indicator of the creation of economic value in the future.

4. The balanced scorecard measures performance from four key perspectives:

a. The *financial perspective* evaluates the profitability of the organization's strategy and the creation of shareholder value. Under the strategy of product differentiation, the financial perspective focuses on how much of operating income results from charging premium selling prices. Under the strategy of cost leadership, the financial perspective focuses on how much of operating income results from reducing costs and selling more units of output.
b. The *customer perspective* identifies the target-market segments and measures the organization's success in these segments. Performance measures for this perspective include market share, number of new customers, and customer satisfaction ratings.
c. The *internal-business-process perspective* focuses on internal operations that create value for customers that, in turn, helps achieve

the financial perspective. Performance measures for this perspective include improving product quality, reducing delivery time, and meeting specified delivery dates.

d. The *learning-and-growth perspective* identifies the capabilities the organization must excel at to achieve superior internal processes that, in turn, create value for customers and shareholders. Performance measures for this perspective include employee education and skill levels, employee satisfaction ratings, number of suggestions per employee, and percentage of suggestions implemented.

These four perspectives are linked in a cause-and-effect chain, moving backward from (d) to (a). That is, gains in learning and growth lead to improvements in internal business processes, which in turn lead to higher customer satisfaction and market share, and finally result in superior financial performance. In this chain, many nonfinancial measures serve as leading indicators of future financial performance.

5. A useful first step in designing a balanced scorecard is to develop a **strategy map**. A strategy map is a diagram that describes how an organization creates value by connecting strategic objectives in explicit cause-and-effect relationships with each other in the financial, customer, internal business process, and learning and growth perspectives. EXHIBIT 13-2, text p. 471, presents the strategy map for Chipset, Inc., a manufacturer of devices used in modems and communication networks. Chipset uses a strategy of cost leadership.

6. In the strategic map, empowering the workforce helps align employee and organization goals and improves processes. Employee and organizational alignment also helps improve processes that improve manufacturing quality and productivity, reduce customer delivery time, meet specified delivery dates, and improve post-sales services—all of which increase customer satisfaction. Improving manufacturing quality and productivity directly increases operating income and customer satisfaction that, in turn, drives increases in market share, operating income and shareholder value.

7. EXHIBIT 13-3, text p.473, presents the balanced scorecard for Chipset, Inc. For each of the four perspectives, Chipset's balanced scorecard for 2011 specifies the "objectives," "measures," "initiatives," and "target performance" (the first four columns in the exhibit). Comparing "actual performance" (the last column in the exhibit) to "target performance" shows that Chipset met most of its targets in 2011.

8. One of Chipset's initiatives under the internal business process perspective is to reengineer its order delivery process. **Reengineering** is the fundamental rethinking and redesign of business processes to achieve improvements in critical measures of performance, such as cost, quality, service, speed, and customer satisfaction. Reengineering tends to be more beneficial when it cuts across functional lines in the organization to focus on an entire business process (as in the Chipset example). Successful reengineering efforts focus on changing roles and responsibilities, eliminating unnecessary activities and tasks, using information technology, and developing employee skills.

9. As noted above, Chipset uses a strategy of cost leadership. One of its competitors, Visilog, uses a strategy of product differentiation. What are the contents of Visilog's balanced scorecard? Likely possibilities are:

- The financial perspective measures how much of operating income and the creation of shareholder value result from charging premium selling prices.
- The customer perspective measures the percentage of revenues from new products and new customers.
- The internal business process perspective measures the development of advanced manufacturing capabilities to produce custom products.
- The learning and growth perspective measures new product development time.

Of course, Visilog also uses some of the measures in Chipset's balanced scorecard, such as revenue growth, customer satisfaction ratings, on-time delivery rate, and employee satisfaction ratings.

10. Features of a good balanced scorecard include:

a. Each measure in the balanced scorecard is part of a cause-and-effect sequence, from strategy formulation to financial outcomes.
b. The balanced scorecard helps communicate the strategy to all members of the organization by translating the strategy into a linked set of understandable and measurable operational targets.
c. In for-profit companies, the balanced scorecard must motivate managers to take actions that eventually result in improvements in financial performance.
d. The balanced scorecard limits the number of measures, identifying only the most critical ones.

11. Pitfalls in implementing a balanced scorecard include:

a. Managers should not assume the cause-and-effect linkages are precise; they are merely hypotheses. With experience, organizations should alter their scorecards to include those nonfinancial strategic objectives and measures that are the best leading indicators (the causes) of subsequent financial performance (a lagging indicator of the effect).
b. Managers should not seek improvements across all of the measures all of the time. For example, strive for quality and on-time performance but not beyond a point at which further improvement in these objectives may be inconsistent with long-run profit maximization.
c. Managers should not use only objective measures in the balanced scorecard. When using subjective measures, though, managers must be careful that the benefits of this potentially rich information are not lost by using measures that are inaccurate or that can be easily manipulated.
d. Despite challenges of measurement, top management should not ignore nonfinancial measures when evaluating managers and other employees.

12. To evaluate how successful an organiza-tion's strategy and its implementation have been, management compares the target performance and actual performance in the balanced scorecard. A more detailed aspect of the evaluation is to subdivide the change in operating income from one period to the next into a **growth component**, a **price-recovery component**, and a **productivity component**.

- The *growth component* measures the change in operating income attributable solely to the change in the quantity of output sold from period 1 to period 2.
- The *price-recovery component* measures the change in operating income attributable solely to changes in prices of inputs and outputs from period 1 to period 2.
- The *productivity component* measures the change in costs attributable to a change in the quantity of inputs used in period 2 relative to the quantity of inputs that would have been used in period 1 to produce the period 2 output.

A company is considered to be successful in implementing its cost leadership or product differentiation strategy if the amounts of the three components align closely with the strategy.

13. Because subdividing the change in operating income into the growth, price-recovery, and productivity components is similar to variance analysis, a component is labeled favorable (F) if it increases operating income and unfavorable (U) if it decreases operating income. The following table shows the variances—*called revenue effects and cost effects in this context*—measured for each component:

Component	Revenue Effect	Cost Effect
Growth	Yes	Yes
Price recovery	Yes	Yes
Productivity	No	Yes

14. In the Chipset example, text p.479, operating income is $2,750,000 in 2010 and $5,725,000 in 2011, an increase of $2,975,000. Based on the formulas, beginning text p.479, the increase is explained as follows:

Growth component		
Revenue effect	$3,450,000 F	
Cost effect	630,000 U	$2,820,000 F
Price-recovery component		
Revenue effect	1,150,000 U	
Cost effect	607,500 U	1,757,500 U
Productivity component		1,912,500 F
Change in operating income		$2,975,000 F

This analysis indicates that Chipset was successful in implementing its cost leadership strategy: productivity contributed $1,912,500 to the increase in operating income and growth contributed $2,820,000. Operating income decreased by $1,757,500 because Chipset was unable to raise selling prices to pass along increases in input prices. Had Chipset been able to differentiate its product, the price-recovery effects would have been less unfavorable or perhaps even favorable.

15. To further evaluate the success of Chipset's strategy and its implementation, the $2,975,000 increase in operating income can be analyzed more closely. For example was Chipset's growth helped by an increase in industry market size? If so, at least part of the increase in operating income may be attributable to favorable economic conditions in the industry rather than to Chipset successfully implementing its strategy. Some of the growth also may have resulted from a management decision to take advantage of the productivity gains by reducing selling price. Using additional information, text p.483, the $2,975,000 increase in operating income can be analyzed based on three main factors: growth/decline in industry market size, product differentiation, and cost leadership. The box on the next page presents the results of this analysis

16. Because a company's fixed costs are tied to its capacity, managers must understand, measure, and manage **unused capacity** in order to reduce these fixed costs. Unused capacity is the amount of productive capacity available over and above the productive capacity employed to meet customer demand in the current period. To understand unused capacity, it is necessary to distinguish **engineered costs** from **discretionary costs**.

- Engineered costs result from a cause-and-effect relationship between the cost driver, output, and the (direct or indirect) resources used to produce that output. For example, direct material costs are direct engineered costs, and conversion costs are indirect engineered costs. Although some conversion costs are fixed in the short run, over time there is a cause-and-effect relationship between output and manufacturing capacity required (and conversion costs needed). Therefore, engineered costs can be variable or fixed in the short run.
- Discretionary costs have two important features: (a) They arise from periodic (usually annual) decisions regarding the maximum amount to be incurred, and (b) They have no measurable cause-and-effect relationship between output and resources used. Some examples of discretionary costs are advertising, executive training, and R&D. The most noteworthy aspect of discretionary costs is that managers are seldom confident the "correct" amounts are being spent.

Identifying unused capacity is easier for engineered costs than for discretionary costs because engineered costs have a cause-and-effect relationship with the cost driver.

17. When a company has identified its unused capacity, attempts can be made to either eliminate it or utilize it to grow revenues. In recent years, many companies have downsized in an attempt to eliminate unused capacity. **Downsizing** (also called **rightsizing**) is an integrated approach of configuring processes, products, and people to match costs to the activities that need to be performed to operate effectively and efficiently in the present and future. Downsizing often means eliminating jobs, which can have an adverse effect on employee morale and the culture of the organization. Downsizing, therefore, is best done in the context of the company's overall strategy, and by retaining individuals who have strong management, leadership, technical skills, and experience.

18. (Appendix) **Productivity** measures the relationship between actual inputs used (both quanti-

ties and costs) and actual output produced. Measuring productivity improvements over time highlights the specific input-output relationships that contribute to cost leadership. Two measures of productivity are **partial productivity** and **total factor productivity**.

- Partial productivity, the most frequently used productivity measure, compares the quantity of output produced with the quantity of an individual input used. Although partial productivity is easily understood by operations person-nel, it does not allow managers to evaluate the effect of input substitutions on overall productivity.

- Total factor productivity is the ratio of the quantity of output produced to the costs of all inputs used based on current-period prices. It considers all inputs simultaneously and the tradeoffs among inputs based on current input prices. A drawback of total factor productivity is operations personnel find it difficult to understand and less useful than partial productivity measures.

Many companies use both partial productivity and total factor productivity to evaluate performance. The two measures of productivity work well together because the strengths of one offset the weaknesses of the other.

The amounts in this box are from the Chipset example, text p.485.

Analysis of the Change in Chipset's Operating Income (OI)
from 2010 to 2011

Change in OI due to the growth in industry market size		$1,504,000 F
Product differentiation factor:		
Change in OI due to increases in input prices		
(same as cost effect of price-recovery component)	$ 607,500 U	
Change in OI due to product differentiation		607,500 U
Cost leadership factors:		
Productivity component		
(same as in previous analysis)	1,912,500 F	
Strategic decision to reduce selling price	1,150,000 U	
Growth in market share due to productivity component		
and strategic decision to reduce selling price	1,316,000 F	
Change in OI due to cost leadership		2,078,500 F
Change in OI		$2,975,000 F

This analysis shows that, consistent with its cost leadership strategy, Chipset's productivity gains in 2011 are key to the increase of $2,975,000 in OI.

Featured Exercise

Castleton Company makes a chemical fertilizer, Turfgro. The market for Turfgro is highly competitive. As a result, managing costs is critical for long-run profitability and growth. Information on Turfgro for 2010 and 2011 is as follows:

		2010	2011
1.	Tons of Turfgro produced and sold	10,000	10,400
2.	Selling price per ton	$300	$315
3.	Direct materials used in tons	11,500	12,000
4.	Direct material cost per ton	$120	$123
5.	Tons of Turfgro manufactured per batch	40	40
6.	Manufacturing capacity in batches	350	345
7.	Conversion costs	$1,050,000	$1,069,500
8.	Conversion costs per batch of capacity		
	(row 7 ÷ row 6)	$3,000	$3,100
9.	Number of advertisements run	1,400	1,395
10.	Advertising costs	$350,000	$351,540
11.	Advertising costs per advertisement run		
	(row 10 ÷ row 9)	$250	$252

Each year's conversion costs depend on production capacity (defined in terms of number of batches of Turfgro that can be produced), not the actual number of batches produced. At the start of each year, management uses its discretion in deciding how many advertisements to run for the year. The number of advertisements run has no direct cause-and-effect relationship with the quantity of Turfgro produced and sold.

a. Is Castleton using a strategy of product differentiation or cost leadership? Explain briefly.
b. Compute the change in operating income from 2010 to 2011.
c. Compute the growth, price-recovery, and productivity components of the change in operating income from 2010 to 2011.

Solution (on next page)

Solution

a. Castleton's strategy is cost leadership. The reason: the company operates in a highly competitive market in which managing costs is critical to its long-run profitability and growth.

b.

	2010	2011
Revenues,		
10,000 × $300; 10,400 × $315	$3,000,000	$3,276,000
Costs:		
Direct material costs,		
11,500 × $120; 12,000 × $123	1,380,000	1,476,000
Conversion costs	1,050,000	1,069,500
Advertising costs	350,000	351,540
Total costs	2,780,000	2,897,040
Operating income	$ 220,000	$ 378,960

$158,960 F

c. *Growth Component*

Revenue effect, (10,400 − 10,000) × $300	$120,000 F
Cost effect:	
Direct material costs	
(11,960* − 11,500) × $120	55,200 U
Conversion costs	
(350 − 350) × $3,000	0
Advertising costs	
(1,400 − 1,400) × $250	0
Change in operating income due to growth component	$ 64,800 F
*(11,500 ÷ 10,000) × 10,400 = 11,960	

Price-Recovery Component

Revenue effect, ($315 − $300) × 10,400	$156,000 F
Cost effect:	
Direct material costs	
11,960* × ($123 − $120)	35,880 U
Conversion costs	
350 × ($3,100 − $3,000)	35,000 U
Advertising costs	
1,400 × ($252 − $250)	2,800 U
Change in operating income due to price-recovery component	$ 82,320 F
*Same as computed for growth component	

Productivity Component

Direct material costs	
(12,000 − 11,960*) × $123	$ 4,920 U
Conversion costs	
(345 − 350) × $3,100	15,500 F
Advertising costs	
(1,395 − 1,400) × $252	1,260 F
Change in operating income due to productivity component	$11,840 F
*Same as computed for growth component	

Recap:

Change in operating income due to growth component	$ 64,800 F
Change in operating income due to price-recovery component	82,320 F
Change in operating income due to productivity component	11,840 F
Change in operating income from 2007 to 2008	$158,960 F

Review Questions and Exercises

Completion Statements

Fill in the blank(s) to complete each statement.

1. An organization's ability to offer products or services perceived by its customers to be superior and unique relative to the products or services of its competitors is the strategy called _____.

2. The _____ translates an organization's mission and strategy into a set of performance measures that provides the framework for implementing its strategy.

3. The fundamental rethinking and redesign of business processes to achieve improvements in critical measures of performance such as cost, quality, service, speed, and customer satisfaction is called _____.

4. A _____ is a diagram that describes how an organization creates value by connecting strategic objectives in explicit cause-and-effect relationships with each other in the financial, customer, internal business process, and learning and growth perspectives.

5. In subdividing the change in operating income from 2010 to 2011 into components, the _____ component measures the change in operating income attributable solely to the change in the quantity of output sold from 2010 to 2011.

6. _____ costs result from a cause-and-effect relationship between the cost driver, output, and the (direct or indirect) resources used to produce that output.

7. _____ is an integrated approach of configuring processes, products, and personnel to match costs to the activities that need to be performed to operate effectively and efficiently in the present and future.

8. (Appendix) The ratio of the quantity of output produced to the costs of all input used based on current period prices is called _____ _____.

True-False

Indicate whether each statement is true (T) or false (F).

_____ 1. The balanced scorecard has separate columns for objectives, initiatives, performance measures, target performance, and actual performance.

_____ 2. The balanced scorecard gets its name because it balances short-run and long-run financial performance measures in a single report.

_____ 3. Under the strategy of product differentiation, the financial perspective of a well-designed balanced scorecard focuses on how much operating income results from charging premium selling prices.

_____ 4. The cause-and-effect relationship built into the balanced scorecard is that gains in learning and growth lead to improvements in internal business processes, which in turn lead to higher customer satisfaction and market share, and finally result in superior financial performance.

_____ 5. In a well-designed balanced scorecard, many financial performance measures serve as leading indicators of future nonfinancial performance.

_____ 6. Successful reengineering efforts involve changing roles and responsibilities, eliminating unnecessary activities and tasks, using information technology, and developing employee skills.

_____ 7. A well-designed balanced scorecard

uses only objective financial and nonfinancial performance measures.

___ 8. The most noteworthy aspect of engineered costs is that managers are seldom confident that the "correct" amounts are being spent.

___ 9. (Appendix) The lower the inputs for a given quantity of output or the higher the output for a given quantity of inputs, the higher the level of productivity.

___ 10. (Appendix) Fluctuations in input prices affect partial productivity measures.

Multiple Choice

Select the best answer to each question. Space is provided for computations after the quantitative questions.

___ 1. Brand loyalty is associated closely with:
   a. cost leadership but not product differentiation.
   b. product differentiation but not cost leadership.
   c. both cost leadership and product differentiation.
   d. neither cost leadership nor product differentiation.

___ 2. The percentage of manufacturing processes with real-time feedback is a performance measure under which perspective in the balanced scorecard?
   a. Financial perspective
   b. Customer perspective
   c. Internal business process perspective
   d. Learning and growth perspective

___ 3. Reengineering relates to which perspective in the balanced scorecard?
   a. Financial perspective
   b. Customer perspective
   c. Internal business process perspective
   d. Learning and growth perspective

___ 4. In analyzing the change in a company's operating income from one year to the next, which effect(s) is computed for the price-recovery component?

	Revenue Effect	Cost Effect
a.	Yes	Yes
b.	Yes	No
c.	No	Yes
d.	No	No

___ 5. Nesbitt Company analyzed the change in its operating income from 2010 to 2011 into three components as follows:

Growth component	$684,000 favorable
Price-recovery component	604,000 unfavorable
Productivity component	450,000 favorable

If operating income is $1,050,000 in 2011, operating income in 2010 is:
a. $212,000.
b. $520,000.
c. $1,580,000.
d. Cannot be determined from the information given.

6. Drummond Enterprises had an increase in its operating income from 2010 to 2011 of $200,000. Two of the three factors accounting for the increase are:

Change due to cost leadership $498,500 favorable
Change due to product differentiation 454,500 unfavorable

The third factor to complete this analysis is:
a. Change due to a strategic decision that affected selling price, $156,000 favorable.
b. Change due to a strategic decision that affected selling price, $156,000 unfavorable.
c. Change due to industry market size, $156,000 favorable.
d. Change due to input prices, $156,000 favorable.

7. (Appendix, CMA) Fabro Inc. produced 1,500 units of Product RX-6 last week. The inputs for this production are:

450 pounds of Material A at a cost of $1.50 per pound
300 pounds of Material Z at a cost of $2.75 per pound
300 labor-hours at a cost of $15.00 per hour

The total factor productivity for Product RX-6 is:
a. 2.00 output units per pound.
b. 1.00 output unit per dollar of input costs.
c. 5.00 output units per hour.
d. 0.25 output units per dollar of input costs.
e. 0.33 output units per dollar of input costs.

Review Exercises

1. The following information is from the Solution to the Featured Exercise, pp.172-173:

   - Castleton Company's strategy is cost leadership.
   - Change in operating income due to growth component $ 64,800 F

Change in operating income due to price-recovery component	82,320 F
Change in operating income due to productivity component	11,840 F
Change in operating income from 2010 to 2011	$158,960 F

During 2011 the unit sales for Castleton's fertilizer product, Turfgro, increased by 4% (from 10,000 tons in 2010 to 10,400 tons in 2011). A trade association reports the industry market size for this type of fertilizer increased by 3% in 2011. The increase in Turfgro's market share (that is, its unit sales grew by more than the 3% growth in industry market size) and the increase in its selling price are due to customers perceiving this product to be a superior fertilizer.

a. Compute the change in operating income from 2010 to 2011 that is due to three factors: industry market size, product differentiation and cost leadership.

b. How successful has Castleton been in implementing its cost leadership strategy for Turfgro? Explain.

2. (Appendix) Vander Lind Industries makes a chemical product using direct materials and direct manufacturing labor, which are partial substitutes for each other. The company reported the following data for the last two years of operations:

	2010	2011
Output units	8,500	10,200
Direct materials used (in kilograms)	5,700	7,000
Direct material cost per kilogram	$3.20	$3.00
Direct manufacturing labor-hours used	700	800
Wages per labor-hour	$14	$15
Manufacturing capacity in output units	12,000	11,500
Manufacturing overhead costs	$15,000	$14,950
Manufacturing overhead costs per unit of capacity	$1.25	$1.30

a. Compute the partial productivity ratios for each input for each year, and compute the change in partial productivity for each input from 2010 to 2011.

b. Compute the change in total factor productivity from 2010 to 2011.

Answers and Solutions to Chapter 13 Review Questions and Exercises

Completion Statements

1. product differentiation
2. balanced scorecard
3. reengineering
4. strategy map
5. growth
6. Engineered
7. Downsizing (Rightsizing)
8. total factor productivity

True-False

1. T
2. F   The statement is incomplete; it does not include an important aspect of the balanced scorecard, *nonfinancial performance measures*. That is, the balanced scorecard gets its name because it balances financial *and* nonfinancial measures to evaluate both short-run and long-run performance in a single report.
3. T
4. T
5. F   The statement is reversed. That is, as a result of the cause-and-effect relationship described in question 4, many nonfinancial measures serve as leading indicators of future financial performance.
6. T
7. F   One of the pitfalls in implementing a balanced scorecard is using only objective performance measures. When using subjective measures, though, management must be careful that the benefits of this potentially rich information are not lost by using measures that are imprecise or that can be easily implemented.
8. F   The statement describes *discretionary costs*, not *engineered costs*. Discretionary costs have two important features: (a) they arise from periodic (usually annual) decisions regarding the maximum amount to be incurred, and (b) they have no measurable cause-and-effect relationship between output and resources used. Examples of discretionary costs include advertising, executive training, and R&D. In contrast, engineered costs result from a cause-and-effect relationship between the cost driver, output, and the (direct or indirect) resources used to produce that output. For example, direct material costs are direct engineered costs, and conversion costs are indirect engineered costs.
9. T
10. F   Partial productivity compares the quantity of output produced with the quantity of an individual input used. Therefore, fluctuations in input prices do *not* affect partial productivity measures.

Multiple Choice

1. b   Product differentiation is an organization's ability to offer products or services perceived by its customers to be superior and unique relative to the products or services of its competitors. Product differentiation, therefore, increases brand loyalty and the prices that customers are willing to pay.
2. d   EXHIBIT 13-3, text p.473, shows the "percentage of manufacturing processes with real-time feedback" is a performance measure under the learning and growth perspective. The related objective is "enhance information system capabilities," and the related initiative is "improve on-line and off-line data gathering."

3. c EXHIBIT 13-3, text p.473, shows "reengineer order delivery process" is an initiative under the internal business process perspective. The related objective is "reduce delivery time to customers" and the related performance measure is "order delivery time."

4. a Paragraph 13 of the Highlights shows the price-recovery component computes both the revenue and cost effects.

5. b
Growth component	$684,000 F
Price-recovery component	604,000 U
Productivity component	450,000 F
Change in operating income	$530,000 F

Operating income in 2010 = Operating income in 2011 − $530,000
= $1,050,000 − $530,000 = $520,000

Proof:

Operating income in 2010	$ 520,000
Add increase in operating income	530,000
Operating income in 2011	$1,050,000

6. c
Change due to cost leadership	$498,500 F
Change due to industry market size	156,000 F
Change due to product differentiation	454,500 U
Change in operating income	$200,000 F

If, in fact, a strategic decision were made that affected the selling price, its effects are already included in the cost leadership and product differentiation factors. Likewise, these two factors already include the effects of a change in input prices.

7. d Let TFP = Total factor productivity

$$TFP = \frac{Output\ units}{Cost\ of\ all\ inputs\ used}$$

$$TFP = \frac{1,500}{(450 \times \$1.50) + (300 \times \$2.75) + (300 \times \$15)}$$

$$TFP = \frac{1,500}{\$675 + \$825 + \$4,500} = \frac{1,500}{\$6,000} = 0.25 \text{ output units per dollar of input costs}$$

Review Exercise 1

a. Effect of industry-market-size factor

   Of the 400-ton increase in sales, 300 (3% × 10,000) tons is due to the growth in industry market size. The other 100 tons is due to the growth in market share.

$64,800 F growth component × (300 ÷ 400) =		$48,600 F

   Effect of product-differentiation factor

Price-recovery component	$82,320 F
Growth in market share due to product differentiation	
$64,800 F growth component × (100 ÷ 400)	16,200 F
Total	$98,520 F

   Effect of cost-leadership factor

Productivity component	$11,840 F

Change in operating income from 2010 to 2011	= $48,600 F + $98,520 F + $11,840 F
	= $158,960 F

b. The analysis shows that $98,520 of the $158,960 (approximately 62%) is due to customers perceiving Turfgro to be a superior product. As a result, Castleton was able to pass along all input price increases in the form of a higher selling price. The strong product differentiation could be linked to Castleton's effective advertising or the lack of effective advertising by its competitors. If, however, Castleton believes the benefits of product differentiation are only temporary—either because it expects competitors to advertise more effectively or because customers will soon realize that Turfgro is not really superior to competitors' products—management should be concerned. The reason: Castleton has achieved little success with its cost leadership strategy ($11,840 F). The company needs to improve productivity both in its use of direct materials and by reducing its manufacturing capacity. Currently, Castleton has manufacturing capacity for 345 batches or 13,800 (345 × 40) tons of Turfgro. Unless the company expects to grow its business significantly in the short run, management may want to downsize, reducing its manufacturing capacity from 13,800 tons to, say, 12,000 tons, or 300 (12,000 ÷ 40) batches.

Review Exercise 2

a. Inputs that would have been used in 2011 to produce 2011 output, assuming the 2010 input-output relationship continued in 2011, are as follows:

Direct materials	$5,700 \times (10,200 \div 8,500)$	$= 6,840$ kilograms
Direct manufacturing labor	$700 \times (10,200 \div 8,500)$	$= 840$ labor-hours
Manufacturing capacity	Remains the same because adequate capacity is available	$= 12,000$ units

Input	Partial Productivity in 2011	Partial Productivity in 2010	Percentage Change from 2010 to 2011
Direct materials	$10,200 \div 7,000 = 1.46$	$10,200 \div 6,840 = 1.49$	$(1.46 - 1.49) \div 1.49 = -2.0\%$
Direct manufacturing labor	$10,200 \div 800 = 12.75$	$10,200 \div 840 = 12.14$	$(12.75 - 12.14) \div 12.14 = 5.0\%$
Manufacturing OH	$10,200 \div 11,500 = 0.89$	$10,200 \div 12,000 = 0.85$	$(0.89 - 0.85) \div 0.85 = 4.7\%$

b.

$$\text{Total factor productivity for 2011 using 2011 prices} = \frac{10,200}{(7,000 \times \$3.00) + (800 \times \$15) + (11,500 \times \$1.30)}$$

$$= \frac{10,200}{\$21,000 + \$12,000 + \$14,950}$$

$$= \frac{10,200}{\$47,950} = 0.213 \text{ output units per dollar of input costs}$$

$$\text{Benchmark total factor productivity} = \frac{10,200}{(6,840 \times \$3.00) + (840 \times \$15) + (12,000 \times \$1.30)}$$

$$= \frac{10,200}{\$20,520 + \$12,600 + \$15,600}$$

$$= \frac{10,200}{\$48,720} = 0.209 \text{ output units per dollar of input costs}$$

The change in total factor productivity from 2010 to 2011 = $(0.213 - 0.209) \div 0.209 = +0.019$, or an increase of 1.9%. The fact that total factor productivity increased means that the partial productivity increases in direct manufacturing labor (5.0%) and manufacturing overhead (4.7%) more than offset the partial productivity decrease in direct materials (−2.0%).

CHAPTER 14

Cost Allocation, Customer-Profitability Analysis, and Sales-Variance Analysis

Overview

This chapter begins by explaining the purposes of cost allocation and the criteria that guide cost-allocation decisions. Next, customer-profitability analysis explores issues related to customer revenues and customer costs. Then, the chapter describes how the sales-volume variance (introduced in Chapter 7) can be subdivided when a company has multiple products or multiple channels of distribution. Finally, the Appendix to this chapter analyzes cost variances for multiple types of substitutable materials or labor.

Highlights

1. Four purposes of allocating indirect costs to cost objects are:

a. To provide information for economic decisions
b. To motivate managers and other employees
c. To justify costs or compute reimbursement amounts
d. To measure income and assets for reporting to external parties.

The allocation of a particular cost need not satisfy all four purposes simultaneously because different costs are used for different purposes. The key is to determine which purpose of cost allocation is dominant in the given situation. EXHIBIT 14-1, text p.504, gives illustrations of each of the four purposes of cost allocation.

2. Four criteria guide cost-allocation decisions: (a) cause and effect, (b) benefits received, (c) fairness or equity, and (d) ability to bear. Managers must first choose the purpose of a particular cost allocation and then select the appropriate criterion to implement the allocation. The chapter emphasizes the superiority of the cause-and-effect and the benefits-received criteria, especially when the purpose of cost allocation is economic decisions or motivation.

3. Companies place great importance on the cost-benefit approach in designing and implementing cost allocations. The costs of cost allocation—collecting data and educating management—are highly visible, and companies work to reduce them. However, the benefits of cost allocation—managers being able to make better informed decisions—are less visible and difficult to measure. Today's information technology enables companies to make more detailed cost allocations.

4. The Consumer Appliances Inc. (CAI) illustration, beginning text p.504, explains how product costs can be determined for the company's two products, refrigerators and clothes dryers. The illustration allocates the corporate costs to the two divisions and reallocates them to each division's product. The corporate costs (and their allocation bases) are: corporate treasury costs (cost of new assembly equipment), corporate human resource management costs (salary and labor costs), and corporate administration costs (division administration costs).

5. A key decision in the CAI illustration is how many cost pools should be used in allocating corporate costs to the divisions. The concept of homogeneity is important in making this decision. In a **homogeneous cost pool**, all of the costs in the cost pool have the same or a similar cause-and-effect or benefits-received relationship with the cost-allocation base. Using homogeneous cost pools results in determining more accurate costs of a given cost object.

6. Companies that prosper have a strong customer focus in their decisions. Accordingly, management accountants are giving increased attention to **customer-profitability analysis**, the reporting and assessment of revenues earned from customers and the costs incurred to earn those revenues. Customer-profitability analysis helps managers in two main ways. First, it frequently shows that a small percentage of customers accounts for a large per-

centage of the company's operating income. Sufficient resources need to be devoted to maintaining and expanding relationships with customers that make significant contributions to profitability. Second, it identifies low-profitability and loss-category customers. Ways can be explored to make these customers more profitable in the future.

7. Two variables explain revenue differences among customers: the quantity of units they purchase and the magnitude of price discounts. A **price discount** is the reduction in selling price below list selling price to encourage customers to purchase more. Tracking the amount of price discounts by customer, and by salesperson, can help to improve customer profitability.

8. A **customer cost hierarchy** categorizes costs related to customers into different cost pools on the basis of different types of cost drivers (or cost-allocation bases) or different degrees of difficulty in determining cause-and-effect or benefits-received relationships. In the Spring Distribution example, beginning text p.510, there are five categories in the customer cost hierarchy:

a. *Customer output unit-level costs* are resources used for activities performed to sell each unit to a customer. An example is product-handling costs of each unit sold.
b. *Customer batch-level costs* are resources used for activities related to a group of units sold to a customer. An example is delivery costs for a customer order.
c. *Customer-sustaining costs* are resources used for activities to support individual customers, regardless of the number of units or orders delivered to the customer. An example is the costs of sales visits to a customer.
d. *Distribution-channel costs* are resources used for activities related to a particular distribution *channel*. An example is the salary of the manager of the retail distribution channel.
e. *Corporate-sustaining costs* are resources used for activities *that* cannot be traced to individual customers or distribution channels. An example is general administration costs.

Customer-level operating costs are the costs incurred in the first three categories of the cost hierarchy. EXHIBIT 14-5, text p.513, shows the customer-level operating income for four of Spring Distribution's customers.

9. The activity-based costing system in EXHIBIT 14-5 indicates that costs would be reduced if individual customers use smaller quantities of the cost drivers. For example, delivery costs assigned to a customer will decrease by combining some orders and making fewer deliveries. Another opportunity for cost reduction is to take actions that lower the costs in the individual activity areas. For example, improving efficiency of the ordering process can reduce costs even if customers place the same number of orders.

10. Customer-profitability analysis often focuses on a single accounting period. Short-run profitability is one of several factors that managers consider in deciding how to allocate resources among customers. Other factors managers should consider include likelihood of customer retention, potential for customer growth, long-run customer profitability, increases in overall demand from having well-known customers, and ability to learn from customers.

11. When a company has multiple products or multiple channels of distribution, several sales variances help managers gain insight into why actual results differ from budgeted amounts. (Sales variances are measured in terms of contribution margin.) The least detailed of the sales variances is the *static-budget variance*, which subdivides into the *flexible-budget variance* and the *sales-volume variance*.

12. The sales-volume variance subdivides into the **sales-mix variance** and the *sales-quantity variance*.

• The sales-mix variance is the difference between (a) budgeted contribution margin for the *actual sales mix* and (b) budgeted contribution margin for the *budgeted sales mix*. A favorable (unfavorable) sales-mix variance arises for an individual product when its actual sales-mix percentage is greater (less) than its budgeted sales-mix percentage.

- The sales-quantity variance is the difference between (a) budgeted contribution margin based on *actual units sold of all products* at the budgeted mix and (b) contribution margin in the static budget, which is based on *budgeted units of all products to be sold* at the budgeted mix. A favorable (unfavorable) sales-quantity variance arises when actual units sold of all products is greater (less) than budgeted units of all products to be sold.

EXHIBIT 14-10, text p.522, calculates the sales-mix and sales-quantity variances using a columnar solution format.

13. The sales-mix variance of all products and the sales-quantity variance of all products can be computed two ways: (a) by algebraically summing the respective variances for the individual products or (b) by using the budgeted contribution margin per **composite unit**. A composite unit is a hypothetical unit with weights based on the mix of individual units. The box below illustrates (b).

Product	Budgeted Contribution Margin per Unit (1)	Actual Sales-Mix Percentage (2)	Budgeted Contribution Margin per Composite Unit for Actual Mix (3) = (1) × (2)	Budgeted Sales-Mix Percentage (4)	Budgeted Contribution Margin per Composite Unit for Budg. Mix (5) = (1) × (4)
X	$3,200	0.10	$ 320	0.05	$ 160
Y	2,400	0.25	600	0.15	360
Z	900	0.65	585	0.80	720
		1.00	$1,505	1.00	$1,240

Sales volume of all three products:

Actual units	24,000
Budgeted units	20,000

Total sales-mix variance	= 24,000 × ($1,505 − $1,240)	= $6,360,000 F
Total sales-quantity variance	= (24,000 − 20,000) × ($1,505 − $1,240)	= $1,060,000 F

The sales-mix variance is favorable because budgeted contribution margin per composite unit is greater for the actual mix ($1,505) than for the budgeted mix ($1,240). The sales-quantity variance is favorable because actual sales volume of all three products (24,000 units) is greater than budgeted sales volume of all three products (20,000 units).

14. (Appendix) When a company uses multiple types of substitutable material or labor inputs in producing a finished good, insight about performance can be gained by subdividing the efficiency variance into the **mix variance** and the **yield variance.**

EXHIBIT 14-13, text p.527, calculates the direct materials mix and yield variances using a columnar solution format.

Featured Exercise

Cambridge Industries collects information on two customers for the fiscal year just ended:

	Langley Supply	Sweeney, Inc.
Revenues	$1,492,000	$640,000
Cost of goods sold	$1,164,000	$486,000
Number of in-stock orders	14	4
Number of out-of-stock orders	12	24

Cambridge estimates the following activity-based costs:

Cost of processing and delivering an in-stock order	$1,200
Cost of processing and delivering an out-of-stock order	$3,500

For an in-stock order, all the items included in the order are in inventory at the time the order is received.

Compute the customer-level operating income of each customer for the fiscal year using:

a.   16% of revenues as the allocation rate for customer-related costs.
b.   Activity-based costing.

Solution

a.

	Langley	Sweeney
Revenues	$1,492,000	$640,000
Costs:		
Cost of goods sold	1,164,000	486,000
Customer-related costs, 16% of revenues	238,720	102,400
Total costs	1,402,720	588,400
Customer-level operating income	$ 89,280	$ 51,600

b.

	Langley	Sweeney
Revenues	$1,492,000	$640,000
Costs:		
Cost of goods sold	1,164,000	486,000
In-stock costs		
14 × $1,200; 4 × $1,200	16,800	4,800
Out-of-stock costs		
12 × $3,500; 24 × $3,500	42,000	84,000
Total costs	1,222,800	574,800
Customer-level operating income	$ 269,200	$ 65,200

Review Questions and Exercises

Completion Statements

Fill in the blank(s) to complete each statement.

1. In a _____ cost pool, all of the costs in the cost pool have the same or a similar cause-and-effect or benefits-received relationship with the cost-allocation base.
2. The reduction in selling price below list selling price in order to encourage customers to purchase more is called a

   _____.
3. A _____ categorizes costs related to customers into different cost pools on the basis of different types of cost drivers (or cost-allocation bases) or different degrees of difficulty in determining cause-and-effect or benefits-received relationships.

4. A _____ unit is a hypothetical unit with weights based on the mix of individual units.
5. The sales-volume variance subdivides into which two variances?
   _____ and

   _____.
6. (Appendix) The direct materials (DM) efficiency variance subdivides into which two variances?
   _____ and
   _____.

True-False

Indicate whether each statement is true (T) or false (F).

___ 1. One of the four purposes of cost allocation is to measure income and assets for reporting to external parties.

___ 2. The fairness criterion is superior to other criteria used for guiding cost-allocation decisions when the purpose of the allocation is either to provide information for economic decisions or to motivate managers and other employees.

___ 3. When the degree of homogeneity is greater among costs, more cost pools are required to explain accurately the differences in how products use the resources of a company.

___ 4. Customer-profitability analysis often shows that a small percentage of customers accounts for a large percentage of the company's operating income.

___ 5. In the customer cost hierarchy, delivery cost for a customer order is a customer-sustaining cost.

___ 6. An unfavorable sales-mix variance arises for an individual product when its actual sales-mix percentage is less than its budgeted sales-mix percentage.

___ 7. (Appendix) When multiple inputs of direct materials can be combined in varying proportions within specified limits, they are called substitutable inputs.

___ 8. (Appendix) An unfavorable direct materials mix variance for an individual type of direct material arises when its actual mix percentage is less than its budgeted mix percentage.

Multiple Choice

Select the best answer to each question. Space is provided for computations after the quantitative questions.

___ 1. (CPA) Of most relevance in deciding how indirect costs should be allocated to products is the degree of:
a. avoidability.
b. causality.
c. controllability.
d. linearity.

___ 2. In a customer cost hierarchy, the cost of a sales visit to a customer is:
a. a customer output unit-level cost.
b. a customer batch-level cost.
c. a customer-sustaining cost.
d. a distribution-channel cost.

___ 3. The following information is for Eucha Corp. for the first quarter of the current fiscal year:

	Actual Results	Static Budget
Unit sales:		
Product X	15,000	40,000
Product Y	65,000	60,000
Total	80,000	100,000

Contribution margin per unit:

Product X	$4	$5
Product Y	$3	$2

The sales-mix variance for both products together is:
a. $51,000 unfavorable.
b. $64,000 unfavorable.
c. $115,000 unfavorable.
d. $115,000 favorable.

4. Using the information in question 3, the sales-quantity variance for Product Y is:
   a. $40,000 unfavorable.
   b. $40,000 favorable.
   c. $24,000 unfavorable.
   d. $24,000 favorable.

7. (Appendix) Using the information in question 6, the mix variance for skilled labor is:
   a. $1,200 favorable.
   b. $4,000 unfavorable.
   c. $2,800 unfavorable.
   d. $2,800 favorable.

5. Using the information in question 3, the amount of the budgeted contribution margin per composite unit is:
   a. $3.50.
   b. $3.20.
   c. $2.5625.
   d. none of the above.

6. (Appendix) The following information is for Kershaw Company for last month:

   Budgeted direct labor mix at budgeted prices for actual output produced

   3,825 skilled hours at $16 per hour
   1,275 unskilled hours at $12 per hour
   5,100 total hours

   Actual results

   4,000 skilled hours at $19 per hour
   1,000 unskilled hours at $9 per hour
   5,000 total hours

   The direct labor yield variance for both types of labor together is:
   a. $1,500 favorable.
   b. $1,000 unfavorable.
   c. $1,000 favorable.
   d. $500 favorable.

Review Exercises

1. (CMA) Cosmo Inc.'s income statement by segments for November 2011 is as follows:

	Total	Mall Store	Town Store
Revenues	$200,000	$80,000	$120,000
Variable costs	116,000	32,000	84,000
Contribution margin	84,000	48,000	36,000
Direct fixed costs	60,000	20,000	40,000
Contribution by store	24,000	28,000	(4,000)
Indirect fixed costs	10,000	4,000	6,000
Operating income	$ 14,000	$24,000	$(10,000)

Additional information regarding Cosmo's operations is as follows:

- One-fourth of each store's direct fixed costs will continue through December 31, 2012, even if either store is closed.
- Cosmo allocates indirect fixed costs to each store on the basis of revenues. These costs are regarded as unavoidable.
- Management estimates that closing the Town Store would result in a 10% decrease in the Mall Store's sales volume, whereas closing the Mall Store would not affect the Town Store's sales volume.
- The operating results for November 2011 represent the average for all months.

a. Compute the increase/decrease in Cosmo's monthly operating income for 2012 if the Town Store is closed.

b. Cosmo is considering a promotion campaign at the Town Store that would not affect the Mall Store. Compute the increase/decrease in Cosmo's monthly operating income in 2012, assuming annual promotion costs at the Town Store are increased by $60,000 and its sales volume increases by 10%.

c. One-half of Town Store's revenues are from items sold at variable cost in order to attract customers to the store. Cosmo is considering discontinuing these items, a decision that would reduce the Town Store's direct fixed costs by 15% and result in the loss of 20% of its remaining revenues and variable costs. This change would not affect the Mall Store. Compute the increase/decrease in Cosmo's monthly operating income for 2012, assuming the items sold at variable cost are discontinued.

2. (CMA) Given the following information for Xerbert Company (in thousands):

	Static Budget for 2008			Actual Results for 2008		
	Xenox	Xeon	Total	Xenox	Xeon	Total
Units sold	150	100	250	130	130	260
Revenues	$900	$1,000	$1,900	$780	$1,235	$2,015
Variable costs	450	750	1,200	390	975	1,365
Contribution margin	$450	$ 250	$ 700	$390	$ 260	$ 650
Fixed costs:						
Manufacturing			200			190
Marketing			153			140
Customer service			95			90
Total fixed costs			448			420
Operating income			$ 252			$ 230

a. Compute the sales-volume variance for both products together.
b. Compute the sales-mix variance for both products together.
c. Compute the sales-quantity variance for both products together.

Answers and Solutions to Chapter 14 Review Questions and Exercises

Completion Statements

1. homogenous
2. price discount
3. customer cost hierarchy
4. composite
5. sales-mix variance, sales-quantity variance
6. DM mix variance, DM yield variance

True-False

1. T

2. F   The cause-and-effect criterion is superior to other criteria used for guiding cost-allocation decisions when the purpose of the allocation is to provide information for economic decisions or to motivate managers and other employees. When the cause-and-effect criterion is not operational, the benefits-received criterion is often used.

3. F   When the degree of homogeneity is greater among costs, *more* cost items have the same or a similar cause-and-effect relationship with the individual allocation bases. Therefore, *fewer* cost pools are required to explain accurately the differences in how products use the resources of a company.

4. T

5. F   In the customer cost hierarchy, delivery cost for a customer order is a customer batch-level cost because the cost is incurred for activities related to a group of units sold to a customer.

6. T

7. T

8. F   An unfavorable direct materials mix variance for an individual type of direct material arises when its actual mix percentage is *greater than* its budgeted mix percentage. Note, this question is worded in a parallel manner to question 6. Question 6 is true, however, because it refers to *contribution margin* rather than *input cost*. In other words, in the income statement contribution margin almost always has a *positive* algebraic sign while input cost has a *negative* algebraic sign.

Multiple Choice

1. b   Decisions on cost allocation are preferably guided by the cause-and-effect criterion. That is, it is desirable that all of the individual activities whose costs are included in a cost pool have the same or a similar cause-and-effect relationship with the cost-allocation base.

2. c   Customer-sustaining costs are incurred for activities undertaken to support an individual customer.

For illustrative purposes, *formulas* are used to answer questions 3 and 4, and the *columnar solution format* is used to answer questions 6 and 7.

3. a   Let SMV-X = Sales-mix variance for Product X
        Let SMV-Y = Sales-mix variance for Product Y
        Let SMV-T = Total sales-mix variance

$$\text{SMV-X} = 80,000 \times \left[(15,000 \div 80,000) - (40,000 \div 100,000) \right] \times \$5$$
$$\text{SMV-X} = 80,000 \times (0.1875 - 0.40) \times \$5$$
$$\text{SMV-X} = 80,000 \times (-0.2125) \times \$5 = -\$85,000, \text{ or } \$85,000 \text{ U}$$

$$\text{SMV-Y} = 80,000 \times \left[(65,000 \div 80,000) - (60,000 \div 100,000) \right] \times \$2$$
$$\text{SMV-Y} = 80,000 \times (0.8125 - 0.60) \times \$2$$
$$\text{SMV-Y} = 80,000 \times (0.2125) \times \$2 = \$34,000, \text{ or } \$34,000 \text{ F}$$

$$\text{SMV-T} = \text{SMV-X} + \text{SMV-Y}$$
$$\text{SMV-T} = \$85,000 \text{ U} + \$34,000 \text{ F} = \$51,000 \text{ U}$$

Alternative solution:

Budgeted contribution margin per composite unit at actual mix:

$$\frac{(\$15,000 \times \$5) + (\$65,000 \times \$2)}{15,000 + 65,000} = \frac{\$75,000 + \$130,000}{80,000} = \frac{\$205,000}{80,000} = \$2.5625$$

Budgeted contribution margin per composite unit at budgeted mix:

$$\frac{(\$40,000 \times \$5) + (\$60,000 \times \$2)}{40,000 + 60,000} = \frac{\$200,000 + \$120,000}{100,000} = \frac{\$320,000}{100,000} = \$3.20$$

$$\begin{aligned}\text{Sales-mix variance} &= (\$2.5625 - \$3.20) \times 80,000 \\ &= -\$0.6375 \times 80,000 = -\$51,000, \text{ or } \$51,000 \text{ U}\end{aligned}$$

4. c   Let SQV-Y = Sales-quantity variance for Product Y

$$\text{SQV-Y} = (80,000 - 100,000) \times (60,000 \div 100,000) \times \$2$$
$$\text{SQV-Y} = -20,000 \times 0.60 \times \$2 = -\$24,000, \text{ or } \$24,000 \text{ U}$$

5. b   The alternative solution in answer 3 shows the budgeted contribution margin per composite unit is $3.20.

6. a

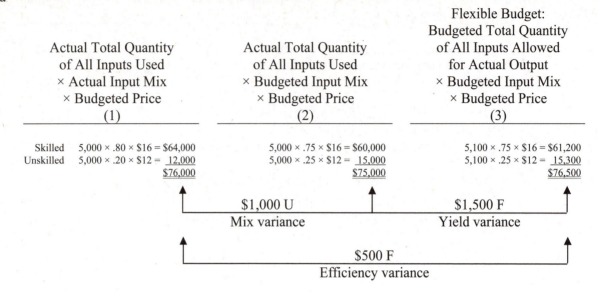

	Actual Total Quantity of All Inputs Used × Actual Input Mix × Budgeted Price (1)	Actual Total Quantity of All Inputs Used × Budgeted Input Mix × Budgeted Price (2)	Flexible Budget: Budgeted Total Quantity of All Inputs Allowed for Actual Output × Budgeted Input Mix × Budgeted Price (3)
Skilled	5,000 × .80 × $16 = $64,000	5,000 × .75 × $16 = $60,000	5,100 × .75 × $16 = $61,200
Unskilled	5,000 × .20 × $12 = 12,000	5,000 × .25 × $12 = 15,000	5,100 × .25 × $12 = 15,300
	$76,000	$75,000	$76,500

$1,000 U
Mix variance

$1,500 F
Yield variance

$500 F
Efficiency variance

Supporting computations:

Actual labor mix:
Skilled = 4,000 ÷ 5,000 = 80%
Unskilled = 1,000 ÷ 5,000 = 20%

Budgeted labor mix:
Skilled = 3,825 ÷ 5,100 = 75%
Unskilled = 1,275 ÷ 5,100 = 25%

7. b Using the amounts for skilled labor in columns 1 and 2 from the preceding answer, the mix variance = $64,000 − $60,000 = $4,000 U

Review Exercise 1

a. Compare the company's total operating income at present, $14,000, and the amount of operating income from the proposed situation of operating only the Mall Store:

		Proposed Situation
Contribution margin of Mall Store		
$48,000 × 90%		$43,200
Deduct:		
Direct fixed costs of Mall Store	$20,000	
Unavoidable direct fixed costs of Town Store, $40,000 × 25%	10,000	
Indirect fixed costs of company as a whole	10,000	
Total fixed costs		40,000
Operating income of company as a whole		$ 3,200

Closing the Town Store, therefore, decreases operating income for the year by $10,800 ($14,000 − $3,200).

b. The two items affected in the proposed situation are the Town Store's contribution margin and its promotion costs. Monthly contribution margin increases by $36,000 × 10% = $3,600. *Monthly* promotion costs are $60,000 ÷ 12 = $5,000. Monthly operating income of the Town Store, therefore, decreases by $5,000 − $3,600 = $1,400.

c. Compare the Town Store's contribution at present, −$4,000, and the amount of its contribution with the proposed changes:

	Proposed Situation
Revenues, $0.50 \times \$120,000 \times (1 - 0.20)$	$48,000
Deduct:	
Variable costs	
50% of original revenues of $120,000	
are variable and would be avoided;	
also there will be a 20% reduction	
in the *remainder of the original*	
variable costs,	
$(\$84,000 - \$60,000) \times (1 - 0.20)$	$19,200
Direct fixed costs,	
$\$40,000 \times (1 - 0.15)$	34,000
Total costs	53,200
Contribution by store	$(5,200)

The proposed situation, therefore, decreases the Town Store's contribution by $1,200 (from −$4,000 to −$5,200). This $1,200 decrease is also the effect on the company's operating income because indirect fixed costs in total will remain the same, regardless of how they are allocated between the two stores.

Review Exercise 2

See the Solution Exhibit on the next page.

SOLUTION EXHIBIT

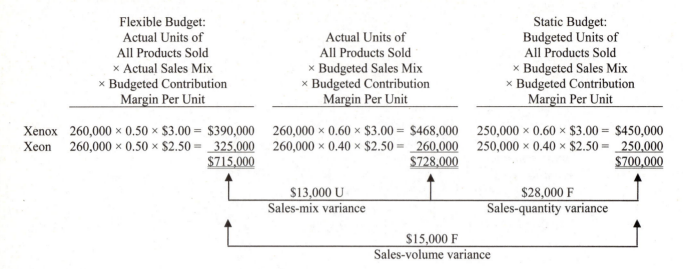

	Flexible Budget: Actual Units of All Products Sold × Actual Sales Mix × Budgeted Contribution Margin Per Unit	Actual Units of All Products Sold × Budgeted Sales Mix × Budgeted Contribution Margin Per Unit	Static Budget: Budgeted Units of All Products Sold × Budgeted Sales Mix × Budgeted Contribution Margin Per Unit
Xenox	$260,000 \times 0.50 \times \$3.00 = \$390,000$	$260,000 \times 0.60 \times \$3.00 = \$468,000$	$250,000 \times 0.60 \times \$3.00 = \$450,000$
Xeon	$260,000 \times 0.50 \times \$2.50 = \underline{325,000}$	$260,000 \times 0.40 \times \$2.50 = \underline{260,000}$	$250,000 \times 0.40 \times \$2.50 = \underline{250,000}$
	$\underline{\$715,000}$	$\underline{\$728,000}$	$\underline{\$700,000}$

$13,000 U
Sales-mix variance

$28,000 F
Sales-quantity variance

$15,000 F
Sales-volume variance

Supporting computations:

Actual sales mix:
Xenox = $130,000 \div 260,000 = 50\%$
Xeon = $130,000 \div 260,000 = 50\%$

Budgeted sales mix:
Xenox = $150,000 \div 250,000 = 60\%$
Xeon = $100,000 \div 250,000 = 40\%$

Budgeted contribution margin per unit:
Xenox = $\$450,000 \div 150,000 = \$3.00$
Xeon = $\$250,000 \div 100,000 = \$2.50$

Alternative solution:

Budgeted contribution margin per composite unit at actual mix:

$$\frac{(130,000 \times \$3) + (130,000 \times \$2.50)}{260,000} = \frac{\$390,000 + \$325,000}{260,000} = \frac{\$715,000}{260,000} = \$2.75$$

Budgeted contribution margin per composite unit at budgeted mix:

$$\frac{(150,000 \times \$3) + (100,000 \times \$2.50)}{250,000} = \frac{\$450,000 + \$250,000}{250,000} = \frac{\$700,000}{250,000} = \$2.80$$

Sales-volume variance $= (260,000 \times \$2.75) - (250,000 \times \$2.80) = \$715,000 - \$700,000 = \$15,000$, or $15,000 F

Sales-mix variance $= (\$2.75 - \$2.80) \times 260,000 = -\$0.05 \times 260,000 = -\$13,000$, or $13,000 U

Sales-quantity variance $= (260,000 - 250,000) \times \$2.80 = 10,000 \times \$2.80 = \$28,000$, or $28,000 F

Allocation of Support-Department Costs, Common Costs, and Revenues

Overview

Most of this chapter explores additional cost-allocation issues: allocating costs under the single-rate and dual-rate methods, allocating support-department costs to operating departments—using the direct, step-down, and reciprocal methods—and then to products, and allocating common costs to cost objects. These issues are often debatable and the results of the allocations are seldom clearly right or clearly wrong. The final section of the chapter examines revenue-allocation issues that arise when companies sell bundles of multiple products or services.

Highlights

1. Two alternative cost-allocation methods are the **single-rate method** and **dual-rate method**.

- The single-rate method, which makes no distinction between fixed and variable costs, allocates costs in each pool to cost objects using the same rate per unit of the single allocation base. The single-rate method is easy to implement. However, it may lead department or division managers to make outsourcing decisions that are in their own best interests but are not in the best interest of the organization as a whole.

- The dual-rate method partitions the cost of each cost pool into two pools—a variable-cost pool and a fixed-cost pool—and allocates each pool using a different cost-allocation base. Because the dual-rate method focuses on cost-behavior, it guides department or division managers to make decisions that are in their own best interests as well as in the best interest of the organization as a whole.

2. Under either the single-rate or dual-rate method, the decision whether to use *budgeted cost rates* or *actual cost rates* affects the level of uncertainty user departments (or divisions) face. Budg-eted cost rates let user departments know, in advance, the rates they will be charged. User departments are in a better position to determine the amount of service to request and, if the option exists, whether or not to outsource. Budgeted cost rates also help motivate managers of the supplier departments to improve efficiency. In contrast, actual cost rates are not known until the end of the budget period and do not promote efficiency in the supplier departments.

3. Under the dual-rate method, the decision whether to use *budgeted usage* or *actual usage* for allocating fixed costs can affect how managers behave. Budgeted usage lets user departments know, in advance, their allocated costs, which is especially helpful for long-run planning. When fixed costs are allocated on the basis of budgeted long-run usage, however, managers of user departments may be tempted to underestimate their planned usage. That's because a user department that underestimates its planned usage bears a lower percentage of the fixed costs, assuming all other managers do not similarly underestimate their usage. This temptation can be countered by offering incentives to managers whose actual usage does not exceed their budgeted usage. There are two disadvantages of allocating fixed costs based on actual usage: (a) the amount of fixed costs allocated to a given user department is affected by the usage of other user departments, and (b) the actual fixed costs allocated to user departments are not known until the end of the budget period.

4. Companies distinguish **operating departments** from **support departments**. An operating department (also called a **production department**) directly adds value to a product or service. A support department (also called a **service department**) provides the services that assist other internal departments (operating departments and other support departments) in the company. Support departments create special cost-allocation problems if they provide reciprocal services to

each other as well as services to operating departments.

5. Support department costs can be allocated to operating departments by using the **direct method**, **step-down method**, or **reciprocal method**.

- The direct method allocates each support department's costs to the operating departments only. *This method ignores any services provided by a support department to other support departments.* The advantage of the direct method is its simplicity— there is no need to predict the usage of support department services by other support departments. The direct method is the most widely used method of allocating support department costs.

- The step-down method (also called the **sequential allocation method**) allocates support department costs to other support departments and to operating departments in a sequential manner that *partially recognizes the mutual services provided among all support departments.* This method requires the support departments to be ranked (sequenced) in the order that the step-down allocation is to proceed. Different sequences result in different allocations of support department costs to operating departments. A popular step-down sequence begins with the support department that provides the highest percentage of its total services to other support departments. The sequence continues with the department that provides the next-highest percentage of its total services to other support departments, and so on, ending with the support department that provides the lowest percentage of its total services to other support departments. Once a support department's costs are allocated under the step-down method, no support department costs are allocated back to it.

- The reciprocal allocation method (also called the **matrix method**) allocates support-department costs to operating departments by *fully recognizing the mutual services provided among all support departments.* Exhibit 15-5, text p.553, illustrates the reciprocal method by using repeated iterations. The reciprocal method also can be applied by expressing support-department costs and support-department reciprocal service relationships in the form of linear equations (one equation for each support department). Solving these equations simultaneously gives the **complete reciprocated costs** (also called **artificial costs**) of each support department. The complete reciprocated costs of a support department are the department's own costs plus any interdepartmental cost allocations. The reciprocal method is conceptually the most appealing of the three methods because it *fully recognizes the mutual services provided among all support departments.*

6. Another type of cost allocation concerns a **common cost**, which is a cost of operating a facility, activity, or like cost object that is shared by two or more users. Common costs exist because each obtains a lower cost by sharing than the separate cost that would result if such user were an independent entity. Two methods for allocating a common cost are the **stand-alone cost-allocation method** and the **incremental cost-allocation method**. The stand-alone cost-allocation method determines the weights for cost allocation by considering each user of the cost as a separate entity. The incremental cost-allocation method ranks the individual users of a cost object in the order of users most responsible for a common cost, and then uses this ranking to allocate the cost among those users. The first-ranked user of the cost object is the *primary user*, the second-ranked user is the *first incremental user*, the third-ranked user is the *second incremental user*, and so on. Under the incremental method, the primary user typically receives the highest allocation of the common costs.

7. Cost data are important in contracts. Contract disputes arise often, usually in regard to cost allocation. The areas of dispute between contracting parties can be reduced by making the "rules of the game" explicit and in writing when the contract is signed. These rules include details such as the definition of allowable cost items, definitions of terms used, the permissible cost-allocation bases, and how differences between budgeted and actual costs are to be accounted for.

8. An **allowable cost** is a cost that the contract parties agree to include in the costs to be reimbursed. For example, only economy-class airfares are allowable in many U.S. government contracts. Some contracts identify cost categories that are not allowable. For example, costs of lobbying activities and alcoholic beverages are not allowable costs in U.S. government contracts.

9. The U.S. government reimburses most contractors in either of two ways: (a) the contractor is paid a set price without analysis of actual contract cost data (such as in competitive bidding situations) or (b) the contractor is paid after analysis of actual contract cost data (such as reimbursement of allowable costs plus a fixed fee). All contracts with U.S. government agencies must comply with cost accounting standards issued by the **Cost Accounting Standards Board (CASB)**. The standards are designed to achieve *uniformity* and *consistency* in regard to measurement, assignment, and allocation of costs to contracts within the U.S.

10. Allocation issues also can arise with revenues. **Revenue allocation** occurs when revenues are related to a particular **revenue object** but cannot be traced to it in an economically feasible (cost-effective) way. A revenue object is anything for which a separate measurement of revenue is desired. Examples of revenue objects are products, customers, and divisions.

11. In cases where managers have revenue or profit responsibility for individual products (or services), an important revenue allocation issue arises when **bundled products** are sold. A bundled product is a package of two or more products (or services) that is sold for a single price but whose individual components may be sold as separate items at their own "stand-alone" prices. The price of a bundled product is typically less than the sum of the prices of the individual products sold separately.

12. There are two main methods for allocating bundled product revenues to the individual products in the bundle.

- The **stand-alone revenue-allocation method** uses product-specific information on the products in the bundle as weights for allocating the bundled revenues to the individual products. Three types of weights for the stand-alone method are selling prices, unit costs, and physical units. Selling prices are preferred because they better capture the benefits received by customers who purchase a bundled product.

- The **incremental revenue-allocation method** ranks individual products in a bundle according to criteria determined by management—such as the product in the bundle with the most sales—and then uses this ranking to allocate bundled revenues to the individual products. The first-ranked product in the bundle is the *primary product*, the second-ranked product is the *first incremental product*, the third-ranked product is the *second incremental product*, and so on.

Featured Exercise

The following information is for Moran Manufacturing Company:

	Support Departments		Operating Departments	
	T	V	1	2
Budgeted manufacturing overhead before allocation of support dept. costs	$60,000	$80,000	$30,000	$25,000
Proportions of service provided by T	–	30%	50%	20%
Proportions of service provided by V	10%	–	60%	30%

a. Complete the schedule below using the direct method to allocate the costs of the support departments to Departments 1 and 2.

	T	V	1	2	Total
Budgeted manufacturing overhead before allocation of support dept. costs	$60,000	$80,000	$30,000	$25,000	$195,000
Allocation of T					
Allocation of V					
	$ 0	$ 0			
Total budgeted manufacturing overhead of operating departments			$_____	$_____	$195,000

b. Complete the schedule below using the step-down method to allocate the costs of the support departments to Departments 1 and 2. Allocate Department T first.

	T	V	1	2	Total
Budgeted manufacturing overhead before allocation of support dept. costs	$60,000	$80,000	$30,000	$25,000	$195,000
Allocation of T					
Allocation of V					
	$ 0	$ 0			
Total budgeted manufacturing overhead of operating departments			$_____	$_____	$195,000

c. Complete the schedule below using the reciprocal method to allocate the costs of the support departments to Departments 1 and 2. (Hint: the first step is to formulate and solve two linear equations).

	T	V	1	2	Total
Budgeted manufacturing overhead before allocation of support dept. costs	$60,000	$80,000	$30,000	$25,000	$195,000
Allocation of T					
Allocation of V					
	$ 0	$ 0			
Total budgeted manufacturing overhead of operating departments			$_____	$_____	$195,000

Solution

a. Direct method:

	T	V	1	2	Total
Budgeted manufacturing overhead before allocation of support dept. costs	$60,000	$80,000	$ 30,000	$25,000	$195,000
Allocation of T (5/7, 2/7)[1]	(60,000)		42,857	17,143	
Allocation of V (6/9, 3/9)[2]		(80,000)	53,333	26,667	
	$ 0	$ 0			
Total budgeted manufacturing overhead of operating departments			$126,190	$68,810	$195,000

[1]50%/(50% + 20%); 20%/(50% + 20%)
[2]60%/(60% + 30%); 30%/(60% + 30%)

b. Step-down method:

	T	V	1	2	Total
Budgeted manufacturing overhead before allocation of support dept. costs	$60,000	$80,000	$ 30,000	$25,000	$195,000
Allocation of T (30%, 50%, 20%)	(60,000)	18,000	30,000	12,000	
Allocation of V (6/9, 3/9)[1]		(98,000)	65,333	32,667	
	$ 0	$ 0			
Total budgeted manufacturing overhead of operating departments			$125,333	$69,667	$195,000

[1]60%/(60% + 30%); 30%/(60% + 30%)

c. Reciprocal method:

	T	V	1	2	Total
Budgeted manufacturing overhead before allocation of support dept. costs	$60,000	$80,000	$ 30,000	$25,000	$195,000
Allocation of T: (see below)	(70,103)	21,031[1]	35,051[2]	14,021[3]	
Allocation of V: (see below)	10,103[4]	(101,031)	60,619[5]	30,309[6]	
	$ 0	$ 0			
Total budgeted manufacturing overhead of operating departments			$125,670	$69,330	$195,000

$T = \$60,000 + 0.10V$
$V = \$80,000 + 0.30T$

$T = \$60,000 + 0.10(\$80,000 + 0.30T)$
$T = \$60,000 + \$8,000 + 0.03T$
$0.97T = \$68,000$
$T = \$70,103$

$V = \$80,000 + 0.30(\$70,103)$
$V = \$80,000 + \$21,031 = \$101,031$

[1]30% × $70,103 = $21,031
[2]50% × $70,103 = $35,051
[3]20% × $70,103 = $14,021
[4]10% × $101,031 = $10,103
[5]60% × $101,031 = $60,619
[6]30% × $101,031 = $30,309

Review Questions and Exercises

Completion Statements

Fill in the blank(s) to complete each statement.

1. The _____ method of cost allocation uses a variable-cost pool and a fixed-cost pool.

2. The _____ method allocates support departments costs to other support departments and to operating departments in a sequential manner that partially recognizes the mutual services provided among all support departments.

3. The _____ method allocates support department costs to operating departments by fully recognizing the mutual services provided among support departments.

4. The cost of operating a facility, activity, or like cost object that is shared by two or more users is called a _____ cost.

5. An _____ cost is a cost that the contract parties agree to include in the costs to be reimbursed.

6. CASB stands for _____ _____.

7. A _____ is anything for which a separate measurement of revenue is desired.

8. A _____ is a package of two or more products (or services) that is sold for a single price but whose individual components may be sold as separate items at their own "stand-alone" prices.

True-False

Indicate whether each statement is true (T) or false (F)

_____ 1. To allocate the fixed costs of a supplier department so that fluctuations of usage in one user department do not affect charges to other user departments, the allocation should be based on actual usage in the current accounting period.

_____ 2. For a given support department providing services to other support departments, its complete reciprocated costs are always larger than its actual costs.

_____ 3. A major reason for allocating support department costs to operating departments in a manufacturing company is to compute budgeted department overhead cost rates.

_____ 4. If two users share a facility such as a mailroom, the primary user prefers the common costs be allocated using the incremental cost-allocation method.

_____ 5. Expenditures for lobbying activities are not allowable costs in U.S. government contracts.

_____ 6. If a manager is deciding whether to keep or discontinue a product, the product is both the revenue object and the cost object.

_____ 7. The selling price of a bundled product is typically less than the sum of the prices of the individual products sold separately.

_____ 8. The stand-alone revenue-allocation method ranks individual products in a bundle according to criteria determined by management and then uses this ranking to allocate bundled revenues to individual products.

Multiple Choice

Select the best answer to each question. Space is provided for computations after the quantitative questions.

_____ 1. The most accurate and most widely used method for allocating support department costs is:
   a. the direct method.
   b. the step-down method.
   c. the reciprocal method.
   d. none of the above.

2. (CPA adapted) Boa Corp. allocates support department overhead costs to operating departments X and Y by means of the reciprocal method. Information for the current month is as follows:

| | Support Departments | |
	A	B
Overhead costs	$20,000	$10,000

Services provided
to departments:

	A	B
A	–	10%
B	20%	–
X	40%	30%
Y	40%	60%
	100%	100%

The linear equation to be used in the allocation of Department A's costs is:
a. A = $20,000 + 0.20B.
b. A = $10,000 + 0.10B.
c. A = $10,000 + 0.20B.
d. A = $20,000 + 0.10B.

3. Bixler Manufacturing Company uses the step-down method for allocating its support department costs to operating departments. The overhead costs of support Department A are to be allocated first, followed by the costs of B, and then those of C. The distribution of services is:

Service Supplied By	Support Depts.			Operating Depts.	
	A	B	C	X	Y
A	–	10%	50%	20%	20%
B	40%	–	15%	30%	15%
C	25%	25%	–	20%	30%

The percentage of B's costs that should be allocated to Y is:
a. 15%.
b. 33⅓%.
c. 25%.
d. none of the above.

4. Using the information in question 3, the percentage of C's costs that should be allocated to B under the step-down method is:
a. 0%.
b. 20%.
c. 33⅓%.
d. none of the above.

5. (CMA adapted) The Cost Accounting Standards Board's purpose is to:
a. develop accounting principles and standard practices for industry.
b. develop uniform cost accounting standards to be used in pricing, administration, and settlement of negotiated government contracts.
c. work in conjunction with the Securities and Exchange Commission in examining registration forms and financial statements filed by corporations.
d. aid the Financial Accounting Standards Board in establishing accounting standards.

6. Revenue objects include:

	Customers	Distribution Channels
a.	No	No
b.	No	Yes
c.	Yes	No
d.	Yes	Yes

7. Under the stand-alone revenue-allocation method, which weights better capture the benefits received by customers who purchase a bundled product?
a. Selling prices and physical units
b. Selling prices and unit costs
c. Selling prices and stand-alone product revenues
d. Stand-alone product revenues and physical units

Review Exercises

1. Hanover Company's power plant provides electricity for its two operating departments, A and B. The 2011 budget for the power plant shows:

Budgeted fixed costs $80,000
Budgeted variable cost
   per kilowatt hour (kwh) $0.20

Additional data for 2011:

	Budget (kwh)	Actual (kwh)
Department A	240,000	215,000
Department B	160,000	195,000

Actual power-plant costs: fixed $92,000, variable $88,000

a. Compute the budgeted power-plant costs allocated to A and B using the single-rate method with budgeted usage as the allocation base.
b. Compute the budgeted power-plant costs allocated to A and B using the dual-rate method with actual usage as the allocation base for variable costs and budgeted usage as the allocation base for fixed costs.
c. From the standpoint of Departments A and B, what are the two main benefits of the dual-rate method described in (b)?

2. Adams Company and Baker Company are in noncompeting lines of business and use a common database for marketing purposes. The variable costs associated with accessing the database are readily identifiable and kept in separate cost pools that are charged to each user. The fixed costs of maintaining the database, however, cannot be identified by user on a cause-and-effect basis. These fixed costs for next year are budgeted at $55,000. If Baker does not use the database, the fixed costs to Adams are $48,000. An outside vendor offers to provide Adams access to a comparable database for a fixed fee of $60,000 per year plus variable costs of accessing the database. The same vendor offers to provide Baker access to that database for a fixed fee of $20,000 per year plus variable costs of accessing the database.

Compute how much of the $55,000 fixed costs of maintaining the database are charged to each user:
a. Under the stand-alone cost-allocation method.
b. Under the incremental cost-allocation method, assuming Adams is regarded as the primary user.

3. Van Sickle Tours is located in Atlanta. The company sells "mini-vacation" travel packages. A travel package consists of air travel, lodging, and a multiple-day scenic bus tour of the local sights. Each of the three revenue components of travel packages is the responsibility of a different manager. One of Van Sickle's most popular travel packages is the two-person, three-day "Fall Foliage of Vermont" priced at $849. This package consists of:

- Two round-trip airline tickets (Atlanta to Burlington, Vermont)—separately priced at $330 per person.
- Three nights' lodging—separately priced at $130 per night for two people.
- Three-day sightseeing bus tour—separately priced at $125 per person.

Allocate the $849 Vermont-package revenue to the three components of the travel package using:
a. The stand-alone revenue-allocation method.
b. The incremental revenue-allocation method (with the bus tour as the primary product, lodging as the first incremental product, and air travel as the second incremental product).
For both methods, use selling prices as the weights. Round all computations to the nearest dollar.

Answers and Solutions to Chapter 15 Review Questions and Exercises

Completion Statements

1. dual-rate
2. step-down
3. reciprocal (matrix)
4. common
5. Allowable
6. Cost Accounting Standards Board
7. revenue object
8. bundled product

True-False

1. F   Exhibit 15-1, text p.549, shows that using *actual usage* does affect the allocation of fixed costs to departments when fluctuations occur in actual usage. Allocation is not affected by fluctuations in usage, however, if the allocation base is *budgeted usage*.

2. T

3. T

4. F   The example, text pp.557-558, allocates the Albany employer (the primary user) $1,200 under the incremental method but only $900 under the stand-alone method.

5. T

6. T

7. T

8. F   The statement describes the *incremental revenue-allocation method*, not the *stand-alone revenue-allocation method*. The stand-alone method uses product-specific information on products in the bundle as weights for allocating bundled revenues to the individual products.

Multiple Choice

1. d   The reciprocal method is the most accurate method for allocating support department costs because it fully recognizes the mutual services provided among all support departments. The direct method is the most widely used method because of its simplicity.

2. d   The equation must include A's own costs *plus its percentage use of B's services*, which is 10%.

3. c   Department A's costs have already been allocated, so its usage of B's services (40%) should be disregarded in answering this question: $0.15 \div (0.15 + 0.30 + 0.15) = 0.15 \div 0.60 = 0.25$, or 25%. Note, the sequence of allocating the costs of the support departments in the question is consistent with the popular step-down sequence based on the percentage of a support department's total services provided to other support departments.

Order of Allocation	% of a Support Department's Total Services Provided to Other Support Departments
1st A	10% to B + 50% to C = 60%
2nd B	40% to A + 15% to C = 55%
3rd C	25% to A + 25% to B = 50%

4. a Once a support department's costs are allocated under the step-down method, no support department costs are allocated back to it.

5. b The purpose of the CASB is to promulgate cost accounting standards to achieve *uniformity* and *consistency* in regard to measurement, assignment, and allocation of costs to contracts. Note, answer (a) is incorrect because only *cost* accounting standards (as distinguished from *financial* accounting standards) are promulgated by the CASB.

6. d A revenue object is anything for which a separate measurement of revenues is desired. Examples of revenue objects are products, customers, divisions, distribution channels, and the like.

7. c Three types of weights for the stand-alone revenue-allocation method are selling prices, unit costs, and physical units. Selling prices are preferred because they better capture the benefits received by customers who purchase a bundled product.

Review Exercise 1

a.
$$\text{Total pool of budgeted costs} = \$80,000 + (240,000 + 160,000)\$0.20$$
$$= \$80,000 + \$80,000 = \$160,000$$
$$\text{Budgeted cost per kwh} = \$160,000 \div (240,000 + 160,000)$$
$$= \$160,000 \div 400,000 = \$0.40$$
$$\text{Total costs allocated to A} = 215,000 \times \$0.40 = \$86,000$$
$$\text{Total costs allocated to B} = 195,000 \times \$0.40 = \$78,000$$

b. Fixed cost allocation:
$$\text{To A} = \left[240,000 \div (240,000 + 160,000)\right] \times \$80,000 = 0.60 \times \$80,000 = \$48,000$$
$$\text{To B} = \left[160,000 \div (240,000 + 160,000)\right] \times \$80,000 = 0.40 \times \$80,000 = \$32,000$$

Total cost allocation:
$$\text{To A} = \$48,000 + (215,000 \times \$0.20) = \$48,000 + \$43,000 = \$91,000$$
$$\text{To B} = \$32,000 + (195,000 \times \$0.20) = \$32,000 + \$39,000 = \$71,000$$

c. First, costs allocated to each department are not affected by the kwh usage of the other department. Second, inefficiencies in the power plant are not charged to Departments A and B because both variable and fixed costs are allocated using budgeted rates.

Review Exercise 2

a. Total individual stand-alone costs = $60,000 + $20,000 = $80,000
   Allocated to Adams = ($60,000 ÷ $80,000) × $55,000 = $41,250
   Allocated to Baker = ($20,000 ÷ $80,000) × $55,000 = $13,750

b. Adams, the primary user, bears $48,000.
   Baker, the incremental user, bears $55,000 − $48,000 = $7,000.

Review Exercise 3

a. Stand-alone revenues:

Air travel, $330 × 2	$ 660
Lodging, $130 × 3	390
Bus tour, $125 × 2	250
Total	$1,300

Stand-alone revenue-allocation method:

Allocation to air travel = ($660 ÷ $1,300) × $849 = $431
Allocation to lodging   = ($390 ÷ $1,300) × $849 =   255
Allocation to bus tour = ($250 ÷ $1,300) × $849 =   163
Total Vermont-package revenue $849

b. Incremental revenue-allocation method:

Components Listed in Order of Allocation	Revenue Allocated	Revenue Remaining to Be Allocated to Other Components
Bus tour, $125 × 2	$250	$849 − $250 = $599
Lodging, $130 × 3	390	$599 − $390 = $209
Air travel	209	$209 − $209 = $0
Total Vermont-package revenue	$849	

CHAPTER 16

Cost Allocation: Joint Products and Byproducts

Overview

The main focus of this chapter is to explain methods of allocating **joint costs** to products. Joint costs are the costs of a production process that yields multiple products simultaneously (for example, the costs of processing raw milk into cream and skim milk). The purpose of allocating joint costs to individual products is to measure income and assets for external reporting. For economic decisions, allocating joint costs provides misleading information to managers. These decisions should be guided by the relevant-revenue and relevant-cost analysis introduced in Chapter 11. The chapter concludes with a description of accounting for byproducts.

Highlights

1. In a joint-production process, the juncture where two or more products become separately identifiable is the **splitoff point**. **Separable costs** are all costs—manufacturing, marketing, distribution, and so on—incurred beyond the splitoff point that are assignable to each of the specific products identified at the splitoff point. For example, the joint production process of milling timber (logs) yields various grades of lumber as well as sawdust and wood chips. The splitoff point is where individual boards are cut from the timber. The costs of planing these boards into finished lumber are separable costs of the finished lumber.

2. A joint production process can yield **joint products** (or a **main product**) and **byproducts**. Joint products are two or more products that have high total sales values compared with the total sales values of other products of a joint production process. When a joint production process yields only one product that has a high total sales value, compared to the total sales values of the other products of the process, that product is called a main product. Byproducts are products of a joint production process that have low total sales values compared with the total sales value of the main

product or joint products. A joint product can become a byproduct (or vice versa) if its market price increases or decreases by, say, 30% or more in a year.

3. Four methods of allocating joint costs are the **sales value at splitoff method**, **physical measure method**, **net realizable value (NRV) method**, and **constant gross-margin percentage NRV method**. All of the methods except the physical measure method base their allocations on market-price data.

4. The *sales value at splitoff method* allocates joint costs to joint products produced during the accounting period on the basis of the relative total sales value at the splitoff point. Joint products *produced during the accounting period* is used because joint costs are incurred for *all units produced*, not just those sold in the current period. The sales value at splitoff method exemplifies the benefits-received criterion of cost allocation: costs are allocated to products in proportion to their ability to contribute revenues. This method is widely used when market prices for the individual products are available at the splitoff point, even if further processing occurs.

5. The *physical measure method* allocates joint costs to joint products produced during the accounting period on the basis of the relative weight, volume, or other physical measure at the splitoff point. The major criticism of this method is that the physical measure used for allocating joint costs may have no relationship to the revenue-generating power of the individual products.

6. The *net realizable value (NRV) method* allocates joint costs to joint products produced during the accounting period on the basis of their relative NRV—final sales value minus separable costs. Because separable costs are used in the computations, the NRV method does not meet the benefits-received criterion as well as the sales value at split-off method. However, it is impossible to

use the sales value at splitoff method unless market prices for the individual products are available at the split-off point.

7. The *constant gross-margin percentage NRV method* allocates joint costs to joint products produced during the accounting period in such a way that the overall gross-margin percentage is identical for the individual products. The rationale for the constant gross-margin percentage NRV method is that, given the arbitrary nature of joint-cost allocation under any method, none of the individual products show a loss.

8. All the methods for allocating joint costs to individual products are subject to criticism. As a result, some companies refrain entirely from this allocation. Instead, they carry their inventories at NRV, which recognizes income on each product when production is completed. Industries that use variations of the no-allocation approach include meatpacking, canning, and mining.

9. In joint-cost situations, managers must often decide whether to sell joint products (or a main product) at the splitoff point or process them (it) further. *Because joint costs incurred up to the splitoff point are past (sunk) costs, they are irrelevant to the sell-or-process further decision.* In other words, the sell-or-process further decision should *not* be influenced either by the total amount of joint costs or by the portion of joint costs allocated to individual products. *It is profitable to process a product beyond the splitoff point when the incremental revenues resulting from that processing exceed the incremental costs.* Note: separable costs of a product (defined in paragraph 1) are usually greater than incremental costs of further processing the product beyond the splitoff point. That's because separable costs include an allocated amount of fixed manufacturing overhead, but total fixed manufacturing overhead often remains the same whether or not the product is processed further.

10. Joint production processes may yield not only joint products or a main product but byproducts as well. Byproducts are accounted for under either the *production method* or the *sales method*.

- The production method recognizes byproducts in the financial statements *at the time their production is completed*: increase (debit) Byproduct Inventory and decrease (credit) Work in Process for the NRV of the byproducts produced. Crediting Work in Process reduces the amount of joint costs allocated to the joint products (or the main product). When sales of byproducts occur, increase (debit) Cash or Accounts Receivable and decrease (credit) Byproduct Inventory.
- The sales method recognizes byproducts in the financial statements *at the time they are sold*: increase (debit) Cash or Accounts Receivable and increase (credit) Byproduct Revenues. Under this method, no joint costs are allocated to the byproducts, and there is no general-ledger account for Byproduct Inventory.

The production method is conceptually superior but the sales method is widely used because the amount of revenues from byproducts tends to be immaterial.

Featured Exercise

Cascade Sawmill manufactures two lumber products in a joint milling process. The products are mine support braces (MSB) and commercial building lumber (CBL). A production run results in 60,000 units of MSB and 90,000 units of CBL at the splitoff point. The joint costs are $300,000. MSB and CBL can be sold at splitoff for $1.50 per unit and $4 per unit, respectively.

a. Compute the amount of total joint costs allocated to MSB and CBL using the physical measure method.
b. Compute the amount of total joint costs allocated to MSB and CBL using the sales value at splitoff method.
c. Assume CBL is not salable at the splitoff point; it must be further planed and sized, requiring separable costs of $200,000. During this process, 10,000 units are unavoidably spoiled; this spoilage has zero sales value. The good units of CBL can be sold at $10 per unit. The MSB is coated with a tar-like preservative requiring separable costs of $100,000. After further processing, MSB can be sold for $5 per unit. Compute the inventoriable cost per unit of MSB and CBL using the net realizable value method.
d. Assume incremental costs of further processing are 90% of separable costs. Compute the change in operating income that results from further processing of MSB.

Solution (on next page)

Solution

a.

	MSB	CBL	Total
Physical measure of production (units)	60,000	90,000	150,000
Weighting (60,000 ÷ 150,000; 90,000 ÷ 150,000)	0.40	0.60	
Joint costs allocated (0.40 × $300,000; 0.60 × $300,000)	$120,000	$180,000	$300,000

b.

	MSB	CBL	Total
Sales value at splitoff (60,000 × $1.50; 90,000 × $4)	$90,000	$360,000	$450,000
Weighting ($90,000 ÷ $450,000; $360,000 ÷ $450,000)	0.20	0.80	
Joint costs allocated (0.20 × $300,000; 0.80 × $300,000)	$60,000	$240,000	$300,000

c.

	MSB	CBL	Total
Final sales value of production 60,000 × $5;[(90,000 − 10,000) × $10]	$300,000	$800,000	$1,100,000
Deduct separable costs to complete and sell	100,000	200,000	300,000
Net realizable value at split-off point	$200,000	$600,000	$ 800,000
Weighting ($200,000 ÷ $800,000; $600,000 ÷ $800,000)	0.25	0.75	
Joint costs allocated (0.25 × $300,000; 0.75 × $300,000)	$75,000	$225,000	$300,000
Inventoriable cost per unit ($75,000 + $100,000) ÷ 60,000	$2.92		
($225,000 + $200,000) ÷ (90,000 − 10,000)		$5.31	

d.

Incremental revenues, (60,000 × $5) − (60,000 × $1.50)	$210,000
Deduct incremental costs, $100,000 × 0.90	90,000
Increase in operating income	$120,000

Review Questions and Exercises

Completion Statements

Fill in the blank(s) to complete each statement.

1. The juncture in a joint production process at which two or more products become separately identifiable is called the _____ _____.

2. When a joint production process yields only one product that has a high total sales value, compared with the total sales values of the other products of the process, that product is called a _____.

3. All costs—manufacturing, marketing, distribution, and so on—incurred beyond the splitoff point that are assignable to each of the specific products identified at the splitoff point are called _____ costs.

4. _____ are products of a joint production process that have low total sales values compared with the total sales value of the main product or joint products.

5. The _____ of a product is equal to its final sales value minus its separable costs.

6. Of the methods for allocating joint costs to products, which three use market-price data:

_____

_____

_____

True-False

Indicate whether each statement is true (T) or false (F).

____ 1. Joint products have high total sales values compared with the total sales values of other products of the joint production process and must be salable at the splitoff point.

____ 2. The amount of joint costs to be allocated should not be considered in choosing the allocation method.

____ 3. The net realizable value (NRV) method recognizes the revenue-generating power of the individual products and presupposes management decisions on further-processing steps to be undertaken after the splitoff point.

____ 4. The constant gross-margin percentage NRV method is sometimes preferred to set a fair selling price in rate-regulation situations because it avoids the circular reasoning of other methods.

____ 5. The sales value at splitoff method allocates joint costs on the basis of the relative total sales value at the splitoff point of the units sold during the accounting period.

____ 6. The main criticism of the physical measure method is that the measure used may have no relationship to the revenue-generating power of the individual products.

____ 7. Allocation of joint costs assists managers in deciding whether joint products should be sold at the splitoff point or processed further.

____ 8. Byproducts are the portion of production of a main product or joint products that has been further processed.

____ 9. In accounting for byproducts, when no joint costs are allocated to them, there will be no Byproduct Inventory account in the general ledger.

Multiple Choice

Select the best answer to each question. Space is provided for computations after the quantitative questions.

____ 1. (CPA) O'Connor Company manufactures Products J and K from a joint process. For Product J, 4,000 units are produced having a total sales value at splitoff of $15,000. If Product J were processed further, the separable costs would be $3,000 and the final total sales value would be $20,000. For Product K, 2,000 are produced having a total sales value at splitoff of $10,000. If Product K were processed further, the separable costs would be $1,000 and the final total sales value would be $12,000. Using the sales value at splitoff method, the portion of the total joint costs allocated to Product J is $9,000. The total joint costs are:
   a. $14,400.
   b. $15,000.
   c. $18,400.
   d. $19,000.

____ 2. If the constant gross-margin percentage NRV method is used and the overall gross margin of the joint products is 40%, the amount of joint costs allocated to a joint product with a final total sales value of $1,800 and separable costs of $400 is:
   a. $1,080.
   b. $780.
   c. $720.
   d. $680.

3. (CPA adapted) Ohio Corporation manufactures liquid chemicals A and B from a joint process. Joint costs are allocated on the basis of sales value at splitoff. It costs $13,680 to process 500 gallons of A and 1,000 gallons of B up to the splitoff point. The sales value at splitoff is $10 per gallon for A and $14 per gallon for B. B requires additional processing beyond splitoff at separable cost of $1 per gallon before it can be sold. Assuming the 1,000 gallons of B are processed further and sold for $18 per gallon, Ohio's gross margin on this sale is:
   a. $7,920.
   b. $7,420.
   c. $7,880.
   d. $6,920.

4. (CPA) Actual total sales values at the split-off point for joint Products Y and Z are not known. For purposes of allocating joint costs to Products Y and Z, the net realizable value method is used. Assume an increase in the separable costs beyond splitoff for Product Z occurs, while those of Product Y remain constant. If the selling prices of finished Products Y and Z remain constant, the percentage of the total joint costs allocated to Product Y and Product Z:
   a. decreases for both products.
   b. increases for Y and decreases for Z.
   c. decreases for Y and increases for Z.
   d. increases for both products.

5. (CMA) Copeland Inc. produces X-547 in a joint production process. The company is considering whether to sell X-547 at the splitoff point or process the product further to produce Xylene. The following information is available.

   (1) Selling price per pound of X-547.
   (2) Variable manufacturing costs of further processing.
   (3) Avoidable fixed costs of further processing.
   (4) Selling price per pound of Xylene.
   (5) Joint costs to produce X-547.

   Which items are relevant to the upgrade decision?
   a. 1, 2, 4.
   b. 1, 2, 3, 4.
   c. 1, 2, 3, 4, 5.
   d. 1, 2, 4, 5.
   e. 2, 3.

6. (CPA) Crowley Company produces joint Products A and B from a process that also yields a byproduct, Y. The byproduct requires additional processing before it can be sold. The cost assigned to the byproduct is its market value minus additional costs incurred after splitoff. Information concerning a batch produced in the current month at joint costs of $40,000 is as follows:

Product	Units Produced	Market Value	Costs After Splitoff
A	800	$44,000	$4,500
B	700	32,000	3,500
Y	500	4,000	1,000

   How much of the joint costs should be allocated to the joint products?
   a. $36,000
   b. $37,000
   c. $39,000
   d. $40,000

Review Exercises

1. The Tri-Ken Corporation incurred $3,000 to produce the following products in a joint production process:

	Product T	Product K
Quantity produced and processed beyond splitoff point	130 units	390 units
Separable costs	$1,000	$1,460
Selling price of a fully processed unit	$40	$10

    a. Compute the amount of joint costs allocated to each product using the physical measure method.

    b. Based on your allocation of joint costs in part (a), compute the gross margin of Product T, Product K, and both products together, assuming all units are sold.

    c. Compute the amount of joint costs allocated to each product using the NRV method.

    d. Compute the amount of joint costs allocated to each product using the constant gross-margin percentage NRV method.

    e. If the selling prices at splitoff are $34 per unit for Product T and $4 per unit for Product K, is it profitable to further process either or both products? Assume incremental costs are 80% of separable costs. Show your computations.

2. The Cambridge Chemical Company prepared the following data for the month just ended:

Total manufacturing costs of a joint production process	$75,000
Revenues of main product	100,000
Net realizable value of byproduct produced	2,000
Beginning inventories	none

Ending inventory of the main product is 10% of the quantity produced. Ending inventory of the byproduct is 30% of the quantity produced.

Compute the gross margin of the main product, assuming the sales method is used to account for the byproduct.

Answers and Solutions to Chapter 16 Review Questions and Exercises

Completion Statements

1. splitoff point
2. main product
3. separable
4. Byproducts
5. net realizable value (NRV)
6. sales value at splitoff method, net realizable value (NRV) method, constant gross-margin percentage NRV method

True-False

1. F Joint products have high total sales values compared to the total sales values of other products of the joint production process, but joint products may or may not be salable at the splitoff point.
2. T
3. T
4. F The methods using market-price data-sales value at splitoff, NRV, and constant gross-margin percentage NRV involve circular reasoning for setting prices. That is, they use selling prices to allocate joint costs that serve, in turn, as a basis for setting selling prices. Only the physical measure method avoids this circular reasoning because it does not use market-price data.
5. F The sales value at splitoff method allocates joint costs on the basis of the relative total sales value of total units *produced* during the accounting period. This method exemplifies the benefits-received criterion of cost allocation: costs are allocated to products in proportion to their ability to contribute revenues.
6. T
7. F Allocation of joint costs is irrelevant to the decision of whether joint products or a main product should be sold at the splitoff point or further processed. That's because the *total amount* of the joint costs remains the same whether or not further processing occurs. Only *incremental revenues and incremental costs beyond the splitoff point* are relevant to the sell-or-process-further decision.
8. F Byproducts are products of a joint production process that have low total sales values compared with the total sales values of joint products or a main product. Byproducts are identified at the splitoff point; they may or may not require further processing.
9. T

Multiple Choice

1. b   Total sales value at splitoff of the two products together = $15,000 + $10,000 = $25,000; the portion of joint costs allocated to Product J = $15,000 ÷ $25,000 = 60%, so total joint costs = $9,000 ÷ 0.60 = $15,000. Note: it is a coincidence the sales value at splitoff of Product J is the same amount as total joint costs, $15,000. Also note: in using the sales value at splitoff method, ignore information regarding processing of the products beyond the splitoff point.

2. d
Final total sales value of joint product	$1,800
Deduct gross margin, $1,800 × 0.40	720
Cost of goods sold	1,080
Deduct separable costs	400
Joint costs allocated	$ 680

3. d   Total sales value at splitoff:
A, 500 × $10	$ 5,000
B, 1,000 × $14	14,000
Total sales value at splitoff	$19,000
Cost of Product B (fully processed):	
Allocation of joint costs,	
($14,000 ÷ $19,000) × $13,680	$10,080
Separable costs, 1,000 × $1	1,000
Cost of goods sold	$11,080
Revenues, 1,000 units of B × $18	$18,000
Cost of goods sold	11,080
Gross margin of B	$ 6,920

4. b An effective way to answer this question is to assume a set of "before change" figures. Next, select an amount for the increase in separable costs of Product Z; $2,000 is used in the following computations. Then, compute "after change" amounts by incorporating the increase in the separable costs of Product Z.

	Before Change	
	Y	Z
Final sales value of total production	$9,000	$8,000
Deduct separable costs	3,000	4,000
Net realizable value	$6,000	$4,000
Joint cost allocation percentage:		
$6,000 ÷ ($6,000 + $4,000)	60%	
$4,000 ÷ ($6,000 + $4,000)		40%

	After Change	
	Y	Z
Final total sales value of total production	$9,000	$8,000
Deduct separable costs	3,000	6,000
Net realizable value	$6,000	$2,000
Joint cost allocation percentage:		
$6,000 ÷ ($6,000 + $2,000)	75%	
$2,000 ÷ ($6,000 + $2,000)		25%

The percentage of total joint costs allocated to Product Y increases to 75% from 60%—as a result of its separable costs increasing to $6,000 from $4,000—and decreases for Product Z to 25% from 40%.

5. b The first four items are relevant to the decision because they will differ depending on whether X-547 is sold at the splitoff point or processed further. Item 5 is irrelevant to the decision because it is the same under either alternative.

6. b This question uses the production method to account for the byproduct.
Joint costs allocated to the byproduct = $4,000 − $1,000 = $3,000
Joint costs allocated to the joint products = $40,000 − $3,000 = $37,000

Review Exercise 1

a. Allocation of joint costs:
To T: 130 ÷ (130 + 390) × $3,000 = $750
To K: 390 ÷ (130 + 390) × $3,000 = $2,250

b.

	T	K	Total
Revenues, 130 × $40; 390 × $10	$5,200	$3,900	$9,100
Cost of goods sold			
Joint costs (computed above)	750	2,250	3,000
Separable costs	1,000	1,460	2,460
Cost of goods sold	1,750	3,710	5,460
Gross margin	$3,450	$ 190	$3,640

c.

	T	K	Total
Final sales value of total production			
130 × $40; 390 × $10	$5,200	$3,900	$9,100

Deduct separable costs	1,000	1,460	2,460
Net realizable value	$4,200	$2,440	$6,640
Allocation of $3,000 joint costs:			
To T: ($4,200 ÷ $6,640) × $3,000	$1,898		
To K: ($2,440 ÷ $6,640) × $3,000		$1,102	

d.

			Total
Final sales value of total production			
(130 × $40) + (390 × $10)			$9,100
Cost of goods sold			
Total joint costs		$3,000	
Total separable costs		2,460	5,460
Gross margin of both products together			$3,640
Gross margin percentage of both products			
together, $3,640 ÷ $9,100			40%

	T	K	Total
Final sales value of total production	$5,200	$3,900	$9,100
Deduct gross margin at 40%	2,080	1,560	3,640
Total manufacturing costs	3,120	2,340	5,460
Deduct separable costs	1,000	1,460	2,460
Joint costs allocated	$2,120	$ 880	$3,000

	T	K
Incremental revenue beyond splitoff		
($40 − $34) × 130; ($10 − $4) × 390	$780	$2,340
Incremental costs beyond splitoff, which		
are 80% of separable costs		
$1,000 × 0.80; $1,460 × 0.80	800	1,168
Operating income (loss) from further processing	$(20)	$1,172

Review Exercise 2

Revenues		
Main product		$100,000
Byproduct, $2,000 × 0.70		1,400
Total revenues		101,400
Cost of goods sold		
Total manufacturing costs	$75,000	
Deduct ending inventory		
of main product, $75,000 × 0.10	7,500	67,500
Gross margin		$ 33,900

CHAPTER 17 | Process Costing

Overview

This chapter explains how process-costing systems determine the cost of products or services. In the simplest case, a process has no beginning or ending work-in-process inventory. Considerable complexity is added when a process has both beginning and ending work-in-process inventory; this case necessitates selecting an inventory cost-flow method. The chapter illustrates two of these methods: the weighted-average method and the first-in, first-out (FIFO) method. Many detailed exhibits are included in the chapter because *process costing is highly procedural*. The chapter also explains how operation-costing systems determine the cost of products. The Appendix to the chapter describes the standard-costing method of process costing.

Highlights

1. In a *process-costing system*, the unit cost of a product (or service) is obtained by assigning total costs to many identical or similar units of output. A process-costing system separates costs into cost categories according to the timing of when costs are introduced into the process. Often only two cost classifications—direct materials and conversion costs—are necessary to assign costs to products. *The key feature of process costing is that it averages production costs over all units produced.* Industries using process costing include chemical, pharmaceutical, and semiconductor.

2. The chapter uses three cases to illustrate process costing of cell-phone model SG-40 in the Assembly Department of Pacific Electronics. The following table shows the cases differ in regard to whether or not the Assembly Department has work-in-process inventory.

	Beginning Inventory	Ending Inventory
Case 1	No	No
Case 2	No	Yes
Case 3	Yes	Yes

3. Case 1 is simple because there is no work-in-process inventory in the Assembly Department. That is, all units of SG-40 are started and completed during the accounting period. The unit cost of the 400 units of SG-40 in this case is computed as follows:

Direct material costs	
$32,000 ÷ 400	$ 80
Conversion costs	
$24,000 ÷ 400	60
Cost per unit	$140

4. Case 2 has some unfinished units of SG-40 in the Assembly Department at the end of the accounting period but no beginning work-in-process inventory. Whenever there is an ending work-in-process inventory (*with or without beginning work-in-process inventory*), use a five-step procedure to compute the cost of fully completed and partially completed units:

Step 1: Summarize the flow of physical units of output.
Step 2: Compute output in terms of **equivalent units**.
Step 3: Summarize total costs to account for.
Step 4: Compute cost per equivalent unit.
Step 5: Assign total costs to units completed and to units in ending work in process.

Steps 1 and 2 deal only with units, whereas Steps 3, 4, and 5 incorporate costs. Step 1 tracks where *physical units* come from and where they go to during the accounting period. That is, units in beginning inventory + units started = units completed + units in ending inventory. In Step 2, *equivalent units* is a derived amount of output units that (a) takes the quantity of each input (factor of production) in units completed and in incomplete units of work in process, and (b) converts the quantity of input into the amount of completed output units that could be produced with that quantity of input. For SG-40, direct materials are added at the beginning of the process in the Assembly Department, and conversion costs are added evenly throughout the process. EXHIBIT 17-1, text p.611, shows the details for Steps 1 and 2 in Case 2.

5. The accuracy of the completion percentages used for partially completed units in equivalent unit computations depends on the care and skill of the estimator and the nature of the process. Estimating the degree of completion is usually easier for direct materials than for conversion costs. *That's* because the quantity of direct materials needed for a completed unit and a partially completed unit can be measured accurately, whereas it is more difficult to measure what proportion of the total conversion costs needed to complete units has been used for the units still in process. Because of the difficulties in estimating completion percentages for conversion costs, department supervisors and line managers—individuals most familiar with the process—often make these estimates.

6. Steps 3, 4, and 5 together are called the *production cost worksheet*. In Step 3, total costs to account for are equal to the sum of the amounts debited to the department's Work in Process account. When there is no beginning inventory, the Assembly Department's debits are for direct materials used and conversion costs incurred during the period. Step 4 computes cost per equivalent unit by dividing the costs in each input cost category by the respective quantity of equivalent units. Step 5 assigns total costs to account for from Step 3 (a) to units completed and transferred out of the process and (b) to units remaining in process at the end of the period. EXHIBIT 17-2, text p.612, shows the details for Steps 3, 4, and 5 in Case 2.

7. Using dollar amounts from EXHIBIT 17-2, journal entries for the Assembly Department for February are as follows:

Work in Process–Assembly	32,000	
Accounts Payable Control		32,000

Work in Process–Assembly	18,600	
Various accounts		18,600

Work in Process–Testing	24,500	
Work in Process–Assembly		24,500

Because the Assembly Department had no beginning inventory in February, Work in Process—Assembly has a balance at the end of February of $26,100 ($0 + $32,000 + $18,600 − $24,500).

8. Case 3 adds complexity: there is both beginning and ending work-in-process inventory of SG-40 in the Assembly Department. Under these conditions it is necessary to select an *inventory cost-flow method*. The chapter illustrates two of these methods:

- The **weighted-average process-costing method** calculates cost per equivalent unit of all *work done to date* (regardless of the accounting period in which it is done) and assigns this cost (a) to equivalent units completed and transferred out of the process and (b) to equivalent units in ending work-in-process inventory.
- The **first-in, first-out (FIFO) process-costing method** (a) assigns the cost of the *previous* accounting period's equivalent units in beginning work-in-process inventory to the first units completed and transferred out of the process, and (b) assigns the cost of equivalent units worked on during the *current period* first to complete beginning inventory, next to start and complete new units, and finally to units in ending work-in-process inventory.

Both methods use the five-step procedure presented in paragraph 4.

9. The key difference in computing equivalent units (Step 2) under the two methods concerns work done on the physical units to account for in the process.

- *The weighted-average method combines work done to date, regardless of whether it is performed in the previous period or the current period.* Thus, the stage of completion of the current period's beginning work in process is *not* used in computing equivalent units.

- *The FIFO method separates work done on beginning inventory in the* previous *period from work done on it in the current period.*

EXHIBIT 17-4, text p.614, shows the details of Steps 1 and 2 for the weighted-average method. EXHIBIT 17-6, text p.618, is a parallel presentation for the FIFO method.

10. To compute cost per equivalent unit (Step 4), the weighted-average method divides *costs incurred to date in each cost category by the respective amount of work done to date*, whereas the FIFO method divides *costs incurred in the current period in each cost category by the respective amount of work done in the current period.* The assignment of costs (Step 5) is more complicated under FIFO because units completed and transferred out of the process have both a beginning inventory component and a started and completed component, instead of a single component for these units under weighted average. The major advantage of FIFO is that it provides managers with information about changes in cost per unit from one period to the next. This information can be used for evaluating performance in the current period by comparing actual costs and budgeted costs. EXHIBIT 17-5, text p.615, shows the details of Steps 3, 4, and 5 for the weighted-average method. EXHIBIT 17-7, text p.619, is a parallel presentation for the FIFO method.

11. The cost of units completed, and hence operating income, can differ materially between the weighted-average and FIFO methods if (a) the direct materials or conversion costs per unit vary significantly from period to period, and (b) the physical unit levels of beginning and ending work in process are large in relation to the total number of units transferred out of the process. Thus, as companies move toward long-term procurement contracts to reduce differences in unit costs from period to period, and reduce inventory levels, the difference in cost of units completed under the weighted-average and FIFO methods decreases.

12. Many process-costing systems have two

or more departments or processes in the production cycle. In the Pacific Electronics example, beginning text p.621, the SG-40 component moves from the Assembly Department to the Testing Department and then to Finished Goods. In the Testing Department, direct materials (crating and other packing materials) are added at the *end* of the process, and conversion costs are added evenly throughout the process. Because the Testing Department is not the first process in the production cycle, it has an input cost category called **transferred-in costs** (also called **previous department costs**). Transferred-in costs are costs incurred in previous departments that are carried forward as the product's cost when it moves to a subsequent process in the production cycle. That is, as units move from one department to the next, their costs are transferred with them. SG-40's cost, therefore, consists of the transferred-in costs as well as the direct materials and conversion costs added in the Testing Department.

13. As in a first-department situation, the five-step procedure assigns the costs of a subsequent department to units completed and transferred out, and to units in ending inventory. In calculating a subsequent department's equivalent units (Step 2), *transferred-in costs are treated as if they are a separate type of direct material added at the* beginning *of the process.* Recall that the weighted-average equivalent units are work done to date, whereas the FIFO equivalent units are work done in the current period. EXHIBIT 17-8, text p.623, and EXHIBIT 17-10, text p.624, show this contrast in the computation of equivalent units.

14. Steps 3, 4, and 5 are basically the same for a subsequent department as for a first department, except transferred-in costs must be accounted for. These steps under the weighted-average and FIFO methods, as described for a first department in paragraph 10, are applied in a similar manner to a subsequent department. EXHIBIT 17-9, text p.623, shows the details of Steps 3, 4, and 5 for weighted average. EXHIBIT 17-11, text p.625, is a parallel presentation for FIFO.

15. Product-costing systems do not always fall neatly into either job-costing or process-costing categories. A **hybrid-costing system** blends

characteristics from both job-costing and process-costing systems. Manufacturers of a relatively wide variety of closely related standardized products tend to use hybrid-costing systems. Examples are televisions, dishwashers, and washing machines.

16. An **operation-costing system** is a hybrid-costing system applied to batches of similar, but not identical, products. Individual batches of products are often a variation of a single design and proceed through a sequence of selected, though not necessarily the same, **operations**. An operation is a standardized method or technique that is performed repetitively, often on different materials, resulting in different finished goods. Within each operation, all product units are treated exactly alike, using identical amounts of the operation's resources. Manufacturers of clothing and shoes commonly use operation-costing systems.

17. (Appendix, paragraphs 17-19) Under the *standard-costing method* of process costing, standards are set for quantities of inputs needed to produce output. Standard costs per input unit can be assigned to these physical quantities to develop standard costs per output unit. The standard-costing method is especially useful for companies manufacturing a *wide variety of similar products,* such as rubber products, textiles, ceramics, paints, and packaged food products. Identifying standard costs for each individual product overcomes the disadvantage of costing all products at a single average actual cost amount.

18. Variances arise under the standard-costing method when the standard costs assigned to products on the basis of work done in the current period do not equal the actual costs incurred in the current period. As described in Chapters 7 and 8, variances can be analyzed in little or much detail for planning and control purposes.

19. In addition to their role in planning and control, standard costs make it easier to use the five-step procedure presented in paragraph 4. Steps 1 and 2 are the same under standard costing as under FIFO, but *Step 4 requires no computations under standard costing because cost per equivalent unit is* the *standard cost per unit of output.* Step 5 assigns the total standard costs to account for from Step 3 to units completed and transferred out of the process and to units in ending work-in-process inventory.

Featured Exercise

Rogers Company manufacturers a component, Y-28, in a two-process production cycle, Departments 1 and 2. In Department 2, direct materials are added at the beginning of the process and conversion costs are added evenly throughout the process. Conversion costs were 60% complete for the 6,000 units in process on May 1, and 75% complete for the 8,000 units in process on May 31. Twelve thousand units were completed and transferred out of Department 2 during May. Department 2's costs for May are as follows:

	Transferred-in Costs	Direct Materials	Conversion Costs
Work in process, May 1	$140,000	$ 28,000	$ 72,000
Costs added in May	280,000	112,000	216,000

a. Using the weighted-average method in Department 2 for May:
   - Summarize the flow of physical units of output.
   - Compute output in terms of equivalent units.
   - Compute cost per equivalent unit.
   - Summarize total costs to account for.
   - Assign total costs to units completed and transferred out and to units in ending work-in-process inventory.
   - Prepare the journal entry to record the transfer of completed work to Finished Goods.
b. Using the FIFO method, repeat part (a).

Solution (on p. 229)

Solution

a. Weighted-average method:

Flow of Production	Physical Units	Equivalent Units		
		Trans.-in Costs	Direct Materials	Conversion Costs
Work in process, beginning	6,000			
Transferred-in during May	14,000*			
Physical units to account for	20,000			
Completed and transferred out during May	12,000	12,000	12,000	12,000
Work in process, ending	8,000			
8,000 × 100%; 100%; 75%		8,000	8,000	6,000
Physical units accounted for	20,000			
Work done to date		20,000	20,000	18,000

*A plug figure: 20,000 units accounted for minus 6,000 units in beginning inventory.

	Total Production Costs	Trans.-in Costs	Direct Materials	Conversion Costs
Work in process, beginning	$240,000	$140,000	$ 28,000	$ 72,000
Costs added in May	608,000	280,000	112,000	216,000
Costs incurred to date		$420,000	$140,000	$288,000
Divide by equivalent units		÷ 20,000	÷ 20,000	÷ 18,000
Equivalent unit costs		$ 21	$ 7	$ 16
Total costs to account for	$848,000			
Assignment of costs:				
Completed and trans. out	$528,000	12,000 × ($21 + $7 + $16)		
Work in process, ending				
Transferred-in costs	168,000	8,000 × $21		
Direct materials	56,000	8,000 × $7		
Conversion costs	96,000	6,000 × $16		
Total work in process	320,000			
Total costs accounted for	$848,000			

The journal entry to record the transfer of completed work:

Finished Goods	528,000	
Work in Process—Dept. 2		528,000

b. FIFO method:

Flow of Production	Physical Units	Trans.-in Costs	Direct Materials	Conversion Costs
			Equivalent Units	
Work in process, beginning	6,000			
Transferred-in during May	14,000*			
Physical units to account for	20,000			
Completed and transferred				
out during May:				
Work in process, beginning	6,000			
6,000×0%; 0%; (100%−60%)		0	0	2,400
Started and completed	6,000			
6,000×100%; 100%; 100%		6,000	6,000	6,000
Work in process, ending	8,000			
8,000×100%; 100%; 75%		8,000	8,000	6,000
Physical units accounted for	20,000			
Work done in May		14,000	14,000	14,400

*A plug figure: 20,000 units accounted for minus 6,000 units in beginning inventory.

	Total Production Costs	Trans.-in Costs	Direct Materials	Conversion Costs
Work in process, beginning	$240,000	(costs of work done before May)		
Costs added in May	608,000	$280,000	$112,000	$216,000
Divide by equivalent units		÷ 14,000	÷ 14,000	÷ 14,400
Equivalent unit costs		$ 20	$ 8	$ 15
Total costs to account for	$848,000			
Assignment of costs:				
Work in process, beginning	$240,000			
Direct materials added in May	-0-	0 × $8		
Conversion costs added in May	36,000	2,400 × $15		
Total work in process, beg.	276,000			
Started and completed	258,000	6,000 × ($20 + $8 + $15)		
Total completed and trans. out	534,000			
Work in process, ending				
Transferred-in costs	160,000	8,000 × $20		
Direct materials	64,000	8,000 × $8		
Conversion costs	90,000	6,000 × $15		
Total work in process, ending	314,000			
Total costs accounted for	$848,000			

The journal entry to record the transfer of completed work:

Finished Goods	534,000	
Work in Process—Dept. 2		534,000

Review Questions and Exercises

Completion Statements

Fill in the blank(s) to complete each statement.

1. The overall objective of the five-step procedure to process costing is to assign the total costs to account for to units _____ _____ and to units _____.

2. _____ is a derived amount of output units that takes the quantity of each input (factor of production) in units completed and in incomplete units of work in process, and converts the quantity of input in-to the amount of completed output units that could be produced with that quantity of input.

3. The journal entry to transfer completed goods out of Painting, the final processing department in the production cycle, is:
   Debit: _____
   Credit: _____

4. A hybrid-costing system applied to batches of similar, but not identical, products is called an _____ system.

True-False

Indicate whether each statement is true (T) or false (F).

_____ 1. A process-costing system separates costs into cost categories according to the timing of when costs are introduced into the process.

_____ 2. In a process for a given month, physical units are always equal to or greater than equivalent units.

_____ 3. In terms of physical units in a processing department, the sum of units completed and transferred out and units in ending work in process is equal to the sum of units in beginning inventory and units started during the current period.

_____ 4. In process costing, estimating the degree of completion of units is usually more accurate for conversion costs than for direct materials.

_____ 5. The weighted-average method focuses on the total costs and total equivalent units completed to date, whereas the FIFO method computes unit costs by confining equivalent units to work done in the current period.

_____ 6. The weighted-average method uses the stage of completion of the current period's beginning work in process in computing equivalent units.

_____ 7. The FIFO method does not use the costs of beginning inventory in computing cost per equivalent unit for the current period.

_____ 8. In computing equivalent units, transferred-in costs are treated as if they are a separate type of direct material added at the beginning of the process.

_____ 9. Transferred-in costs for Process Two in the current period cannot include conversion costs that are incurred in Process One in the current period.

_____ 10. An operation-costing system allocates different amounts of conversion costs to different products that undergo a given operation.

_____ 11. (Appendix) Standard costing uses "work done during the current period" as the basis to compare actual costs and standard costs for control purposes.

Multiple Choice

Select the best answer to each question. Space is provided for computations after the quantitative questions.

_____ 1. (CPA) Kew Co. had 3,000 units in work in process at April 1 of the current fiscal year, which were 60% complete as to conversion costs. During April, 10,000 units are completed. At April 30, 4,000 units remain in work in process and are 40% complete as to conversion costs. Direct materials are added at the beginning of the process. Conversion costs are added evenly throughout the process. Assuming Kew uses the weighted-average method, how many units were started during April?
   a. 9,000
   b. 9,800
   c. 10,000
   d. 11,000

2. (CPA) Under which of the following conditions will the first-in, first-out method of process costing yield the same cost per equivalent unit as the weighted-average method?
   a. If units produced are homogeneous in nature.
   b. If there is no beginning inventory.
   c. If there is no ending inventory.
   d. If beginning and ending inventories are each 50% complete.

3. (CPA) Walton, Incorporated, had 8,000 units of work in process in Department A on October 1 of the current fiscal year. These units were 60% complete as to conversion costs, which are added evenly throughout the process. Direct materials are added at the beginning of the process. During October, 34,000 units are started and 36,000 units completed. Walton has 6,000 units of work in process on October 31. These units are 80% complete as to conversion costs. For October, how much did the equivalent units under the weighted-average method exceed the equivalent units under the first-in, first-out method?

	Direct Materials	Conversion Costs
a.	0	3,200
b.	0	4,800
c.	8,000	3,200
d.	8,000	4,800

4. (CMA) Kimbeth Manufacturing uses a process-costing system to manufacture Dust Density Sensors for the mining industry. The following information pertains to operations for May 2010:

	Units
Beginning work-in-process inventory, May 1	16,000
Started in production during May	100,000
Completed production during May	92,000
Ending work-in-process inventory, May 31	24,000

The beginning inventory was 60% complete for direct materials and 20% complete for conversion costs. The ending inventory is 90% complete for direct materials and 40% complete for conversion costs.

Costs pertaining to the month of May are as follows:

- Beginning inventory costs are direct materials, $54,560; conversion costs, $35,560.
- Costs incurred during May are direct materials used, $468,000; conversion costs, $574,040.

Using the weighted-average method, the total cost of the units in the ending work-in-process inventory at May 31, 2010, is:
a. $86,400.
b. $153,960.
c. $154,800.
d. $155,328.
e. $156,960.

5. Using the information in question 4 and the FIFO method, the total cost of units in the ending work-in-process inventory at May 31, 2010, is:
   a. $153,168.
   b. $154,800.
   c. $155,328.
   d. $156,960.
   e. $159,648.

6. (CPA) The Wiring Department is the second stage of Flem Company's production cycle. On May 1 of the current fiscal year, the beginning work-in-process inventory consisted of 25,000 units that are 60% complete as to conversion costs. During May, 100,000 units are transferred in from the first stage of Flem's production cycle. On May 31, the ending work-in-process inventory consists of 20,000 units that are 80% complete as to conversion costs. Direct materials are added at the end of the process, and conversion costs are added evenly throughout the process. Using the weighted-average method, the equivalent units are:

	Transferred-in Costs	Direct Materials	Conversion Costs
a.	100,000	125,000	100,000
b.	125,000	105,000	106,000
c.	125,000	105,000	121,000
d.	125,000	125,000	121,000

7. Using the information in question 6 and the FIFO method, the equivalent units are:

	Transferred-in Costs	Direct Materials	Conversion Costs
a.	100,000	100,000	111,000
b.	100,000	105,000	106,000
c.	100,000	105,000	111,000
d.	125,000	125,000	106,000

8. (CPA) An error is made in estimating the percentage of completion of the current month's ending work-in-process inventory. The error results in understating the percentage of completion of conversion costs. What is the resulting effect of this error on:
   1. Equivalent units of conversion costs?
   2. Cost per equivalent unit?
   3. Costs assigned to work completed during the period?

	1	2	3
a.	Understate	Overstate	Overstate
b.	Understate	Understate	Overstate
c.	Overstate	Understate	Understate
d.	Overstate	Overstate	Understate

9. (Appendix, CPA) Under the standard-costing method, how (if at all) are equivalent units used in the computations for process costing?
   a. Equivalent units are not used.
   b. Actual equivalent units are multiplied by the standard cost per unit.
   c. Standard equivalent units are multiplied by the standard cost per unit.
   d. Standard equivalent units are multiplied by the actual cost per unit.

1. Ozark Company uses a process-costing system. The following information is for the Testing Department for January 2011:

	Units
Work in process, January 1,	
40% complete	300
Transferred in during January	600
Completed and transferred out	
of the department during January	700
Work in process, January 31,	
50% complete	200
January 1 inventory costs:	
Transferred-in costs	$28,200
Conversion costs	5,560
Current costs in January:	
Transferred-in costs	51,000
Conversion costs	36,040

No direct materials are added in the Testing Department.

a. Using the weighted-average method:
   (1) Compute total physical units accounted for.
   (2) Compute equivalent units of transferred-in costs and conversion costs.
   (3) Compute cost per equivalent unit of transferred-in costs and conversion costs.
   (4) Compute cost of units completed and transferred out of the department.
   (5) Compute cost of work-in-process inventory, January 31.
b. Repeat part (a) using the FIFO method.

2. (Appendix) Fisher Company manufactures two models of aircraft subassemblies, X and Y. The following information is for November 2010:

	Production Orders	
	2,000 Units of Model X	1,000 Units of Model Y
Direct materials	$48,000	$64,000
Conversion costs (allocated on the basis of machine-hours used)		
Operation 1	20,000	10,000
Operation 2	?	?
Operation 3	–	5,000
Total manufacturing costs	$?	$?

For Operation 2, budgeted costs for the year 2010 are $200,000 for direct manufacturing labor and $880,000 for manufacturing overhead. Budgeted machine-hours are 36,000. Each product unit requires 10 minutes of machine time in Operation 2.

a. Compute the total conversion costs allocated to each model in Operation 2.
b. Compute the total manufacturing costs and the unit cost of each model in finished form.
c. Assume at the end of November that 100 units of Model X are in process through Operation 1 only, and that 200 units of Model Y are in process through Operation 2 only. Assume no direct materials are added in Operation 2 and that $8,000 (of the $64,000) direct materials are added to the 1,000 units of Model Y in Operation 3. Compute the cost of ending work-in-process inventory for each model.

Answers and Solutions to Chapter 17 Review Questions and Exercises

Completion Statements

1. completed and transferred out of the process, in ending work in process
2. Equivalent units
3. Finished Goods Control, Work in Process—Painting
4. operation-costing

True-False

1. T
2. T
3. T
4. F   In process costing, estimating the degree of completion of units is usually more accurate for direct materials than for conversion costs. That's because the quantity of direct materials needed for a completed unit or a partially completed unit can be measured accurately, whereas it is more difficult to measure what proportion of the total conversion costs needed to complete units has been used for units still in process.
5. T
6. F   Under the weighted-average method, the stage of completion of the current period's beginning work in process is *not* used in computing equivalent units. For example, the 225 units of beginning work in process in Exhibit 17-4, text p.609, are 40% complete on March 1, but this stage of completion is disregarded in computing equivalent units under the weighted-average method.
7. T
8. T
9. F   Transferred-in costs always include conversion costs incurred in the current period and may include some conversion costs incurred in the previous period. That's because, if none of these conversion costs are incurred in the current period, the transfer would have taken place in the previous period.
10. F   Under an operation-costing system, *identical* amounts of conversion costs are allocated to all the different products that undergo a given operation.
11. T

Multiple Choice

1. d   Total physical units accounted for $= 10,000 + 4,000 = 14,000$
   Units started during current period $= 14,000 - 3,000 = 11,000$
   This answer is *not* affected by the process-costing method used.
2. b   Either of two conditions must be met for the two costing methods to produce the same cost per equivalent unit: (i) no beginning inventory or (ii) no period-to-period changes in the cost per equivalent unit of direct materials and conversion costs. Condition (i) is illustrated in Cases 1 and 2, text pp.602-607. Condition (ii) rarely exists.
3. d   The differences in equivalent units between the two methods are attributable to work done in the *previous* period (that is, work done to date minus work done in the current period). The differences can be calculated directly by multiplying physical units in October 1 work-in-process inventory by the percentage of work done in September.
   Direct materials: $8,000 \times 100\% = 8,000$
   Conversion costs: $8,000 \times 60\% = 4,800$
   Alternative solution: Compare the equivalent units computed under each method. These comparisons are as follows (detailed calculations not shown):

	Direct Materials	Conversion Costs
Equivalent units under weighted average	42,000	40,800
Equivalent units under FIFO	34,000	36,000
Difference in equivalent units	8,000	4,800

4. e Three steps are used to obtain the answer. First, compute equivalent units of work done to date:

Direct materials = 92,000 + 24,000(90%) = 92,000 + 21,600 = 113,600
Conversion costs = 92,000 + 24,000(40%) = 92,000 + 9,600 = 101,600

Second, compute equivalent unit costs of work done to date:

$$\text{Direct materials} = \frac{\$54,560 + \$468,000}{113,600} = \frac{\$522,560}{113,600} = \$4.60$$

$$\text{Conversion costs} = \frac{\$35,560 + \$574,040}{101,600} = \frac{\$609,600}{101,600} = \$6.00$$

Third, compute the total cost of units in ending work in process:

Direct materials = 24,000(90%) × $4.60 = 21,600 × $4.60 = $ 99,360
Conversion costs = 24,000(40%) × $6.00 = 9,600 × $6.00 = 57,600
Work in process, May 31, 2010 $156,960

5. a Three steps are used to obtain the answer. First, compute equivalent units of work done in the current period:

Direct materials = 92,000 + 24,000(90%) − 16,000(60%)
= 92,000 + 21,600 − 9,600 = 104,000
Conversion costs = 92,000 + 24,000(40%) − 16,000(20%)
= 92,000 + 9,600 − 3,200 = 98,400

Second, compute equivalent unit costs of work done in the current period:

Direct materials = $468,000 ÷ 104,000 = $4.50
Conversion costs = $574,040 ÷ 98,400 = $5.83

Third, compute the total cost of units in ending work in process:

Direct materials = 24,000(90%) × $4.50 = 21,600 × $4.50 = $ 97,200
Conversion costs = 24,000(40%) × $5.83 = 9,600 × $5.83 = 55,968
Work in process, May 31, 2008 $153,168

6. c

			Equivalent Units	
Flow of Production	Physical Units	Trans.-in Costs	Direct Materials	Conversion Costs
Work in process, May 1	25,000			
Transferred-in during May	100,000			
Physical units to account for	125,000			
Completed and transferred out during May, 125,000 − 20,000	105,000	105,000	105,000	105,000
Work in process, May 31, 20,000×100%; 0%; 80%	20,000	20,000	-0-	16,000
Physical units accounted for	125,000			
Work done to date		125,000	105,000	121,000

The equivalent units of direct materials for the May 31 inventory is zero because materials are added at the *end* of the process.

7. b

Flow of Production	Physical Units	Equivalent Units Trans.-in Costs	Direct Materials	Conversion Costs
Work in process, May 1	25,000			
Transferred-in during May	100,000			
Physical units to account for	125,000			
Completed and transferred out during May				
From work in process, May 31, 25,000×0%; 100%; 40%	25,000	-0-	25,000	10,000
Started and completed 100,000 − 20,000	80,000			
80,000 × 100%		80,000	80,000	80,000
Work in process, May 31 20,000×100%; 0%; 80%	20,000	20,000	-0-	16,000
Physical units accounted for	125,000			
Work done to date		100,000	105,000	106,000

8. a Regardless of whether the FIFO or weighted-average method is used, the effects of this error are the same because *both methods treat ending inventory exactly alike*. To illustrate the effects of the error, use assumed figures to satisfy the situation described. For example, assume ending inventory is estimated to be 50% complete as to conversion costs instead of the correct figure of 70%. Using assumed figures, the effect of this error on each of the three items specified in the question is as follows:

(1) Equivalent units of conversion costs are understated:

	Physical Units	Equivalent Units Before Correction	After Correction
Work in process, beginning	-0-		
Started during current period	1,100		
Physical units to account for	1,100		
Completed and transferred out during current period, 1,100 − 200	900	900	900
Work in process, ending, 200 × 50%; 200 × 70%	200	100	140
Physical units accounted for	1,100	1,000	1,040

(2) Cost per equivalent unit is overstated:
   Before correction: $2,080 ÷ 1,000 = $2.08 per unit
   After correction: $2,080 ÷ 1,040 = $2.00 per unit

(3) Cost of work completed and transferred out is overstated:
   Before correction: 900 units × $2.08 = $1,872
   After correction: 900 units × $2.00 = $1,800

If this illustration had been based on *direct materials* instead of *conversion costs*, the conclusions would be the same; however, an error in computing the percentage of completion of direct materials is less likely to occur because the quantity of direct materials needed for a completed unit or a partially completed unit can be measured accurately.

9. b Under the standard-costing method, costs are computed by multiplying actual equivalent units for each cost category by the respective standard cost per unit, as shown in Exhibit 17-13, text p.634.

Review Exercise 1

a. (1) Total physical units accounted for = 300 + 600 = 900
    (2) Equivalent units of work done to date:
    Transferred-in costs = 700(100%) + 200(100%) = 900
    Conversion costs = 700(100%) + 200(50%) = 800
    (3) Cost per equivalent unit:
    Transferred-in costs = ($28,200 + $51,000) ÷ 900
                         = $79,200 ÷ 900 = $88
    Conversion costs = ($5,560 + $36,040) ÷ 800
                     = $41,600 ÷ 800 = $52
    (4) Costs transferred out = 700($88 + $52) = $98,000
    (5) Cost of ending work in process = 200($88) + 200(50%)($52)
                                       = $17,600 + $5,200 = $22,800

b. (1) Same as a(1) above, 900.
    (2) Equivalent units of work done in current period:
    Transferred-in costs = (700 − 300)100% + 200(100%) = 600
    Conversion costs = 300(100% − 40%) + (700 − 300)100% + 200(50%)
                     = 180 + 400 + 100 = 680
    (3) Cost per equivalent unit:
    Transferred-in costs = $51,000 ÷ 600 = $85
    Conversion costs = $36,040 ÷ 680 = $53
    (4) Costs transferred out = ($28,200 + $5,560) + 300(100% − 40%)$53 + (700 −
                               300(100%)($85 + $53)
                             = $33,760 + $9,540 + $55,200 = $98,500
    (5) Cost of ending work in process = 200(100%)($85) + 200(50%)($53)
                                       = $17,000 + $5,300 = $22,300

Review Exercise 2

a. $\text{Budgeted allocation rate for conversion costs} = \dfrac{\$200,000 + \$880,000}{36,000} = \$30 \text{ per machine-hour}$

Units produced per hour = 60 minutes ÷ 10 minutes per unit = 6 units
Conversion costs allocated per unit = $30 ÷ 6 = $5
Conversion costs allocated to 2,000 units of Model X = 2,000 × $5 = $10,000
Conversion costs allocated to 1,000 units of Model Y = 1,000 × $5 = $5,000

b.

	Model X	Model Y
Direct materials	$48,000	$64,000
Conversion costs:		
Operation 1	20,000	10,000
Operation 2	10,000	5,000
Operation 3	-0-	5,000
Total manufacturing costs	$78,000	$84,000
Divide by number of units	÷2,000	÷1,000
Manufacturing cost per unit	$ 39	$ 84

c.

	Model X	Model Y
Direct materials:		
$48,000 \times (100 \div 2,000)$	$2,400	
$($64,000 - $8,000) \times (200 \div 1,000)$		$11,200
Conversion costs:		
Operation 1:		
$20,000 \times (100 \div 2,000)$	1,000	
$10,000 \times (200 \div 1,000)$		2,000
Operation 2:		
$5,000 \times (200 \div 1,000)$		1,000
Ending work in process ($17,600)	$3,400	$14,200

CHAPTER 18

Spoilage, Rework, and Scrap

Overview

This chapter focuses on accounting for the costs of manufacturing outputs that fail to meet established production specifications—called spoilage and rework—and residual materials that result from the production process—called scrap. As companies strive to improve product quality, managers learn that rates of spoilage, rework, and scrap regarded as normal in the past are no longer tolerable. The Appendix to the chapter illustrates the standard-costing method and spoilage.

Highlights

1. **Spoilage** is units of production—whether fully or partially completed— that do not meet the specifications required by customers for good units and that are discarded or sold at reduced prices. **Rework** is units of production that do not meet the specifications required by customers but which are subsequently repaired and sold as good finished goods. **Scrap** is residual material (such as wood shavings) that results from manufacturing a product; it has low sales value compared with the total sales value of the product.

2. When accounting for spoilage, it is necessary to distinguish the costs of **normal spoilage** from the costs of **abnormal spoilage**.

- Normal spoilage is spoilage inherent in a particular production process that arises even when the process is operated in an efficient manner. The cost of normal spoilage is typically included as a component of the cost of good units manufactured (that is, normal spoilage is an inventoriable cost) because good units cannot be made without simultaneously producing normally spoiled units.

- Abnormal spoilage is spoilage that is not inherent in a particular production process and would not arise under efficient operating conditions. Abnormal spoilage is usually regarded as avoidable and controllable. Abnormal spoilage costs are written off as a loss of the accounting period in which detection of the spoiled units occurs.

3. Spoilage might actually occur at various stages of the production process, but it is typically detected only at one or more inspection points. An **inspection point** is the stage of the production process at which products are examined to determine whether they are acceptable or unacceptable units. There is often a single inspection at the completion of the production process. The cost of spoiled units is assumed to be all costs incurred by spoiled units prior to inspection. When spoiled goods have a disposal value, net cost of spoilage is calculated by deducting disposal value from the costs of the spoiled goods up to the inspection point. Unit costs of normal and abnormal spoilage are the same when the two are detected simultaneously. When abnormal spoilage is detected at a different point in the production process than normal spoilage, however, the unit cost of abnormal spoilage would differ from unit cost of normal spoilage.

4. In process costing, all spoiled units should be counted and classified as normal and abnormal spoilage. For example, assume a process has 10,000 physical units to account for, 7,000 good units completed and transferred out, 2,000 units in ending inventory, and normal spoilage of 10% of good output. Then:

$$\text{Total spoilage} = 10,000 - 7,000 - 2,000$$
$$= 1,000 \text{ units}$$
$$\text{Normal spoilage} = 7,000 \times 10\% = 700 \text{ units}$$
$$\text{Abnormal spoilage} = 1,000 - 700 = 300 \text{ units}$$

5. The weighted-average and FIFO methods of process costing can incorporate both normal and abnormal spoilage by making only slight modifications to the five-step procedure used in

Chapter 17. The five steps (with the modifications shown in parenthesis) are:

Step 1: Summarize the flow of physical units of output. (Identify both normal spoilage and abnormal spoilage.)

Step 2: Compute output in terms of equivalent units. (Compute equivalent units for spoilage in the same way as for good units.)

Step 3: Summarize total costs to account for. (None)

Step 4: Compute equivalent unit costs. (None)

Step 5: Assign total costs to units completed, to spoiled units, and to units in ending work-in-process inventory. (Compute the cost of each type of spoiled units and the cost of good units.)

6. The weighted-average method of process costing combines costs in beginning inventory with costs in the current period to determine the cost of good units (including a normal spoilage amount) and the cost of abnormal spoilage. EXHIBIT 18-2, text p.650, illustrates the five-step procedure for the weighted-average method. Using dollar amounts from this exhibit, journal entries for the completed work of the Forming Department for July are:

Finished Goods	152,075	
Work in Process—Forming		152,075
Loss from Abnormal Spoilage	5,925	
Work in Process—Forming		5,925

7. The FIFO method of process costing keeps costs in beginning inventory separate from costs in the current period to determine the cost of good units (including a normal spoilage amount) and the cost of abnormal spoilage. EXHIBIT 18-3, text p.651, illustrates the five-step procedure for the FIFO method.

8. The equivalent units of spoilage computed in EXHIBITS 18-2 and 18-3 are based on the fact that the inspection point is at the *completion of the production process* in the Forming Department. In this situation, all the cost of normal spoilage is allocated to good units completed and transferred out of the department because none of the units in ending work-in-process inventory passed the inspection point. On the other hand, the cost of normal spoilage is allocated to units in ending inventory (in addition to completed units), if the units in ending inventory did pass the inspection point.

9. In process costing, the inspection point be-ing at different stages of the production process affects the respective amounts of normal and abnormal spoilage. Regardless of where inspection occurs in the production process, normal spoilage is computed on the basis of the number of good units that pass the inspection point during the current period. The table, text p.653, computes the number of physical units of normal spoilage and abnormal spoilage with the inspection point being at three different stages of the production process. EXHIBIT 18-4, text p.654, computes the equivalent units under the weighted-average method when the inspection point is at the 50% stage of production.

10. The concepts of normal and abnormal spoilage or rework also apply to job costing, but job costing requires more detailed classifications of spoilage or rework than those used in process costing. That's because an item such as normal spoilage or normal rework can be either *attributable to a specific job* or *common to all jobs*. Process costing classifies normal spoilage or normal rework only as common to a process. Job costing uses the following classifications, with journal entries recorded for each "Yes":

	Attributable to a Specific Job	Common to All Jobs
Normal spoilage	Yes	Yes
Abnormal spoilage	Yes	No
Normal rework	Yes	Yes
Abnormal rework	Yes	No

In the example (beginning text p.655) the journal entries are as follows:

Normal spoilage attributable to a specific job

Materials Control	3,000	
Work-in-Process Control		3,000

The $3,000 is the disposal value of spoiled goods.

Normal spoilage common to all jobs
Materials Control (disposal value)	3,000	
Manuf. OH Control (normal spoilage cost)	7,000	
Work-in-Process Control (gross spoilage cost)		10,000

Here the net cost of spoilage is allocated to production via the budgeted manufacturing overhead cost rate, which includes a provision for normal spoilage.

Abnormal spoilage
Materials Control (disposal value)	3,000	
Loss from Abnormal Spoilage (net spoilage cost)	7,000	
Work-in-Process Control (gross spoilage cost)		10,000

Normal rework attributable to a specific job
Work-in-Process Control (rework cost)	3,800	
Materials Control		800
Wages Payable Control		2,000
Manuf. OH Allocated		1,000

Normal rework common to all jobs
Manuf. OH Control (rework cost)	3,800	
Materials Control		800
Wages Payable Control		2,000
Manuf. OH Allocated		1,000

Abnormal rework
Loss from Abnormal Rework (rework cost)	3,800	
Materials Control		800
Wages Payable Control		2,000
Manuf. OH Allocated		1,000

11. Initial entries to scrap records are commonly in physical terms by weighing, counting, or some other measure. Scrap records not only help measure efficiency, but also help keep track of scrap and so reduce the chances of theft. Companies use scrap records to prepare periodic summaries of the amounts of actual scrap compared with the budgeted amounts. Scrap is either sold or disposed of quickly, or stored for later sale, disposal, or reuse.

12. Accounting for scrap requires that two questions be answered:

a. When should the value of scrap be recognized in the accounting records—at the time scrap is *produced* or at the time scrap is *sold*?
b. How should revenue from scrap be accounted for?

To illustrate, assume the scrap from a job has a value of $900.

- Recognizing Scrap at the Time of Its Sale

    When the value of scrap is *immaterial*, the simplest approach is to make a note of the quantity of scrap returned to the storeroom and to regard the sales as scrap revenues. The only journal entry is:

Cash or Accounts Receivable	900	
Scrap Revenues		900

When the value of scrap is *not immaterial* and the scrap is sold quickly after it is produced, the accounting depends on whether the scrap is attributable to a specific job or is common to all jobs:

Scrap attributable to a specific job
Cash or Accounts Receivable	900	
Work-in-Process Control		900

Unlike spoilage and rework, there is no cost attached to the scrap, and hence no distinction is made between normal scrap and abnormal scrap.

Scrap common to all jobs
Cash or Accounts Receivable	900	
Manuf. OH Control		900

When scrap is common to all jobs, the expected sales of scrap are considered in setting the budgeted manufacturing overhead cost rate. Thus, budgeted overhead is lower than if the overhead budget had not been reduced for expected sales of scrap.

- Recognizing Scrap at the Time of Its Production

When the value of scrap is *not immaterial* and the time between storing it and selling or reusing it can be long, scrap can be inventoried at a conservative estimate of its net realizable value. In this way, production costs and related scrap recovery are recognized in the same accounting period.

Scrap attributable to a specific job

Materials Control	900	
Work-in-Process Control		900

Cash or Accounts Receivable	900	
Materials Control		900

If scrap is reused rather than sold, debit Work-in-Process Control in the preceding journal entry.

Scrap common to all jobs

Materials Control	900	
Manuf. OH Control		900

Cash or Accounts Receivable	900	
Materials Control		900

Accounting for scrap under process costing is like that under job costing when scrap is common to all jobs.

13. (Appendix) The standard-costing method of process costing uses standard costs to determine the cost of good units (including a normal spoilage amount) and the cost of abnormal spoilage. EXHIBIT 18-5, text p.662, illustrates the five-step procedure for the standard-costing method.

Featured Exercise

Tyler Company uses a process-costing system. Selected information about the Molding Process for December 2010 follows:

	Units
Beginning work in process, 60% complete as of 12/1/10	100
Transferred in	620
Normal spoilage	40
Abnormal spoilage	50
Good units completed and transferred out	550
Ending work in process, 75% complete as of 12/31/10	80

Conversion costs in beginning inventory	$160,000
Current period conversion costs	$960,000

Spoilage is detected when the units are inspected at the end of the process.

a. Using the weighted-average method:
   (1) Compute equivalent units of conversion costs.
   (2) Compute conversion costs per equivalent unit.
   (3) Compute the conversion costs component of normal spoilage.
   (4) Compute the conversion costs component of abnormal spoilage.
   (5) Compute the total conversion costs transferred out to the next process.
   (6) Compute the conversion costs component of ending work in process.
b. Using the FIFO method, repeat part (a).

Solution (on next page)

Solution

a. Weighted-average method:

(1)

Flow of Production	Physical Units	Equivalent Units of Conversion Costs
Good units completed and transferred out during December	550	550
Normal spoilage	40	
40 × 100%		40
Abnormal spoilage	50	
50 × 100%		50
Work in process, December 31	80	
80 × 75%		60
Physical units accounted for	<u>720</u>	
Work done to date		<u>700</u>

(2) $$\text{Conversion cost per equivalent unit} = \frac{\$160,000 + \$960,000}{700} = \frac{\$1,120,000}{700} = \$1,600$$

(3) $$\text{Conversion costs component of normal spoilage} = 40 \times \$1,600 = \$64,000$$

(4) $$\text{Conversion costs component of abnormal spoilage} = 50 \times \$1,600 = \$80,000$$

(5) Conversion costs transferred out to next process

Good units completed, 550 × $1,600	$880,000
Normal spoilage, answer (3) above	64,000
Total	$944,000

(6) $$\text{Conversion costs component of ending inventory} = 60 \times \$1,600 = \$96,000$$

b. FIFO method:

(1)

Flow of Production	Physical Units	Equivalent Units of Conversion Costs
Good units completed and transferred out during December:		
From work in process, December 1	100	
100 × (100% − 60%)		40
Started and completed, 550 − 100	450	450
Normal spoilage	40	
40 × 100%		40
Abnormal spoilage	50	
50 × 100%		50
Work in process, December 31	80	

	80 × 75%		60
Physical units accounted for		720	
Work done in December			640

(2) $\dfrac{\text{Conversion cost per}}{\text{equivalent unit}} = \dfrac{\$960,000}{640} = \$1,500$

(3) $\dfrac{\text{Conversion costs component}}{\text{of normal spoilage}} = 40 \times \$1,500 = \$60,000$

(4) $\dfrac{\text{Conversion costs component}}{\text{of abnormal spoilage}} = 50 \times \$1,500 = \$75,000$

(5) Conversion costs transferred out to next process
    Good units completed:

Work in process, December 1	$160,000
Conversion costs added in December	
40 × $1,500	60,000
Started and completed	
450 × $1,500	675,000
Normal spoilage, answer (3) above	60,000
Total	$955,000

(6) $\dfrac{\text{Conversion costs component}}{\text{of ending inventory}} = 60 \times \$1,500 = \$90,000$

Review Questions and Exercises

Completion Statements

Fill in the blank(s) to complete each statement.

1. Units of production that do not meet the specifications required by customers for good units and that are discarded or are sold at reduced prices are called _____.
2. Units of production that do not meet the specifications required by customers for finished goods that are subsequently repaired and sold as good finished goods are called _____.
3. _____ is residual material that results from manufacturing a product; it has low sales value compared with the total sales value of the product.
4. _____ is inherent in a particular production process that arises even under efficient operating conditions.
5. The cost of abnormal spoilage is debited to which account? _____
6. Accounting for spoilage or rework in job-costing systems uses what three classifications?

   _____
   _____
   _____

True-False

Indicate whether each statement is true (T) or false (F).

____ 1. Normal spoilage is a period cost.
____ 2. In computing equivalent units for process costing, it is more accurate to include normal spoilage and exclude abnormal spoilage.
____ 3. The appropriate base to use in computing normal spoilage is actual units started in production.
____ 4. When a company adheres to a goal of zero defects, all of its spoilage is regarded as abnormal.
____ 5. The cost of normal spoilage should never be allocated to units in ending work-in-process inventory.
____ 6. Regardless of the point in the production process that inspection occurs, normal spoilage is computed on the basis of the number of good units that pass the inspection point during the current period.
____ 7. Unlike spoilage and rework, no cost is assigned to scrap, and hence scrap is not classified as normal or abnormal.

Multiple Choice

Select the best answer to each question. Space is provided for computations after the quantitative questions.

1. (CPA) The Forming Department is the first of a two-stage production process. Spoilage is detected at the end of the Forming Department. Costs of spoiled units are assigned to units completed and transferred to the second department in the period spoilage is detected. The following information concerns Forming's conversion costs in May 2011:

	Units	Conv. Costs
Beginning work in process (50% complete)	2,000	$10,000
Units started during May	8,000	75,500
Spoilage—normal	500	
Units completed and transferred out	7,000	
Ending work in process (80% complete)	2,500	

   Using the weighted-average method, how much of Forming's conversion costs were transferred to the second production department?
   a. $59,850
   b. $64,125
   c. $67,500
   d. $71,250

2. Using the information in question 1 and the FIFO method, how much of the Forming Department's conversion costs were transferred to the second production department? (Round equivalent unit cost to four decimal places.)
   a. $58,853
   b. $66,618
   c. $67,735
   d. $69,603

3. (CMA) During March of the current fiscal year, Mercer Company completed 50,000 units costing $600,000, exclusive of spoilage allocation. Of these completed units, 25,000 were sold during the month. An additional 10,000 units, costing $80,000, are 50% complete at March 31. The inspection point is at the end of the production process. For the month, normal spoilage is $20,000 and abnormal spoilage is $50,000. The portion of total spoilage costs that should be charged against revenues in March is:
   a. $50,000.
   b. $20,000.
   c. $70,000.
   d. $60,000.
   e. $30,000.

4. If spoilage occurs that is normal and Control should be credited with:
   a. nothing.
   b. the disposal value of the spoiled goods.
   c. the net spoilage cost.
   d. the gross spoilage cost.

5. In a job-costing system, Work-in-Process Control should be debited with the cost of rework that is:
   a. abnormal.
   b. normal and common to all jobs.
   c. normal and attributable to a specific job.
   d. discarded.

6. (CPA) Simpson Company manufactures electric drills to the exacting specifications of various customers. During April, Job 403 for the production of 1,100 drills is completed at the following cost per unit:

Direct materials	$10
Direct manufacturing labor	8
Manufacturing overhead allocated	12
Total manufacturing cost	$30

   Final inspection of Job 403 discloses 50 defective units and 100 units of normal spoilage attributable to this specific job. The defective drills are reworked at a total cost of $500 and the spoiled drills are sold to a jobber for $1,500. What is the unit cost of the good units produced on Job 403?
   a. $33
   b. $32
   c. $30
   d. $29

7. (CPA) Under Heller Company's job-costing system, the budgeted manufacturing overhead cost rate includes the estimated costs of defective work (considered normal in the manufacturing process). During March, Job No. 210 for 2,000 hand saws is completed at the following cost per unit:

Direct materials	$ 5
Direct manufacturing labor	4
Manufacturing overhead allocated (at 150% of direct manufacturing labor cost)	6
Total manufacturing cost	$15

Final inspection of Job No. 210 discloses 100 defective saws were reworked at a cost of $2 per unit for direct manufacturing labor, plus manufacturing overhead at the budgeted cost rate. The defective units on Job No. 210 are considered normal. What is the total rework cost and to which account should it be debited?

	Rework cost	Account debited
a.	$200	Work-in-Process Control
b.	$200	Manuf. OH Control
c.	$500	Work-in-Process Control
d.	$500	Manuf. OH Control

8. (CPA adapted) If the value of scrap is not immaterial, the scrap is sold soon after its production, and the scrap is common to all jobs in a manufacturing process, the scrap is recorded as a:
a. credit to Manufacturing Overhead Control.
b. debit to Manufacturing Overhead Control.
c. credit to Finished Goods Control.
d. credit to Work-in-Process Control.

Review Exercises

1. (CMA) JC Company uses a process-costing system. A unit of product passes through three departments—Molding, Assembly, and Finishing—before it is completed. The following activity took place in the Finishing Department during May:

	Units
Work in process, May 1	1,400
Transferred in from the Assembly Department	14,000
Spoilage	700
Completed and transferred out to finished goods inventory	11,200

Direct materials are added at the beginning of the processing in the Finishing Department without changing the number of units processed. Conversion costs are added evenly throughout the process. The work-in-process inventory was 70% complete as to conversion costs on May 1 and 40% complete as to conversion costs on May 31. All spoilage is detected at the inspection point, which occurs at the end of the production process; 560 of the units spoiled are considered normal spoilage.

JC Company uses the weighted-average method. The equivalent unit costs for May are as follows:

	Equivalent Unit Cost
Transferred-in costs	$5.00
Direct materials	1.00
Conversion costs	3.00
Total manufacturing cost	$9.00

a. Compute the equivalent units of transferred-in costs, direct materials, and conversion costs.

b. Compute the cost of units completed and transferred from the Finishing Department to finished goods inventory during May.

c. Compute the cost assigned to the Finishing Department's work-in-process inventory on May 31.

d. Compute the cost of abnormal spoilage.

e. Compute the total transferred-in costs of the Finishing Department during May, assuming the transferred-in costs component of the work-in-process inventory of the Finishing Department on May 1 amounted to $6,300.

2. Boucher Company uses a job-costing system. During November, the following costs are incurred on Job 109 to manufacture 200 motors:

Original costs:

Direct materials	$ 6,600
Direct manufacturing labor	8,000
Manufacturing overhead allocated	
(150% of direct manufacturing labor)	12,000
Total	$26,600

Direct costs of reworking 10 motors:

Direct materials	$1,000
Direct manufacturing labor	1,600
Total	$2,600

a. Prepare the journal entry to record the rework costs, assuming the rework is attributable specifically to Job 109.
b. Compute the cost per finished motor for Job 109, assuming the rework is attributable specifically to this job.
c. Prepare the journal entry to record the rework costs, assuming the rework is common to all jobs.
d. Compute the cost per finished motor for Job 109, assuming the rework is common to all jobs.

Answers and Solutions to Chapter 18 Review Questions and Exercises

Completion Statements

1. spoilage
2. rework
3. Scrap
4. Normal spoilage
5. Loss from Abnormal Spoilage
6. normal spoilage (rework) attributable to a specific job, normal spoilage (rework) common to all jobs, and abnormal spoilage (rework)

True-False

1. F Normal spoilage is an inventoriable cost. Abnormal spoilage is a period cost.
2. F In computing equivalent units for process costing, it is more accurate to include both normal and abnormal spoilage. Exhibit 18-1, text p. 647, illustrates this approach.
3. F The appropriate base to use in computing normal spoilage is total units of good output. Actual units started in production is an inappropriate base because it can include both normal and abnormal spoilage.
4. T
5. F A portion of normal spoilage cost should be allocated to units in ending work-in-process inventory, if those units have passed the inspection point. For example, when the inspection point is at the 50% stage of the production process and ending work in process is 70% complete, normal spoilage cost should be allocated to this inventory. The Appendix to this chapter illustrates the effects of the inspection point being at three different stages of the production process.
6. T
7. T

Multiple Choice

1. c Three steps are used to obtain the answer. First, compute equivalent units of conversion costs:

$$7,000 + 500 + 2,500(80\%) = 7,000 + 500 + 2,000 = 9,500$$

Second, compute equivalent unit cost of conversion costs:

$$\frac{\$10,000 + \$75,500}{9,500} = \frac{\$85,500}{9,500} = \$9$$

Third, compute the conversion costs transferred from the Forming Department to the second production department:

$$(7,000 + 500) \times \$9 = 7,500 \times \$9 = \$67,500$$

Alternative solution:
   Let X = Conversion costs transferred out of Forming
      X = Total conversion costs − Conversion costs in ending work in process
      X = ($10,000 + $75,500) − (2,500 × 80% × $9)
      X = $85,500 − (2,000 × $9)
      X = $85,500 − $18,000 = $67,500

2. c Three steps are used to obtain the answer. First, compute equivalent units of conversion costs:

Beginning work in process = 2,000 × 50% = 1,000
Work done in current period = 7,000 + 500 + 2,500(80%) − 2,000(50%)
                           = 7,500 + 2,000 − 1,000 = 8,500

Second, compute the equivalent unit cost of conversion costs:

Beginning work in process   = $10,000 ÷ 1,000 = $10
Work done in current period = $75,500 ÷ 8,500 = $8.8824

Third, compute the conversion costs transferred from the Forming Department to the second production department:

Beginning work in process:	
Previous period costs, $1,000 \times \$10$	$10,000
Current period costs, $(2,000 - 1,000) \times \$8.8824$	8,882
Started and completed	
Good units, $(7,000 - 2,000) \times \$8.8824$	44,412
Normal spoilage units, $500 \times \$8.8824$	4,441
Conversion costs transferred from the Forming Department	$67,735

Alternative solution:

Let X = Conversion costs transferred out of Forming

X = Total conversion costs − Conversion costs in ending work in process

$X = (\$10,000 + \$75,500) - (2,500 \times 80\% \times \$8.8824)$

$X = \$85,500 - (2,000 \times \$8.8824)$

$X = \$85,500 - \$17,765 = \$67,735$

3. d   Normal spoilage included in cost of goods sold

$\$20,000 \times (25,000 \div 50,000)$	$10,000
Abnormal spoilage	50,000
Total spoilage costs charged against revenues	$60,000

4. d   This question refers to the second journal entry in paragraph 10 of the Highlights.

5. c   This question refers to the fourth journal entry in paragraph 10 of the Highlights.

6. b   Because the electric drills are manufactured to the exacting specifications of various customers, the rework and normal spoilage are *attributable specifically to Job 403*. Thus, rework costs increase the cost of good units produced, and the disposal value of spoilage decreases the cost of good units produced.

Let X = Unit cost of good units produced

$X = [(1,100 \times \$30) + \$500 - \$1,500] \div (1,100 - 100)$

$X = (\$33,000 - \$1,000) \div 1,000$

$X = \$32,000 \div 1,000 = \$32$

Note: had the rework and normal spoilage been *common to all jobs*, an allowance for these costs would be included in the budgeted manufacturing overhead cost rate. In that case,

Let Y = Unit cost of good units produced

$Y = [(1,100 \times \$30) - (100 \times \$30)] \div (1,100 - 100)$

$Y = (\$33,000 - \$3,000) \div 1,000$

$Y = \$30,000 \div 1,000 = \$30$

7. d   Total rework cost $= [\$2 + (\$2 \times 150\%)] \times 100$

$= (\$2 + \$3) \times 100 = \$500$

Because normal rework is included in the budgeted overhead cost rate, this means the normal rework is *common to all jobs*. Thus, debit Manufacturing Overhead Control, as shown in the fifth journal entry in paragraph 10 of the Highlights.

8. a   If the value of scrap is not immaterial, the scrap is sold soon after its production, and the scrap is common to all jobs in a manufacturing process, the scrap is recorded as a credit to Manufacturing Overhead Control. The debit in the journal entry is to Cash or Accounts Receivable. If all of the conditions are the same except the scrap is attributable to a specific job, the debit remains the same but Work-in-Process Control is credited.

Review Exercise 1

a.

Flow of Production	Physical Units	Trans.-in Costs	Direct Materials	Conversion Costs
		Equivalent Units		
Work in process, May 1	1,400			
Transferred-in during May	14,000			
To account for	15,400			
Good units completed and				
transferred out	11,200	11,200	11,200	11,200
Normal spoilage	560	560	560	560
Abnormal spoilage, 700 − 560	140	140	140	140
Work in process, May 1,				
15,400 − 140 − 560 − 11,200	3,500			
3,500 × 100%; 100%, 40%		3,500	3,500	1,400
Physical units accounted for	15,400			
Work done to date		15,400	15,400	13,300

b. Because spoilage is detected at the completion of work in the Finishing Department, the cost of all normal spoilage should be allocated to the good units completed and transferred out of Finishing: $(11,200 \times \$9.00) + (560 \times \$9.00) = \$105,840$. This amount is debited to Finished Goods and credited to Work in Process—Finishing.

c. Using the equivalent unit amounts for the May 31 work-in-process inventory from the schedule in part (a) above, the costs of this inventory are: $(3,500 \times \$5) + (3,500 \times \$1) + (1,400 \times \$3) = \$17,500 + \$3,500 + \$4,200 = \$25,200$.

d. The cost of abnormal spoilage $= 140 \times \$9.00 = \$1,260$. This amount is debited to Loss from Abnormal Spoilage and credited to Work in Process—Finishing.

e. Under the weighted-average method, the equivalent unit cost for each cost category is computed by dividing costs incurred to date by work done to date.
Let X = Transferred-in costs of Finishing during May (that is, costs transferred out of Assembly)

$$(X + \$6,300) \div 15,400 = \$5.00$$
$$X + \$6,300 = \$5.00 \times 15,400$$
$$X = \$77,000 - \$6,300$$
$$X = \$70,700$$

Review Exercise 2

a.

Work-in-Process Control	5,000	
Materials Control		1,000
Wages Payable Control		1,600
Manuf. Overhead Allocated		
($1,600 × 150%)		2,400

b. Cost per finished motor $= \dfrac{\$26,600 + \$5,000}{200} = \dfrac{\$31,600}{200} = \$158$

c. Manuf. Overhead Control   5,000
    Materials Control   1,000
    Wages Payable Control   1,600
    Manuf. Overhead Allocated
      ($1,600 × 150%)   2,400

d. Cost per finished motor = $26,600 ÷ 200 = $133

Balanced Scorecard: Quality, Time, and the Theory of Constraints

Overview

This chapter examines how management accounting helps managers to take initiatives that improve quality and shorten delivery times, and to make production decisions when faced with multiple constraints. Quality and time are powerful competitive tools, and the theory of constraints and throughput-margin analysis are used in making the aforementioned production decisions. The chapter uses the relevant-revenues and relevant-cost analysis introduced in Chapter 11.

Highlights

1. **Quality** is the total features and characteristics of a product or service made or performed according to specifications to satisfy customers at the time of purchase and during use. Companies throughout the world emphasize quality as an important strategic initiative. Several high-profile awards—such as the Malcolm Baldrige Quality Award in the United States—are given to companies that have produced high quality products and services. International quality standards have also emerged. For example, ISO 9000, adopted by more than 85 countries, enables companies to effectively document and certify the elements of their production processes that lead to quality.

2. Two basic aspects of quality are **design quality** and **conformance quality**.

- Design quality refers to how closely the characteristics of a product or service meet the needs and wants of customers. For example, if customers of photocopying machines need copiers that copy and fax, machines that do not meet these consumer needs would be a design quality failure.
- Conformance quality is the performance of a product or service relative to its design and product specifications. For example, if a pho-

tocopying machine mishandles paper or breaks down, it fails to satisfy conformance quality.

To ensure that actual performance achieves customer satisfaction, companies must first design products to satisfy customers through design quality and then they must meet design specifications through conformance quality.

3. Companies incur the **costs of quality (COQ)** to prevent, or the costs arising as a result of, the production of a low-quality product. These costs occur in all business functions of the value chain. COQ programs use four cost categories:

a. **Prevention costs** are incurred to preclude the production of products that do not conform to specifications.
b. **Appraisal costs** are incurred to detect which of the individual units of products do not conform to specifications.
c. **Internal failure costs** are incurred on defective products *before* they are shipped to customers.
d. **External failure costs** are incurred on defective products *after* they have been shipped to customers.

COQ reports give more insight when managers compare trends over time. In successful quality programs, decreases occur over time in (i) the COQ as a percentage of revenues and (ii) the sum of internal and external failure costs as a percentage of the COQ. Many companies believe they should eliminate all failure costs and have zero defects.

4. A seven-step activity-based approach determines the COQ:

Step 1: Identify the product that is the chosen cost object.
Step 2: Identify the direct COQ of the product.

Step 3: Select the activities and cost-allocation bases to use for allocating indirect COQ to the product.

Step 4: Identify the indirect COQ associated with each cost-allocation base.

Step 5: Compute the rate per unit of each cost-allocation base.

Step 6: Compute the indirect COQ allocated to the product.

Step 7: Compute the total COQ by adding all direct and indirect COQ assigned to the product.

The total COQ in step 7 typically exclude some important items such as opportunity costs of the contribution margin and income forgone from lost sales, lost production, or lower prices resulting from poor quality. Why are opportunity costs typically excluded? Because they are not recorded in financial accounting systems and are difficult to estimate.

5. Three common techniques to identify and analyze quality problems are **control charts**, **Pareto diagrams**, and **cause-and-effect diagrams** (also called *fishbone diagrams*).

- A control chart, an important tool in statistical quality control (SQC), is a graph of a series of successive observations of a particular step, procedure, or operation taken at regular intervals of time. Each observation is plotted relative to specified ranges that represent the limits within which observations are expected to fall. Only those observations outside the control limits are ordinarily regarded as nonrandom and worth investigating.
- Observations outside the control limits serve as inputs for a Pareto diagram. This diagram is a chart that indicates how frequently each type of defect occurs, ordered from the most frequent to the least frequent.
- The most frequently recurring and costly problems identified by the Pareto diagram are analyzed using a cause-and-effect diagram (also called a *fishbone diagram*) that identifies potential causes of defects—human factors, methods and design factors, machine-related factors, and materials and component factors;

this diagram resembles the bone structure of a fish.

6. A cause-and-effect diagram can help engineers identify alternative solutions to quality problems. Then, these alternatives can be analyzed in terms of relevant costs and relevant benefits. The relevant costs of quality improvement are the incremental costs incurred to implement the quality program. The relevant benefits are lower internal and external failure costs and greater contribution margin from higher sales attributable to the quality improvements.

7. Prevention costs, appraisal costs, and internal failure costs are the financial measures of quality performance inside the company. Nonfinancial measures of internal quality—such as number of defects for each product line and process yield (the ratio of good output to total output)—supplement the financial measures. Other nonfinancial measures help managers gauge customer satisfaction: for example, number of customer complaints, number of defective units shipped to customers as a percentage of total units shipped, and products that experience early or excessive failure. For a single reporting period, financial and nonfinancial measures of quality have limited meaning. They are more informative when managers examine trends over time.

8. Financial and nonfinancial measures of quality have different advantages. COQ reports serve as a summary measure of quality performance for evaluating trade-offs among prevention costs and failure costs. Nonfinancial measures of quality are often easy to quantify and understand. They direct attention to physical processes and hence focus attention on the precise problem areas that need improvement.

9. Companies increasingly view *time* as a driver of strategy. Conducting business correctly and quickly helps increase revenues and decrease costs. Two common operational measures of time are **customer-response time** and **on-time performance**.

- Customer-response time is how long it takes from the time a customer places an order for a product or service to the time the product or service is delivered to the customer. Paragraph 10 discusses customer-response time.

- On-time performance is delivery of a product or service by the time it was scheduled to be delivered. On-time performance increases customer satisfaction.

Note that there is a trade-off between customer-response time and on-time performance: simply scheduling longer customer-response times makes achieving on-time performance easier (although this tactic would displease customers).

10. Three components of customer-response time are (a) *receipt time*, (b) **manufacturing cycle time** (also called **manufacturing lead time**), and (c) *delivery time*. Receipt time is how long it takes the Marketing Department to specify to the Manufacturing Department the exact requirements in the customer's order. Manufacturing cycle time is how long it takes from the time an order is received by the Manufacturing Department to the time a finished good is produced. Manufacturing cycle time is the sum of waiting time and manufacturing time for an order. Delivery time is the time it takes to deliver a completed order to a customer.

11. Some companies evaluate their response time improvement efforts using a measure called **manufacturing cycle efficiency (MCE)**. MEC equals value-added manufacturing time divided by manufacturing cycle time. As discussed in Chapter 12, value-added manufacturing activities are tasks that customers perceive as adding value or utility to a product.

12. A **time driver** is any factor that causes a change in the speed of an activity when the factor changes. Two important time drivers are (a) uncertainty about when customers will order products or services and (b) **bottlenecks** due to limited capacity. A bottleneck occurs in an operation when the work to be performed approaches or exceeds the capacity available to do it. For example, a bottleneck results and causes delays when products that need to be processed at a particular machine arrive while the machine is being used to process other products. **Average waiting time** is the aver-

age amount of time that an order will wait in line before the machine is set up and the order is processed. Average waiting time is inversely related to the amount of unused capacity. That is, the smaller the unused capacity, the greater the likelihood that an order arrives when an operation is in use. The formula, text p.683, computes average waiting time if only one product is manufactured.

13. In some instances, introducing a new product causes delays in the delivery of all of the products. That's because the new product can cause unused capacity to shrink, increasing the probability that (at any point in time) new orders will arrive while existing orders are being manufactured or are waiting to be manufactured. Because time is a key factor in competitiveness, the management accountant needs to identify and analyze the cost of delays for all products in calculating the relevant costs and relevant revenues of adding a new product.

14. The extended example, text p.683, considers whether to add a new product: pistons. Interestingly, even though the new product has a positive contribution margin of $1,600 per order, the analysis of relevant revenues and relevant costs indicates *not* to add the new product, because of the negative effects it has on the existing product—increased inventory carrying costs caused by a higher average manufacturing cycle time and decreased revenues caused by customers who are unwilling to pay as high a price for slower delivery. EXHIBIT 19-8, text p.685, presents the relevant revenues and relevant costs for this decision.

15. When products are made from multiple parts and processed on different machines, interdependencies arise among operations. Some operations cannot be started until parts from a previous operation are available. In these cases, waiting time occurs for two reasons. First, parts that require processing at a bottleneck machine must wait until the bottleneck machine is available. Second, parts made on nonbottleneck machines subsequent to the bottleneck machine must wait until parts coming from the bottleneck machine arrive.

16. The **theory of constraints (TOC)** describes methods to maximize operating in-come when faced with some bottleneck and some non bottleneck operations. The TOC defines three measurements:

- **Throughput margin** equals revenues minus the direct material costs of the goods sold.

- *Investments* equal the sum of materials costs in direct materials, work-in-process, and finished goods inventories; R&D costs; and costs of equipment and buildings.

- *Operating costs* equal all costs of operations (other than direct materials) incurred to earn throughput margin. Operating costs include salaries and wages, rent, utilities, depreciation, and the like.

The objective of the TOC is to increase throughput margin while decreasing investments and operating costs. The TOC considers a short-run time horizon and assumes operating costs are fixed.

17. The TOC emphasizes the management of bottleneck operations as the key to improving performance of the production system as a whole. Desirable actions in managing a bottleneck operation include:

a. Eliminate idle time at the bottleneck operation (that is, time when a machine is neither being set up to process products nor actually processing products).

b. Process only those parts or products that increase throughput margin, not parts or products that will be placed in finished goods or spare parts inventory.

c. Shift products that do not have to be made on the bottleneck operation to nonbottleneck operations or to outside processing facilities.

d. Reduce setup time and processing time at bottleneck operations (for example, by reducing the number of parts in a product).

e. Improve the quality of parts or products manufactured at the bottleneck operation.

18. It is insightful to use the four perspectives of the balanced scorecard to summarize how financial and nonfinancial measures of time relate to one another, reduce delays, and increase output of bottlemeck operations. See the listing of items for each perspective, text pp. 688-689.

Featured Exercise

Moran Company expects to spend $100,000 in 2011 for appraisal costs if it does not change its inspection method for incoming materials. If Wellington decides to implement a new inspection method, it will save fixed appraisal costs of $10,000 and variable appraisal cost of $0.30 per pound of materials inspected. The new method requires annual training costs of $15,000 and equipment rental of $40,000 per year. Each unit of finished product requires two pounds of materials.

Internal failure cost averages $40 per failed unit of finished product. During 2010, 10% of all completed units had to be reworked. External failure cost averages $100 per failed unit of finished product. The company's average external failure rate is 2% of units sold. Assume there are no inventories.

a. If the new method is used, how much will appraisal costs change in 2011 if 200,000 pounds of materials are inspected?

b. Assume the new inspection method reduces failed units of finished product by 20%. How much will internal failure costs change in 2011 if 200,000 pounds of materials are inspected?

c. Assume the new inspection method reduces external product failures by 50%. How much will external failure costs change in 2011 if 200,000 pounds of materials are inspected?

Solution

a. Savings in existing appraisal costs:

Fixed portion	$10,000
Variable portion, 200,000 × $0.30	60,000
Total	70,000
Deduct additional appraisal costs:	
Training ($15,000) and equipment rental ($40,000)	55,000
Decrease in appraisal costs	$15,000

b. Production of finished product = 200,000 pounds ÷ 2 pounds per unit = 100,000 units

Internally failed units with original inspection method = 100,000 × 0.10 = 10,000 units

Decrease in internal failure costs with new inspection method = 10,000 × 0.20 × $40
= $80,000

c. Production of finished product (including reworked units), from (b) = 100,000 units

Externally failed units with new inspection method = 100,000 × 0.02 = 2,000 units

Decrease in external failure costs with new inspection method = 2,000 × 0.50 × $100
= $100,000

Review Questions and Exercises

Completion Statements

Fill in the blank(s) to complete each statement.

1. _____ quality refers to how closely the characteristics of a product or service meet the needs and wants of customers.
2. _____ quality is the performance of a product or service relative to its design and product specifications.
3. Costs of quality (COQ) are classified into which four categories? _____ _____ _____
4. The time it takes from the time a customer places an order for a product or service to the time the product or service is delivered to the customer is called _____ _____.
5. _____ is the time it takes from the time an order is received by the Manufacturing Department to the time a finished good is produced.
6. An operation in which the work required to be performed approaches or exceeds the capacity available to do it is called a _____.
7. Under the theory of constraints, throughput margin equals _____ _____.

True-False

Indicate whether each statement is true (T) or false (F).

____ 1. Costs of quality incurred to detect which of the individual units of a product do not conform to specifications are called internal failure costs.
____ 2. All the costs of quality entail cash outflows.
____ 3. Costs of quality are incurred across the entire value chain.
____ 4. Statistical quality control often uses Pareto diagrams to distinguish random variation from nonrandom variation in an operating process.
____ 5. A Pareto diagram helps to identify the potential causes of product failure.
____ 6. Customer-response time is an example of a nonfinancial measure of performance used in quality-improvement programs.
____ 7. Average waiting time is inversely related to the amount of unused capacity.
____ 8. Considering only quantitative factors, it may be undesirable to introduce a new product that has a positive contribution margin, even though machine capacity is available.
____ 9. It is undesirable to have unused capacity at the bottleneck operation in a manufacturing plant.

Multiple Choice

Select the best answer to each question. Space is provided for computations after the quantitative questions.

____ 1. (CMA adapted) The costs of rework in a quality-improvement program are categorized as:
   a. external failure costs.
   b. internal failure costs.
   c. training costs.
   d. prevention costs.
   e. appraisal costs.

____ 2. (CMA) The costs of using statistical quality control in a quality-improvement program are categorized as:
   a. external failure costs.
   b. internal failure costs.
   c. training costs.
   d. prevention costs.
   e. appraisal costs.

____ 3. (CMA) All of the following costs are generally included in a costs of quality report except:
   a. warranty claims.
   b. forgone contribution margin on lost sales.
   c. supplier evaluations.
   d. design engineering.
   e. quality training.

4. (CMA) The following selected line items are from the Cost of Quality Report for Watson Company for May.

Cost	
Rework	$ 725
Equipment maintenance	1,154
Product testing	786
Product repair	695

Watson's total prevention and appraisal costs for May are:
a. $786.
b. $1,154.
c. $1,849.
d. $1,940.
e. $2,665.

5. John's Custom Shirts has variable demand. Historically, demand has ranged from 20 to 40 shirts a day with an average of 30. John works 8 hours a day, 5 days a week. Each order he receives is to custom print one shirt and each shirt takes 12 minutes to print. The average waiting time (rounded to nearest tenth of a minute) is:
a. 1.8 minutes.
b. 14.1 minutes.
c. 18.0 minutes.
d. 36.0 minutes.

6. Ashmore Company has two production departments, Cutting and Finishing. The Cutting Department is constrained by the speed of the cutting machines. The Finishing Department is constrained by the speed of the workers. The Finishing Department normally waits on work coming from the Cutting Department. Each department works an 8-hour day. If the Cutting Department were to begin work 2 hours earlier than the Finishing Department each day (thereby working a 10-hour day), the two departments would finish their work at about the same time. Not only would this change eliminate the bottleneck, but also it would increase production by 40 finished units per day. The number of units in finished goods inventory would remain the same. It costs $400 to operate the Cutting Department 2 more hours per day. The contribution margin is $15 per unit. If the Cutting Department operates 10 hours per day, the total production per day is:
a. 160 units.
b. 200 units.
c. 220 units.
d. 400 units.

7. Using the information in question 6, and assuming the Cutting Department operates 10 hours per day, the total contribution margin per day:
a. increases by $200.
b. remains the same.
c. decreases by $200.
d. decreases by $400.

___ 8. Which of the following is *not* an action
in managing bottleneck operations under the theory of constraints?
  a. Reduce setup time and processing
     time at bottleneck operations.
  b. Increase the efficiency and capacity
     of the bottleneck operation.
  c. Process only those products that in-
     crease throughput margin.
  d. Increase the efficiency and capacity
     of nonbottleneck operations.

Review Exercises

1. Palmateer Company manufactures two products, C and P. Pertinent information is as follows:

	Product C	Product P
Selling price	$90	$100
Market demand per week	100 units	50 units
Direct material costs	$45	$40
Time required to produce one unit:		
Operation 1	18 minutes	10 minutes
Operation 2	15 minutes	30 minutes
Operation 3	10 minutes	5 minutes
Operation 4	12 minutes	10 minutes

Each operation has a capacity of 2,400 minutes per week.

What production schedule for C and P maximizes Palmateer's weekly throughput margin? Show your computations.

2. Huntington Industries makes an electronic component in two departments, Machining and Assembly. The capacity per month is 30,000 units in the Machining Department and 20,000 units in the Assembly Department. The only variable cost of the product is direct material of $100 per unit. All direct material cost is incurred in the Machining Department. All other costs of operating the two departments are fixed costs. Huntington can sell as many units of this electronic component as it produces at a selling price of $300 per unit.

Assuming any defective units produced in either department must be scrapped:
a. Compute the loss that occurs if a defective unit is produced in the Machining Department.
b. Compute the loss that occurs if a defective unit is produced in the Assembly Department.
c. How do your answers in parts (a) and (b) relate to the theory of constraints? Explain.

Answers and Solutions to Chapter 19 Review Questions and Exercises

Completion Statements

1. Design
2. Conformance
3. prevention costs, appraisal costs, internal failure costs, external failure costs
4. customer-response time
5. Manufacturing cycle time (Manufacturing lead time)
6. bottleneck
7. revenues minus direct material cost of the goods sold

True-False

1. F   The statement describes *appraisal costs*, not *internal failure costs*. Internal failure costs are incurred on defective products before they are shipped to customers.
2. F   The opportunity-cost portion of external failure costs—estimated forgone contribution margin on lost sales (shown in Panel B of EXHIBIT 19-2, text p.674)—does not entail cash outflows.
3. T
4. F   Statistical quality control often uses *control charts* to distinguish random variation from nonrandom variation in an operating process.
5. F   The statement describes a *cause-and-effect diagram* (also called a *fishbone diagram*), not a *Pareto diagram*. A Pareto diagram indicates how frequently each type of failure (defect) occurs, ordered

from the most frequent to the least frequent. EXHIBIT 19-5, text p.677, shows a cause-and-effect diagram, and EXHIBIT 19-4, text p.677, shows a Pareto diagram.

6. T
7. T
8. T
9. F   If the uncertainty of demand is high, some unused capacity at the bottleneck operation is desirable. Increasing the capacity at the bottleneck operation can reduce average waiting time and inventories.

Multiple Choice

1. b   The costs incurred by defective products *before* they are shipped to customers (such as reworked units) are internal failure costs.

2. e   The costs incurred to detect which of the individual units of products do not conform to specifications (such as the costs of product testing) are appraisal costs.

3. b   A COQ report generally does not include opportunity costs. Panel A of EXHIBIT 19-2, text p.674, illustrates the typical COQ report.

4. d   Equipment maintenance is a prevention cost and product testing is an appraisal cost: $1,154 + $786 = $1,940. Rework is an internal failure cost. Product repair is an external failure cost, assuming the repair takes place after the product is shipped to customers.

5. c   The formula for average waiting time (AWT) is:

$$AWT = \frac{\left(\begin{array}{c}\text{Avg. number of}\\\text{orders per day}\end{array}\right) \times \left(\begin{array}{c}\text{Manuf. time}\\\text{per order}\end{array}\right)^2}{2 \times \left[\begin{array}{c}\text{Daily capacity}\\\text{in minutes}\end{array} - \left(\begin{array}{c}\text{Avg. number of}\\\text{orders per day}\end{array} \times \begin{array}{c}\text{Manuf. time}\\\text{per order}\end{array}\right)\right]}$$

$$AWT = \frac{30 \times (12)^2}{2 \times \left[(8 \times 60) - (30 \times 12)\right]}$$

$$AWT = \frac{30 \times 144}{2 \times (480 - 360)}$$

$$AWT = \frac{4,320}{240} = 18 \text{ minutes}$$

6. b   The increase of 2 hours per day in the Cutting Department increases the company's production of finished goods by 40 units per day. Thus, the company's production of finished goods per hour of Cutting Department time is 20 units (40 ÷ 2), and the company's total production of finished goods per day is 200 units (20 × 10). *Alternative solution*: If 40 additional finished units are produced in 20% (2 hours ÷ 10 hours) of the Cutting Department's expanded time per day, the company's total production of finished goods per day is 200 units (40 ÷ 0.20).

7. a   Change in total contribution margin per day = (40 × $15) − $400
                                                                                                          = $600 − $400 = $200 increase

8. d   The theory of constraints emphasizes the management of *bottleneck* operations as the key to improving the performance of the production system as a whole. Increasing the efficiency and capacity of *nonbottleneck* operations does not improve that performance.

Review Exercise 1

Four steps are used to obtain the answer. First, compute throughput margin per unit of each product.

	Product C	Product P
Selling price	$90	$100
Deduct direct material costs	45	40
Throughput margin	$45	$ 60

Second, determine whether there is a bottleneck operation.

Operation	Minutes Required for C	Minutes Required for P	Total Minutes Required
1	$18 \times 100 = 1,800$	$10 \times 50 = 500$	$1,800 + 500 = 2,300$
2	$15 \times 100 = 1,500$	$30 \times 50 = 1,500$	$1,500 + 1,500 = 3,000$
3	$10 \times 100 = 1,000$	$5 \times 50 = 250$	$1,000 + 250 = 1,250$
4	$12 \times 100 = 1,200$	$10 \times 50 = 500$	$1,200 + 1,500 = 1,700$

Operation 2 is the only bottleneck operation. That's because its total minutes required exceed its capacity of 2,400 minutes. (Note that if there were no bottleneck operations, the production schedule to meet market demand would be 100 units of C and 50 units of P.)

Third, determine throughput margin per unit of the bottleneck operation.

Product C $= \$45 \div 15$ minutes $= \$3$ per minute of Operation 2
Product P $= \$60 \div 30$ minutes $= \$2$ per minute of Operation 2

Fourth, determine the production schedule of C and P that maximizes throughput margin.

Given the results in step 3, produce as much C as Operation 2 allows and use the remainder of its capacity to produce P:

Product	Utilization of Operation 2	Production Schedule
C	1,500 minutes (from step 2)	$1,500 \div 15 = 100$ units
P	$2,400 - 1,500 = 900$ minutes	$900 \div 30 = 30$ units

Therefore, the maximum throughput margin $= (100 \times \$45) + (30 \times \$60) = \$6,300$.

Review Exercise 2

a. Direct material cost $100
   Add forgone contribution margin on lost sale,
      $0 because Machining has more capacity
        than Assembly   0
   Loss from producing a defective unit in Machining $100
b. Direct material cost $100
   Add forgone contribution margin on lost sale
      $300 − $100   200
   Loss from producing a defective unit in Assembly $300

c. Under the theory of constraints, the objective is to maximize throughput margin, which equals revenues minus direct material cost of the goods sold. In this case, Huntington Industries should focus on improving quality first in the Assembly Department because poor quality (defective units) in that department is more costly. That is, because the Machining Department has more capacity than the Assembly Department, forgone throughput margin only occurs from poor quality in the Assembly Department.

CHAPTER 20

Inventory Management, Just-in-Time, and Simplified Costing Methods

Overview

This chapter focuses on **inventory management**, which includes planning, coordinating, and controlling activities related to the flow of inventory into, through, and out of a company. Many decisions fall under the umbrella of inventory management: What is the economic order quantity for an item? When is the best time to order an item? Is it desirable for a company to use just-in-time purchasing, just-in-time production, and/or backflush costing? In making these decisions, managers use the relevant-cost analysis introduced in Chapter 11.

Highlights

1. The following cost categories are important when managing goods for sale (or materials):

a. **Purchasing costs** are the cost of goods acquired from suppliers, including incoming freight costs.

b. **Ordering costs** arise in preparing and issuing purchase orders, receiving and inspecting the items included in the orders, and paying the related invoices.

c. **Carrying costs** arise while holding an inventory of goods for sale; these costs include the opportunity cost of the investment tied up in an inventory and costs associated with storage, such as space rental, insurance, obsolescence, and breakage or spoilage. Opportunity cost is not recorded in financial accounting systems.

d. **Stockout costs** arise when a company runs out of a particular item for which there is customer demand, and so the company must act quickly to meet that demand or suffer the costs of not meeting it. Depending on how managers respond to this situation, stockout costs are either the costs of expediting an order from a supplier or the opportunity costs of forgone contribution margin on current and future lost sales.

e. *Costs of quality* are prevention costs, appraisal costs, internal failure costs, and external failure costs (described in paragraph 3 of Chapter 19's Highlights, p.257).

f. **Shrinkage costs** result from theft by outsiders, embezzlement by employees, misclassifications, and clerical errors.

2. One major decision in managing goods for sale (or materials) is deciding *how much of a given item to order*. The **economic order quantity (EOQ)** is a decision model that calculates the optimal quantity of inventory to order under a set of assumptions. The simplest version of this model minimizes only the relevant costs of ordering and carrying inventory. The formula is:

$$EOQ = \sqrt{\frac{2DP}{C}}$$

where:

D = Demand in units for a specified period
P = Relevant ordering cost per purchase order
C = Relevant carrying cost of one unit in stock for the period used for D

Calculate the annual relevant total costs (RTC) for any order quantity, Q (not just the EOQ), as follows:

$$RTC = \left(\frac{D}{Q} \times P\right) + \left(\frac{Q}{2} \times C\right)$$

3. The second major decision in managing goods for sale (or materials) *is when to order a given item*. The **reorder point** is the quantity level of inventory on hand that triggers a new purchase order. The reorder point is simplest to compute if both demand and purchase-order lead time are known with certainty. To illustrate, assume 250 units are sold per week and purchase-order lead time is 2 weeks.

Then,

Reorder point = 250 × 2 = 500 units

In other words, an order should be placed whenever the level of inventory on hand declines to 500 units.

4. When companies holding inventory are uncertain about demand, purchase-order lead time, or the quantity that suppliers can provide, they often hold **safety stock**. Safety stock is inventory held at all times regardless of the quantity of inventory ordered using the EOQ model. Safety stock is used as a buffer against unexpected increases in demand or lead time and unavailability of stock from suppliers. The optimal safety stock level is the quantity of safety stock that minimizes the sum of the annual relevant stockout costs and annual relevant carrying costs.

5. There are three main challenges in estimating inventory-related costs and their effects. First, only relevant outlay (cash) costs and opportunity costs should be used. Second, the parameters in the EOQ model should recognize the impact of improvements in operations and the advent of technologies such as placing purchase orders electronically. Third, goal incongruence occurs if there is an inconsistency between the EOQ decision model and performance evaluation of the managers implementing the inventory management decisions. To illustrate goal incongruence, assume the opportunity cost of investment tied up in inventory is included in the EOQ model (as it should be) but is excluded from annual carrying costs in evaluating the manager's performance. A likely cause of this inconsistency between the EOQ model and performance evaluation is that opportunity costs are not recorded in financial accounting systems, but those systems are the source of information used for performance evaluation. Under these conditions, the manager is inclined to purchase a larger order quantity than the EOQ.

6. An important feature of the EOQ model is that the annual relevant total costs are rarely sensitive to sizable variations in cost predictions. Sensitivity is dampened by the effect of the square root in the EOQ model. A three-step approach, text pp.709-710, determines the cost of a prediction error in ordering costs per purchase order; the prediction error in P is 50% ($100 instead of $200), but the cost of the prediction error is less than 7% of annual relevant total costs of $3,677.

7. Some companies have dramatically reduced their inventories by using **just-in-time (JIT) purchasing**. JIT purchasing is the purchase of materials (or goods) so that they are delivered just as needed for production (or sales). JIT purchasing requires companies to restructure their relationships with suppliers (that is, establish long-run contracts with suppliers and place orders electronically) and place smaller and more frequent purchase orders. Restructuring relationships with suppliers and using computers for order-related activities significantly reduce annual relevant ordering costs, thereby decreasing EOQ. JIT purchasing, however, is not guided solely by the EOQ; in addition to considering the trade-off between carrying costs and ordering costs (which is the full scope of the EOQ model), JIT purchasing includes the other costs of inventory management—purchasing costs, stockout costs, costs of quality, and shrinkage costs. EXHIBIT 20-5, text p.712, compares the annual relevant costs of a company's current purchasing policy with a JIT purchasing policy. EXHIBIT 20-6, text p.713, compares the annual relevant costs of two suppliers under a JIT purchasing policy.

8. The level of inventories held by retailers is influenced by demand patterns of their customers, and supply relationships with their distributors and manufacturers. The term *supply chain* describes the flow of goods, services and information from the initial sources of materials and services to the delivery of products to customers, regardless of whether those activities occur in the

same company or in other companies. There are multiple gains to companies in a supply chain by coordinating activities and sharing information. For example, assume all retailers share daily sales information about a given product. This sales information reduces the level of uncertainty that manufacturers and suppliers face regarding retail demand for the product. The reduced uncertainty leads to fewer stockouts at the retail level, lower inventories being held by each company in the supply chain, and fewer expedited orders.

9. Manufacturing companies face the challenging task of producing high-quality products at competitive cost levels. **Materials requirements planning (MRP)** and **just-in-time (JIT) production** (also called **lean production**) are two widely used types of systems developed to help managers plan and implement production and inventory activities.

- MRP is a "push-through" system that manufactures finished goods for inventory on the basis of demand forecasts. Taking into account the lead time required to purchase materials and to manufacture components and finished products, a master production schedule specifies the quantity and timing of each item to be produced. Once scheduled production starts, the output of each department is pushed through the production line whether or not it is needed. The result is often an accumulation of inventory as workstations receive work they are not yet ready to process. Management accounting assists MRP by (a) maintaining accurate and timely information on inventory and (b) estimating the setup costs for production runs (analogous to the ordering costs in the EOQ model) and downtime costs.
- JIT production is a "demand-pull" system that manufacturers each component in a production line as soon as, and only when, needed by the next step in the production line. Demand triggers each step of the production process, starting with customer demand for a finished product at the end of the process and working all the way back to the demand for direct materials at the beginning of the process. JIT production aims to simultaneously (a) meet customer demand in a timely way, (b) with

high quality products, and (c) at the lowest possible total cost. JIT production emphasizes eliminating the causes of rework and lowering manufacturing lead times.

10. There are five features in a JIT production system. First, organize production in **manufacturing cells**, a grouping of all the different types of equipment used to make a given product. Second, hire and train multi-skilled workers who are capable of performing a variety of operations and tasks. Third, aggressively eliminate defects. Fourth, reduce setup time and manufacturing cycle time. Fifth, select suppliers on the basis of their ability to deliver quality materials in a timely manner. Most companies implementing JIT production also implement JIT purchasing.

11. The success of a JIT system hinges on the speed of information flows from customers to manufacturers to suppliers. Enterprise Resource Planning (ERP) does not concentrate on specific business functions separately; instead it uses a single database that collects data and feeds it into software modules for accounting, distribution, manu-facturing, purchasing, human resources, and other functions. ERP systems give workers, lower-level managers, customers, and suppliers access to operating information. This benefit coupled with tight coordination across business functions enables ERP systems to rapidly shift manufacturing and distribution plans in response to changes in supply and demand.

12. To control and evaluate JIT production, management accounting relies on: (a) personal observation by production line workers and managers, (b) financial performance measures such as inventory turnover ratios, and (c) nonfinancial performance measures of inventory, quality, and time. Rapid, meaningful feedback is critical because the lack of buffer inventories in a demand-pull system creates added urgency to detect and solve problems quickly.

13. Traditional normal and standard costing (described in Chapters 4, 7, 8, and 17) use **sequential tracking**, a costing system in which recording of the journal entries occurs in the same order as actual purchases and progress in production. An

alternative approach to sequential tracking is **backflush costing**, a costing system which omits recording some of the journal entries relating to the stages from purchase of direct materials to the sale of finished goods. Backflush costing then reaches backward and pulls ("flushes") the normal or standard manufacturing costs to units produced and/or sold. Backflush costing dovetails with JIT production and is less costly to operate than sequential tracking systems.

14. There are several versions of backflush costing. They differ with regard to the **trigger points** used. A trigger point is a stage in the production cycle—from purchase of direct materials and recording of conversion costs to sale of finished goods—at which journal entries are recorded in the accounting system. Regardless of the version of backflush costing used, the period-end location of manufacturing costs in the general-ledger accounts is basically the same as in sequential tracking, except backflush costing bypasses the Work in Process Control account. Three examples, beginning text p.719, illustrate different versions of backflush costing; EXHIBIT 20-7 (p.720), EXHIBIT 20-8 (p. 723), and EXHIBIT 20-9 (p. 725) show the related journal entries. In Example 1 the account "Inventory: Materials and In-Process Control" combines materials inventory and materials in work-in-process inventory. In Example 2 the account "Inventory Control" combines direct materials inventory and any direct materials in work-in-process and finished goods inventories. In Example 3, there are two trigger points: completion of good finished units and sale of those units.

15. The financial accounting procedures in backflush costing do not strictly adhere to generally accepted accounting principles (GAAP) and do not leave sufficient audit trails. For example, work in process (an asset) exists but is not recognized in the financial statements under backflush costing. Advocates of backflush costing, however, cite the materiality concept in support of their pro-

cedures. That is, they maintain that when inventories are low or when total costs are not subject to significant change from one accounting period to the next, operating income reported under backflush costing does not differ materially from operating income reported in traditional normal or standard costing. If the amount of difference is material, an adjusting entry is recorded to satisfy GAAP.

16. Successful JIT production requires companies to focus on the entire value chain of business functions (from suppliers to manufacturing to customers) in order to reduce inventories, lead times, and waste. The emphasis on improvements throughout the value chain has led some JIT companies to develop organization structure and costing systems that focus on **value streams**. Value streams are all the value-added activities needed to design, manufacture, and deliver a given product or product line to customers.

17. **Lean accounting** is a costing method that supports creating value for customers by costing the value streams, as distinguished from individual products or departments. Tracing direct costs to value streams is simple because companies using lean accounting dedicate resources to individual value streams. The Allston Company example, text pp. 727-728, illustrates lean accounting.

Featured Exercise

Catalina Stores, a retail chain, sells small appliances. Information for one of these appliances is as follows:

Total annual demand in units	3,000
Relevant carrying cost per unit per year	$5
Relevant ordering cost per purchase order	$300
Inventory level when each order arrives	zero
Maximum daily sales	80 units
Average daily sales	70 units
Minimum daily sales	60 units
Purchase-order lead time	22 days

a. Compute EOQ.
b. Compute the total of annual relevant ordering costs and annual relevant carrying costs at the EOQ level.
c. Compute the minimum safety stock needed to be certain a stockout does not occur.
d. Compute the reorder point.

Solution

a. $\text{EOQ} = \sqrt{\dfrac{2(3,000)(\$300)}{\$5}} = \sqrt{\dfrac{\$1,800,000}{\$5}} = \sqrt{360,000} = 600 \text{ units}$

b. Let TRC = Total of annual relevant ordering costs and annual relevant carrying costs at the EOQ level

$$\text{TRC} = \frac{DP}{Q} + \frac{QC}{2} = \frac{3,000(\$300)}{600} + \frac{600(\$5)}{2} = \$1,500 + \$1,500 = \$3,000$$

c. Minimum safety stock to prevent a stockout $= (80 - 70) \times 22 = 220$ units

d. Reorder point $= 220 + (70 \times 22)$
$= 220 + 1,540 = 1,760$ units

Alternative solution: $\quad 80 \times 22 = 1,760$ units

Review Questions and Exercises

Completion Statements

Fill in the blank(s) to complete each statement.

1. Which six categories of costs pertaining to inventory are distinguished for management purposes?

   _____
   _____
   _____.

2. Which two of the cost categories in the preceding answer are considered in the EOQ model?

   _____
   and _____

3. What do each of the letters in the EOQ model stand for?

   D = _____
   _____
   P = _____
   _____
   C = _____
   _____
   _____

4. In purchasing materials or goods, ordering costs are equivalent to _____ costs for a production run.

5. A system of production that manufacturers each component in a production line as soon as, and only when, needed by the next step in the production line is called _____
   _____.

6. Traditional normal and standard costing record the journal entries in the same order as actual purchases and progress in production occurs, which is called _____
   _____.

7. _____ omits recording some of the journal entries relating to the stages from purchase of direct materials to the sale of finished goods; it then uses normal or standard costs to work backward to assign manufacturing costs to units produced and/or sold.

8. A stage in the cycle, from purchase of direct materials to sale of finished goods, at which journal entries are recorded in the accounting system is called a _____.

True-False

Indicate whether each statement is true (T) or false (F).

_____ 1. Examples of carrying costs of inventory are obsolescence, opportunity cost of investment tied up in inventory, and inspection.

_____ 2. The EOQ model does not include quantity discounts lost on inventory purchases.

_____ 3. EOQ minimizes the annual relevant total carrying costs of inventory.

_____ 4. An example of a cost pertaining to inventory that usually is irrelevant to the decision of how much to order is salaries of stockroom workers.

_____ 5. The reorder point decreases if the ordering costs per purchase order increase.

_____ 6. JIT purchasing should be guided by the EOQ decision model.

_____ 7. Adopting JIT purchasing is likely to result in fewer suppliers for each item and more paperwork.

_____ 8. JIT production operates as a push-through system.

_____ 9. A key feature of backflush costing is that it tracks manufacturing costs sequentially.

_____ 10. When a single Inventory Control account is used in backflush costing, this account is restricted solely to direct materials, whether they are in storerooms, in process, or in finished goods.

_____ 11. Although backflush costing may not strictly adhere to generally accepted accounting principles, the accounting principle of materiality works in favor of backflush costing when inventories are low.

Multiple Choice

Select the best answer to each question. Space is provided for computations after the quantitative questions.

____ 1. (CPA) Barter Corporation has been buying Product A in lots of 1,200 units, a four months' supply. The cost per unit is $100; the ordering cost is $200 per purchase order; and the annual inventory carrying cost for one unit is $25. Assume the units are required evenly throughout the year. The EOQ is:
    a. 144 units.
    b. 240 units.
    c. 600 units.
    d. 1,200 units.

____ 2. (CPA) Garmar, Inc., determines the following information for a given year:

EOQ in units	5,000
Total annual ordering costs	$10,000
Ordering cost per	
purchase order	$50
Cost of carrying	
one unit for one year	$4

What is Garmar's estimated annual demand in units?
    a. 1,000,000
    b. 2,000,000
    c. 4,000,000
    d. Cannot be determined from the information given.

____ 3. (CPA adapted) A manufacturer expects to produce 200,000 widgets during the fiscal year ending June 30, 2011, to supply the demand that is uniform throughout the year. The setup costs for each production run of widgets are $144. The cost of carrying one widget in inventory is $0.20 per year. After a batch of widgets is produced and placed in inventory, it is sold at a uniform rate and inventory reaches zero when the next batch of widgets is completed. The quantity of widgets (rounded to the nearest one hundred widgets) that would be produced in each run in fiscal year 2011 to minimize total annual relevant setup and carrying costs is:
    a. 12,000.
    b. 12,500.
    c. 16,000.
    d. 17,000.
    e. 19,000.

____ 4. (CPA) For its EOQ model, a company has ordering cost per purchase order of $10, and annual cost of carrying one unit in stock of $2. If the ordering cost per purchase order increases by 20%, and the annual cost of carrying one unit in stock increases by 25%, while all other considerations remain constant, EOQ:
    a. remains unchanged.
    b. decreases.
    c. increases.
    d. either increases or decreases depending on the reorder point.

5. (CMA) Canseco Enterprises uses 84,000 units of Part 256 in manufacturing activities over a 300-day work year. The usual purchase-order lead time for the part is six days; occasionally, however, the lead time has been as high as eight days. The company now desires to adjust the size of its safety stock. The size of the safety stock and the likely effect on stockout costs and carrying costs, respectively, are:
   a. 560 units, decrease, increase.
   b. 560 units, decrease, decrease.
   c. 1,680 units, decrease, increase.
   d. 1,680 units, increase, no change.
   e. 2,240 units, increase, decrease.

6. (CPA adapted) Key Co. changed from a traditional production system with job costing to a just-in-time production system with backflush costing. What are the expected effects of these changes on Key's inspection cost and record-keeping detail of costs tracked to jobs in process?

	Inspection cost	Detail of costs tracked to jobs
a.	Decreases	Decreases
b.	Decreases	Increases
c.	Increases	Decreases
d.	Increases	Increases

7. (CMA) Which one of the following statements best describes material requirements planning (MRP)?
   a. A planning system that is used to determine the amount and timing of the optimal inventory level.
   b. A software tool that is used to forecast the ordering quantities of inventories that tend to be subject to a variable and continual demand.
   c. A planning system that is used to determine the amount and timing of inventories that are dependent on the demand for finished goods.
   d. A software tool that is used to forecast the schedule of material purchases that tend to be subject to a variable and continual demand.
   e. A formal system of ordering and scheduling finished goods inventories.

Review Exercises

1. (CMA) Gerstein Company manufactures a line of deluxe office fixtures. The annual demand for its miniature oak file is estimated to be 5,000 units. The annual cost of carrying one unit in inventory is $10, and the setup cost to initiate a production run is $1,000. There are no miniature oak files on hand and Gerstein has scheduled four equal production runs of this file for the coming year, the first of which is to be run immediately. Gerstein operates 250 business days per year. Assume sales occur uniformly throughout the year.

   a. If no safety stock is held, compute the relevant total carrying costs for the miniature oak file for the coming year.
   b. If two equal production runs are scheduled for the coming year rather than four, compute the amount of change in the sum of annual relevant total carrying costs and setup costs.
   c. Compute the number of production runs that minimizes the sum of relevant total carrying costs and setup costs for the coming year.

2. Quinn Electronics manufactures television sets. Quinn implemented a JIT purchasing policy at the beginning of 2011. One year later, Sandra Lansing is evaluating the effect of this policy on financial performance. She obtains the following information:

- Average inventory declined from $400,000 to $200,000. Pre-JIT insurance costs of $40,000 per year declined by 40% (because of lower average inventory).
- Pre-JIT, 5,000 square feet of warehouse space was leased for $10,000 per year. The lower average inventory allowed Quinn to sublet 40% of the space at $2.50 per square foot.
- The JIT purchasing policy leads to stockouts on 5,000 pieces of direct material per year. Quinn's policy is to handle stockouts with rush orders at a cost of $4 per piece.
- Quinn's required rate of return on investment in inventory is 15%.

Compute the cash savings (loss) from the JIT purchasing policy for 2011.

3. Cumberland Inc. produces video cameras. For November, there were no beginning inventories of direct materials and no beginning and ending work in process. Cumberland uses a JIT production system and backflush costing. Standard costs per unit for November are: direct materials $52, conversion costs $30. The following data are for November:

Direct materials and components purchased	$21,200,000
Conversion costs incurred	$12,320,000
Number of finished units manufactured	400,000
Number of finished units sold	384,000

Assume there are no variances for materials.

a. Prepare summary journal entries for November (without disposing of underallocated or overallocated conversion costs), assuming there are two trigger points: (i) purchase of direct materials and components and (ii) completion of finished goods. The inventory accounts used are Inventory: Materials and In-Process Control, and Finished Goods Control.

General Journal	Debit	Credit

b. Prepare summary journal entries for November, assuming there are two trigger points: (i) purchase of direct materials and components and (ii) sale of finished goods. The only inventory account, Inventory Control, is restricted solely to direct materials and components (whether they are in storerooms, in process, or in finished goods). Underallocated or overallocated conversion costs are written off at the end of each month.

General Journal	Debit	Credit

c. Refer to part (b). Assume conversion costs are regarded as being material in amount. How do your journal entries in part (b) change?

General Journal	Debit	Credit

d. Repeat part (a) with one difference. There is only one trigger point, the completion of good finished units. As a result, there is only one inventory account, Finished Goods Control.

General Journal	Debit	Credit

Answers and Solutions to Chapter 20 Review Questions and Exercises

Completion Statements

1. purchasing costs, ordering costs, carrying costs, stockout costs, costs of quality, shrinkage costs
2. ordering costs, carrying costs
3. D = Demand in units for a specified period
    P = Relevant ordering cost per purchase order
    C = Relevant carrying cost of one unit in stock for the period used for D
4. setup
5. just-in-time (JIT) production (also called lean production)
6. sequential tracking
7. Backflush costing
8. trigger point

True-False

1. F Inspection is an ordering cost. Obsolescence and opportunity cost of investment tied up in inventory are carrying costs.
2. T
3. F EOQ minimizes the sum of annual relevant ordering costs and annual relevant carrying costs (called annual relevant total costs). This minimum occurs where annual relevant ordering costs and annual relevant carrying costs *are equal*.
4. T
5. F $$\text{Reorder point} = \frac{\text{Number of units sold}}{\text{per unit of time}} \times \frac{\text{Purchase-order}}{\text{lead time}}$$

   A change in the ordering cost per purchase order, therefore, has no effect on the reorder point.
6. F To understand the full costs and benefits of JIT purchasing, it is necessary to move outside the confines of the EOQ model because that model does not consider four of the six categories of costs pertaining to inventory: purchasing costs, stockout costs, costs of quality, and shrinkage costs. The EOQ model only considers ordering costs and carrying costs.
7. F Adopting JIT purchasing is likely to result in fewer suppliers for each item and *less* paperwork, such as when purchase orders are placed by means of electronic data interchange (EDI). Other changes associated with JIT purchasing include smaller and more frequent purchase orders, long-term contracts with suppliers, and less inspection of orders received.
8. F JIT production operates as a *demand-pull* system: demand triggers each step of the production process, starting with customer demand for a finished product at the end of the process and working all the way back to the demand for materials at the beginning of the process.
9. F Sequential tracking is not used in backflush costing. Instead, some of the journal entries are delayed until the completion of production or the sale of finished goods, and then manufacturing costs are "flushed back" through the accounting system.
10. T
11. T

Multiple Choice

1. b Demand in units per year = $1,200 \times 3 = 3,600$;

$$EOQ = \sqrt{\frac{2(3,600)(\$200)}{\$25}} = \sqrt{\frac{\$1,440,000}{\$25}} = \sqrt{57,600} = 240 \text{ units}$$

Note: the cost per unit of $100 is not *explicitly* used in this computation. *Implicitly*, however, the required annual return on the investment of $100 per unit, an opportunity cost, is included in the $25 cost of carrying one unit in stock for one year.

2. a Let D = Annual demand in units

$$5,000 = \sqrt{\frac{2D(\$50)}{\$4}}$$

$$25,000,000 = \frac{\$100D}{\$4}$$

$$25,000,000 = 25D$$

$$D = 25,000,000/25 = 1,000,000$$

Alternative solution: Relevant total costs are at a minimum (the EOQ level) where annual ordering costs and annual carrying costs are equal:

$$\frac{D(\$50)}{5,000} = \$10,000$$
$$\$50D = \$50,000,000$$
$$D = \$50,000,000 \div \$50 = 1,000,000$$

3. d Setup costs in production situations are analogous to ordering costs in purchasing situations.

Let EPRQ = Economic production run quantity

$$EPRQ = \sqrt{\frac{2(200,000)(\$144)}{\$0.20}}$$
$$EPRQ = \sqrt{\frac{\$57,600,000}{\$0.20}}$$
$$EPRQ = \sqrt{288,000,000}$$
$$EPRQ = 17,000 \text{ widgets (rounded to nearest hundred widgets)}$$

Note that a production run is, in effect, an *internal* purchase, whereas the two previous questions deal with *external* purchases.

4. b These changes in the variables in the EOQ model can be thought of as an example of the "what if" technique called sensitivity analysis. Assuming an amount for annual demand (say, 9,000 units), the effect of the changes on EOQ is as follows:

Before changes:

$$EOQ = \sqrt{\frac{2(9,000)(\$10)}{\$2}}$$
$$EOQ = \sqrt{90,000} = 300 \text{ units}$$

After changes:

$$EOQ = \sqrt{\frac{2(9,000)(\$12)}{\$2.50}}$$
$$EOQ = \sqrt{86,400} = 294 \text{ units (rounded up)}$$

The changes cause EOQ to decrease. The reorder point, which is mentioned in choice (d), has no bearing on the answer.

5. a Average usage per day = 84,000 ÷ 300 = 280 units
Safety stock = 280 × (8 − 6) = 560 units
By having 560 units of safety stock, stockout costs decrease because stockouts are much less likely to occur; carrying costs increase, however, because the buffer of safety stock increases the level of inventory.

6. a One of the features of JIT production systems is to aggressively eliminate defects; hence inspection cost is decreased, if not eliminated. Under backflush costing, the detail of costs tracked to jobs is decreased, if not eliminated. That's because typically no record of work-in-process inventory is kept in backflush costing.

7. c   Materials requirements planning (MRP)—a push-through system that is distinctly different from the demand-pull system of JIT production—takes into account the lead time required to purchase materials and to manufacture components and subassemblies needed to meet forecast demand for finished goods. The resulting master production schedule specifies the quantity and time of each item to be manufactured.

Review Exercise 1

a.   Number of units per production run   = 5,000 ÷ 4 = 1,250 units
      Relevant total carrying costs per year = (1,250 ÷ 2) × $10 = $6,250

b.

Relevant Costs	4 Runs	2 Runs
Annual carrying costs		
[(5,000 ÷ 4) ÷ 2] × $10	$ 6,250	
[(5,000 ÷ 2) ÷ 2] × $10		$12,500
Annual setup costs		
$1,000 × 4; $1,000 × 2	4,000	2,000
Total annual relevant costs	$10,250	$14,500

Cost increase due to fewer runs $4,250

c.   Economic production run quantity $= \sqrt{\dfrac{2(5,000)(\$1,000)}{\$10}} = \sqrt{1,000,000} = 1,000$ files

      Number of production runs = 5,000 ÷ 1,000 = 5

Review Exercise 2

Relevant Costs	Previous Policy	JIT Policy
Required return on investment		
15% × $400,000; 15% × $200,000	$ 60,000	$30,000
Insurance costs		
$40,000; $40,000(1 − .40)	40,000	24,000
Warehouse rental		
$10,000; $10,000 − (5,000 × .40 × $2.50)	10,000	5,000
Stockout costs		
5,000 × $4		20,000
Annual total relevant costs	$110,000	$79,000

Difference in favor of JIT purchasing policy $31,000

Review Exercise 3

a.   Inventory: Materials and In-Process Control   21,200,000
           Accounts Payable Control   21,200,000
      Conversion Costs Control   12,320,000
           Various Accounts   12,320,000
      Finished Goods Control
      (400,000 × $52) + (400,000 × $30)   32,800,000
           Inventory: Materials & In-Process Control

(400,000 × $52)		20,800,000
Conversion Costs Allocated		
(400,000 × $30)		12,000,000
Cost of Goods Sold		
384,000 ($52 + $30)	31,488,000	
Finished Goods Control		31,488,000

b.
Inventory Control	21,200,000	
Accounts Payable Control		21,200,000
Conversion Costs Control	12,320,000	
Various Accounts		12,320,000
Cost of Goods Sold		
(384,000 × $52) + (384,000 × $30)	31,488,000	
Inventory Control (384,000 × $52)		19,968,000
Conversion Costs Allocated		
(384,000 × $30)		11,520,000
Conversion Costs Allocated	11,520,000	
Cost of Goods Sold	800,000	
Conversion Costs Control		12,320,000

c. The same journal entries as in answer (b) except the last one, which would now include some conversion costs in Inventory, 16,000 units × $30 = $480,000:

Conversion Costs Allocated	11,520,000	
Inventory Control	480,000	
Cost of Goods Sold	320,000	
Conversion Costs Control		12,320,000

d.
Finished Goods Control		
(400,000 × $52) + (400,000 × $30)	32,800,000	
Accounts Payable Control		
(for materials: 400,000 × $52)		20,800,000
Conversion Costs Allocated		
(400,000 × $30)		12,000,000

CHAPTER 21

Capital Budgeting and Cost Analysis

Overview

This chapter explains how managers use capital budgeting methods in making their long-run strategic planning decisions. Capital budgeting methods help managers analyze and select projects that increase the company's value. These projects typically require large amounts of money, span several years or more, and have uncertain cash flows and income over their lives. The relevant-revenue and relevant-cost analysis introduced in Chapter 11 helps managers make capital-budgeting decisions. The Appendix to the chapter describes how inflation is incorporated into capital-budgeting analysis.

Highlights

1. **Capital budgeting** is the process of making long-run planning decisions for investments in projects. This focus on long-run projects contrasts with the accounting-period focus on the income statement and short-run planning and control of operations. This difference is important because of the potential conflict between short-run and long-run performance.

2. Capital-budgeting projects are analyzed on the basis of their expected financial benefits and costs. *The analysis of each project includes only relevant items—future cash flow (or income) amounts that differ between the "accept" and "reject" alternatives.* The conclusion reached from this analysis is reevaluated in light of qualitative factors.

3. This chapter discusses four capital-budgeting methods used to analyze financial information: **net present value**, **internal rate of return**, **payback**, and **accrual accounting rate of return**. *The first three methods use only the expected cash inflows and outflows from a project.* To simplify computations, assume (as the textbook does) that these cash flows occur at the end of the year. *The accrual accounting rate of return method is based on a project's expected average annual income.*

4. **Discounted cash-flow (DCF) methods** measure all expected future cash inflows and outflows of a project discounted back to the present point in time. DCF methods are indifferent as to the origin of a project's relevant cash flows—whether they come from operations, purchase or sale of equipment, or investment in or recovery of working capital. Two DCF methods are net present value and internal rate of return.

5. Calculations under DCF methods incorporate **time value of money**, which takes into account that a dollar (or any other monetary unit) received today is worth more than a dollar received at any future time. Time value of money is the opportunity cost (return forgone) from not having the money today. Because the DCF methods explicitly weight cash flows by the time value of money, they are usually the best (most comprehensive) methods to use for capital-budgeting decisions.

6. The DCF methods use the **required rate of return (RRR)**, the minimum acceptable annual rate of return on an investment. The RRR is the return that on organization could expect to receive elsewhere for an investment of comparable risk. The RRR is also called the **discount rate**, **hurdle rate**, or **cost of capital**.

7. The **net present value (NPV) method** calculates the expected monetary gain or loss from a project by discounting all expected future cash inflows and outflows back to the present point in time (referred to as year 0), using the required rate of return. Only projects with a positive or zero NPV are acceptable because their returns exceed or equal the required rate of return. If other things are equal, the higher NPV, the better. EXHIBIT 21-2, text p.742, shows the computation of NPV; note that the first step in preparing this exhibit is

to draw a sketch of relevant cash inflows and outflows.

8. The **internal rate of return (IRR) method** calculates the discount rate at which an investment's present value of all expected cash inflows equals the present value of its expected cash outflows. That is, IRR is the discount rate that makes NPV = $0. A project is acceptable when IRR exceeds the required rate of return; in that case, the project has a positive NPV. If other things are equal, projects with higher IRRs are better than projects with lower IRRs. The IRR can be determined by calculator, computer, or trial and error. The textbook illustrates the trial-and-error approach when interpolation is not required (top p.743), and when interpolation is required (p.759).

9. The NPV method is preferred over the IRR method. One advantage is that it expresses NPV in dollars, not as a percent. As a result, the NPVs of individual projects can be summed to see the effect of accepting a combination of projects. The IRRs of individual projects cannot be summed or averaged to derive the IRR of a combination of projects. Another advantage of the NPV method is that it can be used when the RRR varies over the life of a project. It is not possible to use the IRR method in those situations.

10. Sensitivity analysis, a "what if" technique introduced in Chapter 3, helps managers focus on those capital-budgeting projects that are most sensitive to a failure to achieve the predicted financial outcomes. For example, sensitivity analysis can examine how the NPV of a project changes if the expected annual cash flow is not achieved. When a project has a positive NPV, sensitivity analysis can determine how much annual cash flow must fall before NPV = $0. Excel spreadsheets enable managers to conduct sensitivity analysis in a systematic and efficient way.

11. A third capital-budgeting method is the **payback method**. This method measures the time it will take to recoup, in the form of expected future cash flows, the net initial investment in a project. Like the NPV and IRR methods, the payback method uses only expected cash inflows and outflows from a project. If the future cash flows of a project are *the same each year*, the payback period is calculated by dividing net initial investment by the uniform increase in annual future cash flows. If those future annual cash flows are *not uniform*, the payback calculation is cumulative; future cash flows are accumulated year by year until fully recouping the amount of the net initial investment.

12. It is relatively simple to adjust the payback method to incorporate the time value of money. The **discounted payback method** calculates the amount of time required for the discounted expected future cash flows to recoup the net initial investment in a project.

13. The payback method highlights liquidity, which is typically an important factor in capital-budgeting decisions. Managers prefer projects with shorter paybacks (more liquid) to projects with longer paybacks, if other things are equal. Projects with shorter paybacks give the organization more flexibility because funds for other projects become available sooner. Also, managers are less confident about cash flow predictions far into the future.

14. Using the payback method, organizations choose a cutoff period for projects. The greater the risks of a project, the shorter the cutoff period. Only projects with a payback period less than the cutoff period are acceptable.

15. The payback method is easy to understand. Payback is a useful measure when (a) preliminary screening of many proposals is necessary, (b) interest rates are high, and (c) the expected cash flows in later years of a project are highly uncertain. A major weakness of the payback method is that it does not consider a project's cash flows after the payback period.

16. A fourth capital-budgeting method is the **accrual accounting rate of return (AARR) method**. Unlike NPV, IRR, and payback, AARR is based on *income* rather than *cash flows*. The AARR method divides the average annual (accrual accounting) income of a project by a measure of the investment in it. AARR indicates the rate at which a dollar of investment generates after-tax operating income. Projects whose AARR exceeds

the required AARR are considered desirable. Managers prefer projects with higher AARRs to projects with lower AARRs, if other things are equal. AARR computations are easy to understand, and they use numbers reported in the financial statements. AARR does not track cash flows, and it ignores time value of money.

17. It is inconsistent to use NPV as best for capital-budgeting decisions and then use AARR to evaluate a manager's performance over short time horizons. For example, consider a project that has a positive NPV but entails a large loss from disposing of an old machine in year 0. Despite the positive NPV, the manager would be tempted to reject this project because the first year's accrual income decreases by the amount of the loss. Such temptations become more pronounced if managers are frequently transferred (or promoted), or if their bonuses are affected by the level of year-to-year accrual income. This conflict can be reduced by evaluating managers on a project-by-project basis and looking at how well managers achieve the amounts and timing of forecasted cash flows.

18. Relevant cash flows are expected future cash flows that differ between two alternatives being considered. Three main categories (with their subcategories) classify the relevant cash flows of capital-budgeting projects. The following table shows these categories and subcategories for a company that is deciding whether to replace an existing ("old") machine with a new machine.

Relevant-Cash Flow Items for a Capital-Budgeting Project

1. Net initial investment
   a. Initial machine investment
   b. Initial working capital investment
   c. After-tax cash flow from current disposal of old machine

2. Cash flow from operations
   a. Annual after-tax cash flow from operations (excluding the depreciation effect)
   b. Income tax cash savings from annual

(continued)
depreciation deduction

3. Terminal disposal of investment
   a. After-tax cash flow from terminal disposal of new machine
   b. After-tax cash flow from terminal recovery of working capital investment

- Items 1a, 1b, and 1c occur at the beginning of the new machine's life (year 0).
- The working capital investment (item 1b) is the incremental investment in current assets minus the incremental amount of current liabilities (for example, the cash outflow to maintain an additional inventory of supplies and spare parts for the new machine).
- Item 2 can result from either a cash savings in operating costs or producing and selling additional output.
- An error in forecasting item 3a is seldom critical for a project with a long life because the present value of the amount to be received in the distant future is usually small.
- *Items 1c, 2a, 2b, and 3a are affected by income taxes*. Item 3b is affected by income taxes *only if there is a gain or loss on the recovery of working capital*.
- For items 1c and 3a, the difference between disposal value and the asset's book value (original cost minus accumulated depreciation at the time of sale) is the gain or loss for tax purposes. For simplicity, assume (as the textbook does) such gains and losses are taxed at the same rate as ordinary income. Using item 1c to illustrate, assume an old machine is sold for $40,000, its book value at the time of sale is $30,000, and the tax rate is 40%. The tax on the gain of $10,000 ($40,000 − $30,000) is $4,000 ($10,000 × 0.40), and the after-tax cash flow from disposing of the old machine is $36,000 ($40,000 − $4,000). Now assume instead that the old machine is sold for $25,000. The loss is $5,000 ($25,000 − $30,000); for a profitable company this loss results in an *income tax saving* of $2,000 ($5,000 × 0.40). That is, *the loss shields $5,000 of the company's income from being taxed*. In turn, income tax outflows would decrease by $2,000, which would increase after-

tax cash flow by that amount. After-tax cash flow from disposing of the old machine for $25,000, therefore, is $27,000 ($25,000 + $2,000)—versus $36,000 in the scenario of selling the old machine for $40,000.

- Item 2a is computed by multiplying annual before-tax cash flow from operations times (1 − tax rate). If annual before-tax cash flow from operations is $80,000 and the tax rate is 30%, annual after-tax cash flow from operations (excluding the depreciation effect) = $80,000(1 − 0.30) = $56,000. In other words, $24,000 is paid in income taxes ($80,000 × 0.30) and the company keeps $56,000 ($80,000 − $24,000).

- Item 2b is computed by multiplying annual depreciation deductions times the tax rate. If the depreciation deduction in year 1 is $50,000 and the tax rate is 30%, the income tax cash savings from the depreciation deduction in that year = $50,000 × 0.30 = $15,000. That is, *the $50,000 depreciation deduction shields this amount of the company's income from being taxed*. In turn, income tax outflows would decrease by $15,000, which means overall cash flow would be higher by that amount.

- The depreciation computations for item 2b are based on the asset's original cost (ignoring terminal disposal value). The schedule of annual depreciation deductions is computed under straight-line or some other method specified by tax law.

19. A post-investment audit is an important aspect of capital budgeting. A post-investment audit compares the actual results for a project to the costs and benefits expected at the time the project was selected. Post-investment audits not only provide management with feedback about performance, but also discourage managers from making unrealistic estimates when seeking approval for capital-budgeting projects. Post-investment audits can identify areas needing corrective action.

20. The Appendix to this chapter uses the *nominal approach* to show how **inflation** can be incorporated into the NPV method. Inflation is the decline in the general purchasing power of the monetary unit, such as dollars. Inflation increases the future cash flows from a project to more than what they would have been had no inflation been expected. These inflated cash flows are called *nominal cash flows*. Under the nominal approach, the inflated cash flows are discounted at the required rate of return stated in nominal terms. The relationship between the **nominal rate of return** (which incorporates investment risk and an inflation component) and the **real rate of return** (which incorporates investment risk but no inflation component) is:

Nominal rate = (1 + Real rate)(1 + Inflation rate) − 1

The real rate of return consists of a risk-free component and a business-risk component. EXHIBIT 21-8, text p.763, illustrates how to compute NPV under the nominal approach.

Featured Exercise

Willet Company provides the following information on a capital-budgeting project:

Net initial investment	$100,000
Estimated useful life	4 years
Estimated before-tax annual cash flow from operations	$33,000
Estimated terminal disposal value	$7,000
Required rate of return	12%
Income tax rate	30%

Willet uses straight-line depreciation and ignores the terminal disposal value in computing depreciation for tax purposes.

Compute present values in this exercise by using either the tables in Appendix A at the back of the textbook or a calculator.

For this project:
a. Compute NPV.
b. Compute IRR (to the nearest tenth of a percent).
c. Compute payback.
d. Compute AARR on net initial investment (to the nearest tenth of a percent).

Solution (on next page)

Solution

a. To compute NPV, a key amount needed is annual after-tax cash flow from operations:

Annual after-tax cash flow from operations (excluding the depreciation effects), $33,000 × (1 − 0.30)	$23,100
Income tax cash savings from annual depreciation deductions, ($100,000 ÷ 4) × 0.30	7,500
Annual after-tax cash flow from operations	$30,600

Net initial investment	−$100,000
Annual after-tax cash flow from operations $30,600 × 3.037	92,932
After-tax cash flow from terminal disposal value $7,000 − $0 book value = $7,000 gain $7,000 × (1 − 0.30) = $4,900; $4,900 × 0.636	3,116
NPV	−$ 3,952

NPV via calculator = −$3,943

b. Given that NPV is −$3,952 when the discount rate is 12%, IRR is lower than 12%. Using trial-and-error:

$$\text{At 10\% NPV} = -\$100,000 + (\$30,600 \times 3.170) + (\$4,900 \times 0.683)$$
$$= -\$100,000 + \$97,002 + \$3,347 = \$349$$

Then using straight-line interpolation:

10%	$ 349	$349
IRR		0
12%	−3,952	
Difference	$4,301	$349

$$IRR = 10\% + \frac{\$349}{\$4,301}(2\%) = 10.2\%$$

IRR via calculator = 10.2%

c. $$\text{Payback} = \frac{\$100,000}{\$30,600} = 3.3 \text{ years}$$

d. $$AARR = \frac{(\$33,000 - \$25,000 \text{ depreciation})(1 - 0.30)}{\$100,000}$$

$$= \frac{\$8,000(1 - 0.30)}{\$100,000} = \frac{\$5,600}{\$100,000} = 5.6\%$$

Review Questions and Exercises

Completion Statements

Fill in the blank(s) to complete each statement.

1. The _____
   method of capital budgeting is based on income
   rather than cash flows.
2. The discount rate that makes the net present value of a project equal to zero is called the
   _____.
3. In a capital-budgeting project, the investment
   required for accounts receivable and inventories
   is called _____.
4. (Appendix) _____ is the
   decline in the general purchasing power of the
   monetary unit.

True-False

Indicate whether each statement is true (T) or false
(F).

____ 1. The planning and control tools used for
        year-to-year operating decisions are
        well suited for capital-budgeting deci-
        sions.
____ 2. The present value of $1 million to be
        received ten years from now is lower if
        computed at a discount rate of 10% ra-
        ther than 14%.
____ 3. Assume a required rate of return of 12%
        is used to compute the NPV of a project.
        If NPV is negative, IRR is less than
        12%.
____ 4. The payback method does not consider
        a project's cash flows after the payback
        period.
____ 5. If the income tax rate for a profitable
        company is 30%, a depreciation deduc-
        tion of $10,000 results in a tax savings
        of $7,000 (before considering time
        value of money).
____ 6. For a profitable company, the gain or
        loss on the recovery of working capital
        in a capital-budgeting project is subject
        to income tax.

____ 7. It is consistent to use NPV as best for
        capital-budgeting decisions and then use
        AARR to evaluate a manager's per-
        formance over short time horizons.

Multiple Choice

Select the best answer to each question. Space is provided for computations after the quantitative questions.

____ 1. (CMA) Amster Corporation has not yet
        decided on its required rate of return for
        use in the evaluation of capital-
        budgeting projects for the current year.
        This lack of information prohibits Am-
        ster from calculating a project's

	AARR	NPV	IRR
a.	no	no	no
b.	yes	yes	yes
c.	no	yes	yes
d.	no	yes	no
e.	yes	no	yes

____ 2. (CPA adapted) Brewster Co. is review-
        ing the following data relating to an en-
        ergy-saving investment proposal:

Net initial investment	$50,000
After-tax cash flow from	
disposal of the investment	
at the end of 5 years	10,000
Present value of an annuity	
of $1 at 12% for 5 years	3.60
Present value of $1 at 12% in	
5 years	0.57

What is the amount of after-tax annual
savings (including the depreciation effects) needed for the investment to provide a 12% return?
a. $ 8,189
b. $11,111
c. $12,306
d. $13,889

3. (CMA) Making the common assumption in capital-budgeting analysis that cash inflows occur in a lump sum at the end of individual years during the life of an investment project when, in fact, they flow more or less continuously during those years:
   a. results in increasingly overstating NPV as the life of the investment project increases.
   b. is done because present value tables for continuous flows cannot be constructed.
   c. results in understating NPV of the investment project.
   d. results in inconsistent errors being made in NPV such that projects cannot be evaluated reliably.
   e. results in a higher IRR of the investment project.

4. (CPA adapted) Apex Corp. is considering the purchase of a machine costing $100,000. The machine's expected useful life is five years. The estimated annual after-tax cash flow from operations is: $60,000 in year 1, $30,000 in year 2, $20,000 in year 3, $20,000 in year 4, and $20,000 in year 5. Assuming these cash flows will be received evenly during each year, the payback is:
   a. 2.50 years.
   b. 3.00 years.
   c. 3.33 years.
   d. none of the above.

5. (CMA) Fast Freight Inc. is planning to purchase equipment to make its operations more efficient. The equipment has an estimated life of six years. At the time of acquiring the equipment, a $9,000 investment in working capital is required. In a discounted cash-flow analysis, this investment in working capital:
   a. should be amortized over the useful life of the equipment.
   b. should be disregarded because no cash is involved.
   c. should be treated as a recurring annual cash outflow that is recovered at the end of six years.
   d. should be treated as an immediate cash outflow.
   e. should be treated as an immediate cash outflow that is recovered at the end of six years.

6. Assume in the current year that a profitable company pays $10,000 for advertising and has depreciation of $10,000. If the income tax rate is 40%, the after-tax effects on cash flow before considering time value of money are a net outflow of:
   a. $4,000 for advertising and a net inflow of $4,000 for depreciation.
   b. $6,000 for advertising and a net inflow of $6,000 for depreciation.
   c. $4,000 for advertising and a net inflow of $6,000 for depreciation.
   d. $6,000 for advertising and a net inflow of $4,000 for depreciation.

7. (CMA) Garfield Inc. is considering a 10-year capital investment project with forecasted cash revenues of $40,000 per year and forecasted cash operating costs of $29,000 per year. The initial cost of the equipment for the project is $23,000, and Garfield expects to sell the equipment for $9,000 at the end of the tenth year. The equipment will be depreciated on a straight-line basis over seven years for tax purposes. The project requires a working capital investment of $7,000 at its inception and another $5,000 at the end of year 5. The working capital is fully recoverable at the end of the life of the project. Assuming a 40% tax rate, expected net after-tax cash flow from the project for the tenth year is:
   a. $32,000.
   b. $24,000.
   c. $20,000.
   d. $11,000.
   e. $12,000.

8. (CMA) Superstrut is considering replacing an old press that cost $80,000 six years ago with a new one with a purchase cost of $225,000. Shipping and installation cost an additional $20,000. The old press has a book value of $15,000 and can be sold currently for $5,000. The increased production of the new press would increase inventories by $4,000, accounts receivable by $16,000, and accounts payable by $14,000. Superstrut's net initial investment for analyzing the acquisition of the new press, assuming a 40% income tax rate is:
   a. $256,000.
   b. $242,000.
   c. $250,000.
   d. $245,000.
   e. $236,000.

9. (CMA) Brownel Inc. currently has annual cash revenues of $240,000 and annual operating costs of $185,000 (all cash items except depreciation of $35,000). The company is considering the purchase of a new mixing machine costing $120,000 that would increase cash revenues to $290,000 per year and operating costs (including depreciation) to $205,000 per year. The new machine would increase depreciation to $50,000 per year. Using a 40% income tax rate, Brownel's annual incremental after-tax cash flow from the new mixing machine is:
   a. $33,000.
   b. $24,000.
   c. $30,000.
   d. $18,000.
   e. $68,000.

10. (Appendix) If the nominal rate of interest is 16% and the inflation rate is 5%, the real rate of interest (rounded to the nearest tenth of a percent) is:
   a. 12.0%.
   b. 11.6%.
   c. 10.5%.
   d. 10.1%.

Review Exercises

1. The following information pertains to a machine recently sold by Powers Enterprises:

Net initial investment	$300,000
Estimated useful life for tax purposes	8 years
Terminal disposal value for tax purposes	zero
Age at the time of sale	6 years
Cash received from the sale	$60,000
Income tax rate	30%

Assuming Powers uses straight-line depreciation and is a profitable company, calculate the after-tax cash flow from the sale of the machine.

2. (CMA adapted) Jasper Company has a payback requirement of three years on new equipment acquisitions. A new sorter is being evaluated that costs $450,000 and has an estimated useful life of five years. Straight-line depreciation will be used with a zero terminal disposal value. Jasper is subject to a 40% income tax rate.

Calculate the amount of savings in after-tax annual cash operating costs that must be generated by the new sorter to meet the company's payback requirement.

3. (Appendix) Massey Company's nominal rate of return for capital-budgeting projects is 20%, which includes a 10% inflation rate. The present value of $1 at 20% for one year is 0.833. Assume a 40% income tax rate.

Calculate the after-tax present value (expressed in nominal dollars) of:
a. Before-tax cash operating savings of $100,000 (expressed in year 0 dollars) to be received at the end of year 1.
b. Year 1 depreciation of $70,000.

Answers and Solutions to Chapter 21 Review Questions and Exercises

Completion Statements

1. accrual accounting rate of return (AARR)
2. internal rate of return (IRR)
3. working capital
4. Inflation

True-False

1. F   The planning and control tools used for year-to-year (short-run) operating decisions distinguish variable costs from fixed costs and generally ignore time value of money. In contrast, capital-budgeting decisions do not distinguish variable costs from fixed costs and often incorporate time value of money.
2. F   Using Table 2 in Appendix A at the back of the textbook:
        At 10%, $1,000,000 × 0.386 = $386,000
        At 14%, $1,000,000 × 0.270 = $270,000
3. T
4. T
5. F   The depreciation deduction of $10,000 is a tax shield that provides a tax savings of $3,000 ($10,000 × 0.30).
6. T
7. F   It is inconsistent to use NPV as best for capital-budgeting decisions and then use AARR to evaluate a manager's performance over short time horizons. For example, a manager being evaluated on AARR might reject a project with a positive NPV simply because it lowers AARR in the short run.

Multiple Choice

1. d   AARR and IRR *calculate* a rate of return, whereas NPV *uses* the required rate of return in making its calculations.

2. c   Net initial investment $50,000

Deduct present value of cash flow from
   disposal, $10,000 × 0.57   5,700

Present value of *total* after-tax savings needed $44,300

Annual after-tax savings needed = $44,300 ÷ 3.60 = $12,306

3. c   Although present value tables for continuous cash flows are available, they are seldom used. Present value tables for end-of-period cash flows are used for convenience. Because *some* cash flows occur only once *sometime* during a period, it is convenient to assume that *all* cash flows during that period occur at the *end* of it. Under this assumption, cash inflows that occur more or less continuously during a period are discounted at the end of the period. As a result, the true present value of these inflows is *understated*, which in turn understates NPV and IRR. Because the errors introduced by making the end-of-period assumption tend to be reasonably consistent from one project to another, capital-budgeting projects can be evaluated with a satisfactory degree of reliability.

4. a   Cumulative after-tax cash flow from operations:

Year 1	$ 60,000
Year 2	30,000
Subtotal	90,000
Year 3	20,000
Total	$110,000

$$\text{Payback} = 2 + \left[(\$100,000 - \$90,000) \div \$20,000 \right]$$
$$= 2 + (\$10,000 \div \$20,000)$$
$$= 2 + 0.5 = 2.5 \text{ years}$$

5. e   In Exhibit 21-7, text p.760, the $9,000 cash outflow for initial working capital occurs in year 0 and is recovered in year 5.

6. d   Advertising: −$10,000 × (1 − 0.40) = −$6,000

Depreciation: $10,000 × 0.40 = $4,000

7. b   Recurring after-tax operating cash
    flows (excluding the depreciation effect)
      ($40,000 − $29,000)(1 − 0.40) $ 6,600

After-tax cash flow from terminal
   disposal of equipment
     ($ 9,000 − $0 book value)(1 − 0.40)   5,400

Recovery of working capital
   $7,000 + $5,000   12,000

Net after-tax cash inflow for year 10 $24,000

Note: there is no tax savings from depreciation for the tenth year because the equipment is fully depreciated at the end of year 7.

8. b   Purchase cost of new press $225,000

Shipping and installation   20,000

Initial working capital

Increase in accounts receivable	$16,000	
Increase in inventories	4,000	
Increase in accounts payable	(14,000)	6,000
Subtotal		251,000

Deduct after-tax cash inflow
   from sale of old press
     $5,000 + ($15,000 − $5,000)(0.40)   9,000

Net initial investment of new press $242,000

9. a

Item	Present Situation	Proposed Situation	Cash-Flow Difference
Cash revenues	$240,000	$290,000	$50,000
Operating costs:			
Cash operating costs (excludes depreciation)			
$185,000 − $35,000	150,000		
$205,000 − $50,000		155,000	(5,000)
Depreciation	35,000	50,000	
Total operating costs	185,000	205,000	
Operating income	55,000	85,000	
Income tax (40%)	22,000	34,000	(12,000)
Net income	$ 33,000	$ 51,000	
Cash-flow difference			$33,000

Alternative solution:

Incremental net income, $51,000 − $33,000	$18,000
Add incremental depreciation, $50,000 − $35,000	15,000
Incremental cash flow from operations, net of income taxes	$33,000

10. c   Nominal rate $= (1 + $ Real rate$)(1 + $ Inflation rate$) - 1$
$0.16 = (1 + $ Real rate$)(1 + 0.05) - 1$
$0.16 = (1 + $ Real rate$)(1.05) - 1$
$0.16 = 1.05 + 1.05($Real rate$) - 1$
$1.05($Real rate$) = 1 - 1.05 + 0.16$
$1.05($Real rate$) = 0.11$
Real rate $= 0.11 \div 1.05 = 0.1048$, or 10.5%

Review Exercise 1

Four steps are used to obtain the answer. First, compute annual depreciation for tax purposes: ($300,000 − $0) ÷ 8 years = $37,500. Second, compute book value at the time of sale:

Net initial investment	$300,000
Deduct accumulated depreciation	
$37,500 × 6 years	225,000
Book value at the time of sale	$ 75,000

Third, compute gain or loss on the sale of the machine:

Cash received from the sale	$60,000
Deduct book value at the time of sale	75,000
Loss on the sale	$15,000

Fourth, compute after-tax cash flow from the sale of the machine:

Cash received from the sale	$60,000
Tax savings from the loss	
$15,000 × 0.30	4,500
After-tax cash flow from the sale	$64,500

Note: the loss shields $15,000 of the company's income from being taxed. In turn, income tax outflows decrease by $4,500, which increases after-tax cash flow by the same amount.

Review Exercise 2

Annual depreciation = ($450,000 − $0) ÷ 5 = $90,000
Annual tax savings from depreciation = $90,000 × 0.40 = $36,000
Let X = Savings in annual after-tax cash operating costs from the new equipment

Using the payback formula and the payback requirement of three years:

$$Payback = \frac{\text{Net initial investment}}{\text{Uniform increase in annual cash flows}}$$

$$3 = \frac{\$450,000}{X + \$36,000}$$

$$3(X + \$36,000) = \$450,000$$
$$3X + \$108,000 = \$450,000$$
$$3X = \$450,000 - \$108,000$$
$$3X = \$342,000$$
$$X = \$342,000 \div 3 = \$114,000$$

Note: the savings in annual before-tax cash operating costs is $190,000 [$114,000 ÷ (1 − 0.40)].

Review Exercise 3

a. $100,000 × 1.10 = $110,000; $110,000 × (1 − 0.40) = $66,000;
   $66,000 × 0.833 = $54,978
b. $70,000 × 0.40 = $28,000; $28,000 × 0.833 = $23,324

Management Control Systems, Transfer Pricing, and Multinational Considerations

Overview

This chapter explains the connection between strategy, organization structure, management control systems, and accounting information. These factors influence the degree of decentralization in the company and the pricing of products or services transferred among its subunits (departments or divisions). Even though this material involves less "number crunching" than most other chapters, the concepts are important because management control systems influence the behavior of managers and other employees.

Highlights

1. A **management control system** is a means of gathering and using information to aid and coordinate the planning and control decisions throughout an organization and to guide the behavior of its managers and other employees. The goal of a management control system is to improve the collective decisions within the company in an economically feasible way.

2. Management control systems consist of both *formal* and *informal* control systems. The formal control system includes those explicit rules, procedures, performance measures, and incentive plans that guide the behavior of managers and other employees. For example, a formal control system provides information on revenues, costs, and income. The informal control system includes shared values, loyalties, and mutual commitments among members of the organization, organization culture, and the unwritten norms about acceptable behavior for managers and other employees.

3. To be effective, management control systems must (a) be closely aligned to the organization's strategies and goals, (b) be designed to fit the organization's structure and the decision-making responsibility of individual managers, and (c) motivate managers and other employees.

4. **Goal congruence** and **effort** are the dual aspects of **motivation**. Goal congruence exists when individuals and groups work toward achieving the organization's goals—that is, managers working in their own best interest take actions that align with the overall goals of top management. Effort is exertion toward achieving a goal. Motivation is the desire to attain a selected goal (the goal-congruence aspect) combined with the resulting pursuit of that goal (the effort aspect).

5. Top management decides how much **decentralization** is optimal for an organization. Decentralization is the freedom for managers at lower levels of the organization to make decisions. (The opposite of decentralization is *centralization*.) Conceptually, the degree of decentralization chosen should maximize the excess of benefits over costs. From a practical standpoint, these benefits and costs can seldom be quantified, but the cost-benefit approach helps managers focus on the key issues.

6. A decentralized organization structure has a number of benefits. It (a) creates greater responsiveness to the needs of a subunit's customers, suppliers, and employees, (b) leads to gains from faster decision making by subunit managers, (c) increases motivation of subunit managers because they can exercise greater individual initiative, (d) assists management development and learning to help develop an experienced pool of management talent to fill higher-level management positions, and (e) sharpens the focus of subunit managers.

7. A cost of a decentralized organization structure is **suboptimal decision making** (also called **incongruent decision making** or **dysfunctional decision making**); it occurs when a decision's benefit to one subunit is more than offset by the costs or loss of benefits to the organization as a whole. *Suboptimal decision making is most likely to occur when the subunits in the organization are highly interdependent,* such as when the end product of one subunit is used or sold by another sub-

unit. Other costs of decentralization: (a) focuses the manager's attention on the subunit rather than the organization as a whole and (b) results in duplication of activities.

8.   Decisions related to sources of suppliers, products to manufacture, and product advertising are likely to be decentralized, whereas decisions on income tax strategies and long-term financing are likely to be centralized. Multinational companies are often decentralized, which enables country managers to make decisions that utilize their knowledge of local business and political conditions.

9.   Responsibility centers—such as cost centers, profit centers, and investment centers—are compatible with either decentralization or centralization. A common misconception is that the term profit center is a synonym for a decentralized subunit, and that cost center is a synonym for a centralized subunit. Profit centers can be coupled with a highly centralized company, and cost centers can be coupled with a highly decentralized company.

10. In decentralized organizations, much of the decision-making power resides in the individual subunits, and the management control system often uses **transfer prices** to coordinate actions and to evaluate performance of the subunits. A transfer price is the price one subunit (department or division) charges for a product or service supplied to another subunit of the same organization. The transfer price creates revenues for the selling subunit and purchase costs for the buying subunit, thereby affecting each subunit's operating income. These operating incomes can be used to evaluate the performance of individual subunits and to motivate their managers.

11. There are three broad categories of methods for determining transfer prices: *market-based transfer prices*, *cost-based transfer prices*, and *hybrid transfer prices*. The chosen transfer price(s) should help achieve a company's strategies and goals, and fit its organization structure. In particular, transfer price(s) should promote goal congruence and a sustained high level of management effort. Subunits selling a product or service should be motivated to hold down their costs, and sub-

units buying the product or service should be motivated to acquire and use inputs efficiently.

12. The Horizon Petroleum example, beginning text p.781, illustrates the three transfer-pricing methods. The following table summarizes Horizon's operating incomes for transporting and refining 100 barrels of crude oil:

| | Transfer-Pricing Method | | |
	Market-Based	Cost-Based	Hybrid
Transportation Division	$ 900*	$ 380	$ 600
Refining Division	300	820*	600
Total company	$1,200	$1,200	$1,200

*The Division's highest operating income.

Total company income is $1,200 regardless of the transfer-pricing method used, but division operating incomes differ. The manager of the Transportation Division prefers the market-based transfer price, while the manager of the Refining Division prefers the cost-based transfer price. Each division manager, therefore, takes considerable interest in the setting of transfer prices, especially those managers whose compensation or promotion directly depends on division operating income. To reduce the excessive focus of subunit managers on their own subunits, many companies compensate subunit managers on the basis of both subunit and companywide operating incomes.

13. In the Horizon Petroleum example, the choice of the transfer-pricing method *does not affect the size of the company's operating income pie ($1,200) but does affect how that pie is divided between the two divisions*. That's because regardless of the transfer price, the Transportation Division sells crude oil to the Refining Division (that is, *this transaction is internal to the company*). On the other hand, assume one of the transfer-pricing methods is chosen and the Refining Division, acting in its own best interest, buys crude oil from an *external supplier*. In this case, the Refining Division's **autonomy** (the manager's degree of freedom to make decisions) is high but could produce suboptimal results. That is, if it is in the best interest of the company as a whole for the Refining Division to buy crude oil internally, the Refining Division's decision to buy from an external sup-

plier *decreases the size of the company's operating-income pie.*

14. Market-based transfer prices generally lead to optimal decisions by subunit managers when three conditions are met: (a) the market for the **intermediate product** (the product transferred between subunits of a company) is perfectly competitive, (b) interdependencies of subunits are minimal, and (c) there are no additional costs or benefits to the company as a whole from buying or selling in the external market instead of transferring internally. A **perfectly competitive market** exists when there is a homogenous product with buying prices equal to selling prices and no individual buyers or sellers can affect those prices by their own actions. By using market-based transfer prices in perfectly competitive markets, a company can achieve (a) goal congruence, (b) management effort, (c) subunit performance evaluation, and (d) subunit autonomy (if desired).

15. When supply exceeds demand, market prices may fall well below their historical average. When the decline in prices is expected to be temporary, these low market prices are called *distress prices*. In the short run, the manager of the selling subunit should meet the distress price as long as it exceeds the incremental cost of supplying the product or service. However, if the price remains low in the long run, the company should use the distress price as the transfer price. If the distress price is lower than the variable and fixed costs that can be saved if manufacturing facilities are shut down, the manager of the selling subunit should dispose of the facilities and the buying subunit should purchase the product from an external supplier.

16. Cost-based transfer prices are helpful when market prices are unavailable, inappropriate, or too costly to obtain. Many companies use full-cost transfer prices even though these prices can lead to suboptimal decisions. Despite this limitation, global surveys indicate managers prefer to use full-cost transfer prices because they (a) yield relevant costs for long-run decisions, (b) facilitate external pricing based on variable and fixed costs, and (c) are the least costly to administer.

17. An alternative cost-based approach is to choose a transfer price that splits, on some equitable basis, the difference between the maximum transfer price the buying subunit is willing to pay and the minimum transfer price the selling subunit is willing to charge. In the example, text p.788, this difference is allocated between the two divisions based on their budgeted variable costs.

18. There is seldom a single cost-based transfer price that simultaneously meets the criteria of goal congruence, management effort, subunit performance evaluation, and subunit autonomy (if desired). As a result, some companies choose **dual pricing**, using two separate transfer-pricing methods to price each transfer from one subunit to another. Dual pricing is not widely used in practice, however, for several reasons; for example, it tends to insulate managers from the frictions of the marketplace because costs, not market prices, affect the revenues of the supplying division.

19. Negotiated transfer prices result from a bargaining process between the selling and buying subunits. A negotiated transfer price preserves division autonomy because the transfer price is the outcome of direct negotiations between subunit managers. It also has the advantage that each subunit manager is motivated to put forth effort to increase the operating income of his or her subunit. Its major disadvantage is the time and energy spent on the negotiations.

20. EXHIBIT 22-3, text p.790, summarizes the properties of the different transfer pricing methods. As the exhibit indicates, there is no all-pervasive rule for transfer pricing that leads toward optimal decisions for the company as a whole. A general guideline formula, however, has proven to be a helpful first step in setting a minimum transfer price in many situations: *Minimum transfer price = Incremental cost per unit incurred up to the point of transfer + Opportunity cost per unit to the selling subunit.* Incremental cost in this context means the additional cost of producing and transferring the product or service. Opportunity cost here is the maximum contribution margin forgone by the selling subunit if the product or service is transferred internally. If the selling subunit has idle capacity, this opportunity cost is zero.

If the selling subunit is operating at capacity, the opportunity cost of transferring a unit internally rather than selling it externally is equal to the market price minus variable cost. Opportunity costs are not recorded in financial accounting systems.

21. When multinational companies transfer products between subunits located in different countries, they must consider additional factors in setting transfer prices, including income taxes, customs duties, tariffs, value-added taxes, and other government levies. With different income tax rates in various countries, companies want to minimize taxable income reported in the higher-taxed countries. Section 482 of the U.S. Internal Revenue Code requires that transfer prices between a company and its foreign division or subsidiary, for both tangible and intangible property, equal the prices that would be charged by unrelated third party in a comparable transaction. Under the U.S. Internal Revenue Code companies can obtain advanced approval of their transfer-pricing arrangements, called advanced pricing agreements (APA). The goal of APAs is to avoid costly transfer pricing disputes between taxpayers and tax authorities.

Featured Exercise

Ajax Division of Carlyle Corporation produces electric motors, 20,000 of which are sold to Bradley Division of Carlyle and the remainder is sold to outside customers. Carlyle treats its divisions as profit centers and allows division managers to choose their sources of supply and to whom they sell. Corporate policy requires variable cost be used as the transfer price for all interdivisional sales and purchases. Ajax Division's estimated revenues and costs for the coming year, based on the full capacity of 100,000 units, are as follows:

	Bradley	External Customers
Revenues	$ 900,000	$8,000,000
Variable costs	900,000	3,600,000
Contribution margin	-0-	4,400,000
Fixed costs	300,000	1,200,000
Operating income	$(300,000)	$3,200,000
Unit sales	20,000	80,000

Ajax Division has an opportunity to sell the 20,000 motors to an external customer at a price of $75 per unit on a continuing basis beginning next year. Bradley can purchase its requirement of 20,000 motors from an external supplier at a price of $85 per unit.

a. Compute the increase/decrease in Ajax Division's operating income if Ajax discontinues the sales to Bradley and adds the new customer for the coming year. Assume Ajax's fixed costs are unavoidable.

b. Instead of using variable cost as the transfer price, assume Carlyle permits the division managers to negotiate the transfer price for next year. The managers agree on a transfer price: $75 per unit minus an equal sharing between the divisions of the additional operating income earned by Ajax from selling Bradley the 20,000 motors at $75 per unit. Compute the transfer price for next year.

Solution (on next page)

Solution

a. In making this decision, the manager of Ajax Division needs to determine the difference between the total relevant operating income of selling externally and of selling internally. The variable manufacturing cost per unit is ($900,000 + $3,600,000) ÷ (20,000 + 80,000) = $45.

Total relevant operating income on external sale	
20,000 × ($75 − $45)	$600,000
Total relevant operating income on internal sale	
20,000 × ($45 − $45)	-0-
Difference in favor of external sale	$600,000

Alternative solution: Compare the financial statement results for the 20,000 units in question:

	Internal Sale (the Present Situation)	External Sale
Revenues, given; 20,000 × $75	$ 900,000	$1,500,000
Variable costs	900,000	900,000
Contribution margin	-0-	600,000
Fixed costs	300,000	300,000
Operating income	$(300,000)	$ 300,000

Difference in favor of external sale $600,000

b. Two steps are used to obtain the answer. First, determine the amount of additional operating income that results from the internal sale at $75 per unit:
$75 − $45 = $30 per unit
Second, reduce the $75 by a 50%:50% split between the divisions of the additional operating income:
Transfer price = $75 − 0.50($30) = $75 − $15 = $60 per unit

Review Questions and Exercises

Completion Statements

Fill in the blank(s) to complete each statement.

1. A means of gathering and using information to aid and coordinate the planning and control decisions throughout the organization and to guide the behavior of its managers and other employees is called a _____.

2. _____ exists when individuals and groups work toward achieving the organization's goals—that is, managers working in their own perceived best interest take actions that align with the overall goals of top management.

3. The desire to attain a selected goal combined with the resulting pursuit of that goal is called _____.

4. _____ is the freedom for managers at lower levels of an organization to make decisions.

5. _____ refers to the degree of freedom to make decisions.

6. _____ arises when the benefit of a decision to a subunit is more than offset by the costs or loss of benefit to the organization as a whole.

7. Products transferred between subunits of a company are called _____.

8. What four criteria help in choosing a transfer price? _____
_____
_____ and
_____.

9. In many situations, a general guideline formula has proven to be a helpful first step in setting a minimum transfer price. This minimum transfer price is equal to the sum of which two per-unit costs?

_____

_____
_____ and _____
_____.

True-False

Indicate whether each statement is true (T) or false (F).

___ 1. The informal control system in an organization is likely to include a human resources system that provides information on recruiting, training, absenteeism, and accidents.
___ 2. Conceptually, the degree of decentralization in a company depends primarily on determining the optimal number of profit centers.
___ 3. Suboptimal decisions are often associated with a lack of goal congruence.
___ 4. Decentralization is likely to be most beneficial when a company's subunits are highly interdependent.
___ 5. One way to limit decentralization is to impose restrictions on the ability of subunits to outsource products that are available from internal subunits.
___ 6. Profit centers are compatible with high centralization or high decentralization.
___ 7. The choice of a transfer-pricing method can affect how a company's operating-income pie is divided among the individual subunits as well as the size of the operating-income pie itself.
___ 8. If top management imposes insourcing on its subunit managers, total company operating income will be unaffected by the transfer-pricing method used.

___ 9. Full-cost transfer prices are frequently used in practice to help avoid the pitfalls of suboptimal decision making.
___ 10. Compared to domestic companies, multinational companies must consider additional factors in setting their transfer prices, including different income tax rates in various countries and promotion of goal congruence.

Multiple Choice

Select the best answer to each question. Space is provided for computations after the quantitative questions.

___ 1. (CMA adapted) Which of the following is decentralization *least likely* to accomplish?
  a. Provide a pool of management talent.
  b. Shorten decision time.
  c. Heighten goal congruence.
  d. Increase motivation of subunit managers.
___ 2. (CPA) Brent Co. has intracompany service transfers from Division Core, a cost center, to Division Pro, a profit center. Under stable economic conditions, which of the following transfer prices is likely to be most conducive to evaluating whether both divisions have met their responsibilities?
  a. Actual cost
  b. Standard variable cost
  c. Actual cost plus a markup
  d. Negotiated price
___ 3. Designing the transfer-pricing system is most difficult in organizations that are:
  a. highly decentralized with many interdependencies among subunits.
  b. highly centralized with many interdependencies among subunits.
  c. highly decentralized with few interdependencies among subunits.
  d. highly centralized with few interdependencies among subunits.

4. (CMA) Parkside Inc. has several divisions that operate as decentralized profit centers. Parkside's Entertainment Division manufactures video arcade equipment using the products of two of Parkside's other divisions. The Plastics Division manufactures plastic components; one type is made exclusively for the Entertainment Division, while other less complex components are sold to external markets. The products of the Video Cards Division are sold in a competitive market, but one video card model is also used by the Entertainment Division. The actual manufacturing cost per unit of the Entertainment Division is as follows:

	Plastics Components	Video Cards
Direct materials used	$1.25	$2.40
Direct manuf. labor	2.35	3.00
Variable overhead	1.00	1.50
Fixed overhead	.40	2.25
Total cost per unit	$5.00	$9.15

The Plastics Division sells its commercial products at full cost plus a 25% markup based on cost and believes the proprietary plastic component made for the Entertainment Division would sell for $6.25 per unit on the open market. The market price of the video card used by the Entertainment Division is $10.98 per unit.

Assuming the Video Cards Division has no unused capacity, a transfer price to the Entertainment Division of $9.15 per unit will:
   a. allow evaluation of both divisions on a competitive basis.
   b. satisfy the Video Cards Division's profit desire by allowing recovery of opportunity costs.
   c. not motivate the Entertainment Division and will cause mediocre performance.
   d. provide no incentive for the Video Cards Division to control or reduce costs.
   e. encourage the Entertainment Division to purchase video cards from an external source.

5. Use the information in question 4 but assume the Entertainment Division is able to purchase a large quantity of video cards from an external supplier at $8.70 per unit. The Video Cards Division, having unused capacity, agrees to lower the transfer price to $8.70 per unit. This action will:
   a. optimize the profit goals of the Entertainment Division while subverting the profit goals of Parkside Inc.
   b. provide no profit incentive for the Video Cards Division.
   c. subvert the profit goals of the Video Cards Division while optimizing the profit goals of the Entertainment Division.
   d. cause mediocre performance in the Video Cards Division because opportunity costs increase.
   e. optimize the overall profit goals of Parkside Inc.

6. Use the information in question 4 and assume the Plastics Division has unused capacity and negotiates a transfer price of $5.60 per plastic component with the Entertainment Division. This price will:
   a. cause the Plastics Division to reduce the number of commercial plastic components it manufactures.
   b. motivate both divisions.
   c. encourage the Entertainment Division to seek an external supplier for plastic components.
   d. not motivate the Plastics Division, causing mediocre performance.
   e. satisfy the Plastics Division's profit desire by allowing recovery of opportunity costs.

7. (CPA adapted) Mar Company has two decentralized divisions, X and Y. Division X has been purchasing certain component parts from Division Y at $75 per unit. Because Division Y plans to raise the price to $100 per unit, Division X desires to purchase these parts from ex-

ternal suppliers for $75 per unit. The following information is available:

Y's variable cost per unit	$70
Y's annual fixed costs	$15,000
Y's annual production of these parts for X	1,000 units

If Division X buys from an external supplier, the facilities Division Y uses to manufacture these parts will be idle. Assuming Division Y's fixed costs cannot be avoided, what is the result if Mar requires Division X to buy from Division Y at a transfer price of $100 per unit?

a. It is suboptimal for the company as a whole because X should buy from external suppliers at $75 per unit.
b. It is more profitable for the company as a whole than allowing X to buy from external suppliers at $75 per unit.
c. It provides higher overall company operating income than a transfer price of $75 per unit.
d. It provides lower overall company operating income than a transfer price of $75 per unit.

Review Exercises

1. During the current year, Division A of Galloway Company incurred the following manufacturing costs for 5,000 units of a component part:

	Total	Per Unit
Variable costs	$200,000	$40
Fixed costs	40,000	8

a. Compute the advantage/disadvantage to the company as a whole (in terms of next year's operating income) if there are no alternative uses for Division A's facilities, and if Division B purchases 5,000 units of this part from an external supplier at a price of (1) $43 per unit (2) $36 per unit.

b. Compute the advantage/disadvantage to the company as a whole (in terms of next year's operating income) if there are alternative uses for Division A's facilities by other Galloway operations that would otherwise require additional outlay costs of $26,000, and if Division B purchases 5,000 units of this part from an external supplier at a price of (1) $43 per unit (2) $36 per unit.

2. Empire Company has two divisions. Division A is located in the United States where the income tax rate is 40%. Division K is located in Korea where the income tax rate is 30%. Division A produces an intermediate product at a variable cost of $100 per unit, and transfers the product to Division K where it is finished and sold for $500 per unit. Variable cost in Division K is $80 per unit. Fixed costs are $75,000 per year in Division A and $90,000 per year in Division K. Assume 1,000 units are transferred annually and the minimum transfer price allowed by the U.S. tax authorities is the variable cost. Also assume operating income in each country is equal to taxable income.

   a. What transfer price should be set for Empire to minimize its total income taxes? Show your calculations.
   b. If Empire desires to minimize its total income taxes, calculate the amount of tax liability in each country.

Answers and Solutions to Chapter 22 Review Questions and Exercises

Completion Statements

1. management control system
2. Goal congruence
3. motivation
4. Decentralization
5. Autonomy
6. Suboptimal decision making (Incongruent decision making, Dysfunctional decision making)
7. intermediate products
8. goal congruence, management effort, subunit performance evaluation, and subunit autonomy (if desired)
9. incremental cost per unit incurred up to the point of transfer, opportunity cost per unit to the selling subunit

True-False

1. F A human resources system is part of the *formal control system* in the company. The *informal control system* includes shared values, loyalties, mutual commitments among members of the company, and unwritten norms about acceptable behavior for managers and employees.
2. F To decide how much decentralization is optimal, top management tries conceptually to choose the degree of decentralization that maximizes the excess of benefits over costs. From a practical stand-

point, these benefits and costs can seldom be quantified, but the cost-benefit approach helps top management focus on the central issues.

3. T

4. F Decentralization is likely to be most beneficial if an organization's subunits are *independent*. If the subunits are highly *interdependent*, suboptimal decisions are most likely to occur because the decisions affecting one subunit influence the decisions and performance of one or more other subunits.

5. T

6. T

7. T

8. T

9. F Although full-cost transfer prices are frequently used in practice, this method can lead to suboptimal decisions, as explained in the Horizon Petroleum example, text p.785. The main rationale for using full-cost transfer prices is that they allow subunits to recover their fixed costs.

10. F All companies (whether multinational or domestic) need to consider the promotion of goal congruence in setting their transfer prices. Compared to domestic companies, however, multinational companies must consider several additional factors in setting their transfer prices: (i) different income tax rates in various countries, (ii) tariffs, custom duties, value-added taxes, and the like, and (iii) other government levies.

Multiple Choice

1. c A cost of decentralization is suboptimal decision making. One reason this phenomenon occurs is that the goals of subunit managers may not be congruent with top management goals. For example, a division manager, who is acting to maximize his or her division's operating income, might decide to buy a component part from an external supplier when it is in the company's best interest to buy the part internally. Note that answers (a), (b), and (d) refer to *benefits* of decentralization.

2. b By using standard variable cost as the transfer price, Division Core is motivated to improve its efficiency in providing services to Division Pro. Under this transfer price, none of Core's cost variances will be allocated to Pro; therefore, Pro's performance could be appropriately measured by its operating income. A negotiated price could not be used in this case because Core is a cost center, not a profit center or investment center.

3. a The transfer-pricing problem is the most troublesome in organizations that are highly decentralized with many interdependencies among subunits. That's because, under conditions of considerable freedom in decision making, decisions made by one subunit manager affect the decisions and performance of one or more other subunit managers.

4. d The market price of the video card used by the Entertainment Division is $10.98. Because the Video Cards Division has no unused capacity, it obviously has no profit incentive in selling this video card to the Entertainment Division for $9.15. The Video Cards Division would forgo $1.83 ($10.98 − $9.15) on each unit sold to the Entertainment Division. In contrast, the Entertainment Division would be very pleased to buy the video card internally at $1.83 less than the market price.

5. e Because the Video Cards Division has unused capacity, a selling price of $8.70 contributes $1.80 ($8.70 − $2.40 − $3.00 − $1.50) per unit sold to the recovery of its fixed overhead and then to its operating income. The Entertainment Division is indifferent about buying internally or from an external supplier at the price of $8.70. Given the benefit to the Video Cards Division and the indifference of the Entertainment Division, the $8.70 transfer price is in the best interest of the company as a whole.

6. b The negotiated transfer price of $5.60 lies between the Plastics Division's variable cost per unit of $4.60 ($1.25 + $2.35 + $1.00) and its regular selling price of $6.25. Because the Plastics Division has unused capacity, the transfer price of $5.60 motivates both divisions. The Plastics Division receives $1.00 ($5.60 − $4.60) more than its variable cost on each unit sold. The Entertainment Division buys the plastic component for $0.65 ($6.25 − $5.60) per unit less than the market price.

7. b If Mar requires transfers be made at $100 per unit, Division X pays Division Y 1,000 × $100 = $100,000. This transaction is intracompany (interdivisional) in nature (that is, money goes out of one corporate pocket into another corporate pocket). *The $100,000, therefore, has no effect on operating income of the company as a whole.* The effect of purchasing internally on the operating income of the company as a whole is:

Total relevant costs of external purchase		
1,000 × $75		$75,000
Deduct total relevant costs of internal purchase:		
Avoidable costs, 1,000 × $70	$70,000	
Opportunity costs to the selling division	-0-	70,000
Difference in favor of buying internally		$ 5,000

This analysis indicates that operating income of the company as a whole is $5,000 higher if Division X buys from Division Y. Given that transfers are required, *this conclusion holds regardless of the transfer price used.* Of course, performance evaluation of the subunit managers is likely to be affected by the transfer price used.

Review Exercise 1

a.

	(1)	(2)
Variable cost per unit, $200,000 ÷ 5,000	$ 40	$ 40
External market price per unit	43	36
Advantage (disadvantage) per unit	$(3)	$ 4
Multiply by number of units	× 5,000	× 5,000
Next year's annual operating income advantage (disadvantage) to the company as a whole	$(15,000)	$20,000

Fixed costs are irrelevant because they remain the same whether Division B buys internally or externally.

b.

	(1)	(2)
Advantage (disadvantage) as above, before considering alternative use of facilities	$(15,000)	$20,000
Advantage from alternative use of facilities	26,000	26,000
Next year's operating income advantage to the company as a whole	$ 11,000	$46,000

As in part (a), fixed costs are irrelevant.

Review Exercise 2

a. To minimize its total income taxes, the company should report no operating income in the U.S., the country with the higher income tax rate. This outcome occurs if the transfer price is set at full cost: $100 + ($75,000 ÷ 1,000) = $175 per unit.

b. Using the $175 transfer price from part (a), the company's tax liability in the U.S. is $0 and in Korea is $46,500:

Division A (U.S.)	
Revenues, 1,000 × $175	$175,000
Variable costs,	
1,000 × $100	(100,000)
Fixed costs	(75,000)
Operating income	0
Income tax	0
Net income	$ 0

Division K (Korea)	
Revenues, 1,000 × $500	$500,000
Transferred-in costs,	
$1,000 × $175	(175,000)
Variable costs, 1,000 × $80	(80,000)
Fixed costs	(90,000)
Operating income	155,000
Income tax (at 30%)	(46,500)
Net income	$108,500

CHAPTER 23 — Performance Measurement, Compensation, and Multinational Considerations

Overview

This chapter examines issues related to designing performance measures for managers at different levels of the organization. Performance measures are a central component of management control systems, and performance evaluation and rewards (salaries, bonuses, and career advancement) are key elements to motivate managers. Much of the chapter focuses on decentralized companies in which the divisions are investment centers.

Highlights

1. Management control systems use both financial and nonfinancial performance measures. Many widely used performance measures, such as operating income and return on investment, are based on internal financial information. Increasingly, companies are supplementing internal financial measures with measures based on external financial information (such as stock price), internal nonfinancial information (such as manufacturing lead time), and external nonfinancial information (such as customer satisfaction ratings). Companies often benchmark their financial and nonfinancial measures against the best levels of performance available within the company or in other companies.

2. Some companies present financial and nonfinancial performance measures for their subunits in a single report called the *balanced scorecard* (described in Chapter 13). Although different companies emphasize different elements in their scorecards, most scorecards include (a) profitability measures, (b) customer-satisfaction measures, (c) internal measures of efficiency, quality, and time, and (d) innovation measures. The balanced scorecard highlights trade-offs among the performance measures and avoids overemphasis on a single measure.

3. Designing accounting-based performance measures requires three steps:

Step 1: Choose performance measures that align with top management's financial goals.
Step 2: Choose the details of each performance measure in step 1.
Step 3: Choose a target level of performance and feedback mechanism of each performance measure in step 1.

Discussion of these steps is keyed to paragraphs 4 through 18.

4. (Step 1) A subunit's operating income should be evaluated by considering the size of the investment (assets) used to generate this income. One way to do this evaluation is by computing **return on investment (ROI)**:

$$\text{ROI} = \frac{\text{Income}}{\text{Investment}}$$

ROI has conceptual appeal because it blends all of the ingredients of profitability (revenues, costs, and investment) into a single percentage. ROI can be compared with the rate of return on investment opportunities available elsewhere, inside or outside the company. Like any single performance measure, however, ROI should be used cautiously and in conjunction with other performance measures.

5. (Step 1) Under an approach known as the *DuPont method of profitability analysis*, the ROI computation is separated into two components:

$$\frac{\text{Income}}{\text{Revenues}} \times \frac{\text{Revenues}}{\text{Investment}} = \text{ROI}$$

also written as:

Return on sales × Investment turnover = ROI

The DuPont method recognizes the two basic ingredients in profit making: (a) increasing income per dollar of revenues and (b) using assets to generate more revenues. ROI increases by improving one or both of these ingredients.

6. (Step 1) ROI highlights the benefits that managers can obtain by reducing their subunits' investments in current or long-term assets. Some managers are conscious of the need to boost revenues or to control costs but pay less attention to reducing their investment base. Reducing the investment base means decreasing idle cash, managing credit judiciously, determining proper inventory levels, and spending carefully on long-term assets.

7. (Step 1) Another way to consider the size of the investment used to generate income is by computing **residual income (RI)**:

$$RI = Income - (RRR \times Investment)$$

where:

RRR = Required rate of return

In this formula, RRR multiplied by investment is the **imputed cost** of the investment, which is an opportunity cost—the return forgone as a result of tying up cash in the investment rather than earning returns elsewhere on investments of similar risk. Being an opportunity cost, an imputed cost is not recorded in financial accounting systems.

8. (Step 1) By maximizing RI, managers are induced to expand their subunits as long as the rate of return earned is greater than the required rate of return. In contrast, maximizing ROI may cause managers of highly profitable subunits to reject projects that, from the standpoint of the company as a whole, should be accepted (that is, the ROI on these projects exceeds the company's required rate of return). *Goal congruence, therefore, is more likely to be promoted by using RI, rather than ROI, as a measure of the subunit manager's performance.*

9. (Step 1) Another way to consider the size of the investment used to generate income is by computing **economic value added (EVA)**. This performance measure, a specific type of RI calculation, is used by many companies.

$$EVA = \begin{matrix} \text{After-tax} \\ \text{operating} \\ \text{income} \end{matrix} - \left[WACC \times (TA - CL) \right]$$

where:

WACC = Weighted-average cost of capital on an after-tax basis
TA = Total assets
CL = Current liabilities

WACC is the counterpart of "required rate of return" in the computation of RI. To increase EVA, managers must earn more after-tax operating income with the same capital, use less capital to earn the same after-tax operating income, or invest capital in high-return projects. The example, text pp.812-813, computes EVA.

10. (Step 1) The income-to-revenues ratio—often called *return on sales (ROS)*—is a frequently used financial performance measure. ROS is one component of ROI in the DuPont method of profitability analysis. ROS provides the most meaningful indicator of a subunit manager's performance in markets where revenue growth is limited and investment levels are fixed.

11. (Step 2) Managers could make decisions that cause short-run increases in ROI, RI, EVA, and ROS but are in conflict with the long-run interest of the company. For this reason, many companies evaluate subunit managers on the basis of these measures over a multiple-year time horizon. Another reason for evaluating subunit managers over multiple years is that the benefits of decisions made in the current period may not show up in short-run performance measures.

12. (Step 2) Using a multiple-year time horizon highlights another advantage of RI: the net present value (NPV) of all the cash flows over the life of an investment equals the NPV of the RIs. This characteristic means that when managers use the NPV method to make capital-budgeting decisions (as advocated in Chapter 21), using multiple-year RIs to evaluate managers' performance achieves goal congruence.

13. (Step 2) Another way to motivate managers to take a long-run perspective is by compensating them on the basis of changes in the market price of the company's stock (in addition to using accounting-based performance measures over multiple years). This approach extends managers' time horizons because stock prices incorporate the expected future period effects of current decisions.

14. (Step 2) Companies that use ROI or RI as performance measures generally define "investment" as *total assets available*. When top management directs a subunit manager to carry extra assets, however, *total assets employed* can be more informative than total assets available. Companies that use EVA define investment as *total assets employed minus current liabilities*. The most common rationale for using this definition of investment is that the subunit manager often influences decisions on current liabilities of the subunit.

15. (Step 2) Two alternative ways to measure assets included in the investment base are: *historical cost* or **current cost**. Current cost is the cost of purchasing an asset today identical to the one currently held, or the cost of purchasing an asset that provides services like the one currently held if an identical asset cannot be purchased. Adjusting assets to recognize current costs negates differences in the investment base that are caused solely by different construction price levels over time. Compared to historical-cost ROI, current-cost ROI is a better measure of the current economic returns from the investment. A drawback of using current cost is it can be difficult to obtain current-cost estimates for some assets. EXHIBIT 23-2, text p.817, illustrates a step-by-step approach for incorporating current-cost estimates of long-term assets and depreciation expense into the ROI calculation.

16. (Step 2) Because historical cost of assets is often used to calculate ROI, there has been much discussion about the relative merits of using *gross book value* (original cost) or *net book value* (original cost minus accumulated depreciation). Those who favor using gross book value claim that it enables more accurate comparisons across subunits. They point out that if net book value is

used, ROI can increase as an asset ages solely because periodic depreciation expense decreases the investment base. Those who favor using net book value maintain that it is less confusing because (a) it is consistent with the amount of total assets shown in the conventional balance sheet and (b) it is consistent with income computations that include deductions for depreciation expense. Global surveys of company practice report net book value to be the dominant asset measure used by companies in their internal performance evaluations.

17. (Step 3) Despite the fact that accounting measures based on historical cost are often inadequate for evaluating economic returns on new investments and sometimes create disin-centives for expansion, *historical-cost ROIs can be used to evaluate current performance by establishing target (budgeted) ROIs*. The target ROI should be carefully negotiated with a full knowledge of the pitfalls of historical cost.

18. (Step 3) Performance feedback can be reported daily, weekly, monthly, or at some other time interval. The timing of feedback depends largely on how critical the information is for the success of the company, the specific level of management receiving the feedback, and the sophistication of the company's information technology.

19. Comparing performance of the divisions of a multinational company (that is, a company operating in different countries) is difficult because of economic, legal, political, cultural, and currency differences. For example, when divisions of a multinational company record their performance in different currencies, issues of inflation and fluctuations in foreign currency exchange rates become important. The illustration, text pp.819-820, explains how a U.S. multinational company should compute the ROI of its Mexico division for the current year during which the peso steadily declined in value relative to the dollar.

20. Regardless of whether ROI, RI, EVA, or ROS is used, distinguish measuring the performance of a *manager* from measuring the performance of a *subunit*. For example, the most skillful manager may be put in charge of the division producing the poorest economic returns in an attempt

to change its fortunes. In this case, the manager is more appropriately evaluated by comparing his or her performance against a budget rather than against the performance of other divisions. The manager's performance is the basis of his or her compensation, future job assignments, and career advancement, whereas the division's performance is key to allocating resources within the company.

21. The total compensation of subunit managers usually consists of both a salary and a performance-based incentive (bonus). An important consideration in designing compensation arrangements is the trade-off between creating incentives to get the manager to work hard and imposing risk on the manager. The manager is subject to risk when actual performance depends partially on factors he or she cannot control, such as economic conditions. In this case, the difficulty of monitoring the manager's efforts causes **moral hazard**: a situation in which an employee prefers to exert less effort (or report distorted information) compared with the effort (or accurate information) desired by the owner, because the employee's effort (or validity of the reported information) cannot be accurately monitored and enforced.

22. The size of the incentive component in a compensation plan relative to the amount of salary should depend on how well the performance measures capture the manager's ability to influence the desired results. *Preferred performance measures are ones that are sensitive to or change significantly with the manager's performance, and do not change much with changes in factors that are beyond the manager's control.* Performance measures that are sensitive to the manager's performance motivate the manager but limit his or her exposure to uncontrollable risk. For example, assume a division manager has no control over revenues and investment but can control costs. Using a cost-based performance measure is desirable because it captures the manager's effort, whereas using ROI as the performance measure is undesirable because it does not capture the manager's effort. If owners have performance measures available to them that are sensitive to the manager's performance, owners place greater reliance on incentive compensation in those cases.

23. Global surveys show that division managers' compensation plans include a mix of salary and long-term compensation tied to the income and stock price of the company. The goal is to balance division and companywide incentives, as well as short-run and long-run incentives.

24. It can be cost effective to benchmark a manager's performance against the best levels of performance available within the company or in other companies. This approach is called *relative performance evaluation*; it filters out the effects of common uncontrollable factors. Benchmarking the performance of two managers responsible for similar operations within a company, however, may not lead to goal congruence. That's because one manager might improve his or her performance by making the other manager look bad. Managers being unwilling to cooperate and work together is not in the best interest of the company as a whole.

25. Many manufacturing, marketing, and design problems require employees with multiple skills, knowledge, and experiences to pool their talents. In these situations, companies often reward individuals based on team performance. Team incentives encourage individuals to help one another as they strive toward a common goal.

26. The principles of performance evaluation described in paragraphs 21 through 25 also apply to executive compensation plans. These plans are based on both financial and nonfinancial performance measures and consist of a mix of (a) base salary, (b) annual incentives such as cash bonuses based on achieving a target annual RI, (c) long-run incentives such as stock options based on stock performance over, say, a five-year period, and (d) fringe benefits.

27. Stock options motivate executives to improve a company's long-run performance by linking executive compensation to increases in the company's stock price. Accounting rules in force at the time of writing the textbook require U.S. companies to, at the very least, disclose in a note to the financial statements the effect on net income and earnings per share if the company had recognized an expense equal to the estimated fair market value of the stock options on the grant date.

28. The Securities and Exchange Commission (SEC) requires disclosures of the compensation arrangements of top-level executives. The SEC rules require companies to disclose the principles underlying their executive compensation plans and the performance criteria used in determining compensation. Another SEC requirement is to disclose how well the company's stock performed relative to the overall stock market and relative to stocks of other companies in the same industry.

29. In implementing strategies and achieving financial and nonfinancial performance goals, it is essential for companies to use four levers of control:

a. **Diagnostic control systems** track how a company is performing compared to expectations for measures such as ROI, RI, EVA, customer satisfaction, and employee satisfaction.

b. **Boundary systems** describe standards of behavior and codes of conduct expected of all employees, especially actions that are off-limits—for example, (i) "cooking the books" such as by overstating assets or reporting fictitious revenues, (ii) bribery, and (iii) environmental violations such as water and air pollution.

c. **Belief systems** articulate the mission, purpose, and core values of a company. They describe the accepted norms and patterns of behavior expected of all managers and other employees with respect to one another, shareholders, customers, and communities.

d. **Interactive control systems** focus the company's attention and learning on key strategic issues—emerging threats and opportunities—such as changes in technology, customer preferences, regulations, and competitors.

Why four levers of control? Because holding managers and other employees accountable for and rewarding them for achieving performance goals in diagnostic control systems needs to be counterbalanced with the other three levers of control. It is unacceptable for managers to misreport numbers to make their performance look better that it really is—as happened in the last few years at companies such as Enron and WorldCom.

Featured Exercise

The following information is from the financial statements of Duke Company for the fiscal year just ended:

Total assets	$6,000,000
Current liabilities	1,250,000
Operating income	1,140,000

a. Calculate return on investment (ROI).
b. Calculate residual income (RI), assuming the required rate of return is 18%.
c. Calculate economic value added (EVA) assuming (1) Duke has two sources of funds—long-term debt with a market value of $2,500,000 and an interest rate of 10%, and equity capital with a market value of $5,000,000 and a cost of equity of 16%—and (2) Duke's income tax rate is 30%.

Solution (on next page)

Solution

a.   ROI = $1,140,000 ÷ $6,000,000 = 19%
b.   RI = $1,140,000 − ($6,000,000 × 0.18)
     RI = $1,140,000 − $1,080,000 = $60,000

c.   Three steps are used to obtain the answer. First, compute the after-tax cost of debt financing:

> After-tax cost of debt financing = (1.00 − 0.30) × 10% = 7%
> (The after-tax cost of equity, 16%, is given.)

Second, compute the weighted-average cost of capital (WACC) on an after-tax basis:

$$\text{WACC} = \frac{(0.07 \times \$2,500,000) + (0.16 \times \$5,000,000)}{\$2,500,000 + \$5,000,000}$$

$$\text{WACC} = \frac{\$175,000 + \$800,000}{\$7,500,000} = \frac{\$975,000}{\$7,500,000} = 13\%$$

Third, compute EVA:

> EVA = ($1,140,000 × 0.70) − [0.13 × ($6,000,000 − $1,250,000)]
> EVA = $798,000 − (0.13 × $4,750,000)
> EVA = $798,000 − $617,500 = $180,500

Review Questions and Exercises

Completion Statements

Fill in the blank(s) to complete each statement.

1. Designing accounting-based performance measure for an organization subunit requires three steps. Step 1 is to choose performance measures that

    _____

    _____ financial goals.

2. In the formula to calculate residual income, the required rate of return multiplied by investment is called the _____ cost of the investment.

3. _____ cost is the cost of purchasing an asset today identical to the one currently held, or the cost of purchasing an asset that provides services like the one currently held if an identical asset cannot be purchased.

4. An important consideration in designing compensation arrangements is the trade-off between creating _____ to get the manager to work hard and imposing _____ on the manager.

5. _____ describes situations in which an employee prefers to exert less effort (or report distorted information) compared to the effort (or accurate information) desired by the owner, because the employee's effort (or validity of the reported information) cannot be accurately monitored and enforced.

6. Name the four levers of control. _____

    _____

    _____

    _____

True-False

Indicate whether each statement is true (T) or false (F).

___ 1. A company's market share is an example of external nonfinancial information.

___ 2. A good reason for using ROI as a performance measure rather than RI is that goal congruence is more likely to be promoted by using ROI.

___ 3. The DuPont method of profitability analysis recognizes two basic ingredients to profit making: increasing income per dollar of revenues and using assets to generate more revenues.

___ 4. If companies compensate managers on the basis of changes in the market price of the company's stock, this approach tends to shorten managers' time horizon because stock prices incorporate the expected future period effects of current decisions.

___ 5. Those who favor using net book value as the investment base in ROI calculations claim this approach enables more accurate comparisons to be made across subunits.

___ 6. Comparing performance of the divisions of a multinational company is difficult because of economic, legal, political, cultural, and currency differences.

___ 7. The necessary and sufficient condition for moral hazard to exist in a company is that the employee's interest differs from the owner's interest.

___ 8. Performance measures that are sensitive to the manager's performance motivate the manager but limit his or her exposure to uncontrollable risk.

___ 9. It can be cost effective to benchmark a manager's performance against the best levels of performance available within the company or in other companies.

___ 10. Holding managers and other employees accountable for and rewarding them for achieving performance goals in diagnostic control systems needs to be counterbalanced with boundary systems, belief systems, and interactive control systems.

Multiple Choice

Select the best answer to each question. Space is provided for computations after the quantitative questions.

___ 1. Roma Bottling Co. has an investment of $3,000,000, an income-to-revenues ratio of 4%, and an ROI of 12%. Its revenues are:
a. $360,000.
b. $9,000,000.
c. $1,440,000.
d. $12,000,000.

___ 2. Using the information in question 1, the revenues-to-investment ratio is:
a. 5 times.
b. 4 times.
c. 3 times.
d. 2 times.

___ 3. (CMA adapted) A company's ROI increases if:
a. revenues increase by the same dollar amount that costs and total assets increase.
b. revenues remain the same, and costs are reduced by the same dollar amount that total assets increase.
c. revenues decrease by the same dollar amount that costs increase.
d. revenues and costs increase by the same percentage that total assets increase.
e. none of the above.

4. For the fiscal year just ended, Fletcher Inc. has an RI of $180,000 and operating income of $500,000. If the required rate of return is 16%, the amount of investment is:
   a. $320,000.
   b. $3,125,000.
   c. $8,000,000.
   d. $2,000,000.
   e. none of the above.

5. Using the information in question 4, ROI is:
   a. 5%.
   b. 10%.
   c. 15%.
   d. 20%.
   e. none of the above.

6. (CPA) Marsh Inc. has an incentive compensation plan under which its president is paid a bonus equal to 10% of Marsh's income after deducting the bonus but before deducting income taxes. For the year ended December 2010, Marsh's income was $110,000 before deducting the bonus and income taxes. Marsh had income taxes of $40,000 in 2010. How much bonus should Marsh pay its president for 2010?
   a. $0
   b. $7,000
   c. $10,000
   d. $11,000

Review Exercises

1. Rochelle Company has just purchased a milling machine at a cost of $200,000. The machine is expected to generate operating income of $18,000 per year during its 10-year useful life. Rochelle uses the straight-line method of depreciation with a zero terminal disposal value.

   Calculate ROI in the following situations:
   a. First year using gross book value as the investment base.
   b. Sixth year using gross book value as the investment base.
   c. First year using net book value at the end of the year as the investment base.
   d. Sixth year using net book value at the beginning of the year as the investment base.

2. The Kline Corporation manufactures pharmaceutical products in the U.S. and China. The operations are organized as decentralized divisions. The following information is available for 2010:

	U.S. Division	China Division
Operating income	$2,400,000	11,400,000 yuan
Total assets	$16,000,000	75,000,000 yuan

The exchange rate at the time of Kline's investment in China on December 31, 2009 was 7.5 Chinese yuan = $1 U.S. During 2010, the yuan declined steadily in value and the exchange rate on December 31, 2010, was 8.5 yuan = $1. The average exchange rate during 2010 was 8 yuan = $1.

a. Calculate the U.S. Division's ROI for 2010 based on dollars.
b. Calculate the China Division's ROI for 2010 based on yuan.
c. Which of Kline's two division's earned the better ROI in 2010? Explain your answer, complete with supporting calculations.

3. Endicott Inc. has four divisions. Each division produces and sells a variety of industrial products. The company is developing a compensation plan for the division managers. Three options are being considered: (a) salary, (b) a performance-based incentive using RI, (c) mix of salary and a performance-based incentive using RI. What factors should be considered in designing this plan?

_____
_____
_____
_____
_____
_____
_____
_____
_____

Answers and Solutions to Chapter 23 Review Questions and Exercises

Completion Statements

1. align with top management's
2. imputed
3. Current
4. incentives, risk
5. Moral hazard
6. diagnostic control systems, boundary systems, belief systems, and interactive control systems

True-False

1. T
2. F   ROI and RI are reversed in the statement. The correct statement is: A good reason for using RI as a performance measure rather than ROI is that goal congruence is more likely to be promoted by using RI.
3. T
4. F   The statement is true except for one point. The approach described helps to *extend* managers' time horizon, not *shorten* it.
5. F   The argument cited is used by those who favor using *gross book value*, not *net book value*.
6. T
7. F   The statement accurately describes one of the two necessary conditions for moral hazard to exist. The other condition is that the employee's effort cannot be accurately monitored and enforced.
8. T
9. T
10. T

Multiple Choice

1. b   Income = 12% × $3,000,000 = $360,000
   Revenues = $360,000 ÷ 0.04   = $9,000,000
2. c $9,000,000 ÷ $3,000,000 = 3 times
3. b   To answer this question, use assumed amounts. Suppose the present ROI is 20% as follows:

$$\frac{\text{Income}}{\text{Revenues}} \times \frac{\text{Revenues}}{\text{Investment}} = \text{ROI}$$

$$\frac{\$100,000 - \$90,000}{\$100,000} \times \frac{\$100,000}{\$50,000} = 20\%$$

Using assumed amounts for the changes specified in the question, the effect on ROI in each of the answers is as follows:

a.   Revenues increase by $30,000, which is the amount that costs and total assets increase:

$$\frac{\$130,000 - \$120,000}{\$130,000} \times \frac{\$130,000}{\$80,000} = 12.5\%$$

b. Revenues remain the same, costs decrease by $6,000, and total assets increase by $6,000:

$$\frac{\$100,000 - \$84,000}{\$100,000} \times \frac{\$100,000}{\$56,000} = 28.6\%$$

c. Revenues decrease by $5,000, costs increase by $5,000, and total assets remain the same:

$$\frac{\$95,000 - \$95,000}{\$95,000} \times \frac{\$95,000}{\$50,000} = 0\%$$

d. Revenues and costs increase by 15% and total assets increase by 15%:

$$\frac{\$100,000(1.15) - \$90,000(1.15)}{\$100,000(1.15)} \times \frac{\$100,000(1.15)}{\$50,000(1.15)} = \frac{\$115,000 - \$103,500}{\$115,000} \times \frac{\$115,000}{\$57,500} = 20\%$$

ROI increases in answer (b).

4. d   Imputed interest cost = $500,000 − $180,000 = $320,000
   Investment = $320,000 ÷ 0.16 = $2,000,000
5. e $500,000 ÷ $2,000,000 = 25%
6. c   Let B = Bonus
   B = ($110,000 − B) × 0.10
   B = $11,000 − 0.10B
   1.10B = $11,000
   B = $11,000 ÷ 1.10 = $10,000
   The income taxes of $40,000 should not be used in computing the bonus.

Review Exercise 1

a. ROI based on gross book value in the first year = $18,000 ÷ $200,000 = 9%
b. ROI based on gross book value in the sixth year= $18,000 ÷ $200,000 = 9%
c. ROI based on net book value at the end of the first year:

$$\text{Net book value at end of first year} = \$200,000 - \left[(\$200,000 - \$0) \div 10 \right]$$
$$= \$200,000 - \$20,000 = \$180,000$$

   ROI = $18,000 ÷ $180,000 = 10%

d. ROI based on net book value at the beginning of the sixth year:

$$\text{ROI} = \$18,000 \div (0.50 \times \$200,000)$$
$$= \$18,000 \div \$100,000 = 18\%$$

Review Exercise 2

a. U.S. Division's ROI for 2010 $= \dfrac{\$2,400,000}{\$16,000,000} = 15\%$

b. China Division's ROI for 2010 $= \dfrac{11,400,000 \text{ yuan}}{75,000,000 \text{ yuan}} = 15.2\%$

c. Three steps are used to determine the answer. First, convert total assets in the China Division into dollars at the December 31, 2009, exchange rate, the rate prevailing when these assets were acquired (7.5 yuan = $1):

$$\text{Total assets} = \dfrac{75,000,000 \text{ yuan}}{7.5 \text{ yuan per dollar}} = \$10,000,000$$

Second, convert operating income in the China Division into dollars at the average exchange rate prevailing during 2010 when the operating income was earned;

$$\dfrac{11,400,000 \text{ yuan}}{8 \text{ yuan per dollar}} = \$1,425,000$$

Third, compute the China Division's comparable ROI for 2010 $= \dfrac{\$1,425,000}{\$10,000,000} = 14.25\%$

The China Division's ROI measured in yuan is helped by the inflation that occurred in China during 2010 because inflation boosted the China Division's operating income. Given that the assets were acquired on December 31, 2009, the asset values should not be increased to reflect the inflation that occurred during 2010. The net effect of inflation on ROI computed in yuan is to use an inflated value in the numerator relative to the denominator. Adjusting for inflation using currency differences that represent differential inflation negates the effects of any differences in inflation rates between the two countries on the computation of ROI. After these adjustments, the U.S. Division shows a higher ROI (15% from part (a) above) than the China Division (14.25%).

Review Exercise 3

The basic trade-off to consider in designing the compensation plan for division managers is between creating incentives to get managers to work hard and imposing risk on them. Compensation based on RI creates incentives for the managers to work hard, but they also bear risk because RI is affected by some factors outside their control. For example, a division manager may work hard but uncontrollable factors (such as economic conditions) may cause RI to be reduced, thereby reducing the manager's compensation. A salary, independent of RI performance, does not impose any risk on managers but it also creates no incentives for them. For this reason, many companies use a mix of salary and a performance-based incentive—the salary component reduces risk while the performance-based component creates incentives.

Check Figures for Review Exercises

Chapter 1
1. No check figure
2. No check figure
3. No check figure

Chapter 2
1. (a) $7.20 (b) $747,000
2. 50,000 units
3. (a) $195,000 (b) $230,000 (c) $585,000

Chapter 3
1. (a) $135,000 (b) 3,000 tons
2. 2,025 units of T; 10,125 units of U
3. 833,334 units
4. (a) 10,200 units (b) 0.40

Chapter 4
1. (a) $11,000 underallocated (b) $91,700 (c) $205,800 (d) $12,600
2. No check figure
3. $4,250

Chapter 5
1. $59.57 per case
2. (a) Jason $7 undercosted
3. (b) Fuentes audit $36,000
4. (b) $0.849 per box (c) $1.362 per box

Chapter 6
1. (a) 665,720 units (b) $3,034,320
2. Budgeted operating income $3,516,000
3. $161,280

Chapter 7
1. (a) Price variance $800 F, Efficiency variance $1,000 U
2. (a) $1,460 U (b) $10,660 F (c) 50,700 kilograms (d) $4.985 (e) $252,000 (f) $309,960

Chapter 8
1. (a) $2 per machine-hour (b) 600 hours (c) Spending variance $50 F
2. (a) $6 per machine-hour (b) Production-volume variance $120 U
3. (a) 121,000 machine-hours (b) 115,000 machine-hours

Chapter 9
1. (a) $1,200,000 (b) $2,600,000 (c) $1,000,000 (d) $700,000 U (e) $2,400,000 (f) $1,400,000
   (g) $122,000 increase (h) $157,000 increase (i) 91,804 units (j) 72,414 units
2. (a1) $60 per machine-hour (a2) $780,000 (a3) $40,000 overallocated (a4) $60,000 F (b) $135,000 U
   (c) $252,000 U

Chapter 10

1. $2 variable cost per unit
2. (a) $896,000 (b) $1,022,480
3. No check figure

Chapter 11

1. 1,440 machine-hours used for T
2. $14,000 decrease per month
3. (a) $900 increase (b) $1,250 decrease (c) $1,515 decrease

Chapter 12

1. (a) $240 prospective selling price (b) 25% markup
2. (a) Operating income of Quick Tax $700,000

Chapter 13

1. (a) Industry-market-size factor $48,600 F
2. (a) Change in partial productivity for direct materials −2.0% (b) Change in total factor productivity +1.9%

Chapter 14

1. (a) $10,800 decrease (b) $1,400 decrease (c) $1,200 decrease
2. (a) Langley $89,280 (b) Langley $269,200
3. (a) Sales-volume variance $15,000 F (b) Sales-mix variance $13,000 U (c) Sales-quantity variance $28,000 F

Chapter 15

1. (a) $86,000 allocated to A (b) $91,000 allocated to A
2. (a) $41,250 allocated to Adams (b) $48,000 allocated to Adams
3. (a) $163 allocated to bus tour (b) $209 allocated to air travel

Chapter 16

1. (a) T $750 (b) T $3,450 (c) T $1,898 (d) T $2,120 (e) T $20 decrease
2. Gross margin $33,900

Chapter 17

1. (a4) $98,000 costs transferred out (b4) $98,500 costs transferred out
2. (a) Model X $10,000 (b) Model X $39 per unit (c) Model X $3,400

Chapter 18

1. (a) 13,300 equivalent units of conversion costs (b) $105,840 (c) $25,200 (d) $1,260 (e) $70,700
2. (b) $158 cost per finished motor (d) $133 cost per finished motor

Chapter 19

1. Produce 100 units of C and 30 units of P
2. (a) $100 loss from producing a defective unit in Machining (b) $300 loss from producing a defective unit in Assembly

Chapter 20

1. (a) $6,250 relevant total carrying costs per year (b) $4,250 cost increase (c) 5 production runs
2. JIT saves $31,000
3. (a) credit Finished Goods Control $31,488,000 (b) debit Cost of Goods Sold twice: $31,488,000 and $800,000 (c) debit Inventory Control $480,000 (d) debit Finished Goods Control $32,800,000

Chapter 21

1. $64,500 after-tax cash flow from the sale of the machine
2. $114,000 savings in annual after-tax cash operating costs from the new equipment
3. (a) $54,978 after-tax present value of expected cash operating savings before tax (b) $23,324 after-tax present value of depreciation deduction

Chapter 22

1. (a1) $15,000 disadvantage (a2) $20,000 advantage (b1) $11,000 advantage (b2) $46,000 advantage
2. (a) $175 per unit (b) U.S. $0 income tax; Korea $46,500 income tax

Chapter 23

1. (a) 9% (b) 9% (c) 10% (d) 18%
2. (a) 15% (b) 15.2% (c) U.S. Division 15% versus China Division 14.25%
3. No check figure